W/D

c/w

GEORGIAN POETRY 1911-1922

THE CRITICAL HERITAGE SERIES

GENERAL EDITOR: B. C. SOUTHAM, M.A., B. LITT. (OXON.)
Formerly Department of English, Westfield College, University of London

For a list of books in the series see the back end paper

GEORGIAN POETRY
1911–1922

THE CRITICAL HERITAGE

Edited by
TIMOTHY ROGERS
Principal, The Bosworth College
Leicestershire

ROUTLEDGE & KEGAN PAUL
LONDON, HENLEY AND BOSTON

First published in 1977
by Routledge & Kegan Paul Ltd
39 Store Street,
London WC1E 7DD,
Broadway House,
Newtown Road,
Henley-on-Thames,
Oxon RG9 1EN and
9 Park Street,
Boston, Mass. 02108, USA
Printed in Great Britain by
Redwood Burn Limited
Trowbridge and Esher
© Timothy Rogers 1977

ISBN 0 7100 8278 9

General Editor's Preface

The reception given to a writer by his contemporaries and near-contemporaries is evidence of considerable value to the student of literature. On one side we learn a great deal about the state of criticism at large and in particular about the development of critical attitudes towards a single writer; at the same time, through private comments in letters, journals or marginalia, we gain an insight upon the tastes and literary thought of individual readers of the period. Evidence of this kind helps us to understand the writer's historical situation, the nature of his immediate reading-public, and his response to these pressures.

The separate volumes in the *Critical Heritage Series* present a record of this early criticism. Clearly, for many of the highly productive and lengthily reviewed nineteenth- and twentieth-century writers, there exists an enormous body of material; and in these cases the volume editors have made a selection of the most important views, significant for their intrinsic critical worth or for their representative quality— perhaps even registering incomprehension!

For earlier writers, notably pre-eighteenth century, the materials are much scarcer and the historical period has been extended, sometimes far beyond the writer's lifetime, in order to show the inception and growth of critical views which were initially slow to appear.

In each volume the documents are headed by an Introduction, discussing the material assembled and relating the early stages of the author's reception to what we have come to identify as the critical tradition. The volumes will make available much material which would otherwise be difficult of access and it is hoped that the modern reader will be thereby helped towards an informed understanding of the ways in which literature has been read and judged.

B.C.S.

Contents

CONTENTS

CONTENTS

Preface

In the fairest, most scholarly account of Georgian Poetry
yet published, Robert H. Ross writes: (1)

> ..... perhaps no group of poets since the Pre-
> Raphaelites has suffered more, or more ignominiously,
> from the widespread acceptance of over-simplified
> stereotypes and critical half-truths, even among
> readers who should know better.

One of the objects of this volume is to trace the history
of a movement which, though 'fortuitous and informal' in
its inception, (2) 'more or less casual and entirely un-
theoretical', (3) came to represent for later generations
a literary establishment of the most reactionary kind.
As Professor Ross shows, that ambitious adjective
'Georgian' which 'had been applied proudly by Marsh in
1912 to mean "new", "modern", "energetic"' had, by 1922,
'come to connote only "old-fashioned", "outworn", or
worse'. (4)   It was one of the objects of his book to
rescue the better Georgians from the obloquy which the
weaknesses of a few had brought upon them.   A similar
object must have prompted two recent anthologies, Alan
Pryce-Jones 'Georgian Poets' (1959) and James Reeves's
'Georgian Poetry' (1962).   It is Mr Reeves's laudable
aim 'to make a selection of Georgian poetry which will
appeal to the unprejudiced modern reader'. (5)   Un-
fortunately both he and to a lesser degree Professor Ross
have been guilty of further confusions by their use of
'Georgian'.   A first purpose, then, of the present book
must be to define.
    'Georgian Poetry' is here taken literally to mean the
five volumes edited by E[dward]. M[arsh]. and published
by Harold Monro at the Poetry Bookshop from 1912 to 1922,
and 'Georgian Poets' those forty poets whom Marsh

anthologized in them.   A full list of them with some
contemporary comments is given as an Appendix (pp. 395-417).
Poets such as Housman (who was invited by Marsh but de-
clined: see p. 18) and Edward Thomas (who is frequently
thought of as a Georgian, but did not appear in the an-
thologies: see p. 19), are excluded, though each appears
in the Reeves anthology;   conversely, D.H. Lawrence, who
is excluded by Reeves but appeared in four of Marsh's
volumes, is by definition included.   It may be noted that
Alan Pryce-Jones departs even further from such a literal
definition.   He frankly admits that he has 'not stuck
closely to the very poems, or even the very poets, whom
Marsh either did include, or might have included, in his
five volumes', (6) and prints one poem each by twenty-
nine poets, of whom only nineteen had appeared in
'Georgian Poetry'.

In the obvious respect that it is concerned, not with
a single writer, but with forty poets, diverse both in
quality and kind, the present volume differs from others
in the Critical Heritage series.   The difference in sub-
ject has given rise to a number of special problems in
the selection, introduction and presentation of material;
and, although solutions have been sought within the gen-
eral framework of the series, there have been small but
necessary changes of balance and emphasis.   In particular
I have allowed more space than usual in the Introduction
to a survey of contemporary literary magazines, especially
those of the period immediately preceding the First World
War, for it is in them that one can discern most clearly
the currents and cross-currents of the Georgian literary
scene.   The poets have been considered chiefly within
the context of 'Georgian Poetry'.   It would have been an
interesting exercise to consider the individual fortunes
of a representative few as they were affected by assoc-
iation with the anthology.   To have done so, however,
would have lengthened and diversified the book, and might
have duplicated (or perhaps anticipated) others in the
series.

A further concern in writing historically on a subject
so controversial must be to document it fully.   An
abundance of footnotes may not make for easy reading (it
certainly has not made for easy writing);   but sources
are important, albeit that only a selection even of
remembered ones can be included.   References to them
serve both as milestones and signposts in a landscape
which has been despoiled by earlier travellers and often
deceptively mapped.   If, during my own thirty years of
travelling in it, some sources have become obscured so
that I have sometimes failed to make due acknowledgment,
I offer apologies to those concerned.

Notes

1 Robert H. Ross 'The Georgian Revolt', 1967, 15.
2 Harold Monro, 'Some Contemporary Poets', 1920, 150.
3 James Reeves (ed.), 'Georgian Poetry', 1962, xii.
4 Ross, op. cit., 254-5.
5 Reeves (ed.), op. cit., xxi.
6 Alan Pryce-Jones (ed.), 'Georgian Poets', 1959, 9.

Acknowledgments

The editor and publishers would like to thank the following for permission to reprint material within their copyright or other control:

Associated Newspapers Group Ltd for No. 44; 'Daily Herald' for No. 48; 'The Daily Telegraph' for Nos 7, 46 and 47; Mr Geoffrey Grigson for No. 67; 'The Guardian' for Nos 2 and 53; David Higham Associates Ltd for No. 70; The Literary Trustees of Walter de la Mare, and The Society of Authors as their representative, for No. 13; Macmillan, London and Basingstoke, for Nos 63 and 64; 'The New Statesman' for Nos 9, 18, 19, 24, 27, 31, 33 and 56; 'The New York Times' for No. 38, © 1920 by The New York Times Company; Mr Peter Newbolt for No. 11; 'The Observer' for Nos 52 and 72; A.D. Peters & Co. for Nos 21, 47 and 62; Laurence Pollinger Ltd, the Estate of the late Mrs Frieda Lawrence and The Viking Press Inc. for No. 12; 'Punch' for No. 23; 'The Saturday Review' for Nos 41 and 49; The Society of Authors, as the literary representative of the estate of John Middleton Murry, for No. 34; 'The Spectator' for Nos 6, 16, 20, 36 and 39, and Lady Williams-Ellis for No. 50; Mrs Myfanwy Thomas for Nos 4 and 10; 'The Times' for No. 43; 'The Times Literary Supplement' for Nos 8, 17, 28, 35, 55, 68, 71 and 74; 'The Sunday Times' for Nos 51 and 73; Twentieth Century Magazine Ltd for Nos 22 and 65; 'Yorkshire Post' for No. 54.

It has proved difficult in certain cases to locate the proprietors of copyright material. However all possible care has been taken to trace ownership of the selections included and to make full acknowledgment of their use.

Warmest thanks are due also to the staffs of The British Library, The Newspaper Library (Colindale), The New York Public Library (Berg Collection), The University

of California Library, The Bodleian, the University
Libraries of Cambridge, London and Leicester, The London
Library, the Library of King's College, Cambridge and
the Resources Centre of the Bosworth College.

Finally to my friend William F. Gosling, teacher and
scholar, I owe thanks for his proof-reading and - in the
Eddie Marsh tradition - 'diabolization' of this and two
previous books.   Any faults remaining are, of course,
my responsibility.

                                                    T.R.

Introduction

'Who were the Georgians?'

'Who were the Georgians?' asks John Press, and it is a
convenient starting point.   'Some writers', he continues,
'are at pains to deny this title to any poet of merit who
flourished between 1912 and 1922.' (1)

> Robert Graves, we are assured, was not a Georgian, nor
> were D. H. Lawrence, Edward Thomas, Siegfried Sassoon,
> Wilfred Owen, Isaac Rosenberg, and Edmund Blunden.
> Whether or not they appeared in 'Georgian Poetry' is,
> according to such critics, totally irrelevant.   What
> matters is the quality of their work: if it is good
> it cannot be Georgian; if it is Georgian it must,
> *ipso facto*, be feeble.

Sandra Gilbert is only the most recent of the writers on
D. H. Lawrence to find that, 'Reading the bucolic
warblings of the rather cosily domesticated Georgians,
one is immediately struck by the force of some of [his]
verses as by an alien wind.   The demon, certainly, was
no Georgian.' (2)   Vivien de Sola Pinto writes that
Lawrence and Robert Graves 'really had no connection with
the Georgian fold';   (3)   Jon Silkin that 'Rosenberg was
not a Georgian', (4)   David Daiches that Rosenberg and
the other 'trench poets' were an alien presence in the
Georgian anthologies;   (5)   and Masefield's latest
biographer, Muriel Spark, after citing Herbert Palmer's
view that 'he is certainly no true-blue Georgian', (6)
sets out on her first page to show that 'he is no
Georgian at all'. (7)   James Reeves names W. H. Davies,
together with de la Mare and Blunden, as 'among those
poets who are central to the Georgian movement at its
best', (8) and one would not quarrel with the judgment.

Predictably, however, in his critical biography of Davies,
Richard J. Stonesfier finds that even he, 'by and large,
was an exception'. (9)   Dr F.R. Leavis argues that Edmund
Blunden deserves to be distinguished from the group
'because he has some genuine talent and is an interesting
case'. (10)   Edith Sitwell would likewise make exception
of him ('Of the less violent of the Georgian poets, Edmund
Blunden is the best'), (11) and offers special pleas for
'three poets whose work had its place in Sir Edward
Marsh's "Georgian Poetry", but whose work bears no family
resemblance to the other poets in that anthology': Walter
de la Mare, W.H. Davies, and Ralph Hodgson. (12)
    It is interesting to set beside this mere sample of
attempts made by protagonists of individual Georgians to
separate them from the fold, the comments of three
contemporaries.   Richard Aldington addresses his audience
in 'The Egoist' (1 June 1914) on Modern Poetry and the
Imagists: (13)

> Do you, most honourable reader, who are fed upon the
> works of Mr Wells, and Mr Henry James, and Mr
> Bennett ......, do you take no interest in the works
> of Mr Yeats, Mr Sturge Moore, Mr Bridges, Mr James
> Stevens [sic] , Mr Brooke, Mr Flint, Mrs Meynell
> and Mr Pound?

(Messrs Sturge Moore, Stephens and Brooke, be it noted,
had appeared in the first anthology of 'Georgian Poetry',
which had been dedicated to Mr Bridges; the fifth
anthology was to be dedicated to Mrs Meynell.) In the
same year, Harold Monro lectures to a Cambridge audience
on the Contemporary Poet, by which he means 'the poet
[who] has caught the spirit of Darwin, that spirit which
has so altered our attitude, and rendered obsolete so
many ways of talking about life'.   He calls these poets,
not Georgians, but 'Impressionists': chief among whom is
Ezra Pound; but highly to be commended are Flecker,
Gibson, and Brooke. (14)   Finally, Monro's friend and
assistant editor, Arundel del Re, wrote reminiscently in
the 1930s of 'Ezra Pound, W.W. Gibson, Lascelles
Abercrombie, John Drinkwater and others who were after-
wards to form the nucleus of the Georgian group'. (15)
The juxtaposition of Pound, whom del Re calls 'the
Troubadour of the Georgians', (16) with poets whom
Mrs Gilbert would find more 'cosily domesticated' may
seem less strange when we have examined the background
history.

The background c. 1909-12

King George V succeeded to the throne on 6 May 1910.
A.R. Orage, who edited 'The New Age' from 1907 until
1922, and made it the most influential radical weekly of
its time, wrote in the first issue of the new reign: (17)

> At each successive death of the great men who lived
> during the reign of Queen Victoria, the public has
> been instructed to believe that each was indeed the
> close of his age.   Tennyson was the last, so was
> Lord Salisbury.   Then it was Meredith, and only
> recently it was Swinburne.   But all of these
> announcements of the real close of the Victorian era
> have been premature.   The last genuine link with the
> Victorian age has been broken with the death of
> King Edward VII.

Tennyson had died in 1892, and there was still, said
A.C. Ward, 'a widespread impression that English poetry
had died with him'; (18)   Swinburne had died in April
1909, Meredith in May.   In June 'The English Review'
commented: 'Mr Meredith follows Mr Swinburne into the
shadows; and now indeed the whole Round Table is dis-
solved'. (19)   Yeats said, 'And now I am King of the
Cats' - 'forgetting perhaps', as John Press has reminded
us, 'that Thomas Hardy was still in the plenitude of his
poetical genius': (20)   'The Dynasts' had come out in
three volumes in 1903, 1906 and 1908; 'Time's Laughing
Stocks' was published in 1910.   In 1909 Yeats published
his 'Collected Poems', and, with new books by Kipling,
Noyes, Watson, and Newbolt, 'The English poetic scene
offered a rather spiritless Yeats, and a collection of
public-spirited versifiers'. (21)   The neglect of John
Davidson (who drowned himself in the same year) and the
overvaluing of Stephen Phillips (who seems never to have
recovered from the rapturous reception of his first poems)
are in their different ways symptomatic of the poetic
barrenness of the time.   Galsworthy could write optim-
istically of a renaissance in his Vague Thoughts on Art,
(22) and Ezra Pound, in one of nearly 300 articles he
contributed to 'The New Age', could look characteristic-
ally for a *risorgimento*, though he thought of course that
it would originate in America. (23)   But Orage wrote
some two years after the earlier article quoted: 'If I
were asked upon what I rely for the renaissance of England,
I should say a miracle'. (24)   And almost a half century
later T.S. Eliot reflected that 'the situation in poetry
in 1909 or 1910 was stagnant to a degree difficult for
any poet of today to conceive'. (25)

Yet, with hindsight, 1909 might be seen to mark the
beginning of a new age in poetry.   Eliot, who had
ordered the works of Laforgue in the previous year, was
in 1909-10 writing 'Preludes', 'Portrait of a Lady' and
a first draft of 'Prufrock' (though the poems were not to
appear until 1915).   His fellow American, Pound, dined in
March at the club founded by F.S. Flint, and 'Imagism' was
born. (26)   'Personae', Pound's second book, his first to
be published in England, appeared in the following month,
and was favourably reviewed by Rupert Brooke.   In the
same year Pound met Yeats, and by the middle of the year
was attending Yeats's 'Monday evenings'.   Although
Harold Monro, writing in 1920, thought that 'Yeats had
already published most of his best work' with the appear-
ance of 'Collected Poems', (27) C.K. Stead can see in
later perspective that their publication 'put an outworn
style and restricted sensibility behind him, making way
for the new, more robust poetry that was to emerge'. (28)

If Blériot's flying the Channel, which preceded King
George's accession by some ten months, had less symbolic
value for the new reign than had the conquest of Everest
for the 'new Elizabethans', it had wider cultural signif-
icance.   As Wallace Martin shows in his admirable study
of '"The New Age" under Orage', the art and thought of
the continent provided the impetus for change. (29)

> This impetus was transmitted, not through the
> recognition and emulation of defined artistic canons,
> but as an emotion, a sudden expansion of the realm of
> imaginative possibility, which was to find its own
> forms of expression in England.

Professor Martin identifies Post-Impressionism, the
philosophy of Bergson, psycho-analysis, and Russian
culture as among the sources of this emotion, and judges
that 'collectively, they appear to imply cultural changes
of such magnitude as to justify comparisons with the
Renaissance'. (30)   T.E. Hulme introduced readers of 'The
New Age' to Bergson in 1909, (31) and two years later
wrote five articles on him. (32)   Hulme himself wrote
pseudonymously in 'The Saturday Westminster Gazette': (33)

> There have been stirring times lately for those
> peculiar people amongst us who take an interest in
> metaphysics.   We have not been able to buy even a
> sporting evening paper without finding in it an
> account of a certain famous philosopher.

Eliot and Pound were anti-Bergsonians; but an aesthetic
which exalted personality was to find an impressionable
disciple in the young Middleton Murry, (34) and to be a
cause of dispute on that account between the editor of
'Rhythm' and the editor of 'The New Age'. This was only
the beginning of an aesthetic split which found further
expression in the 1920s when Murry's 'Adelphi' and Eliot's
'Criterion' continued the debate.

    Diaghilev's Russian Ballet (1911), the first perform-
ance of 'The Cherry Orchard' (1911), Constance Garnett's
translation of 'The Brothers Karamazov' (1912), A.A.
Brill's translation of 'The Interpretation of Dreams'
(1913) - although this last was at first available only
to 'Members of the Medical, Scholastic, Legal, and
Clerical professions' - were contributions to the 'subtle
expansion of the realm of imaginative possibility'; but
no event contributed more to it than the two Post-
Impressionist exhibitions. It was probably to the first
of them that Virginia Woolf was alluding when she wrote:
'On or about December, 1910, human character changed.'(35)
Some poets wrote 'Post-Impressionist' poems; (36) and
Robert Bridges, thanking Marsh for his presentation copy
of 'Georgian Poetry, 1911-1912', felt 'sometimes as if I
were reminded of the Post-Impressionists' pictures'.
Marsh, who thought he 'had kept out all that kind of
thing', supposed it had 'become so much of the London air
that one doesn't notice it'. (37) Middleton Murry admits
in his autobiography that the somewhat vague ideal which
inspired 'Rhythm' was transmitted to him in Paris by the
Scottish painter, J.D. Fergusson, an enthusiastic spokes-
man for Post-Impressionists. (38) Murry wanted 'Rhythm'
to do in words what the Post-Impressionists had done in
paint. His first wife, Katherine Mansfield, wrote
indeed that two of the Van Gogh paintings in the 1910
exhibition 'taught me something about writing, which was
queer, a kind of freedom - or rather, a shaking free'.(39)

    When one has been working for a long stretch one begins
    to narrow one's vision a bit, to fine things down too
    much. And it's only when something else breaks
    through, a picture or something seen out of doors,
    that one realises it.

In a perceptive review of the second exhibition (1912),
Rupert Brooke wrote of Matisse: (40)

    The great glory of this exhibition is that it gives
    us at length a chance of judging and appreciating
    Matisse. Some twenty pictures and nearly as many

drawings.   The pure bright and generally light colour,
and the stern simplicity and unity of design, fascinate
the beholder .....   There are moments in the life of
most of us when some sight suddenly takes on an inex-
plicable and overwhelming importance - a group of
objects, a figure or two, a gesture, seem in their
light and position and colour to be seen in naked
reality, through some rent in the grotesque veil of
accidental form and hue - for a passing minute.

A still stronger feeling than Katherine Mansfield's of a
sense of 'freedom' or 'shaking free' was that expressed
by D.H. Lawrence in the March 1913 issue of 'Rhythm'
(No. 12); but this was prompted by another and more
literary occasion.

Georgian Poetry: birth of an idea

Some three weeks before Orage's pessimistic thoughts on
the chances of a renaissance, a luncheon party had been
held in the rooms of a civil servant who was then private
secretary to Winston Churchill at the Admiralty.   The
beginnings of the Georgian Poetry venture have been often
related.   The earliest account is that of Edward Marsh
himself in his 'Memoir' of Rupert Brooke: (41)

There was a general feeling among the younger poets
that modern English poetry was very good, and sadly
neglected by readers.   Rupert announced one evening,
sitting half-undressed on his bed, that he had con-
ceived a brilliant scheme.   He would write a book of
poetry, and publish it as a selection from the works
of twelve different writers, six men and six women,
all with the most convincing pseudonyms.   That, he
thought, *must* make them sit up.   It occurred to me
that as we both believed there were at least twelve
flesh-and-blood poets whose work, if properly thrust
under the public's nose, had a chance of producing
the effect he desired, it would be simpler to use the
material which was ready to hand.   Next day
(September 20th it was) we lunched in my rooms with
Gibson and Drinkwater, and Harold Monro and Arundel
del Re (editor and sub-editor of the then 'Poetry
Review', since re-named 'Poetry and Drama'), and
started the plan of the book which was published in
December under the name of 'Georgian Poetry'.

In his own memoirs Marsh referred to two other events of
1911 which had 'put it past a doubt that a golden age was

beginning': they were the publication of Rupert Brooke's
'Poems' in December of that year and of Masefield's 'The
Everlasting Mercy' in October. (42)   In an appendix to
his biography of Brooke, Hassall makes a useful survey of
the contemporary reviews of the only book of Brooke's
writing to be published during his lifetime. (43)
Almost all the critics seem to have given their chief
attention to those few poems which came to be known as
'unpleasant', notably 'A Channel Passage' in which, in
Byronic vein, Brooke emulated Don Juan's retching fare-
well to Spain and Donna Julia, and 'Lust' which his
publisher, Frank Sidgwick, persuaded him to retitle
'Libido'. (44)   Criticism ranged from J.C. Squire's
complaint in 'The New Age' that 'the appalling narrative
of a cross-Channel voyage should never have been included
in the volume.   It spreads its aroma all round', (45) to
the kindlier comments of 'The Times Literary Supplement':

> Mr Rupert Brooke's swagger and brutality we are inclined
> to take much more leniently [than those of James
> Stephens, one of the six other poets reviewed in the
> article]; they are so obviously boyish.   His dis-
> gusting sonnet on love and seasickness ought never to
> have been printed; but we are tempted to like him for
> writing it.   Most people pass through some such
> strange nausea on their stormy way from romance to
> reality.

The same review   paid tribute to 'a rich nature -
sensuous, eager, brave - fighting towards the truth', and
concluded: 'We shall watch Mr Brooke's development with
high hopes; but he must remember that swagger and
brutality are no more poetry than an unripe pear is
fruit.' (46)   Congratulating him on the book's appear-
ance, Marsh wrote to Brooke: (47)

> I had always in trembling hope reposed that I should
> like the poems, but at my wildest I never looked
> forward to such magnificence ..... The 'Channel
> Passage' is so clever and amusing that in spite of a
> prejudice in favour of poetry that I can read at meals,
> I can't wish it away - but ..... I must protest against
> the 'smell' line in 'Libido' ..... there are some
> things too disgusting to write about, especially in
> one's own language.

Among those with whom Marsh shared his enthusiasm was the
poet, Francis Meynell.   Meynell suggested that he should
write an article on the 'Poems' for 'The Poetry Review'

which was edited by his friend, Harold Monro.   Marsh
agreed to do so, and Meynell's initiative was the means
of first bringing together the future editor and the
future publisher of 'Georgian Poetry'.

More immediately successful had been the publication
of 'The Everlasting Mercy'.   Robert H. Ross attributes
its widespread popularity to the fact that 'it was the
first book of verse since "Barrack-Room Ballads" to
succeed in titillating the British public by poetry which
managed to be at once both ribald and respectable'. (48)
In his early study of Masefield, Cecil Biggane wrote: (49)

> It is difficult now to recall, and it will in later
> years be still more difficult to realise the shock
> with which 'The Everlasting Mercy' came upon the
> literary world.   It was something quite new, in
> matter, in spirit, in style.   Its amazing vitality,
> its startling candour, something large in the design,
> something swift in the pace, which made its frequent
> carelessness of detail seem not merely negligible but
> inevitable, took the public by storm.

The poem was first printed in 'The English Review',
whose editor, Austin Harrison, recalled in a reminiscent
article twelve years later that a large section of
readers had been hostile to the 'Review' at that time on
the grounds that it was corrupting morals: (50)

> ..... one morning the fell news came that the trade
> were boycotting us.
> We were off the bookstalls - banned, in disgrace,
> and sales fell by the hundred.   The question was,
> would Sir Alfred Mond [the proprietor] hold on? He
> did gamely, and then, four months after the boycott,
> a man strolled into the office, dripping wet (it was
> raining furiously at the time), unpacked a thick
> manuscript, and told me no publisher would look at it,
> and walked out into the rain.
> The man was John Masefield and the poem was 'The
> Everlasting Mercy'.   I took it home and, after read-
> ing it, decided at once to publish.   But in proof
> form it looked catastrophic - to the editor.   I
> think it contained eighty repetitions of the word
> 'bloody' and ran to eighty pages of print.   I sent it
> to three literary lights for consideration.   One said
> it was 'bloody rot'.   The second said I should be
> locked up if I printed it.   The third: 'It's splendid,
> but it will smash you.'   That decided me.   The poem
> appeared unedited in the following issue.   Two days

later the telephone began to ring continuously. Sir
Alred Mond 'phoned: 'You've done it, but it was worth
doing'; and then it got into the public houses, where
the fight scene was read out aloud to admiring
pugilists.
     Probably no poem ever created such a stir since
Byron's 'Don Juan'. We printed edition after edition.
A society lion-hunter asked me to dinner. A few weeks
afterwards the trade placed us on the bookstalls again,
from which date we never looked back.
     Those eighty bloodies had saved the 'Review', which
we then turned into a company and sold at a shilling.
Masefield's three subsequent poems appeared in its
pages, and each poem was an event. Our enemies were
silenced. We became an institution.

Harrison's facts of publication were disputed by Frank
Sidgwick, who claimed that his firm of publishers had
accepted the poem provisionally when Masefield offered
it, then unfinished, in May of that year. He also
corrected Harrison's inaccuracies about the text: 'The
facts are that the poem occupied forty-four pages of "The
English Review", and as written by the author contained
the said word not eighty but eleven times.' Moreover,
the 'Review' did not print the offending word, preferring
to leave eleven blank spaces to be filled in according to
the taste and fancy of the reader'. (51) Whether or not
the 'Review' was saved by eleven blank spaces, Harrison's
account was true in spirit to the event. Masefield, as
Frank Swinnerton wrote, 'was the first Georgian Poet;
for he did something which at that time no other young
poet could do - he made the general public read what he
had written'. (52)
     The popular success of the poem could fairly have en-
couraged Marsh in his dream of a golden age. The sales
of 'Georgian Poetry' were surpassed only by those of
Brooke and Masefield: thirty-seven impressions of
Brooke's 'Poems' were printed up to May 1932, totalling
nearly 100,000 copies, and Masefield's 'Collected Poems'
of 1923 had sold over 100,000 copies by 1930. No less
important was the influence of such poets as Brooke,
Masefield, and Wilfrid Gibson (whom someone called
'Masefield without the damns') (53) in capturing a wider
public for 'realism'. When, in the second of his anth-
ologies, Marsh (54),

staked the considerable critical reputation of
'Georgian Poetry'on two long works in the realistic
tradition - Abercrombie's 'End of the World' and

Bottomley's 'King Lear's Wife' - he made amply
evident what was in fact true: the kind of realism
first popularised by Masefield was one of the major
facets of the pre-war revolt against the dead hand of
poetic tradition.

Arundel del Re wrote prophetically at the time: (55)

Mr John Masefield is a revolutionary.   His latest
work is a direct assault upon cherished principles and
venerable conventions .....   Its value lies not so
much in sheer audacity - though this indeed has
peculiar interest - as in the influence it may have on
contemporary poetry.

The proud title 'Georgian'

All the literary histories refer to the title 'Georgian
Poetry' as Edward Marsh's coinage, and he himself spoke
of his 'proud, ambiguous adjective'. (56)   There is,
however, some slight evidence, though it is unsupported
by Monro, that the publisher of the anthology rather than
its editor may have first chanced upon the title.   In
'Harold Monro and the Poetry Bookshop', Joy Grant quotes
from the unpublished autobiography of the poet, A.K.
Sabin: (57)

[Sabin and Monro] walked along Brompton Road to
Harrods, and went up in the lift to their newly
decorated refreshment rooms.   'Georgian Restaurant',
shouted the lift-boy, as we reached the top floor.
Hundreds of people were seated at lunch.   'It ought
to be called the *Gorgean* Restaurant', said Harold,
with one of his rare touches of slightly sardonic
humour.   As we followed an attendant to a vacant
table, he continued reflectively: 'This is the first
time since my return that I have been reminded we are
living in a new Georgian era - and, by Jove, Arthur,
we are the new Georgian poets!'

According to Sabin, the event took place on or about
7 June 1911, and Arundel del Re's account confirms that
Monro visited England in the late spring of that year.
Miss Grant continues: (58)

Harrod's [sic] archives confirm that in 1911 a new
restaurant was opened on the fourth floor, 'an oak-
panelled and beamed room with gas chandeliers', origin-

ally to be called the Tudor Restaurant.   The advent of
the new sovereign suggested a more topical if less
appropriate name.

She suggests that it would scarcely have been polite of
Monro, a guest at Marsh's inaugural luncheon, to claim
for himself the invention of the adjective which he had
coined over fifteen months before.   The 1933 Supplement
to the 'Oxford English Dictionary' includes 'Georgian':
'Belonging to the reign of George V', and cites Marsh's
title as a second example.   He is preceded by P[hilip].
Gibbs, who wrote in the 'Lady's Realm' of July 1910
(p. 272) : 'Under the new régime of Georgian England'.(59)
     When Marsh was considering poems for the fifth
anthology, Monro wrote to him about one of the three he
had submitted: 'I feel somehow that "Unknown Country" is
almost too Georgian even for "G.P."!'   This, as Hassall
suggests, was 'possibly the first instance of that
epithet's use in the now familiar, derogatory sense'. (60)
Monro expressed himself publicly in this manner in a pre-
fatory note to his 'Real Property' (1922), and was taken
to task by J.C. Squire in 'The London Mercury': (61)

The poems in the second half are for the most part
earlier than the others.   The poet says of these that
'they have no metaphysical background' and that 'some
of them are tainted with slight Georgian affectations
which no amount of polishing could successfully remove'.
Presumably he is referring to the poem, which is not
good, about the nightingale;   the faults and merits of
the others are distinctly Mr Monro's own.

Interestingly, Monro would seem to have yet another claim
to originality in the useful coinage of 'neo-Georgian' as
applied to Georgianism in decline.   Writing in 'Some
Contemporary Poets' (1920), he suggests that W.J. Turner
'has suffered from learning the "tricks of the trade" in
the neo-Georgian school'. (62)   Robert H. Ross, who
develops a distinction between 'Georgian poets, 1912-17
vintage, and [neo-] Georgian poets, 1917-22', evidently
missed this earlier occasion, and gives Alec Waugh the
credit (63) (see No. 62).   It was taken up by those few
critics who were sensitive enough to appreciate the need
for such a distinction, and further elaborated by Herbert
Palmer in 'Post-Victorian Poetry'. (64)   An anthology of
'Neo-Georgian Poetry, 1936-1937' was published in 1937,
edited anonymously by the poet 'John Gawsworth' (T.I.F.
Armstrong).   In the company of poets who were 'alike in
eschewing both the esoteric and the propagandist tendency

of much modern verse' (65) we find, surprisingly, the
Communist poet 'Hugh MacDiarmid' (C.M. Grieve).

Brooke did not at first like the name 'Georgian';   he
'thought it sounded too staid for a volume designed as the
herald of a revolutionary dawn'. (66)   A.C. Benson wrote
in his review of the first volume (No. 5) that one was
apt to (67)

> connect it with the hapless Hanoverian period, with
> prosaic, shrewd, ethical verse, with solidarity rather
> than fineness.   One thinks of George II's horror of
> 'Boetry' and George III's complaints of all the 'sad
> stuff' there was to be found in Shakespeare.

But no more suitable name could be agreed, and it is
interesting to see how rapidly it gained currency. Frank
Swinnerton, more sympathetic than Benson to its assoc-
iations, thought the title 'a stroke of genius': (68)

> 'Georgian' - with King George barely, you might say,
> upon his throne, a whole literature was announced:
> What! is the age as active as all that?   'Poetry' -
> what! have we, then, some poetry apart from Masefield
> and the old ones?   'Georgian Poetry' - what a claim!
> It suggested that the poetry of the age differed from
> the poetry of all other ages.

It was a cause of confusion that Sir Arthur Quiller-
Couch's 'Oxford Book of Victorian Verse', appearing at
almost the same time as 'Georgian Poetry, 1911-1912',
should have included several of the same contributors.
As Max Plowman said in reviewing Q's anthology: 'No man
can serve Victoria and George at the same time' (69) (see
also No. 2).   When a new book of poems, 'The Sea is Kind',
was published by T. Sturge Moore, the most senior contrib-
utor to 'Georgian Poetry', it was reviewed under the title
'A Victorian Georgian'. (70)   In contrast, one of the
younger contributors to the fifth volume, Edmund Blunden,
had been hailed as a 'Georgian Poet' some six years before
his appearance in it, when his first book, 'Pastorals',
was published in the series produced by one of Marsh's
imitators.   In a notice of the first four volumes of 'The
Little Books of Georgian Verse', the reviewer in 'The Times
Literary Supplement' wrote: 'For a publisher to open at
this moment a series of books by rising poets writing, for
the most part, as if the world was in profound peace,
compels by its very audacity some admiration.' (71)

Although in 1914 an anonymous reviewer in 'The New States-
man' could refer to Georgian literature in an eighteenth-
century context, two years later in the same paper Desmond
MacCarthy reviewed under the heading 'Georgian Plays' the
production at His Majesty's of Bottomley's 'King Lear's
Wife', Gibson's 'Hoops', and Brooke's 'Lithuania'. (72)
Edward Marsh interested a number of contemporary painters
in an idea first suggested by Stanley Spencer for a volume
of reproductions to be called 'Georgian Drawings'. (73)
Rupert Brooke wrote to Russell Loines in New York (6 July
1914): (74)

I'm ..... sending a package which explains itself:
'Georgian Drawings'.   I think, myself, it's going a bit
far to call a lot of beastly artists *Georgian*, when the
name has been appropriated for a nobler clan.   And
it's generally agreed that Marsh has got Georgianism
on the brain, and will shortly issue a series of
Georgian poker-work: and establish a band of Georgian
cooks.   Still, there it is (or will be): and it'll
contain work by most of the good young people in
England.

The idea petered out, partly because of the outbreak of
war, but chiefly for financial reasons. (75)   Rupert
Brooke's Rugby friend, W. Denis Browne, headed his music
criticism for the first issue of 'The Blue Review':
'Georgian Music'. (76)   And a series of 'Georgian
Stories' appeared in five annual volumes from 1922 to
1927 (1923 excepted).   Their anonymous editor, Arnold Lunn,
handed over after two volumes to Alec Waugh.   The series
borrowed more than his proud adjective from 'E.M.'.
The first issue bore on the front of its dust jacket:
'"Georgian Stories" seeks to do for modern English
fiction what "Georgian Poetry" did for modern English
verse .....'; and the editor begins his Preface:
'"Georgian Stories" is published in the hope that the art
of the short story is once again coming into its own
.....' (77)

Edward Marsh: Editor

Herbert Palmer wrote of the first Georgian anthology as
'probably next to Palgrave's the most important and in-
fluential anthology ever published'. (78)   Edmund Gosse
paid its editor the compliment which pleased him most
when, on Monro's announcing the end of the series, he
said in a valedictory tribute, 'He is with Tottel': (79)

see also Gosse's earlier reference to 'Tottel's
Miscellany' (No. 26).   Like his eminent forerunners,
Marsh was not himself a practitioner, and his anthologies
were less subject to a poet's idiosyncrasy than those,
say, of W.B. Yeats, and more recently Philip Larkin.
But like other truly personal collections, their dist-
inction and limitations reflect both the sureness and the
limits of their editor's taste.   It is relevant, then,
to touch upon certain aspects of his life and character.
(See Nos 72, 73 and 74.)

Edward Howard Marsh, known to a wide circle of friends
as 'Eddie', was born in 1872 to Jane (née Percival) and
Howard Marsh.   His father, who became Professor of
Surgery at Cambridge and Master of Downing, entrusted to
his wife the upbringing of his son and second daughter
(an elder had died in infancy), and she was the 'all-
pervading influence in my early life'. (80)   A devout,
puritanical lady, she had cut 'Don Juan' out of her
collected Byron to 'put herself out of temptation'. (81)
Likewise she had thought it necessary to protect her son,
a precocious and avid reader, from 'The Heart of Mid-
lothian' (for the seduction of Effie) and 'David Copper-
field' (for the fate of Emily).   When he committed
'L'Allegro' to his remarkable memory, she made him begin
at 'Haste thee Nymph', 'so as to spare my memory the
contagion of the not-quite-nice line in the preamble
about Zephyr "filling" Aurora with the buxom
Euphrosyne'. (82)   To his mother's distress he was to
find himself incapable of any kind of transcendental
belief. (83)   Moreover he kept throughout life an
almost schoolboyish delight in the ribald.   One of the
earliest letters I received from him included a jingle
he had composed about Henry Moore's 'Three Standing
Figures', followed by: ' - but this will shock you?'(84)

He was educated at Westminster School and at Trinity
College, Cambridge, where he gained a starred First in
the Classical tripos.   The earliest 'portrait' of him in
print appeared in a short-lived undergraduate magazine,
'The Cambridge A.B.C.'.   One of six players in 'A Game
of Croquet' is 'Mr Ethelbert Swamp', an 'Apostle' of
Trinity College.   'Miss Edith Staines' (Ethel Smyth) is
'discussing the rhythm of Baudelaire's poems with Mr
Swamp, an intellectual looking gentleman with a pince-nez;
his hair curls outwards from his collar; he bears a
striking resemblance to Mr Emile Zola'.   While he waits
for Miss Staines to begin, he 'hums a "couplet" of his
own composition (in the manner of Paul Verlaine) in a
delicate falsetto'.   After going through the second hoop,
he muses: 'It is a nice point whether I should get into

position or try and spoil Mrs Tanqueray's game by
croqueting Spur's ball.   I wish McTaggart were here to
ask.   (He plays, and misses both strokes.)' (85)   The
satire is gentle;   more hurtful was that of H.G. Wells's
'Freddie Mush', whose chief characteristic was 'Taste,
Good Taste', and who 'spoke in a kind of impotent
falsetto'. (86)

The falsetto was a direct consequence of a boyhood
attack of mumps complicated by German measles.   'His
speech', wrote his biographer, 'sounded like a witty
aside written in faded pencil.' (87)

> The illness which had left him with a mode of express-
> ion strangely appropriate to his unusual personality
> (though at first it might give a misleading impression
> of weakness of character) had at the same time affected
> his physical constitution in a more serious way.   The
> disease had determined the colour of his personality
> and the course of his life so fundamentally that one
> cannot wish it to have been otherwise, although the
> result was a disability.   So early in life did it
> happen, and the knowledge of it came so gradually,
> there are no grounds for supposing he grieved that he
> was to be incapable of the act of love, or minded at
> all that he was destined from then on to live and die
> as chaste as the day he was born.   It enabled his
> affections to grow more intensely in the mind, and as
> a result he cultivated a capacity for friendship which,
> untroubled by physical desire, could develop into a
> devotion characteristically feminine in its tenderness.

As he wrote at the close of his own reminiscences, he
counted among his advantages in life 'a tendency to take
rather more interest in other people than in myself'.
The title of those reminiscences, 'A Number of People',
was apt;   but 'it seemed a pity', wrote Hassall, 'that
the author himself could hardly be counted as one of their
number'. (88)

In his multiform activities he seems always to have
taken second place.   As private secretary to a success-
ion of cabinet ministers (notably to Winston Churchill:
'I was Ruth to his Naomi'), editor of 'Georgian Poetry'
('Private Secretary, nay, Accoucheur and Wet-Nurse, to
Euterpe in her most respectable modern rebirth'), (89)
biographer of Brooke, translator of Horace and La
Fontaine, proof-reader and book-doctor to Churchill and
Somerset Maugham among many, he gave his time, sympathy,
and artistic judgment to the service of others.   In a
brief parenthesis in his 700-page biography, Hassall

refers to the difficulty of presenting as leading actor
one who was 'off stage even in his own life story'. (90)
Hassall achieved this, however, and gave shape to what
might otherwise have been a mere conglomerate of letters,
tributes, anecdotes and chit-chat, by directing attention
to 'the one unchanging figure - the fastidious and exact-
ing master of pure scholarship'.   Informing the frigid
surface of the public figure - 'Patron of the Arts',
senior civil servant, gentleman of society, 'undeniably
one of the ornaments of his time' (91) - was a mind of
classical symmetry, rational, Horatian, scholarly rather
than intellectual, of wide culture but intensely English,
with something of the elegance, formality and wit that
were more common attributes of the eighteenth century.
It is an indication of his biographer's success that,
although friends as diverse and interesting as Bertrand
Russell, D.H. Lawrence, Henry James, Robert Graves,
Stanley Spencer, and Ivor Novello crowd the pages, one's
chief interest throughout is in him who - to adapt
Swift's maxim - by taking second place has title to the
first.
     An event which occurred some sixty years before
Edward Marsh's birth was to have notable consequences for
himself and many others.   In 1812 his mother's grand-
father, Spencer Perceval, was assassinated while Prime
Minister.   Parliament granted a pension to the family,
and an inherited share of what he called the 'murder
money' was used by Marsh a century later for the benefit
of British art and letters.   'I have never had what any-
one in his right mind could describe as Money', he said
once; (92) but he refused to draw on the pension for his
personal benefit, and shared it instead among struggling
poets and artists.   To call him a patron with its in-
escapable Johnsonian undertones would be to give a false
idea of a relationship in which he felt himself the ser-
vant.   'I should be ashamed', he wrote to one of his
beneficiaries, 'of being comparatively well off, if I
couldn't take advantage of it to help my friends who are
younger and poorer and cleverer and better than I am.'
The pension also provided the means of his guaranteeing
Monro against possible loss on 'Georgian Poetry'.

'Georgian Poetry, 1911-1912'

Such a guarantee was to prove entirely unnecessary.   At
least in its beginnings, 'Georgian Poetry' was a success-
ful business venture rather than a literary movement.
The sales both of the first volume and its successors

were immense by present-day standards for hard-backs.
Marsh estimated that in the final reckoning 'Georgian
Poetry, 1911-1912' sold 15,000 copies. (93)   The second
volume sold 19,000, establishing a record which, as
Hassall conjectures, may never be surpassed.   The third
volume sold 16,000, the fourth 15,000; but sales of the
fifth fell to 8,000, which Marsh himself conceded as an
obvious 'falling off in public receptivity' and 'a pretty
strong hint' that the series had outlived its day. (94)
    Marsh had made one stipulation in accepting Brooke's
suggestion that he should edit the anthology: he would
remain in the background, and not put his name to it.
This was characteristically modest, but it was also
shrewd.   For the private secretary at the Admiralty to
be shepherding a group of poets might be thought absurd
by the uninitiated and so damage the cause (95) - though
such feelings did not prevent Asquith's referring to the
group as 'Eddie Marsh's gang'. (96)   It was agreed with
the luncheon guests that the anthology should be pub-
lished in time for Christmas sales in an edition of 500.
Half the royalties would go to 'The Poetry Review' which
Monro was then editing (when his Poetry Bookshop opened
in the following January, it took over publication) and
half to Marsh who would distribute his share equally
among contributors.   When he accepted this arrangement,
he could have had no idea of the immense administrative
labour he was taking on: the idea of a series had not
then been considered, nor could the demand for success-
ive reprints have been foreseen.   The intermittent des-
patch of royalties over the following decade was a means
of keeping him in touch with his contributors, and,
because he was a thoughtful and painstaking correspondent,
of keeping them in touch with one another. (97)
    No-one was more enthusiastic from the first than the
prime mover of the venture.   John Drinkwater recalled
Brooke's telling his fellow guests at the inaugural
luncheon that 'England must be bombarded with the claims
of the new poets', and offering to use his influence 'as
brazenly as a commercial traveller'. (98)   'Years
before', Marsh noted, 'a cynical young friend of ours at
King's, Francis Birrell, had told me that though
"Rupert's public form was the youthful poet, the real
foundation of his character was a hard business faculty".'
(99)   During November, while staying in Berlin, Brooke
kept Marsh plied with suggestions for promoting sales.
(100)

    'I forget all my other ideas,' he wrote, after
    making some very practical proposals, 'but they each

sold some 25 copies.   I have a hazy vision of in-
credible *réclame*.   You ought to have an immense map
of England (*vide* 'Tono-Bungay') and plan campaigns with
its aid.   And literary charts, each district mapped
out, and a fortress secured.   John Buchan to fill a
page of the 'Spectator':   Filson Young in the P[all].
M[all]. G[azette].   .....   You'll be able to found a
hostel for poor Georgians on the profits'.

(John Buchan filled half a page of 'The Spectator':   see
No. 6.)   It may have been some measure of Brooke's
success that Drinkwater could report: 'the Prime
Minister's car was waiting outside Bumpus's shop in Oxford
Street at opening-time on the day of publication, and
Rupert's strategy was to be seen in it'. (101)
     But if Brooke was an enthusiastic lieutenant, Marsh was
in Robert H. Ross's words, 'the generalissimo in charge
of strategy'. (102)

> So skilful and thorough was his campaign that one is
> tempted to conclude that if there had not been a
> poetic renaissance before publication of 'Georgian
> Poetry' I, it would have been necessary to invent one
> after.   Had 'Georgian Poetry' I turned out to be a
> mediocre anthology or worse, it would nevertheless
> have been assured of creating a considerable critical
> splash.

Marsh's first task was to assemble contributors.   His
normal practice was to make particular requests for what
he wanted rather than allowing choice to the poet.   With
few exceptions, those invited agreed to allow him the
poems he asked for.   Housman refused: he did not think
of himself as belonging to Marsh's 'new era';   'A Shrop-
shire Lad' had appeared sixteen years before, and he had
written nothing in the past two years, the period Marsh
set himself to cover.   Pound was asked for The Goodly
Fere and one other poem (Hassall thinks Portrait d'une
Femme), but refused the first 'as it doesn't illustrate
any *modern* tendency' and the second as it was appearing
shortly in a book of his own. (103)   He invited Marsh to
choose from Canzoni, but Marsh found nothing suitable
there.   Pound hoped that he might appear in the second
volume, but by then Marsh had decided to confine his
choice to British writers, a decision which later de-
prived him of Robert Frost.   Masefield was at first
reluctant, but finally so warmed to the venture that he
held back publication of his 'Biography' so that it
could make its first appearance in 'Georgian Poetry'.

The exclusion of Edward Thomas, who became for a brief
period at the end of his life one of the finest poets of
his day, has sometimes been held against Marsh.   But
Thomas did not begin writing verse until 1914, a year
after Marsh had first met him, and the best of his poems
date from the winter of 1914-15 (see headnote to No. 4).
When in 1917 de la Mare and others tried to persuade
Marsh to include him in the third anthology, de la Mare
offering to stand down in his favour, he was excluded by
the editor's ruling that no poet should appear for the
first time in the series posthumously.
      Publishing schedules were more briskly timed in those
days.   Conceived in late September, the anthology was in
proof by 5 November, and Marsh received advance copies
from Monro later that month.   He sent over a hundred
copies to his friends, and worked by night with a team of
packers (among them, Gilbert Cannan, Elliott Seabrooke,
Abercrombie, Brooke, and Monro), despatching review
copies to all parts of England and to newspapers abroad.
He worked with remarkable skill through friends or
friends of friends, and no subsequent volume was so
widely or so favourably noticed.   At least three of the
notices were written by contributors (Nos 2, 12 and 13).
      While it has seemed important to refer here to the
beginnings of 'Georgian Poetry', to chronicle its develop-
ment through successive volumes would be too large a task
for this Introduction.   In most important respects its
history will appear in the reviews selected and the head-
notes to them.   Biographically the series is well covered
by Christopher Hassall's 'Edward Marsh', and no better
literary account has appeared than that by Robert H. Ross.

Contemporary editors and reviews

In his Introduction to 'Ford Madox Ford' in The Critical
Heritage series, Frank MacShane writes of the 'neglect of
serious imaginative literature ..... during much of the
period that led up to the First World War', and of the
'absence of serious literary people on the staffs of the
literary journals'. (104)   This was truer of the nine-
teenth-century literary journals to which he refers, such
as the 'Quarterly' and 'Edinburgh' reviews, than of some
of the newer magazines which sprang up shortly before the
war, many of them to be killed by it.   Indeed, for one
brief period, just too early to be of service to
'Georgian Poetry', Ford himself brought 'The English
Review' to greatness.   Contributors to his first issue
in 1908 included Conrad, Hardy, Galsworthy, Wells,

W.H. Hudson, and Tolstoy;   and later issues included the
first published work of D.H. Lawrence and Wyndham Lewis.
But, as Samuel Hynes has pointed out, 'Ford ran his
review for little more than a year, lost £5,000, and was
fired, while Orage kept 'The New Age' going for fifteen
years with an initial investment one-fifth the size of
Ford's, and resigned.   Ford was brilliant, but Orage
lasted.'   Elsewhere in his article Hynes is less kind to
'The New Age', which he calls a 'farraginous chronicle':
'It never published an excellent poem, rarely a good
story.   It opened its pages to a good deal of rubbish,
simply because it was *new* rubbish'. (105)   But it is a
measure of Orage's greatness as well as his longevity as
an editor that among writers whose first published work
appeared in his paper were F.S. Flint, T.E. Hulme,
Katherine Mansfield, J. Middleton Murry, Storm Jameson,
Herbert Read, Llewellyn Powys, Ruth Pitter, and Edwin
Muir (under the pseudonym 'Edward Moore'). (106)
    Orage was highly critical of the Georgians;   he
thought little of Brooke, and less of Gibson, Drinkwater
and Abercrombie.   'The New Age' played no direct part in
promoting 'Georgian Poetry';   it seems deliberately to
have neglected the five anthologies, preferring to support
the rival Imagists.   But its importance in the contemp-
orary literary scene has already been suggested.   Shaw
(who had put down half the initial capital for the paper),
Wells, Belloc, Chesterton, Arnold Bennett, and Pound were
regular contributors during the first phase of Orage's
editorship.   In the issue of 19 January 1912 which
noticed Brooke's 'Poems' and W.H. Davies's 'Songs of Joy',
there is a youthful poem by Ruth Pitter (then aged four-
teen), one of a series of verse/prose contributions by
Pound ('I gather the limbs of Isiris'), a reproduction of
de Segonzac's 'Les Boxeurs', a proposal by Huntley Carter
for a circular theatre, a letter on Belloc's anti-
socialism, and part of a lively correspondence on Picasso,
provoked by the publication two months earlier of a Cubist
study by him - all this in 1912!   Not only was Orage
successful at getting people to write for him (usually
for nothing unless, like Pound, they were hard up or, like
Bennett, mercenary);   he was also, according to T.S. Eliot,
'the best literary critic of that time in London'. (107)
For his part Orage wrote a remarkable assessment of Eliot
as a critic at a time when he was comparatively unknown:
'A very serious critic of our day is Mr T.S. Eliot;   and
I commend his essays wherever they are to be found.' (108)
    Orage had been appointed joint editor with Holbrook
Jackson.   They parted amicably after ten months, Jackson
to begin a more literary journalistic career in which he

edited 'T.P.'s Weekly' (1911-16) and 'To-day' (1917-23).
(109)   Belloc founded the 'Eye-Witness' in 1911, and
Cecil Chesterton (brother of G.K.) became editor when it
changed to 'The New Witness' in 1912.   But 'The New Age'
was more directly concerned with the appearance of its
most significant rival, 'The New Statesman', in 1913.
There was a political reason for this: Orage's espousal
of what came to be known as 'Guild Socialism' had alien-
ated his Fabian supporters.   Partisan feelings ran high
between the two papers;   and Wells, writing in 'The New
Witness', declared his feelings towards the upstart:
'One of their best writers is almost good enough for
"The New Age" ..... Ideas!   There is not so much as
the tenth of an *Orage* in the whole enterprise.' (110)
In fact two of their best writers had transferred:
Clifford Sharp as political editor and J.C. Squire as
literary editor.   Squire now took upon himself the
mantle of 'Solomon Eagle' - if mantle be the word
when the original bearer of the name ran naked through
the streets of London at the time of the Great Plague, a
pan of coals on his head, crying: 'Repent, repent!' (111)
Squire's 'Books in General' became a weekly platform for
his wit and entrenched literary tastes, and he developed
also his gifts as a parodist.

   In November 1919, after a well-prepared publicity
campaign had enlisted several thousand subscribers a full
year in advance, 'The London Mercury' was launched with
Squire as editor.   His biographer, Patrick Howarth,
writes (112)

   in the belief that the 'London Mercury' was, arguably,
   the greatest purely literary and artistic magazine
   that this country has ever produced and that the years
   from 1910 to 1925 produced one of the greatest flower-
   ings of the English lyric in history.

Whatever allowance may be necessary for the partiality of
this judgment, 'The London Mercury' took over with remark-
able consistency at the point where Marsh had chosen to
leave off, and became a powerful last bastion of the neo-
Georgians.   In an opening fanfare Squire claimed that
'there has never been in this country a paper with the
scope of the "London Mercury"'.   He referred to 'The
Edinburgh Review' of Jeffrey's and Macaulay's day, to
Thackeray's 'Cornhill', 'The Times Literary Supplement',
and 'weekly papers which review the principal books and
publish original verse and prose'.   But there had been
no paper hitherto which had combined 'all those various
kinds of matter which are required by the lover of books

and the practising writer'.   There followed this state-
ment of his editorial principles: (113)

> As convenient descriptions we do not object (save some-
> times on grounds of euphony) to the terms Futurist,
> Vorticist, Expressionist, Post-Impressionist, Cubist,
> Unamist, Imagist: but we suspect them as banners and
> battle-cries, for where they are used as such it is
> probable that fundamentals are being forgotten.   Our
> aim will be, as critics, to state and to reiterate
> what are the motives, and what must be the dominant
> elements, of all good art, whatever the medium and
> whatever the idiosyncrasies of the artist .....   The
> profoundest truths about art, whether literary or
> pictorial, are crystallised in maxims which may have
> been more often reiterated than understood, but which
> have undeniably been so often repeated that people now
> find them tiresome.   Of such are 'fundamental brain-
> work', 'emotion recollected in tranquillity', 'the
> rhythmical creation of beauty', and 'the eye on the
> object'.   Each of these embodies truths, and there
> is indisputable truth also in the statements that a
> poet should have an ear and that a painter should
> paint what he sees.   These things are platitudes;
> but a thing does not cease to be true merely because
> it is trite, and it is disastrous to throw over the
> obvious merely because it was obvious to one's grand-
> father.

It will be seen that Squire shared a number of Marsh's
preferences and principles: an impatience with schools
of literary theorizing, a concern that 'a poet should
have an ear', and, above all, a wish that writing should
be easily intelligible.   Squire's short review of 'The
Waste Land' began: 'I read Mr Eliot's poem several
times when it first appeared; I have now read it several
times more; I am still unable to make head or tail of
it.' (114)   Which was at least honest.
   To return to the beginning of the period, Middleton
Murry's 'Rhythm', which was first published in summer 1911,
might be regarded as the first of the English 'little
magazines'. (115)   It was founded and edited by Murry
and Michael Sadleir while they were still undergraduates
at Oxford, and exhibited all the bold outspokenness of
youth. '"RHYTHM" is a magazine with a purpose.   Its
title is the ideal of a new art .....   Aestheticism has
had its day .....   Humanity in art in the true sense
needs humanity in criticism .....' and, quoting Synge
without acknowledgment, 'Before art can be human it must

learn to be brutal'. (116)   It was a sitting target for
'The New Age', which made easy fun of the abundance of
naked ladies in linocut (one of whom, an especially buxom
Eve with apples, appeared on each cover), as also of the
literary misjudgments.   There were extravagant reviews
by Murry: 'James Stephens is the greatest poet of our
day .....   Henceforward [he] stands with Sappho, Catullus,
Shakespeare, Coleridge, Heine, Villon and Verlaine';   and
in the same issue Frank Harris is 'the greatest living
English critic and story-writer'. (117)   But the magazine
was a brave venture, expressing a genuine spirit of new-
ness and vitality as well as what Katherine Mansfield
called 'the gentle art of self-consciousness'. (118)   In
the fourth issue Laurence Binyon wrote on 'The Return to
Poetry': (119)

> Slowly we have emerged from the nineteenth century.
> We are breathing a different air.   We are no longer
> *fin de siècle.*   We are being changed, and the world
> with us.   Horizons open and allure us.
>
> How long have we been sitting down before Nature
> and letting her impose herself upon us!   Our imagin-
> ations have been schooled into passivity.   Uncon-
> sciously enslaved, we were growing benumbed.   And now
> we want to stretch our limbs, to move, to dance, to
> feel our life-blood running again.

D.H. Lawrence's 'Georgian·Renaissance' (No. 12), which
develops these ideas, appeared in the final issue.   The
first issue of 'The Blue Review' which followed it for
three issues only (May-July 1913) had as its frontispiece
Max Beerbohm's cartoon of Winston Churchill with his
secretary, 'A Study in Dubiety: Mr Edward Marsh wonder-
ing whether he dare ask his Chief's leave to include in
his anthology of "Georgian Poetry" Mr George Wyndham's
famous and lovely poem: "We want eight and we won't
wait".'   Edward Marsh, who reviewed 'Mr Max Beerbohm's
Exhibition' in the second issue, studiously avoided ref-
erence to the cartoon of himself, but managed to slip in
four lines from Brooke's 'Thoughts on the Shape of the
Human Body'. (120)
In 1920 Arthur Rowntree bought the moribund 'Athen-
aeum' and invited Murry to edit it.   Murry initiated
such new features as 'Marginalia' by 'Autolycus' (Aldous
Huxley) and the publication of fiction: Katherine
Mansfield, Tchekov (in translation), Max Beerbohm,
Virginia Woolf, Stephen Hudson, and Robert Nichols were
prose contributors, and among the poets were Hardy, Edith
Sitwell, Graves, Binyon, Conrad Aiken, T.S. Eliot,

Blunden, W.H. Davies, Wilfred Owen, and W.W. Gibson.
The scene had changed since the days of his two pre-war
magazines.   As some of the names suggest, he was still
happy to print Georgians, but he was discriminating in
his choice of them.   In mid-1919 he had attacked the
whole anthology system (No. 31), and in December he
delivered the most damaging blow to 'Georgian Poetry' by
his review of the fourth volume (see No. 34).   In Feb-
ruary 1921 'The Athenaeum' merged with 'The Nation' and
'The Nation and Athenaeum' was in turn absorbed by 'The
New Statesman' in 1931.

Another poet-critic-editor who showed a somewhat
ambivalent attitude towards 'Georgian Poetry' was, sur-
prisingly, its publisher.   F.S. Flint said that Harold
Munro 'did more to stir up an interest in poetry than any
other man of his generation'. (121)   His life and work,
particularly his support of poetry and poets through the
Poetry Bookshop, have been excellently chronicled by Joy
Grant.   Miss Grant explains in more detail than can be
given here the unhappy agreement he reached with Galloway
Kyle, founder of the Poetry Society, to publish 'The
Poetry Review' in conjunction with the society's
'Gazette'.   It was a misalliance between a man dedicated
to poetry and a society in which, as Miss Grant writes,
'poetry was made an excuse for pleasant social ex-
changes, for irrelevant snobbery, for the disagreeable
consequences of organized association'. (122)   In his
first issue in January 1912 Monro showed his colours.
'Poetry', he wrote in his preface, 'is said to be un-
popular - generally by those who dislike it themselves.
Good poetry is as much read now as at any time since the
invention of printing, and bad poetry is certainly read a
great deal too much.' (123)   In the same issue, an
article on 'The Future of Poetry' is both reflective of
the time and prophetic of the future. (124)

> Something different is necessary in modern poetry than
> sentimental patriotism or a mere delight in poetical
> verbiage.   The modern poet's equipment must include,
> apart from the natural adoration of beauty, a clear
> and sound grasp upon facts, and a stupendous aptitude
> for assimilation.   Moreover he may suffer from no
> illusions as to calling or divine inspiration, but,
> with the simple faith of a forerunner, must work on
> persistently and delightedly towards an invisible
> goal.

Also in the first issue F.S. Flint began a review of
Pound's 'Canzoni' (in which, it will be remembered,

Marsh had been able to find no poems suitable for his
anthology): 'Let it be conceded at once, without cavil,
that the authentic note of poetry sounds throughout this
last book of Mr Ezra Pound's.' (125)   When Pound him-
self launched out in the second issue with 'Prolegomena',
the staider spirits of the society must have been dis-
quieted by his ideas on 'the poetry which I expect to see
written during the next decade or so': (126)

> ..... it will, I think, move against poppycock, it will
> be harder and saner, it will be what Mr Hewlett calls
> 'nearer the bone'.   It will be as much like granite
> as it can be, its force will be in its truth, its
> interpretive power (of course, poetic force does al-
> ways rest there);   I mean it will not try to seem
> forcible by rhetorical din, and luxurious riot.   We
> will have fewer painted adjectives impeding the shock
> and stroke of it.   At least for myself, I want it so,
> austere, direct, free from emotional slither.

The Georgians are well established, with Maurice Browne
reviewing Gibson, and Arundel del Re 'The Everlasting
Mercy', Gibson finding Abercrombie's 'the most signif-
icant voice of our time', (127) Abercrombie and Gibson
writing on poetry in the drama, Abercrombie appreciating
Drinkwater, and Brooke's 'Poems' acclaimed 'The Book of
the Month', reviewed by E. Marsh.   'The Old Vicarage,
Grantchester' was awarded £30 as the best poem printed
in 'The Poetry Review', by a panel of judges consisting
of Monro, Marsh, Ernest Rhys, Edward Thomas and Edward
Plarr.   Among other poets published by Monro were
Gibson, Pound, Drinkwater, James Stephens, Sturge Moore,
F.S. Flint, Abercrombie, W.H. Davies, Walter de la Mare,
Flecker, G.K. Chesterton and himself.   Perhaps the most
significant contribution was F.S. Flint's survey of con-
temporary French poetry which filled most of the August
number (see No. 14).   Pound mentioned it as 'something
which everybody had to get'. (128)
Towards the end of 1912 Monro's conflict with the
Poetry Society came to a head.   In 'The Poetical
Gazette' for December (included in 'The Poetry Review')
appeared the announcement: (129)

> Mr Harold Monro having decided to enlarge the scope
> of his periodical by issuing it quarterly under the
> title POETRY AND DRAMA, THE JOURNAL OF THE POETRY
> SOCIETY beginning with the next number, January,
> will be issued under the Editorship of Mr STEPHEN
> PHILLIPS and a brilliant list of contributors has

been secured, including all the principal leaders of
modern life and thought and criticism who are assoc-
iated with poetry.   In addition to his editorial
functions, the poet-dramatist who thrilled the world
with 'Paolo and Francesca', and fascinated us with the
rare beauty of 'Marpessa', 'Herod', 'Ulysses', 'Nero',
will contribute a monthly article on the eternal sig-
nificance of Poetry.

Confusingly for many contemporary readers, 'The Poetry
Review' continued in name under Phillips's management
while its true successor, Monro's 'Poetry and Drama',
came out in eight quarterly numbers between March 1913
and December 1914.   It is interesting to contrast Monro's
hopes in September 1913 that the laureateship would be
abolished ('officialdom is incompatible with poetry')
(130) with Phillips's disgruntled not to say misinformed
comments on 'The Appointment to the Laureateship' which
appeared in his concurrent issue: (131)

We have ..... as the official representative of English
verse the patron-saint of what one may call 'the blood-
less school' of modern poetry.   The representatives of
this school are a large class of the younger men who
call themselves Georgian poets, and as their leader is
Dr Bridges, so their prophet is Sir Arthur Quiller-
Couch.   Their business in verse is chiefly that of the
present Laureate, a clever cold carpentry of metre and
an intense determination to be 'original'.   But it may
be pointed out that, as in the verse of Dr Bridges,
this technical originality has rather the effect of
irritation than inspiration;   it is fidgety rather
than fiery, and the fact is ignored that what is
called the great 'technique' of verse is rather the
result of an overpowering emotion and sense of glory
than a toying with the inanimate.

In 'Poetry and Drama' Monro felt freer to achieve his
aims as editor, and there is a new note of iconoclasm.
Algar Thorold contributed to the first issue an 'irrevent'
[sic] article attacking the National Anthem;   in the
third issue appeared del Re's translation of the 'New
Futurist Manifesto' together with Monro's own versions
of Futurist poems by Marinetti, Buzzi, and Pallazzeschi.
   Less tolerant than Squire of the 'platitudes' of
literary criticism, Monro commented tersely on the state
of it in the March 1914 issue: (132)

> Reputations are made like those of William Watson or
> Alred Noyes.   Every time such an author publishes a
> book, some trained person has merely to jot down a
> series of the conventional phrases: - 'sustained in-
> spiration', 'finished craftsmanship', 'essential
> quality of high poetry', 'splendid and virile', 'among
> the finest achievements in English poetry', 'most con-
> spicuous achievement of our age', 'sounds depths only
> possible to a master', 'never been surpassed', 'noble',
> 'felicitous' - we all know them so well that we do not
> trouble to pay the slightest attention to them.   The
> criticism of poetry has been degraded and prostituted
> out of all recognition: it still remains genuine in
> only a few periodicals.

Among Monro's other contributors were Ford Madox Ford
(then Hueffer), Remy de Gourmont, Thomas Hardy, and Robert
Bridges;   Edward Thomas reviewed regularly, Brooke wrote
on Webster and the Elizabethan drama, and Newbolt re-
viewed 'Georgian Poetry, 1911-1912' (No. 11).
When 'Poetry and Drama' closed it was with the assur-
ance that it would reappear after the war.   In July 1919
Monro issued a rather different magazine, 'The Monthly
Chapbook', sub-titled 'Poetry and Drama, New Series', and
later renamed 'The Chapbook'.   It appeared monthly for
the first two years, but by early 1922 financial diff-
iculties made its appearances less regular.   The series
ran to forty issues, and concluded with two large annual
volumes in October 1924 and October 1925.   The first
issue announced: (133)

> Each number of 'The Monthly Chapbook' will be of
> separate interest, and complete in itself.   At the
> same time, a definite continuity will be preserved so
> that the six issues for any half-year will form a vol-
> ume combining a record of that half-year's production
> in poetry and drama, a critical survey of contemporary
> literature, and numerous examples of the creative work
> of the present period.....

Joy Grant summarizes the contents of that first issue, and
remarks on the variety of talent represented: (134)

> The inclusion of de la Mare and W.H. Davies harked back
> to the first Georgian anthology, and Thomas Sturge
> Moore and Charlotte Mew hailed from an even greater
> distance;   the old pre-war *avant garde* was represented
> by Aldington, H.D., F.S. Flint and D.H. Lawrence;
> Siegfried Sassoon, W.P.R. Kerr, W.J. Turner and

Robert Nichols were Georgians of the war-time
generation, while the three Sitwells, Aldous Huxley
and Herbert Read were in the very firing-line of post-
war poetry.   Monro contributed 'Underworld'.   'The
Chapbook' was plainly interested in experiment of every
kind, and issued incongruously from the house that, a
few months later, produced 'Georgian Poetry, 1918-1919'.

Monro, who had in 1914 missed the opportunity of publish-
ing 'The Love Song of J. Alfred Prufrock', (135) seems to
have been the only contemporary editor to find 'The Waste
Land' 'as near to poetry as our generation is capable of
reaching'. (136)
An incongruity of a different sort was the publication
in the September 1922 issue of Osbert Sitwell's satire,
'The Jolly Old Squire or Way-Down in Georgia', the Pro-
logue to a 'Mime-Drama, with copious notes by the Author'.
The Heroes were 'J**K C*LL**GS SQ**RE, Poet and Journal-
ist, Editor of the "English Hermes".   ED**RD SH**KS,
Journalist and Poet.   Contributor to the "English Hermes"'
who with FR**M*N and T*RNER were week-end rustic poets
living in London 'where Hawthornden more sweet than haw-
thorn blows' because Shanks and Freeman had both been
awarded the Hawthornden prize.   The Villain, Satan, was
to be impersonated at the first performance by 'Mr
H*R*LD M*NRO'.   (Monro had already been billed in this
unflattering rôle by William Kean Seymour: (137)

> *Monro*, as Mephistopheles, no doubt
> Would be a leading figure in the rout,
> While *Marsh* with all his orders would be there,
> The beau of all the Georgians, and the snare.)

There is also to be a 'Chorus of Critics, Journalists and
Poets, referred to as the Squirearchy, or the Press-Gang'.
The Squirearchy spend half their time playing cricket and
taking in one another's washing, so they do not have time
to do their own work properly, and do not notice when
Satan puts a stanza from Shelley into the desks of Sq**re
and Sh**nks.   Each thinks it his own brainchild, with
predictable consequences.   It is a strange outpouring of
dated wit and doggerel; its inclusion in the body of this
book as a literary curiosity was considered, but its value
as comment seemed too slight to merit this.   Here, how-
ever, are the concluding lines with their echo of the
third and poorest of Brooke's '1914' sonnets: (138)

> Now in the Play which follows you shall see
> The mighty Goddess Mediocrity
> Contrive that naughty Satan's overthrow.
> Meanwhile blow bugles, blow red trumpets, blow!

Two other poets were to echo Sitwell in the early 1930s'.
Robert Nichols also writes of Squire at a village cricket
match (and alludes to Brooke): (139)

> The dawdling 'over' scarce disturbs the flock,
> And oh, how slowly chimes the village clock!

And Roy Campbell pictures him in another sporting
context: (140)

> Nor at his football match is Squire more gay -
> Heart-rending verse describes funereal play;

Part II of Campbell's 'Georgiad' begins: 'Hail,
Mediocrity'. (141)
    In 1921, a year before the appearance of his satire,
Osbert Sitwell published a small pamphlet, 'Who Killed
Cock-Robin?', 'Remarks on Poetry, on its criticism, and
a sad warning, the story of Eunuch Arden'.   In it he
attacked 'the lark-lovers - to whom the antics of some
miserable bull-finch are as important as any poem'. (142)

> *Poetry* is *not* the monopoly of the Lark-lovers, or of
> those who laud the Nightjar, any more than it belongs
> to the elephant or the macaw.
>   Because a good poem has grown out of the emotion
> felt by a poet who realised a lark or a green tree,
> it does not follow that other verse-writers, by
> babbling continually of larks and green trees, will
> write good poems.
>   It is better to leave well alone.
>   The lark has outstayed its welcome, and migrated.
> It may return again one day. (143)

All three Sitwells were to feature noisily in the post-
war chorus of anti-Georgians, quoting one another with
an approval which they bestowed upon few of their con-
temporaries.   Thus Osbert's lark-lovers and the
veritable aviary he derides in the 'Jolly Old Squire'
reappear in Edith's 'Aspects of Modern Poetry' ('Birds
became a cult') together with sheep, beer and the violin
'although this must always be called a fiddle', (144) and
in 'Trio', where we find: (145)

..... certain of the Georgians ..... seem obsessed by
the predilection for sheep.   Sheep became with them
almost a mania, - together with singing-birds, -
(these were heavily patronized), violins (only these
were called fiddles), gaffers, ale-house wits, and
rustic parts of England .....   There were loud and
cheerful if raucous cries for beer and raptures over
cricket.

The oft-quoted dictum of F.R. Leavis that 'the Sitwells
belong to the history of publicity rather than of poetry'
(146) is nowhere more applicable as a half-truth than to
their verse anthology, 'Wheels', which appeared in six
annual 'cycles' from 1916 to 1921.   When the first anth-
ology went into a second edition a few months after its
appearance, it included eight pages of press notices, and
these became an often amusing feature of its successors.
'Wheels' attracted attention from the first because, as
C.K. Stead notes, (147)

so many of its contributors had interesting parents -
a Huxley, three Sitwells, an Hon. Wyndham Tennant, a
daughter of Sir Herbert Beerbohm Tree, a daughter of
Sir Bache and Lady Cunard.   'The names speak for
themselves', the 'Observer' commented;   the 'Sketch'
correctly predicted 'their names are enough to secure
a second edition'.

Besides Aldous Huxley, the three Sitwells, E.W. Tennant,
Iris Tree, and Nancy Cunard, contributors to the first
volume were Arnold James, Victor Tait Peronne, and Helen
Rootham.   The fourth volume was 'dedicated to the memory
of Wilfred Owen M.C.', and seven of his poems were in-
cluded in it.   It is interesting to note in passing that
Owen wrote once of 'We Georgians', and was proud to be
'held peer' by them. (148)
No survey, however brief, could ignore the noisiest
and most extraordinary of the pre-war little reviews,
Wyndham Lewis's 'Blast'.   The first issue appeared in
June 1914, the second and last in July 1915.   It was a
typographical as well as a literary assault on the public,
the first issue carrying an enormous 'BLAST' diagonally
across its puce cover.   Within it proclaimed itself a
'Review of the Great English Vortex', and its editor
announced: (149)

Long live the great art vortex sprung up in the centre
of this town!   We stand for the Reality of the Present
- not for the sentimental Future, or the sacripant Past.
We want to leave Nature and Men alone.

And, triumphantly:

> We believe in no perfectibility except our own.

This was indeed a manifesto to end all manifestos.   Pound
and his sculptor friend, Henri Gaudier-Brzeska, con-
tributed further on the 'Vortex';   there were poems by
Pound, vorticist drawings, and stories by Rebecca West
and Ford Madox Hueffer.

The second issue contained a five-line satirical poem
by Pound on Rupert Brooke (delays in producing the mag-
azine had meant that the poem appeared three months after
Brooke's death and caused much offence), and a moving
piece from the trenches by Gaudier-Brzeska, so soon to die
in them: (150)

> This paltry mechanism, which serves as a purge to over-
> numerous humanity.
> This war is a great remedy.
> In the individual it kills arrogance, self-esteem,
> pride .....

- sentiments not far removed from some expressed by Brooke
in the '1914' sonnets.   Although it contains no specific
reference to Brooke, an article entitled 'The Art of the
Great Race' is remarkably prophetic of his fate at the
hands of his idolaters: (151)

> When a man portrays and gives powerful literary
> expression to a certain type in a nation and milieu,
> he attracts to him that element in the race that he
> symbolizes.   These movements are occasionally
> accompanied with an enthusiasm that resembles a
> national awakening or revival .....   When these free-
> masonries are awoken, they exist without reference to
> their poet.   Some creators, in fact, find themselves
> in the position of the Old Woman who lived in a Shoe.
> This progeny may turn out to be a race of cannibals
> and proceed to eat their poet.

But the chief distinction of 'Blast II' was to give their
first English publication to Eliot's poems, four
'Preludes' and 'Rhapsody on a Windy Night' appearing in
it.   J.C. Squire was characteristically dismissive. (152)

> The first large English enterprise of the Futurist-
> vorticist-Cubist kind was ..... the magenta magazine
> 'Blast'.   It succumbed shortly after a hostile critic,
> consulting his Webster, had discovered the definition:

'Blast: - a flatulent disease of sheep'. (153)   But
it died to give place to countless smaller magazines
and books containing bewildering designs and extra-
ordinary poems.

The 'Men of 1914', as Wyndham Lewis described Pound,
Eliot and himself, owed much to the protagonism of Pound,
and still more to his encouragement and practical initiat-
ive in getting their work in print.   His prolific journ-
alism enlivened the pages of countless periodicals on both
sides of the Atlantic.   Finding that the 'general tend-
ency of British criticism at the time' was, in his own
words, 'towards utter petrification or vitrifaction', (154)
he set himself in racy, arrogant prose to vilify at diff-
erent times almost every one of his literary contempor-
aries.   The antithesis of Marsh who, as an editor, aimed
to woo the reading public and educate its taste, Pound dis-
missed it as too degenerate to deserve consideration. (155)
Typical of his achievements was the persuasion of Dora
Marsden, editor of 'New Freewoman', to change the title of
her paper to 'The Egoist', and transform it from a period-
ical devoted to woman's suffrage and woman's place in
society to one which was to give most of its space to the
support of Imagist poets.   'The Egoist', said Pound, was
'necessary to print Joyce, W. Lewis, Eliot and a lot of
my stuff that Orage would *not* have in "The New Age"' (156)
The change of name took place with the issue of 1 January
1914, and the paper continued as a fortnightly for that
year, appearing thereafter as a monthly under the editor-
ship of its proprietor, Harriet Shaw Weaver.   Among its
contributors were Richard Aldington, F.S. Flint, Robert
Ross, John Gould Fletcher, Amy Lowell, and William Carlos
Williams.   Perhaps its greatest claim to distinction was
the serial publication of Joyce's 'Portrait of the Artist
as a Young Man' after its rejection by all other publish-
ers.   The critical alignment of both the 'New Freewoman'
and 'The Egoist' can be represented by a youthful paean
Rebecca West in praise of the Imagists at the expense of
the Georgian inhabitants of Devonshire Street (it was
there that Monro had his Poetry Bookshop): (157)

Poetry should be burned to the bone by austere fires
and washed white with rains of affliction: the poet
should love nakedness and the thought of the skeleton
under the flesh.   But because the public will not pay
for poetry it has become the occupation of learned
persons, given to soft living among veiled things and
unaccustomed to being sacked for talking too much.
That is why from the beautiful stark bride of Blake

it has become the idle hussy hung with ornaments kept
by Lord Tennyson, handed on to Stephen Phillips and
now supported at Devonshire Street by the Georgian
school.

Similarly representative in satirical vein is Richard
Aldington's 'To a Poet': (158)

> May we not be spared -
> I beseech you -
> The insistent cult of 'Nature',
> This pitiless reiteration?
> . . . . .

or, in its assault on the hymnodists of war, 'Song in
War-Time', possibly by the same hand though signed
'Herbert Blenheim'. (159)

When Richard Aldington, who was one of the assistant
editors, left for military service in mid-1916, (160) his
place was taken briefly by his wife, the American poet,
Hilda Doolittle, who was known always by her initials,
'H.D.'.   In June 1917, however, T.S. Eliot's name
appeared as assistant editor, and from that point 'The
Egoist' became less exclusively an organ of the Imagists.
The last issue appeared in December 1919; but less than
three years later Eliot's 'Criterion' was to take up many
of the same causes and publish many of the same contrib-
utors.   Its first issue was distinguished by the pub-
lication of 'The Waste Land'.   That was in October 1922;
in November, the fifth and last of the Georgian anthol-
ogies appeared.   Monro's already quoted statement that
'The Waste Land' was 'as near to poetry as our generation
is capable of reaching' (161) was, by implication, an
epitaph for his Georgians.

This survey cannot be more than selective and cursory.
It was a period when many literary reviews were born and
many died.   As R.C.K. Ensor said, rich men could become
makers of opinion by publishing sixpenny reviews, for it
was possible then to publish a weekly with a circulation
of 3,000 copies without losing more than £2,000 a year.
'Publication of this class became ..... more numerous and
various than ever before, and from first to last much of
the period's best writing will be found in them.' (162)
Nor has space been allowed to the nineteenth-century
reviews referred to by Frank MacShane, or to daily news-
papers, though each field has provided some useful
material.   For all Rupert Brooke's efforts to promote
'Georgian Poetry' during his American and Canadian tours
in 1912-13, it remained, perhaps appropriately, cis-

Atlantic, not to say insular; and there was little
serious critical attention paid it in America. G.P.
Putnam's Sons of New York issued the 1911-12 anthology in
1914 and each of its four successors in the year follow-
ing its English publication; but the total sales only
just exceeded 5,000. The review of the fourth anthol-
ogy in 'The New York Times' (No. 38) was by one of the
English poets who had contributed to it, and Amy Lowell,
who reviewed it in 'The Dial' (No. 40), had visited the
Poetry Bookshop. One interesting reciprocation of
cross-Channel interest occurred in the Belgian newspaper,
'La Meuse' (No. 14).

Later critical attitudes to the Georgians

D.E.S. Maxwell begins his monograph on Eliot: (163)

> From 1900 until the First World War, poetry in England
> wandered for the most part along country paths opened
> up by the nineteenth-century romantics, unaware that
> the paths had become ruts, and that a more suitable
> track was now the pavement. New forces were appear-
> ing, but their influence was small, and on the Georg-
> ians, who commanded what popular favour there was,
> non-existent.

Commenting on Maxwell as 'typical of most recent critics
of twentieth-century poetry', C.K. Stead writes: (164)

> He shows no awareness that there were poets more
> popular than the Georgians at this time; that [more
> popular poets such as Newbolt, Kipling and Watson]
> considered the Georgians dangerous young innovators;
> that the Georgians were consciously narrowing the scope
> of poetry in order that certain commonl.iterary views
> might be excluded; and that their efforts made poss-
> ible both the war poetry of Wilfred Owen and the
> mature poetry of Robert Graves.

Elsewhere Stead attacks David Daiches (165) on similar
grounds: (166)

> Mr Daiches, like so many critics of the past twenty
> years, has seen the Georgians through spectacles
> provided for him by the later, more vigorous movement
> led by Pound and Eliot. The suggestion is that the
> Georgians set themselves against the natural develop-
> ment of modern poetry: in fact they were its pre-
> cursors.

More recently, in his contribution on Poetry to 'The Twentieth-Century Mind' (1972), John Wain has made a still stronger claim for the Georgians:

> I believe that if the First World War had not happened, the new idiom in English poetry would have been a dev-elopment of Georgianism.   The seeds were there: the honesty, the dislike of cant, the 'selection from the real language of men', the dissatisfaction with a narrow tradition of poetry laid down by the literary Establishment and enforced by teachers and anthologists.

The Georgians, he argues, were already breaking out of the mould of Palgrave's 'Golden Treasury', 'unlearning the literary influence that tended to make poetry an elegant amusement, bringing it closer to everyday speech and the actuality of life'.   He cites Edward Thomas and Wilfred Owen as major poets who 'take off from Georgianism'. (167)

> If their flight had been longer, there would have been no need of a modern poetic idiom imported from France via America.   The Savage God, that daimon of a world without poetry, was already being challenged by Yeats; the seeds planted by Hopkins were still sleeping in the earth;   Owen and Thomas, abetted by the excellent poets who survived the war, by Graves, by Blunden, by the older poets like Hodgson and de la Mare, would have made a living tradition out of English materials aris-ing naturally from English life.   If they had, the Auden generation, coming into a healthier situation for English poetry, might have developed differently, and better.
>
>   But the war came, and nothing as moderate, or as sane, or as hopeful, as Georgian poetry could survive that Gadarene downrush of the nations.   The lyricism of the   early Pound, the Laforguian ironies of the early Eliot, might well have struck an alliance with a Georgian poetry strengthened by Owen, by Thomas, by the maturing Graves and Blunden;   but when the Georgian tree was cut down, these neutrals had to stand alone, their roots in a poisoned soil, faced with the responsibility of devising a poetry that should ask the one remaining question:
>   What are the roots that clutch, what branches grow
>   Out of this stony rubbish?

Professor Wain follows Alec Waugh (No. 62), Herbert Palmer, C.K. Stead, Robert H. Ross and others in dist-inguishing two phases of Georgianism: (168)

in its first, pre-war phase, it was associated with
Edward Marsh; in its second, in the early 1920s, it
was revived in the 'London Mercury' by the altogether
less sensitive J.C. Squire and made into a roadblock
against the advance of 'modern' poetry under Eliot and
Pound.

Harold Monro was making another but related point when
he wrote more than fifty years earlier that, 'in its
infancy, the "Georgian movement" was uncharacterized by
evidence of design': (169)

..... that is, it did not, like other schools, preach
or practise a special degree of the poetic art .....
But the poets subsequently included in the anthologies
devoted much energy to narrowing and hardening what
began as a spontaneous co-operative effort.   They
sought to establish (according to a recent review) 'a
form of literary tyranny, demanding of its own
disciples a complete conformity to certain standards,
and seeking to exclude altogether those who refuse to
do homage to those laws.'

So adversely did the Squirearchy affect response to
their Georgian forerunners that even so sensitive a
critic as Bonamy Dobrée could write in his pioneer study
of Eliot (1929): (170)

For another reason - frankly because I do not think
them of much value, in spite of a deal of charm - I
have passed by those who made their name in immed-
iately pre-war days, namely the 'Georgian Poets';
they walk in the path of an older poetic faith; the
landscape around them has altered, and they have not
noticed the change.

In a study of Eliot published three years after Dobrée's,
Hugh Ross Williamson declared: (171)

Criticism of poetry ..... is in the hands of the
'Georgians', to whom Mr Eliot is very properly ana-
thema, because once his conception of poetry is under-
stood, most of the 'Georgians' will be dismissed for
ever as the negligible versifiers that they are.

Eliot himself, who had of course gone elsewhere to
establish his poetic roots, wrote perceptively about the
Georgians (Nos 25 and 30); but in A Critical Note in
'The Collected Poems of Harold Monro' he could remember
only 'a small number of poems by two or three men'. (172)

Dismissal by a practitioner, whose reading is necess-
arily guided by his own developing art, is more allowable
than that by a newspaper critic or literary historian.
The reviewer of 'Some Poems' by Rupert Croft-Cooke in the
Cambridge magazine, 'The Granta', could write in 1929:
(173)

> I suppose the last word on Georgian poetry has been
> said a great many times, albeit one still lacks a
> succinct formula in which to dismiss it.   Its main
> faults are that it is *facile, sentimental,* socially
> and politically *non-significant,* fit for people of all
> ages and, above all, *popular.*   Probably no poet, not
> even Tennyson, has had such a wide appeal as the
> Georgians.   The erudition and obscurity of the poetry
> which is now considered good in Cambridge have at least
> this in their favour, that they are bound to limit the
> circle of a poet's real admirers.

Do we not hear, three years before the founding of
'Scrutiny', a peculiarly Cambridge tone?   The reviewer
concludes:

> In fact, the author's only radical fault is to have
> copied the wrong people and adopted an idiom that
> everyone is heartily sick of;   and this is a pity
> because I am informed on the cover that he is 'a very
> young man'.   If he would only forget Humbert Wolfe
> and his own ominous (though nice) Christian name, and
> throw off the accent of repressed yearning together
> with the Georgian idiom which, I feel sure, inspired
> it - then he might do something worth while.

In the same year H.W. Garrod, Professor of Poetry at the
other place, could refer to 'that most decaying order of
vulgarity, the Georgian'; (174) while in 1928 A.C. Ward
could write with the same slightly off-hand disdain:
(175)

> The Georgians seemed always on the verge of doing
> something much better than they had done before - but
> the possibilities remained possibilities only.   The
> five volumes - brown, blue, green, orange, red - have
> now a sepulchral air, like five chambers of a maus-
> oleum where faded chaplets hang around the brows of a
> company of the embalmed.

A characteristically more belligerent, less belletrist
note was sounded in the same year by Roy Campbell, who

called the Georgians a 'literary ramification of the Boy
Scout movement or the Open Air League'. (176)

> The homely thoughts of the Georgians on rugger, love,
> or beer: their conversations with dogs;   their bland
> approvals of virtue, restraint, and intellectual dig-
> nity;   their desire to lose their identity in a mus-
> ical blending with nature;   their delight in the
> spring;   their fellow feeling for cows, sheep, dogs,
> and rabbits;   their raptures as walking-tourists and
> globe-trotters.

He listed in the same essay the questions to which any
contributor to 'Georgian Poetry' or the anthologies
which derived from it might be required to answer with
a yes:

> 1.   Have you ever been on a walking tour?
> 2.   Do you suffer from Elephantiasis of the Soul?
> 3.   Do you make friends easily with dogs, poultry,
>   etc.?
> 4.   Are you easily exalted by natural objects?
> 5.   Do you live in one place and yearn to be in
>   another place?
> 6.   Can you write in rhyme and metre?

Campbell's derisive wit was rivalled by that of two other
poets.   In 1934 Edith Sitwell brought to fulness that
catalogue of Georgian attributes from which quotation has
already been made. (177)

> Mr Housman was followed by a school of poets, rather
> loosely held together by their sub-Wordsworthian
> ideals.   To these men rhetoric and formalism were
> abhorrent, partly, no doubt, because to manage either
> quality in verse, the writer must have a certain gift
> for poetry.
>   In the age of which I speak, we find the first shy
> buds of those full-flowered transcriptions of Robert
> Elsmere into blank verse which enliven the pages of a
> certain monthly arbiter of our taste.   In that verse,
> as in much of the verse of our time, the praise of
> early home life is alternated with swollen inflated
> boomings and roarings about the Soul of Man.   These
> beauties reigned triumphant, together with healthy,
> manly, but rather raucous shouts for beer, and advert-
> isements of certain rustic parts of England, to the
> accompaniment of a general clumsy clodhopping with
> hob-nailed boots .....   Any mention of the nest of a

singing-bird threw the community into a frenzy.
Dreary plaster-faced sheep with Alexandra fringes and
eyes like the eyes of minor German royalties, limpid,
wondering, disapproving, uncomprehending, these were
admired, as were bulldogs weeping tears of blood.
Nor was Romance absent.   At one moment, any mention
of 'little Juliet', 'Helen of Troy', or of Troy it-
self, roused a passionate interest.   The names alone
were sufficient .....   Yet with all this romantic
simplicity, the business man's careful logic was
never absent, combined, strangely enough, with the
legendary innocence of the country clergyman (this
last trait being a tribute to the memory of the un-
fortunate Wordsworth).

In the same year, in 'A Hope for Poetry', C. Day Lewis
wrote: (178)

The Georgian poets, a sadly pedestrian rabble, flocked
along the roads their fathers had built, pointing out
to each other the beauty spots and ostentatiously
drinking small-beer in a desperate effort to prove
their virility.   The winds blew, the floods came:
for a moment a few of them showed on the crest of the
seventh great wave;   then they were rolled under and
nothing marks their graves.   One only rode the whirl-
wind: Wilfrid Owen, killed on the Sambre canal, spoke
above the barrage and the gas-cloud, saying to us,
'The poetry is in the pity'.   When it was all over, it
was left to an American, T.S. Eliot, to pick up some
of the fragments of civilization, place them end to
end, and on that crazy pavement walk precariously
through the waste land.

It might seem unkind to quote such youthful rhetoric by
the late Poet Laureate, were it not typical of much that
passed for assured criticism in the years between the
wars·   Although he excepts Hardy and de la Mare in this
'period of very low vitality', Hopkins, Owen and Eliot are
'our immediate ancestors'.   The transition of which
Auden wrote, when (179)

For gasworks and dried tubers, I forsook
The clock at Grantchester, the English rook

came, one suspects, less easily for Day Lewis.   The
title poem of his first book, 'Beechen Vigil and Other
Poems' (1925), begins: (180)

> Come,   dust, spread thine oblivion above
>   My heart and all the words it wove
> For her.   Now in these branches cannot die
>   Remembrance of the hour when I
> Kept vigil with the lady that I love.

Like other poems in the book, notably 'A Creation', this
shows the influence of Brooke, and a still younger Brooke
than wrote 'The Old Vicarage, Grantchester'.   Like other
poets who have 'recovered from an adolescent "phase" of
Brooke', he seems, in Christopher Hassall's phrase, to
have 'lived ever afterwards in a state of resentful con-
valescence'. (181)   But the excepted Hardy (who was
held in high regard by the Georgians, and to whom Marsh
dedicated the fourth of his anthologies) seems at first
and last a prevailing English influence upon Day Lewis.
His voice can be heard in the early 'Rose Pruner', and
it was to sound again in the poems from 'Word Over All'
(1945) onwards, when the 'foreign' influence upon the
Auden generation which John Wain regretted became less
intrusive (see No. 69).   Interestingly, in a 'Letter of
Introduction' to Day Lewis's Bibliography, Auden wrote:
(182)

> ..... I think I am right in saying that I introduced
> you to the poems of Thomas Hardy and Robert Frost,
> for both of which I had developed a passion while
> still at school.   I should like to think I am right
> because I can see what a good influence Hardy's poems
> have had on your own.

Another reason for the Georgians' low reputation in the
1930s and 1940s is suggested by John Press: (183)

> In his influential 'Faber Book of Modern Verse' (1936),
> Michael Roberts omitted every poet, except Graves and
> Owen, whom one could possibly associate with Georgian-
> ism.   Although he specifically named de la Mare,
> Blunden, and Sorley as good poets whom he felt obliged
> to ignore because they had made no notable advance in
> technique, this slightly contemptuous saving clause
> made little impression on his readers, and a generation
> nurtured on this anthology assumed that the Georgians
> were a stagnant creek far from the main current of
> English poetry.

To carry the history further would be dully repetitive:
critical half-truths are no more interesting when they
become clichés, and still less when they become archaisms.

But it would be appropriate to link with John Wain's
speculations on what *might* have happened the hopeful
speculations with which in 1934 Arundel del Re concluded
his 'Georgian Reminiscences': (184)

> The Georgian period in poetry ended with the end of
> the war, or perhaps it would be more correct to say
> that, by 1919, it had exhausted itself.   It was
> inevitable that it should be so owing to the far-
> reaching changes that had affected the spiritual and
> intellectual life of the nation.   To consider it,
> however, as one considers that of the 'Nineties',
> that is as something artificial, outside the main
> current of English poetry, is to misunderstand and
> undervalue it.   My judgement may possibly be biassed
> by the fact that I belong to that earlier generation,
> but when I think of those few years of intense activity,
> full of enthusiasm and supported by the belief that
> poetical creation should and does in effect make life
> complete and beautiful which inspired Georgian poetry,
> and compare it with the intellectual conflicts that
> seem to characterize the poetry of today, - in spite
> of the latter's very real merits, I cannot but look
> forward with confidence to the time when the seeds then
> sown by the Georgians will bear fruit.

NOTES

1   John Press, 'A Map of Modern English Verse', 1969, 105.
2   Sandra Gilbert, 'Acts of Attention: The Poems of
    D.H. Lawrence', 1972, 33.
3   Vivien de Sola Pinto, 'Crisis in English Poetry',
    1951, 134.
4   Jon Silkin, 'Out of Battle: The Poetry of the Great
    War', 1972, 258.
5   Quoted by C.K. Stead in 'The New Poetic', 1964, 88.
6   Herbert Palmer, 'Post-Victorian Poetry', 1938, 133.
7   Muriel Spark, 'John Masefield', 1953, 1.
8   James Reeves (ed.), 'Georgian Poetry', 1962, xix.
9   Richard J. Stonesfier, 'W.H. Davies: A Critical
    Biography', 1963, 101.
10 F.R. Leavis, 'New Bearings in English Poetry', 1932,
    66.
11 Edith Sitwell, Three Eras of Modern Poetry in 'Trio'
    by Osbert, Edith and Sacheverell Sitwell, 1938, 133.
12 Ibid., 121.
13 Richard Aldington in 'The Egoist', 1 June 1914, 201.

14 Quoted by Christopher Hassall in 'Rupert Brooke:
    A Biography', 1964, 365.
15 Arundel del Re, Georgian Reminiscences in 'Studies
    in English Literature' (Tokyo), XII, 1932, 330.
16 Ibid., 329.
17 A.R. Orage in 'The New Age', 12 May 1910, 26.
18 A.C. Ward, 'Twentieth Century Literature', 1928, 139.
19 'The English Review', June 1909, 409.
20 Press, op.cit., 1.
21 Stead, op.cit., 1964, 54. Cf. also Geoffrey Grigson:
    'In 1908 the "Oxford Book of English Verse" was eight
    years old, and Pan had already been christened Peter
    in "The Little White Bird".   England was poetically
    garrisoned by Alfred Austin, Kipling, Newbolt, Noyes;
    by Robert Bridges and two more considerable poets -
    Hardy, an untouched individualist, and Yeats,'
    (Notes on Contemporary Poetry, in 'The Bookman',
    September 1932, 287.)
22 John Galsworthy, Vague Thoughts on Art (1911) in
    'The Inn of Tranquillity', 1912, 260.
23 Ezra Pound, America: Chances and Remedies in 'The
    New Age', 1 May 1913, 9.
24 A.R. Orage, Renaissance in 'The New Age', 10 October
    1912, 569.
25 T.S. Eliot, Introduction to 'Literary Essays of Ezra
    Pound', 1954, xiii.   See also Eliot's A Commentary
    in 'The Criterion', April 1934, 451-2.
26 Necessarily a shorthand statement: the whole truth
    was, of course, more complex, the records of it
    diverse and contradictory.   See Stanley K. Coffman,
    'Imagism: A Chapter for the History of Modern
    Poetry' (Oklahoma), 1951.
27 Harold Monro, 'Some Contemporary Poets', 1920, 20.
28 Stead, op. cit., 54.
29 Wallace Martin, '"The New Age" under Orage'
    (Manchester), 1967, 131.
30. Ibid.
31 T.E. Hulme in 'The New Age', 1 July 1909, 198-9.
32 T.E. Hulme, Notes on Bergson: I, 19 October 1911;
    II, 26 October 1911; III, 23 November 1911; IV,
    30 November 1911; V, 22 February 1912.   These
    articles have been reprinted and discussed in
    Samuel Hynes (ed.), 'Further Speculations'
    (Minneapolis), 1955.
33 [T.E. Hulme,] A Personal Impression of Bergson in
    'The Saturday Westminster Gazette'.   Reprinted in
    Alun R. Jones, 'The Life and Opinions of Thomas
    Ernest Hulme', 1960, 205, and quoted by Martin,
    op. cit., 136.

34   See J. Middleton Murry, Art and Philosophy in
     'Rhythm', summer 1911, 9.
35   Virginia Woolf, 'Mr Bennett and Mrs Brown', 1924, 4.
     Reprinted in 'The Captain's Death Bed and Other
     Essays', 1950, 90-111.
36   E.g. Horace Holly, 'Creation: Post-Impressionist
     Poems', 1914.
37   Quoted by Christopher Hassall in 'Edward Marsh',
     Patron of the Arts: A Biography', 1959, 208.
38   J. Middleton Murry, 'Between Two Worlds', 1935,
     155-8.
39   Quoted by Antony Alpers in 'Katherine Mansfield',
     1954, 135-6.
40   Rupert Brooke in 'The Cambridge Magazine',
     23 November 1912.   Reprinted in Timothy Rogers
     (ed.), 'Rupert Brooke: A Reappraisal and Selection',
     1971, 129-30.
41   Edward Marsh, 'Rupert Brooke: A Memoir', 1918, lxxv.
42   Edward Marsh, 'A Number of People', 1939, 320.
43   Hassall, 'Rupert Brooke: A Biography', 535-9.
44   Marsh, 'Rupert Brooke: A Memoir', lxix-lxx.
45   J.C. Squire in 'The New Age', 18 January 1912, 281.
46   'The Times Literary Supplement', 29 August 1912, 337.
47   Quoted by Hassall, 'Rupert Brooke: A Biography',
     293-4.
48   Robert H. Ross, 'The Georgian Revolt', 1967, 37.
49   Cecil Biggane, 'John Masefield: A Study', Cambridge,
     1924, 9-10.
50   Austin Harrison, The Old 'English' in 'The English
     Review', June 1923, 512-15.
51   Quoted by Charles H. Simmons in 'A Bibliography of
     John Masefield', 1930, 34-5.
52   Frank Swinnerton, 'The Georgian Literary Scene',
     1935, 277.
53   Quoted by Monro, op. cit., 119.
54   Ross, op. cit., 55.
55   Arundel del Re in 'The Poetry Review', January 1912,
     25.
56   Marsh, 'A Number of People', 321.
57   A.K. Sabin, 'Pilgrimage', chapter X: quoted by Joy
     Grant in 'Harold Monro and the Poetry Bookshop',
     1967, 92-3.
58   Grant, op. cit., 93.
59   'Oxford English Dictionary', 1933 Supplement, 411.
60   Hassall, 'Edward Marsh, Patron of the Arts', 493.
61   J.C. Squire in 'The London Mercury', May 1922, 95.
62   Monro, op. cit., 156.
63   Ross, op. cit., 183n.
64   Palmer, op. cit., 197 and passim.

65   'The Times Literary Supplement', 3 July 1937, 498.
66   Hassall, 'Edward Marsh, Patron of the Arts', 190.
67   A.C. Benson in 'The Cambridge Magazine', 18 January
     1913, 209.
68   Swinnerton, op. cit., 283.
69   Max Plowman in 'Poetry and Drama', June 1913, 239.
70   'The Times Literary Supplement', 30 April 1914, 208.
71   Ibid., 8 July 1915, 231.
72   'The New Statesman', 3 January 1914, 96, and 27 May
     1916, 183-4.
73   Hassall, 'Edward Marsh, Patron of the Arts', 280.
74   Geoffrey Keynes (ed.), 'The Letters of Rupert Brooke',
     1968, 597-8.
75   Hassall, 'Edward Marsh, Patron of the Arts', 280.
76   W. Denis Browne in 'The Blue Review', May 1913, 63.
77   'Georgian Stories', 1922, 5.
78   Palmer, op. cit., 94.
79   Quoted by Hassall, 'Edward Marsh, Patron of the Arts',
     533.
80   Marsh, 'A Number of People', 1.
81   Ibid., 5.
82   Ibid., 16.
83   Hassall, 'Edward Marsh, Patron of the Arts', 46.
84   It was sent also, without the apology, to Max
     Beerbohm: see Hassall, 'Edward Marsh, Patron of the
     Arts', 670.
85   A Game of Croquet in 'The Cambridge A.B.C.', 9 June
     1894, 36-40.
86   H.G. Wells, 'Men Like Gods', 1925, 29 and 19.
87   Hassall, 'Edward Marsh, Patron of the Arts', 23.
     (Except where otherwise noted, information in this
     and the two succeeding paragraphs is from the same
     source.)
88   Ibid., xi.
89   Swinnerton, op. cit., 266.
90   Hassall, 'Edward Marsh, Patron of the Arts', 449.
91   Max Beerbohm in Christopher Hassall and Denis
     Mathews (ed.), 'Eddie Marsh: Sketches for a Composite
     Literary Portrait of Sir Edward Marsh, K.C.V.O.,
     C.B., C.M.G.', 1953, 51.
92   Hassall, 'Edward Marsh, Patron of the Arts', xii.
93   Marsh, 'A Number of People', 329.
94   Ibid., 329.
95   Hassall, 'Edward Marsh, Patron of the Arts', 190.
96   Norman Douglas, 'Looking Back: An Autobiographical
     Excursion', 1933, 227.
97   Hassall, 'Edward Marsh, Patron of the Arts', 191.
98   John Drinkwater, 'Discovery: The Second Book of an
     Autobiography', 1932, 228.

99   Marsh, 'Rupert Brooke: A Memoir', lxxvi.
100 Ibid., lxxvi.   See also Keynes (ed.), 'The Letters
     of Rupert Brooke', 406. 'P.F.' (not Filson Young)
     gave the anthology a full column in the 'Pall Mall
     Gazette' (14 January 1913), but the article does not
     merit inclusion here.
101 Drinkwater, op. cit., 229.
102 Ross, op. cit., 123.
103 Hassall, 'Edward Marsh, Patron of the Arts', 193.
     (Much of the information in this paragraph is from
     the same source.)
104 F. MacShane, 'Ford Madox Ford: The Critical
     Heritage' (1972), p. 1.
105 Samuel Hynes, 'The New Age' in 'The Times Literary
     Supplement', 25 April 1968, 436-7.   Reprinted in
     'Edwardian Occasions', 1972, 39-47.
106 A comprehensive survey of 'little reviews' relates
     that most of them 'discovered no more than two
     writers worthy of note' and that only four had
     discovered as many as four or five over the past
     half century (see F.J. Hoffman, Charles Allen and
     Carolyn F. Ulrich, 'The Little Magazine' (Princeton),
     1947, 13-14).
107 T.S. Eliot, letter to 'The New English Weekly',
     15 November 1934, 100.
108 A.R. Orage in 'The New Age', 31 March 1921, 259.
109 Robert H. Ross gives an interesting survey and
     assessment of this comparatively long-lived review:
     'Perhaps no contemporary journal published so much
     poetry or so many different kinds of poetry' ('The
     Georgian Revolt', 204-5).
110 H.G. Wells: quoted in 'The New Age', 1 May 1913, 18.
111 Patrick Howarth, 'Squire: Most Generous of Men',
     1963, 81.
112 Ibid., 285.
113 J.C. Squire in 'The London Mercury', November 1919,
     3.
114 J.C. Squire in 'The London Mercury', October 1923,
     655.
115 See Malcolm Bradbury, 'Rhythm' and 'The Blue Review'
     in 'The Times Literary Supplement', 25 April 1968,
     423.
116 Aims and Ideals in 'Rhythm', summer 1911, 36.
117 J. Middleton Murry in 'Rhythm', June 1912, 34 and
     36.
118 Katherine Mansfield, in a pungent review of a book
     of verse by a writer who seemed to lack this
     quality: see 'Rhythm', July 1912, 71.

119 Laurence Binyon, The Return to Poetry in 'Rhythm',
     spring 1912, 1.
120 Edward Marsh, Mr Max Beerbohm's Exhibition in
     'Rhythm', June 1913, 143-4.
121 F.S. Flint in 'The Criterion', July 1932.
122 Grant, op. cit., 36.
123 Harold Monro in 'The Poetry Review', January 1912,
     3-4.
124 Harold Monro, The Future of Poetry in 'The Poetry
     Review', January 1912, 11.
125 F.S. Flint in 'The Poetry Review', January 1912,
     28-9.
126 Ezra Pound in 'The Poetry Review', February 1912,
     76.
127 W.W. Gibson in 'The Poetry Review', February 1912,
     82.
128 Letter to Harriet Monro, 28 March 1914, in D.D.
     Paige (ed.), 'Letters of Ezra Pound: 1907-1941',
     1951, 74.   Flint's pioneer article together with a
     scholarly account of its original sources and its
     importance are included in Cyrena N. Pondrom, 'The
     Road from Paris: French Influence on English
     Poetry', 1974, 61-145.
129 'The Poetical Gazette', 563, included in 'The Poetry
     Review', December 1912.
130 Harold Monro in 'Poetry and Drama', September 1913,
     270.
131 Stephen Phillips, The Appointment to the Laureate-
     ship in 'The Poetry Review', 3 September 1913, 137.
132 Harold Monro in 'Poetry and Drama', March 1914, 53.
133 Harold Monro in 'The Monthly Chapbook', July 1919,
     1.
134 Grant, op. cit., 138-9.
135 Ibid., 101-3.
136 Harold Monro in 'The Monthly Chapbook', February
     1923, 24.
137 William Kean Seymour in 'Voices', Summer 1921, 86.
138 Osbert Sitwell, The Jolly Old Squire or Way-Down
     in Georgia in 'The Monthly Chapbook', September 1922.
139 Robert Nichols, 'Fisbo: or the Looking-Glass
     Loaned', 1934, 26.
140 Roy Campbell, 'The Georgiad', 1931, 22.
141 Ibid., 29.
142 Osbert Sitwell, 'Who Killed Cock-Robin?', 1921, 8.
143 Ibid., 21.
144 Edith Sitwell, 'Aspects of Modern Poetry', 1934, 19.
145 Edith Sitwell, Three Eras of Modern Poetry in
     Osbert, Edith and Sacheverell Sitwell, 'Trio',
     131-2.

146 Leavis, op. cit., 73.
147 Stead, op. cit., 112.
148 See Letters of 8 January 1918 to his cousin, Leslie
     Gunston, and of 31 December 1917 to his mother,
     Susan Owen, in Harold Owen and John Bell (eds),
     'Wilfred Owen: Collected Letters', 1967, 526 and
     521 respectively.
149 'Blast', June 1914, 7.
150 'Blast', July 1915, 33-4.
151 'Blast', July 1915, 71.
152 J.C. Squire in 'The London Mercury', February 1920,
     386-7.
153 In his earlier guise of 'Solomon Eagle', Squire
     attributed this discovery to 'Truth' (see 'The New
     Statesman', 14 August 1915, 449).
154 Quoted by Hugh Kenner in 'The Poetry of Ezra Pound',
     1951, 308.
155 See Stead, op. cit., 57.
156 Paige (ed.), op. cit., 344.
157 Rebecca West in 'New Freewoman', 15 August 1913, 86.
158 Richard Aldington in 'The Egoist', 1 May 1914, 161.
159 Herbert Blenheim in 'The Egoist', 1 December 1914.
     The poem is reprinted in Ross, op. cit., 164-5.
     Ross reports Christopher Hassall's guess that it was
     by Squire, but Squire was never a contributor to
     'The Egoist', and Ross's suggestion of Aldington can
     be supported by that writer's fondness for attacking
     in review articles the 'tumty tum' school of
     poetastry.
160 Ross (op. cit.) gets this right on p. 192 but wrong
     on p. 69.
161 Harold Monro in 'The Monthly Chapbook', February 1923,
     24.
162 R.C.K. Ensor, 'England, 1870-1914', 1936, 536.
163 D.E.S. Maxwell, 'The Poetry of T.S. Eliot', 1952,
     1 : quoted in Stead, op. cit., 189.
164 Stead, op. cit., 189.
165 See David Daiches, 'Poetry and the Modern World'
     (Chicago), 1940, 40.
166 Stead, op. cit., 80-1.
167 John Wain, Poetry in C.B. Cox and A.E. Dyson (eds),
     'The Twentieth-Century Mind: History, Ideas, and
     Literature in Britain', I, 1900-18, 1972, 396-7.
168 Ibid., 396.
169 Monro, op. cit., 150.
170 Bonamy Dobrée, 'The Lamp and the Lute: Studies in
     Six Modern Authors', 1929, 107.

171   Hugh Ross Williamson, 'The Poetry of T.S. Eliot',
      1932, 11-12.
172   T.S. Eliot, A Critical Note in Alida Monro (ed.),
      'The Collected Poems of Harold Monro', 1933, xiii.
173   J.M.R., A Nice Boy: review of Rupert Croft-Cooke,
      'Some Poems' (1929), in 'The Granta', 8 November
      1929, 95.
174   H.W. Garrod, 'The Profession of Poetry', 1923, 167.
175   Ward, op. cit., 139.
176   Roy Campbell, Contemporary Poetry in Edgell Rickword
      (ed.), 'Scrutinies by Various Writers', 1928,
      168-72.
177   Edith Sitwell, 'Aspects of Modern Poetry', 1934, 18.
178   C. Day Lewis, 'A Hope for Poetry', 1934, 2.
179   W.H. Auden, Letter to Lord Byron in W.H. Auden and
      Louis MacNeice, 'Letters from Iceland', 1937, 209.
180   C. Day Lewis, 'Beechen Vigil' in 'Beechen Vigil and
      Other Poems', 1925, 8.
181   Hassall, 'Rupert Brooke: A Biography', 532.
182   W.H. Auden, Letter of Introduction in Geoffrey
      Handley-Taylor and Timothy d'Arch Smith (compilers),
      'The Poet Laureate: A Bibliography', 1968, v-vi.
183   Press, op. cit., 107.
184   Arundel del Re, Georgian Reminiscences in 'Studies
      in English Literature' (Tokyo), XIV, 1934, 41-2.

Note on the Text

The material in this collection is presented
chronologically, and follows the original text in all
important respects.   Some poems have been omitted where
they are easily referable to the volumes of 'Georgian
Poetry' or to other reasonably accessible sources, and
where the original quotation is for illustration rather
than analysis.   These and other omissions are clearly
shown, five dots representing editorial omissions and
three the author's punctuation.   Punctuation has been
made uniform, the form of reference to titles
regularized, and both typographical and obvious errors
of fact have been silently corrected.   Original titles
of articles have been retained, but sub-titles have
been omitted.

'Georgian Poetry 1911-1912'

Published December 1912
'Dedicated to Robert Bridges by the Writers and the Editor'

Prefatory Note

This volume is issued in the belief that English poetry
is now once again putting on a new strength and beauty.
   Few readers have the leisure or the zeal to
investigate each volume as it appears; and the process
of recognition is often slow.   This collection, drawn
entirely from the publications of the past two years, may
if it is fortunate help the lovers of poetry to realize
that we are at the beginning of another 'Georgian period'
which may take rank in due time with the several great
poetic ages of the past.
   It has no pretension to cover the field.   Every
reader will notice the absence of poets whose work would
be a necessary ornament of any anthology not limited by a
definite aim.   Two years ago some of the writers
represented had published nothing; and only a very few of
the others were known except to the eagerest 'watchers of
the skies'.   Those few are here because within the chosen
period their work seemed to have gained some accession of
power.

[A final paragraph of acknowledgments is omitted from this
and each of the subsequent Prefatory Notes.]

Oct. 1912.   E.M.

1.   'GEORGIAN POETRY OF THE TWENTIETH CENTURY', UNSIGNED
REVIEW, 'THE WESTMINSTER GAZETTE'

4 January 1913, 3

Christopher Hassall in his biography of Edward Marsh
(p. 681) credits Lascelles Abercrombie with the first
review on 8 January (in fact 6 January: see No. 2).
The following just predates it.   In this warm welcome,
reference to 'the disappearance of the adjective' may
sound strange in retrospect (cf. T.S. Eliot, No. 30).

The world always hears a great deal about the blind
arrogance of critics who destroy what they cannot make,
but there is another side to the critic's activity, and
poets no less than all other artists owe whatever of
merely popular success they may enjoy in the first
instance to some critic of established reputation who has
risked that reputation in order to hail the advent of a
new, unrecognised messenger.   The comparatively small
intelligent public cannot, it is true, be persuaded by
the cleverest partisan to accept spurious work, but it is
equally true that in nine cases out of ten people require
to be told authoritatively that the thing is good before
they can begin to appreciate it.   The failure of the
prophet has in some cases meant, if not the disappearance,
at all events the submergence of the poet.   Rossetti's
discovery of 'Pauline', the latter-day rescues of Thomas
Campion and Thomas Traherne, the long obscurity of
Francis Thompson, these and many another instance can be
cited to prove the fundamental necessity for prophetic
criticism.   Of late years it has become more and more
customary for men of taste and insight to collect, with
more or less comment, the poetry they have discovered.
Mr William Archer ten years ago, in a wonderful volume
called 'Poets of the Younger Generation', introduced to
a wider public many poets whose names are now established
or forgotten, and his example has been followed almost
yearly by other anthologists, all of them stimulated by
the true critic's desire to prophesy.   And now, in the
second year of the reign of his Majesty King George the
Fifth, we have an anonymous prophet who boldly states his
'belief that English poetry is ... putting on a new
strength and beauty ... that we are at the beginning of

another Georgian period, which may take rank in due time
with the several great poetic ages of the past'. It has
been objected that the title 'Georgian Poetry' is mis-
leading, to which the anthologist might reply that the
other Georgian age happened largely during the reign of
Queen Anne and is generally called 'Augustan' by histor-
ians, the term 'Georgian' being almost entirely reserved
for eighteenth-century furniture and buildings and snuff-
boxes. For our own part we are sufficiently in agree-
ment with his contention that the second decade of the
twentieth century is seeing a revival of poetry in
England to accept the name, which, as its prophet, he has,
with respectful loyalty, chosen for that revival.
   Of the nature of this new spirit the compiler does not
write, leaving his selections to make their own claim -
we therefore purpose to set forth very briefly one or two
of the aspects of Georgian poetry as they appear through
the work included in the volume before us. Fifteen poets
have been found qualified by the time limit to appear in
its pages. 'Two years ago some of the writers rep-
resented had published nothing; and only a very few of
the others were known ... Those few are here because
within the chosen period their work seemed to have gained
some accession of power.' The few are six in number.
Mr Lascelles Abercrombie has been famous since 1908, when
he published 'Interludes'; Mr Gilbert Chesterton, neg-
lected as a poet, has happily brought himself into the
range of the Georgian period with 'The Ballad of the
White Horse', from which 'The Sons of Elf' is taken for
this anthology; Mr W.H. Davies's unconsciously
Elizabethan lyric gift has been recognised from the
first; Mr Walter de la Mare had Andrew Lang for his
prophet in the days of Victoria; and,'The Vinedresser',
a poem on which we venture to think 'The Sicilian Idyll'
here included makes no great advance, placed Mr Thomas
Sturge Moore also high among the last Victorian poets.
We have kept the name of Mr John Masefield for the end of
our list, because in his case the 'Ballads and Poems' of
1910 closed his first poetical career, and his second,
which opened in 1911 with the publication of 'The Ever-
lasting Mercy', and is represented in this book by
'Biography', summarises in many respects the new move-
ment in poetry which we are now considering.
   The young men of Paris who start new schools each
season are, or were yesterday, eager and convinced about
the 'Unanimistes', a group of poets who recognise human-
ity as one, and desire to express the man in the street
for the man in the street. It is in a spirit akin to
this that the new Masefield writes:

To get the whole world out of bed,
And washed, and dressed, and warmed, and fed,
To work, and back to bed again,
Believe me, Saul, cost worlds of pain.

And it is the same spirit that finds another and a most beautiful individual expression in the swiftly moving verse of Mr Wilfrid Wilson Gibson.   His poem 'The Hare' is as truly the result of a tramp's knowledge and insight touched by the vision of a poet as any work of Mr W.H. Davies.   It is too long and too closely knit for quotation, but a fragment from 'Geraniums' will stand for an example of this latter-day attitude:

Broken with lust and drink, blear-eyed and ill,
Her battered bonnet nodding on her head,
From a dark arch she clutched my sleeve and said:
'I've sold no bunch to-day, nor touched a bite ...
Son, buy six-pennorth; and 't will mean a bed.'
So blazing gaily red
Against the luminous deeps
Of starless London night,
They burn for my delight;
While somewhere, snug in bed,
A worn old woman sleeps.

Mr D.H. Lawrence is even more deeply held by this sense of the significance of hourly life, and one of the few criticisms we have to make on the selection of poems for Georgian Poetry is that Mr Lawrence is represented only by the hyper-erotic 'Snapdragon', whereas, as readers of the 'Saturday Westminster' will remember, a group of poems by him, 'The Schoolmaster', contain very remarkable records of a phase of modern life which hitherto has found no such intimate literary expression.   The choice of 'Snapdragon' for this collection serves to emphasise another particularity of the Georgian Poet.   He is no longer a lover.   Even Mr Rupert Brooke, one of the youngest and most ardent of the young poets, knows that there are forces in Nature before which the blindest passion grows clear-eyed:

[Quotes 'Town and Country', stanzas V-VII.]

And the delicate, sensitive verse of Mr Harold Monro, when it touches the theme on which all poets are supposed to be at one, is still wistfully conscious of the greater themes beyond:

[Quotes 'Child of Dawn', stanzas IV-V.]

There is no escaping the fact that the spread of
scientific knowledge and the enormous modern growth of
interest in sociological and economic questions find a
perceptible reflection in the new poetry.   There is also
no denying that poetry derives from these hard things much
of its novel force, and the poetry in them finds express-
ion in Mr John Drinkwater's long and serious poem 'The
Fires of God', in which the poet recounts that through
his own failures he is brought to see 'this glory long
forgot, This re-discovered triumph of the earth'.   There
is also more than a tinge of scientific annotation in
'Cuckoo-Wood', by Mr E.B. Sargant, a poem curiously
reminiscent of Meredith and yet quick with a new vigour
of its own, and the same comment may be made on Mr Brooke's
poem 'The Fish'.

But all this talk of influences is beside the mark when
it comes to a question of essential poetry.   Knowledge,
observation, tendencies are the mere trappings of verse,
and this book would have no right to claim our attention
did it not contain evidences of the Vision without which
no Poetry can endure.

There is no poem in the whole of this remarkable book
in which evidence of this unchanging essential may not be
traced, but for the purpose of this hurried survey the
work of Mr Gordon Bottomley may be taken as exhibiting to
a marked degree the independent and the creative
qualities by which alone poetry can live.   Those 'watchers
of the skies' who remember the poets of the Unicorn Press
will know his name; they may treasure copies of 'The
Crier by Night' on account of its flexible blank verse,
but they can scarcely have foreseen the power and the
strangeness into which he has grown, and which is here
illustrated in two astonishing poems, 'The End of the
World' and 'Babel'.   The first of these, describing the
final snowfall, betrays that faculty for scientific
observation which we have already noticed as character-
istic of this modern poetry.   The following lines, torn
from their context, will show both the nature of this
annotating tendency and also one of the most marked tech-
nical developments of Georgian verse - the disappearance
of the adjective:

> A butterfly, that hid until the Spring
> Under a ceiling's shadow, dropt, was dead.
> The coldness seemed more nigh, the coldness deepened
> As a sound deepens into silences;
> It was of earth and came not by the air;
> The earth was cooling and drew down the sky.
> The air was crumbling.   There was no more sky.

It is clear from this collection that we have recovered from the influence of Swinburne, that poets are now dealing with the bones and not in the flesh of poetry. There is something stark and icy about the technique of these serious writers. The initial impetus may have come to them from Francis Thompson; it shows itself even in the tumultuous imagery of Mr Lascelles Abercrombie's richest dreams; it gives a firmness to the delicate unearthly beauty of Mr de la Mare's clear verse; it is the outward and visible sign of Mr Masefield's sincerity; the careful coloured lyric by which Mr Ronald Ross is here represented is not without a strain of its austerity; and it finds almost too hard an expression in Mr Robert C. Trevelyan's 'Dirge', with which the book ends:

[Quotes 'Dirge', all three stanzas.]

This desolate sound is only one of the melancholy sighs of youth; technically it has its place here. We are sorry that alphabetical reasons have constrained the editor to close with it, for there is in Georgian poetry another and a higher strain. It is the song of courage and of effort; it is marked by a technical skill inherited from the pupils of Tennyson and of Matthew Arnold; and it has a new sincerity and an intellectual reach which combine to vivify the last aspect on which we can here touch. We have already referred to the present generation of young French poets, and in France of to-day there is, besides a return to common humanity, a very marked revival of formal religion. Readers of 'La Nouvelle Journée' will have freshly in mind the picture M. Romain-Rolland has drawn for us of this new spring of faith, and the same movement is making itself felt in Young Oxford at the present time. We have no space here to follow in detail the traces of this same revival through all the fifteen poets of our collection, and can only refer readers to the madness in which Mr James Stephens, one of the most remarkable of the Georgian poets, shows some of the consequences of the return to Christian and to Celtic mysticism which has followed our long serving of the Pagan ideal.

The fifteen poets of this collection might have been a
score, had not the entire exclusion of women set aside
the Christian Mysticism of Miss Evelyn Underhill, and the
strange, bewildering poetry of Miss E.S. Lorimer.   To
these names we will add, in order to make up our suggested
total, those of Mr Vivian Locke Ellis, Mr Ralph Hodgson,
and Mr John Freeman, in each of whom the new spirit of
poetry has found a voice during this new Georgian Era.
The aim of the compiler, however, was not completeness,
but merely proof of his contention that there is a new
strength stirring in our poets, and in this every reader
of his selection is bound to feel that he is justified.

2.   'VICTORIANS AND GEORGIANS', LASCELLES ABERCROMBIE,
'THE MANCHESTER GUARDIAN'

6 January 1913, 5

Lascelles Abercrombie reviews 'The Oxford Book of
Victorian Verse' (chosen by Sir Arthur Quiller-Couch)
and 'Georgian Poetry, 1911-1912'.
    It has seemed worth quoting in full the first part of
Abercrombie's article to point its contrast with the
second part.   Although one might not judge it from the
tone of his remarks on Q's anthology, he was in fact
included in it, two of his poems occupying the last six
of the near one thousand pages.   The lines'"Why should
not Wattle do ..."' are from 'Under the Wattle', the sole
contribution to that anthology by Douglas Sladen (p. 760).
(Perhaps Abercrombie was particularly sensitive on the
subject: see the last line of the excerpt quoted in No. 8
from 'The Sale of Saint Thomas'.)   An anonymous reviewer
of the 'Poetical Works of Robert Bridges' ('The Times
Literary Supplement', 3 April 1913, 133) wrote:

    No lyrics [than those of Bridges] could be further
    removed from those of the 'Georgian' poets.   Yet, as
    we have seen, they dedicate their book to Mr Bridges.
    And one of the most remarkable among them has lately,
    as if it were a thing undisputed and of course, spoken
    of Mr Bridges in a magazine article as 'the greatest
    living English poet'.   To be the first poet in a
    generation which has so many and is even beginning to
    read them and be proud of them is no small achievement.

For a note on Abercrombie, see Appendix, pp. 395-6.

This sequel to the 'Oxford Book of English Verse' confirms
the precedent set by the second 'Golden Treasury'.
Palgrave's first anthology ranged from the Elizabethans to
the early part of the nineteenth century; his second
anthology took in merely the later nineteenth century.
And it was very little shorter than the first.   Sir
Arthur Quiller-Couch, working on a much larger scale, and
so with more conspicuous results, good and bad, has
accepted the example of the two Golden Treasuries. 'The
Oxford Book of English Verse' covered a period of 650
years; 'The Oxford Book of Victorian Verse' covers a
period of about 100 years; and while the first book ran
to just over a thousand pages, the second only just stops
short of a thousand.   In fact, Sir Arthur Quiller-Couch,
following, as he says in his preface, 'my old rule of
choosing what seems to me the best, and for that sole
reason', has made six centuries yield exactly sixty pages
more of the best English poetry than the last hundred
years.   It is rather too good to be true.   The two
anthologies do, to be sure, overlap somewhat, but that
does not at all affect this astonishing result, since in
the first place the poets who appear in both are rep-
resented by curiously differing selections, and in the
second place we are simply considering the actual length
of the period covered by the two books, both professing
the same standard.   But of course the plain fact is that
Sir Arthur has, consciously or not, amazingly relaxed his
taste and lowered his standard for the Victorian anthol-
ogy.   It seems deplorably unnecessary.   No doubt we
should (to quote Sir Arthur's preface again) be very
severe with 'the habit, constant in fallen Man, of
belittling his contemporaries in particular and the age
next before his own in the gross '.   And we should
certainly be grateful to Sir Arthur for insisting,
generously and courageously, on the importance of much
quite recent poetry.   Still, Sir Arthur's second
anthology is not intended as a comprehensive museum of
what passed, both rightly and wrongly passed, for good
poetry in the Victorian age; it is intended as a genuine
sequel to his first anthology.   And there is no gain, but
decided loss, if 'the best poetry' has a strict meaning
in the first book and in the second is allowed to mean
all sorts of laudable endeavour and amateur earnestness.

However, perhaps we have been going too much on presumpt-
ion so far; perhaps, after all, a difference of sixty
pages does fairly represent the difference between the
total achievement of six hundred and fifty years and the
achievement of a hundred years.   Let us forget all about
the first Oxford anthology and its admirably high standard;
let us simply take the Victorian anthology as a book
claiming to give us nothing but poetry which is at least
good, if not 'the best'.   If the draw-net which Sir
Arthur uses turns out to have a properly wide mesh we may
go on to ask whether his catch tolerably represents the
whole Victorian poetic fauna; if the net has a fine mesh
that question will hardly be necessary, for a net that will
hold almost anything will probably catch the important
fishes as easily as the unimportant.   Well, we start off
with Landor, Rogers, and Ebenezer Elliot, quite decently
selected.   On p. 11, however, we find a very queer fish,
William Stanley Roscoe, with 'To Spring: On the Banks of
the Cam'.   In the first verse of this specimen of the
best Victorian poetry Spring has 'bashful feet' and lifts
her 'soft blue eye'.   The second verse is -

    I woo thee, Spring! - tho' thy dishevell'd hair
    In misty ringlets sweep thy snowy breast,
    And thy young lips deplore
    Stern Boreas' ruthless rage.

In the third verse a thrush 'tunes his song', 'warbling
with unripe throat', and so on.   The poem is simply a
disgusting imitation of Collins; historically it may be
interesting - anything may be interesting historically.
But whatever is it doing in an anthology, unless in an
anthology of the worst poetry?   Clearly if Sir Arthur's
net will catch this debased form of life it will, indeed,
catch anything.   And, truly, as one turns the pages of
his second anthology the wonder grows whether anything
that may justly be called selection has been at work here
at all.   Has not Sir Arthur simply put in every Victorian
thing that has ever appealed to him in some vague way or
another?   Here, for instance, are eleven eight-line
stanzas by Sir Edwin Arnold, feebly pretty, feebly humor-
ous, and withal utterly miserable.   And here, under
Joseph Skipsey (who wrote two good poems, one of which is
left out), Sir Arthur includes a song that is quite lud-
icrously atrocious, formless sentimental ooze that has no
business out of the depths of oblivion.   These are but
typical instances of the low stuff Sir Arthur has admitted.
If the reader thinks these remarks are probably
exaggerated, and certainly ungrateful, let the following

lines be candidly perused (we suppress the name of the
author in kindness, as he still flourishes):

> Why should not Wattle do
>   For Mistletoe?
> Ask'd one - they were but two -
>   Where wattles grow.
>
> He was her lover too,
>   Who urged her so -
> Why should not Wattle do
>   For Mistletoe?

This wash might be very well on an Australian Christmas-
card, but it is in the 'Oxford Book of Victorian Verse'!
And it is by including this kind of verse that the
anthology has been bloated to such absurd proportions.
   The matter is really rather serious.   Here is a book,
published at Oxford and dedicated to Cambridge, put forth,
with unmistakable show of authority, as a compilation of
the best poetry;   and what it most conspicuously
accomplishes is a monstrous degradation of the standards
by which poetry ought to be judged.   Of course, a book
governed by such free-and-easy selection contains pract-
ically all the poets who ought to be here;   it simply
could not miss them.   The choice is not in all cases
very happy, but omissions and inadequacies are in this
case of secondary importance.   A few may be noted.   The
small selection from Whitman does not seem to show any
appreciation of his singular greatness.   A.E. Housman is,
surprisingly, altogether omitted.   So is Walter Headlam;
two of his lyrics should have been in.   Katherine Tynan's
exquisite lark-song is certainly an immortal, but it is
not here.   Bret Harte's 'Fate' is a finer poem than the
one given, 'What the Bullet Sang'.   Mr Shearly Cripps
has a more remarkable talent than is suggested by the only
poem of his the book contains.   To represent Mr Stephen
Phillips by eight lines and the Hon. Roden Noel by five
pages is not only preposterous but undignified.   There is
not enough of Canon Dixon, not enough of Mr Bridges, not
enough of Swinburne.   On the other hand, the book makes
a good deal of rare treasure comfortably accessible.   But
all anthologies have some virtues and commit some offences
against the vagaries of individual taste.   The thing is
that this book is not an anthology at all;   it is simply
a wholesale sweeping up of Victorian remains.   Bad poetry
is quite popular enough as it is;   a book which indust-
riously collects it and authoritatively offers it as 'the
best poetry' is doing something unpardonable.

Sir Arthur Quiller-Couch uses the word 'Victorian' in a
sense more convenient than historical or scientific.
When sovereigns are allowed to give their names to periods
they must not, of course, expect literature to stick
scrupulously to the political time-table; a poetical
period will scarcely begin with an accession and ob-
sequiously end with the royal funeral.   It is clear, then,
that Sir Arthur was quite right to make his Victorian
anthology only vaguely dependent on the Victorian chron-
ology.   Still, a poetical period does end somewhere; and
it is also clear that the Victorian period ends noticeably
a long way before Sir Arthur's anthology ends.   The
matter is nothing to complain of; indeed, by ignoring the
death of Victorianism Sir Arthur has been enabled to
vindicate the worth of contemporary verse, and to have
done that is something more important than the strict use
of a label.   Nevertheless, it is fortunate that almost
simultaneously with the publication of the Oxford
Victorian anthology there should appear another collection
boldly entitled 'Georgian Poetry'.   Perhaps some may think
it too early to talk of a Georgian period; but here
again it is only the use of a label that is in question.
For what is certain is that the poets included in this
book of 'Georgian Poetry' have completely broken away from
Victorianism in manner as well as in matter.   If they
have not yet started a new period, they have at any rate
done with the old.   But the book is not a collection of
merely revolutionary efforts; that is sufficiently
indicated by the fact that it is dedicated both by the
writers and the editor to the greatest of living poets,
the man who has kept the classical tradition of English
poetry nobly alive and vivid among us, Mr Robert Bridges.
On the other hand - granting that a certain negative
quality, an absence of 'Victorianism', is common to the
whole book - it is not easy to find any remarkable
community of purpose in this gathering of seventeen con-
temporary poets.   And that is as it should be, if the
book really declares the beginning of a new period.
There is nothing of a 'school' here, nothing even of a
'movement'; poetry does not willingly classify itself
when it has vital business in hand.   And, though we must
always allow for honest scepticism about the value of
contemporary verse, it does seem pretty obvious that
poetry appears in this Georgian anthology as a spirit,
however variously embodied, throughout intent - eagerly
and delightedly intent - on vital affairs.   No sensible
person will be anxious to compare these Georgians with
the Victorians; it is enough that the book gives us a
chance of judging whether the poetry of to-day is able to

accept the significance of its own time without refusing,
or trying to refuse, the unalterable traditional nature
of its art.   We must not be content with one or the
other of these acceptances; we must have both, if
contemporary poetry is to be worthy of a royal label.
And perhaps the most admirable instance of its way of
achieving both is to be found in the work of Mr Wilfrid
Gibson - poetry dealing frankly and uncompromisingly with
familiar workaday life, using a language which is charged
indeed with the race of common speech, but serenely in-
different to the supposed requirements of customary
ornament, effecting the transformation of reality into art
by the extraordinary certainty of its whole formality -
formality comparable to that of classical music.   And
without attempting in any rashly precise way to estimate
the final value of the poetry this book contains, the most
of it certainly has that double characteristic for which
Mr Gibson's work is notable, and which may easily excuse
those who find in it signs of a new 'period'; it is
finely aware of its time, and it is scrupulous in its art.
Mr Masefield and Mr Sturge Moore are too well known to
need mentioning here.   Sir Ronald Ross and Mr John
Drinkwater are deeply concerned with the modern values of
existence; but they are also concerned with the poetic
value of language.   So it is also with those poets to
whom, at first glance, novelty of craftsmanship seems the
thing; the technical daring of Mr Rupert Brooke, the
elusive elaborate splendour of Mr Bottomley, Mr de la
Mare's subtle rhythms, Mr James Stephens's vigorous
tunes, the fresh simplicity of Mr W.H. Davies, and Mr J.
E. Flecker's delicacy - all these seeming externals need
but a little examination to turn into varying signs of a
general impulse; they betray poetry striving to find
adequate expression for the life of to-day, and so
modifying, but not violating, the traditions of the art.
'Georgian Poetry' is an important book; not because the
poetry in it is entirely satisfactory - a good deal of it
is scarcely that, - but because it is unmistakable
evidence of poetry's determination to undertake new duties
in the old style.

3. 'POETS OF THE HOUR', R. ELLIS ROBERTS,
'THE DAILY NEWS AND LEADER'

8 January 1913, 4

Herbert Palmer ('Post-Victorian Poetry', 1938, 176-7)
includes Ellis Roberts (b. 1879) 'among religious poets
... who made an uncertain contemporary reputation, but
who finally gave up poetry for criticism'. He became
literary editor of 'The New Statesman' (1930-2) and 'Time
and Tide' (1933-4), and editor of 'Life and Letters'
(1934-5). His publications include 'Poems' (1906) and
books on Samuel Rogers, Ibsen, Stella Benson, and Prayer.
    'The Daily News and Leader' is not the same paper as
the 'Daily News'. The latter carried a review of
'Georgian Poetry' by Marjory MacMurchy (26 August 1913),
but it is not of sufficient interest to include here.

The editor of this anthology - he veils his identity
under the initials 'E.M.' - has endeavoured to give not
merely specimens from all the books of good verse pub-
lished during his period, but a collection from the
writing of the younger men and from those of their elders
whose work, in these last two years, has gained in sig-
nificance. So we have Mr Chesterton and Mr Sturge
Moore, Mr Masefield and Mr Trevelyan represented, all of
whom are rather Edwardian than Georgian; while, beside
this comparatively mature work, we have poems by Mr
Rupert Brooke and Mr Harold Monro, so young that it seems
a pity they were not left ungathered.
    'E.M.' hints in his preface that his anthology has a
definite aim; and that this aim is responsible for
certain limitations which he evidently expects will be
the subject of remark. The limitations are glaring;
but it is not easy to guess at the aim which has made
them needful. Where, for instance, is Mr Belloc? or
Mr Madox Hueffer? or Mr Arthur S. Cripps? - to mention
three of the older men, who in their very different ways
have greatly added to their reputation in the two years
past. The omissions among the newer poets are even more
curious. Mr Marjoram is perhaps excluded by dates - but
what about Mr Colum, Mr Freeman, Mr Richard Middleton,
Miss Sweetman, Mr W.A. Mackenzie, Anna Bunston, and Mr
Gerald Gould? No anthology which professes to give any
hint of the revival of beauty in modern English verse can
be even moderately typical of the character of that beauty
if it neglects the contribution made by the poets we have
mentioned.

It is natural to compare this volume to a similar
Victorian publication, the two books of the Rhymers'
Club.   There is one immediate difference between the
books which the most casual reader would be bound to
notice.

In the earlier collections the poetry, particularly
the most perfect in form, such as Mr Symons's, Lionel
Johnson's or Ernest Dowson's, is intensely and anxiously
personal and subjective.   I am not at the moment curious
as to how far that almost passionately subjective note was
sincere; it is enough that it was very prominent, and
that the greatest of that group, Mr Yeats, while he was
never its slave as was Ernest Dowson, was in real danger
of allowing that strange spiritual self-absorption to
hinder the more natural development of his genius.   Now,
from the best verse in this book the subjective note is
singularly absent.   No five poets are more representat-
ive of to-day than Mr Chesterton, Mr Masefield, Mr Davies,
Mr de la Mare, and Mr Abercrombie; no five men writing
have more different styles or more diverse aims; yet they
all are agreed in this one supreme point, an intense
interest in external things, an intense feeling for their
reality and importance.   Their main concern is not with
their own temperament as affected by things outside; they
do not exaggerate the value of their own souls - in brief,
egotism is dethroned from Parnassus.   That this is a gain
few will dispute; it is only the solitary and supreme
people who can afford to be as introspective as was the
habit among Victorian minor poets, and it is surely no
humiliation to go the same way of verse as that trodden
by Chaucer, by Dryden, by Browning, and by Keats.   The
only one of the younger men who seems more akin in this
matter to the previous generation is Mr Monro, whose two
poems are rather out of place.

Many of the poems in this book are familiar already to
all lovers of poetry, and so I will not quote from the
authors whose work is comparatively popular; but take
this from Mr Sargant's 'The Cuckoo Wood':

[Quotes 'The Cuckoo Wood', the first 16 lines of the
last stanza.]

Those lines may give some idea of the charm of a poem
which has affinities with both Keats and Christina
Rossetti, and yet contrives to be a thing altogether
individual and new.   Mr Sargant's poem illustrates
another distinction between the Victorian poets and these
younger men.

Nothing was more noticeable about the generation which
succeeded Swinburne than its love for and its skill in
the use of words.   It is not that poets like Wilde or,
to name an incomparably greater, Rossetti were really
consummate masters of style in the sense in which we give
that title to Milton or Keats or Coleridge.   No, with
the exception of Christina Rossetti the middle Victorian
poets were masters of phrase, of language, rather than of
style.   And this is still truer of the later Victorian
and Edwardian poets.   I can only think of two men whose
work is noteworthy for beauty of style - Lionel Johnson,
who followed the high classical tradition, and W.B. Yeats,
who gave to new experiments in rhythm and music that
touch of eternal dignity which belongs to the classical.
The other poets of that time were lacking, for the most
part, in that simplicity which is the essential of a great
style.   It is arguable that the richness gained by such
daring use of words as Francis Thompson's is worth more
than the effects that follow from a serener sense of lan-
guage, but it cannot be denied that poetry such as Thomp-
son's or Dowson's or Arthur Symons's, in their very diff-
erent kinds, seeks after and achieves a quite dissimilar
splendour from the glory of a simpler and less passionate
style.
Our Georgian poets are following style rather than
words; pursuing the whole rather than the parts.   None
of them, it is true, equal Lionel Johnson - Mr Belloc
might have claims, but he is unrepresented save by an
essay in discipleship by Mr Rupert Brooke - but there is
evident through nearly all the work a stern refusal to be
led astray by the more luxurious side of the poet's art,
by that over-attention to the mere magic of syllables,
which was the cause of so much decadence in recent verse.
For this concentration on unity, on a real effort to
attain some correspondence between the thing said and the
manner of saying, we ought to be thankful; for it means
a wider outlook and a truer spirit than those of the
poetry of the 'eighties and 'nineties.

4.   'GEORGIAN POETS', EDWARD THOMAS, 'THE DAILY CHRONICLE'

14 January 1913, 4

Edward Thomas (1878-1917) was encouraged to write poetry
by Robert Frost, who came to England in 1912, met him in
October 1913, and communed with him in Gloucestershire for
the following twelve months.   On 2 March 1915 Thomas
wrote to Gordon Bottomley, 'I have begun to write in verse
and am impatient of anything else' (R.G. Thomas (ed.),
'Letters from Edward Thomas to Gordon Bottomley', 1969).
In fact Thomas had written a few poems in his earlier
years (see William Cooke, 'Edward Thomas: A Critical
Biography', 1970).   See also Introduction, p. 19.
'Recorder' wrote of him:

> The well-known critic and essayist killed in France in
> 1917.   During most of his life he was well known as
> the reviewer of almost every book of poetry that
> appeared in print.   His pronouncements were treated
> with great respect.   A few months before his death
> some poems from his pen appeared in one or two period-
> icals and an annual, over the name of 'Edward Eastaway'.
> ..... His poetry will remain as an example of those
> principles which he took so much time to discover and
> to present in all his critical essays on the works of
> his contemporaries.   ['The Chapbook', June 1920.]

It has for some time been debatable whether anything
could be done for contemporary poetry which would leave a
little less of its fate to chance.   Anyone with £5 can
get a book of verse printed.   Reviewers and booksellers
have not been able to keep their heads above this stream.
But now there has been opened at 35 Devonshire Street,
Theobald's-road, a Poetry Bookshop, where you can see
any and every volume of modern poetry.   It will be an
impressive and, perhaps, an instructive sight.
    The Poetry Bookshop has, as a good beginning, given
us an anthology of the poetry published under George V.
The editor, 'E.M.' - Mr Edward Marsh - introduces it with
the remarks that 'English poetry is now once again putting
on a new strength and beauty', and that this collection
may help readers to see that 'we are at the beginning of
another "Georgian period", which may take rank in due time
with the several great poetic ages of the past'.   The

authors represented are Messrs Abercrombie, Bottomley,
Brooke, Chesterton, Davies, de la Mare, Drinkwater,
Flecker, Gibson, D.H. Lawrence, Masefield, Monro, Sturge
Moore, Ronald Ross, E.B. Sargant, Stephens and R.C.
Trevelyan.   Not a few of these had developed their
qualities under Victoria and Edward, and it cannot be said
that any uncommon accession of power has very recently
come to Messrs Chesterton, Davies, de la Mare, Sturge
Moore and Trevelyan, though it has to Messrs Bottomley,
Masefield and Gibson (whose 'Queen's Crags' in the
current 'English Review' is a fine thing and his best work).
These three, together with Messrs Abercrombie, Brooke,
Lawrence, Sargant and Stephens, have most of the Georgian
tone, and would alone give a scientific critic material
for defining that tone.   Messrs Brooke, Lawrence and
Sargant, are, as it were, the core of the group.
    Most of the poets are well represented.   The 200 pages
include the whole of Abercrombie's 'Sale of Saint Thomas',
W.H. Davies's 'Child and the Mariner', Masefield's 'Bio-
graphy', James Stephens's 'Lonely God', and the first part
of Sturge Moore's 'Sicilian Idyll'.   Room might have been
made for several other writers whose work has lately
appeared in books and magazines.   There are writers more
Georgian than half a dozen of these, and as worthy of in-
clusion.   Then, to be precise, 'The Kingfisher' of Mr W.
H. Davies, is Edwardian in date.   But the volume is more
representative and striking than if twice the number of
poets had been drawn from.   It shows much beauty,
strength, and mystery, and some magic - much aspiration,
less defiance, no revolt - and it brings out with great
cleverness many sides of the modern love of the simple
and primitive, as seen in children, peasants, savages,
early men, animals, and Nature in general.   Everyone,
except Messrs Davies and de la Mare, is represented
either by narrative or by meditative verse, and by
practically nothing else.

5. 'GEORGIAN POETRY', A.C. BENSON, 'THE CAMBRIDGE
MAGAZINE'

18 January 1913, 209-10

Brooke had written to Marsh: 'My series of inspirations
included these: that "Q" should introduce himself to

Cambridge by reviewing ["Georgian Poetry"] at some length
for "The Review". ..... Failing "Q", Benson.   I'll make
the "Granta" and "Cambridge Magazine" flourish headlines,
too.'   (Geoffrey Keynes (ed.), 'The Letters of Rupert
Brooke', 1968, 406.)

Brooke's 'The Old Vicarage, Grantchester' (under its
earlier and more appropriate title 'The Sentimental Exile')
had already reached a Cambridge audience through its
publication in the King's magazine, 'Basileon' (June 1912,
3-4); T.S. Eliot was to express qualified admiration of
'Fish' (see No. 25).   Benson was the first reviewer to
suggest a sequel to the anthology.

A.C. Benson (1862-1925) was the eldest surviving son
of Edward White Benson, Archbishop of Canterbury, whose
biography he wrote (1899), and brother of the novelists
E.F.B. (1867-1940) and R.H.B. (1871-1914).   Educated at
Eton and King's College, Cambridge, he returned to Eton
as a master, and wrote a book about teaching although he
disliked it.   He resigned in 1903, and went to live in
Cambridge, at first collaborating on an edition of Queen
Victoria's letters, and then accepting without remuner-
ation a fellowship of Magdalene, of which college he later
became Master.   He published books of essays and verse,
but the only verse which is likely to be remembered are
the lines 'Land of Hope and Glory' to Elgar's 'Pomp and
Circumstance'.   'Recorder' described his poetry as 'a
Victorian echo' ('The Chapbook', June 1920, 6).   See also
E.H. Ryle (ed.), 'Arthur Christopher Benson' (1925).

This is an interesting anthology, collected entirely out
of the publications of the last two years, with a fine
touch of personality about the *flair* of the collector,
which adds a zest to the book.

Perhaps the title is a little misleading.   The word
Georgian has become a note of time and date, and one
connects it with the hapless Hanoverian period, with
prosaic, shrewd, ethical verse, with solidity rather than
with fineness.   One thinks of George II's horror of
'Boetry' and George III's complaints of all the 'sad
stuff' there was to be found in Shakespeare.   And so it
is rather a shock, though a pleasant shock, to find that
this quiver is full of such a very different handful of
arrows, so sharp, so light, so nimbly feathered.

Perhaps the first point which strikes one about the
book is the entire absence of any sense of a *school* of
poetry of a dominant tradition, of a 'manner' of any
kind.   That is the most hopeful thing about it, that

there is no echo of other voices here.   Each of these
poets seems to be working wholly on his own line, without
deference or subservience, watching life, feeling, seeing,
recording.   Mr Abercrombie and Mr Sturge Moore, for
instance - one cannot say that their work reminds one of
anyone or anything;   it is perfectly distinct, separate,
peculiar.   Metre, language, thought are all original.
     But on the other hand it is not mere lawless or
anarchical experiment.   There is no sense of revolt, no
hint of a desire to arrest or impress at any cost.   Such
variety of form as occurs seems to spring up naturally
out of subject and mood, not out of a mere wilfulness or
perversity.   It does not give one a feeling, this poetry,
of desiring to kick over the traces out of mere wanton-
ness;   there is rather an instinct of carefulness, of high
accomplishment, of firm conception, of fundamental design.
I do not mean that the work is always equally impressive
or beautiful.   One could criticise and find petty fault;
one may even feel that in cases there is a mistake about
the quality of poetical material.   But for all that, the
verse is adventurous without being disordered.   These
mariners do not merely drift before wind and wave;   they
have mapped out their course, they know whither they are
steering.
     It would be impossible in a short review to survey the
whole galaxy and to weigh their merits critically.   It is
natural here to take the two recent Cambridge poets who
find a place in the book, Mr Rupert Brooke and Mr Flecker.
     First of all comes Mr Brooke's poem on Grantchester,
which is a charming piece of fancy, easy enough, con-
versational, light in hand, and yet every now and then
sending out a sudden gleam of *poetry*, whatever that myst-
erious essential thing is - for we must remember, what
critics often forget, that poetry is a thing all by it-
self, and not to be confused with anything else, a fusion
of sight and mood and language into a flash which cannot
be further analysed:

    Is dawn a secret shy and cold
    Anadyomene, silver-gold?
    And sunset still a golden sea
    From Haslingfield to Madingley?

The poem is full of little touches like that, all seen
and felt in a half-contented, half-mournful nostalgia,
which after all is one of the prettiest moods in the
world!
     And then there is 'The Fish', which I believe is the
finest thing which Mr Brooke has yet done:

Those silent waters weave for him
A fluctuant mutable world and dim,
Where waving masses bulge and gape
Mysterious, and shape to shape
Dies momently through whorl and hollow,
And form and line and solid follow
Solid and line and form to dream
Fantastic down the eternal stream.

That is a fine piece of music, which seems to have
caught the liquid obscurity, the fallen light of moving
waters, the inner life of the dark close tide. That is
poetry, authentic, unquestionable, thought passing into
the element with which it concerns itself, and inter-
preting it in a mystical fashion of its own. It is not
the word, or the stream, but the stream passing into
words.

Mr Flecker is not as well represented as he might be in
this book. I have seen several of his lyrics elsewhere,
which seem to me very fine poetry. He is more of a
lyrist than Mr Brooke, - that is to say the thought con-
denses itself more firmly and definitely into a single
point of light. 'Joseph and Mary' is a pretty dramatic
carol; but in 'The Queen's Song' he is at his very best.

Had I the power
To Midas given of old
To touch a flower
And leave the petals gold,
I might then touch thy face,
Delightful boy,
And leave a metal grace,
A graven joy....

Thus in my love
For nations yet unborn,
I would remove
From our two lives the morn,
And muse on loveliness
In mine armchair
Content should Time confess
How sweet you were.

It is an open secret who 'E.M.', the collector of these
poems, is; and we may be allowed to express our grat-
itude to him for his work. . 'Few readers', he truly says,
'have the leisure or the zeal to investigate each volume
as it appears' - but as art and expression accumulate,
the task of the anthologist will assume an even greater

importance.   To few poets will it be given hereafter to
have all their work reprinted and recognised;   and what
the ordinary reader wants is a volume of this kind, which
gives to those who would like to follow the fortunes of
poetry an idea of what is going on, and what writers are
aiming at.

Criticism at the present day tends more and more to be
conducted on courteous lines;   the old bludgeoning is
happily extinct - it was a cruel and a useless business,
because it directed its audience to revel in what was
worthless and absurd.   We have got to advance still
further to the stage of letting feeble work severely
alone, not making the best of it, but simply not speaking
of it at all;   and the best service that a critical mind
can do is to save excellent poetry from being simply dis-
regarded, by careful selection and generous presentment;
and it is to be earnestly hoped that 'E.M.' will carry on
his valuable work, and that in another two years he may
be able to endow us with another volume, as interesting,
as brilliant, and as hopeful as the present book.

6.   'GEORGIAN POETRY', UNSIGNED REVIEW BY JOHN BUCHAN,
'THE SPECTATOR'

18 January 1913, 107

Again Brooke's hand would seem to have been at work: he
suggested to Marsh that John Buchan should 'fill a page
of the Spectator' (see Introduction, p. 18).

John Buchan (1875-1940), later first Baron Tweedsmuir
and Governor-General of Canada, is of course best known
as a writer of adventure stories.   A scholar of Brase-
nose College, Oxford, he won the Newdigate Prize for
English Verse (1898), and published 'Poems, Scots and
English' (1917).

This anthology, compiled entirely from the publications
of the past two years, has been undertaken by the editor
in the belief that English poetry is on the eve of a ren-
aissance, and that we stand at the beginning of a new
'Georgian period' which in time may rank among the great
poetic ages.   We sincerely hope that he is right, and we

gladly admit that there is some reason for his faith.
The limitations of his purpose make the book a curious
selection, in which well-known names like Mr Chesterton,
Mr Masefield, and Mr Sturge Moore appear side by side with
writers who are familiar only to the most zealous student
of contemporary verse; while some of the best of our
younger poets, like Mr A.S. Cripps and Mr St John Lucas,
do not appear, because they happen to have published
nothing since the beginning of 1911.   It is literally a
review of two years' work, and the result seems to us in
a high degree remarkable.   Many of the pieces selected
have already been praised in these columns, such as Mr
Lascelles Abercrombie's 'The Sale of Saint Thomas', Mr
Sturge Moore's 'Sicilian Idyll', and Mr James Stephens's
wonderful 'The Lonely God'.   We welcome the chance which
brings these and other fine poems into the clearer light
of an anthology.   The selection has been done with great
skill and judgment, but the editor must expect the fate
of all anthologists and have his choice criticised.   We
ourselves should have chosen another extract from Mr
Chesterton's 'Ballad of the White Horse' than the 'Song of
Elf' - probably the verses describing the strange
visitors to Alfred's court; and we should have included
among the pieces from Mr James Stephens's 'The Hill of
Vision' the brilliant 'The Fulness of Time'.   It is
pleasant to welcome again beautiful things like Mr W.H.
Davies's 'The Kingfisher', Mr Walter de la Mare's
'Arabia', Mr Drinkwater's 'The Fires of God', and Mr
Wilfrid Gibson's 'The Hare'.   Of the poems new to us we
like best Mr Gordon Bottomley's 'The End of the World',
Mr Rupert Brooke's 'Grantchester', and Mr Masefield's
'Biography'.   Is there any special quality which is to
mark this new Georgian era?   Perhaps it is too early to
say.   The writers have the old sense of beauty, the love
of lovely words, which are requisite in all eras.   They
seem to us, too, to show a wholesome revolt against
poetic *cliches*, a desire for directness and simplicity
both of feeling and expression.   They are not afraid of
their imaginations or their minds, and though much in
both thought and fancy is crude, there is more that is
bold and fine.   But the most hopeful feature is their
consuming interest in life.   They have little of the idle
singer of an idle day, and set about their work with a gay
seriousness which is full of promise.   Before good poetry
can be written a man must be convinced that there are
things worth writing about.

7. 'KNOCKING AT THE DOOR', EDMUND GOSSE, 'THE MORNING POST'

27 January 1913, 3

Marsh was to follow Gosse's advice, and exclude from his next anthology G.K. Chesterton and Sturge Moore, as well as R.C. Trevelyan, as poets of an older generation. In finding 'an excess of subjectivity' in contrast to the late Victorians' 'objectivity', Gosse would seem in complete disagreement with Ellis Roberts (No. 3). It is interesting to hear his warning that some Georgians are in danger of 'dislocating their verse in ..... striving to make it supple'.

Edmund Gosse (1849-1928) was Librarian at the House of Lords and an influential literary figure of the time. Perhaps best known for his autobiographical 'Father and Son' (1907), he was an early authority on Scandinavian literature, and wrote lives of Gray, Congreve, Donne, and Swinburne.

This attractive volume is at once an anthology and a manifesto. It presents selected examples of the poetry of the latest generation, and at the same time it gives, and so far as I know gives for the first time, an idea of who are considered by that generation itself to be its leaders and most characteristic members. 'Georgian Poetry, 1911-1912', therefore, though put forth with great modesty, deserves the careful attention of all who desire to contemplate without prejudice the moving spectacle of literature. It takes us a step further in the progress of poetry than any previous publication had done, and future historians may place it, if not quite with 'The Germ' of 1850, at least with the Oxford garlands of the Eighties and with the first 'Book of the Rhymers' Club' of 1892. It was high time that we should receive another landmark of this sort. The collection is called 'Georgian', no doubt, in order to point out that it deals solely with bards who have revealed themselves since the accession of King George V. It would have been better if this aim had been more clearly kept in view. What caprice it can be which has introduced Mr G.K. Chesterton, who flourished under Queen Victoria, among the latest candidates for renown it is beyond me to conjecture. Nor is Mr Sturge Moore, whose first volume appeared as long ago as 1899,

in his place with these juveniles.   The others would
present a more consistent front if these two comparative
veterans did not break their rank.

Among the fifteen young poets presented to us by 'E.M.'
there is a considerable inequality of force and skill.
This was inevitable, and at so early a stage of the
career of each it is not to be considered as alarming.
For the present all may be held candidates for immortality.
In every important *cénacle* (1) there are those who are
doomed to eminence and those who will slowly retire.   At
the early meetings of the Mermaid Club there were persons,
no doubt, who considered John Hoskyns a more promising wit
than William Shakespeare;   I should not be surprised to
learn that even Ben Johnson thought so.   All the world
now reads Shakespeare, and the works of Hoskyns have dis-
appeared.   Let us not for that reason doubt that he held
his head high at those miraculous symposia, and that his
sympathy added a lustre to the genius of luckier friends.
It is extraordinary how much sympathy counts in the actual
development of literary talent.   The collective force
which such anthologies as the present exhibit and en-
courage tends directly to the enrichment of the texture of
writing.   The solitary bee may toil all day with great
dexterity and prowess, but for real mollification the hive
is far to be preferred.   What does Ulysses say to Achilles
in the Grecian camp? -

        No man is lord of anything -
  Though in and of him there be much consisting -
  Till he communicate his parts to others:
  Nor doth he of himself know them for aught,
  Till he behold them formed in the applause
  Where they're extended; who, like an arch, reverberates
  The voice again; or, like a gate of steel,
  Fronting the sun, receives and renders back
  His figure and his heat.

The effect of poetry depends on a great many things
besides the formal merit of the verse as it strikes a
reader for the first time.   It is modified by the effect
of 'reverberation', and hence the great importance, to a
new school of poets, of being presented by a graceful
choragus, such as 'E.M.', who is with them but not of
them, and who communicates their 'parts' to one another
and to the world.

It is natural to endeavour to find out, first of all,
what general principles actuate these new poets.   It is
impossible, as it should be, to find in them any distinct
uniformity of purpose, but there is an unconscious unity

of attitude.　Under the fluctuations of taste, under, if
I may say so, the pleasant affectations and caprices
natural to youth, there is nothing here very violently
revolutionary.　Those who expect to find among the new
poets a resemblance to the crazy charlatanries of the
Cubist and Futurist painters will be disappointed.　Like
all their predecessors, from Chaucer downwards, they
pursue the Urphänomen (2) of beauty, as Faust pursues the
phantom of Helena.　But there is for ever proceeding a
wholesome aesthetic change in the direction of this pur-
suit:　and herein resides the immense value of 'revol-
utionary' movements, unjustly so called.　They do not
alter the essential character of poetry, they simply
renovate the outer part of its material, freshening its
surface, burnishing its form.
　Recognising that what is always to be feared and
jealously to be guarded against in any revolution is ab-
surdity, the new poets are careful never to be preposter-
ous.　In the compass of this volume there is no one
piece which errs extravagantly against the ancient laws
of the art.　Yet we find novelties of expression which
are calculated to stir curiosity and to encourage hope.
How are they to be in a few words defined and distin-
guished?　A few extracts, selected with however much
care and piety from the gardens of the new poets, may
give an impression which their larger works may belie.
Yet I seem to detect, as the leading principle of the
action of them all, a desire to render the texture of
poetry more plastic, more sensitive, more independent of
mediocrity.　The plan of bringing poetry closely into
line with prose, and of using it to illustrate popular,
political, 'Imperial' themes, seems to have been entirely
abandoned.　Not one of these new writers but eschews the
loud bassoon.　They are haunted, more than were their
immediate predecessors, by the poignant and feverish
hopes of individuals.　They exchange the romantic, the
sentimental, the fictive conceptions of literature for an
ingenuousness, sometimes a violence, almost a rawness in
the approach to life itself.　There is rich exuberance
of sensibility in Mr Rupert Brooke, a thrilling, tender
sweetness in Mr Walter de la Mare, a sense of the torment
of existence in Mr W.H. Davies, of its melancholy wildness
in Mr W.W. Gibson.　In verse certain things may be pert-
inently, intensely, and even religiously said which in
prose would merely be ridiculous.　This is the great
argument, in our complicated age, for continuing to cult-
ivate the ancient art of poetry.　So Mr John Drinkwater
sings :

Wise of the brief beloved span
Of this our glad earth travelling,
Of beauty's bloom and ordered plan,
Of love and love's compassioning,
Of all the dear delights that spring
From man's communion with man;
We cherish every hour that strays
Adown the cataract of the days.

And Mr Harold Monro expatiates on ecstasies hardly to be
expressed in terms of speech:

O gentle vision in the dawn:
My spirit over faint cool water glides,
Child of the day,
To thee:
And thou art drawn
By kindred impulse over silver tides
The dreamy way
To me.

All good poems, Goethe tells us, are fragments of a great
confession, which can find no sane vehicle but verse.
     There seems to be traceable in most of these poets a
conviction, or a vague belief, that Nature as seen in the
external world and the mind of Man as cultivated within
the human individual are parallel to an extent which may
be partly discerned by our own senses, so far as these
are quickened by imagination and sympathy.   This is a
curious feature of the new school, and stamps them as
Pan-psychical.   The expression of this particular senti-
ment is aided by the nebulous or vitreous diction which
many of them choose to adopt.   They are mysterious and
discreet, as though for ever eavesdropping in the courts
of life.   In short, they are willing to stretch to its
extremest limit the emotional consciousness of the int-
ellect.   It is obvious that this distinguishes poets of
the Georgian group from their predecessors, and leads them
to an excess of subjectivity which is in direct oppos-
ition to the objectivity which marked the poets of the
close of the Victorian age.   This may account for the
want of favour into which the highly-accomplished writers
of that age have now momentarily fallen, but the position
of the Georgian school will to many seem so forced as to
be philosophically untenable, and for purely artistic pur-
poses the new attitude may be held to be not more nor less
acceptable than that of the Seventies and Eighties.
     The only point on which a word of warning may seem to
be required is a technical one.   Many of these new poets,

in their anxiety to be spontaneous, fluid, unfettered, are
afraid to allow the essential character of their metre to
be felt.   There is in many of them an incessant shifting
of the stress, which ends by tiring the ear or even prod-
ucing a sense of weakness.   No doubt there was a great
temptation to avoid the exaggerated sonority of the Late
Victorians.   But the young poets are some of them in
danger of dislocating their verse in the act of striving
to make it supple.   The fatal rock ahead of them is so
to break up the fixed forms of metre as to reduce what is
written to a state of more or less rhythmic prose.   From
this the pilot of their genius must deliver the Georgian
generation.

NOTES

1 Coterie
2 Essential concept

8. 'GEORGIAN POETRY', UNSIGNED REVIEW, 'THE TIMES
LITERARY SUPPLEMENT'

27 February 1913, 81-2

Marsh had of course sent a review copy to Bruce Richmond,
editor of the 'Literary Supplement', together with a
letter suggesting a prominent review, if possible on the
first page.   Richmond was on holiday, but he replied
from Italy:

> I wish I had known earlier about your volume.   Before
> I left, a fortnight ago, I planned out the next five
> front pages - which takes it up to Christmas ..... -
> one of the five was to be Couch's Victorian Verse -
> and my immediate fear is that my colleague may propose
> to tack you on to him.   [Quoted in Robert H. Ross,
> 'The Georgian Revolt', 1967, 125.]

The reviewer is one of the first to recognise that the
Georgians represent, 'though not a revolt, at least a
reaction' from the late Victorians.   Like Gosse (No. 7)
and like Lawrence in his complaints to Marsh about Aber-
crombie (see headnote to No. 17), the reviewer finds 'an
affected and self-conscious brutality' in some of the
poems.

In reviewing on this page, a few weeks ago, the 'Oxford Book of Victorian Verse', we suggested that the later pages of that volume gave evidence of a remarkable poetic revival, though of one in no sense, moral or temporal, to be called Victorian. The quaintly-named anthology before us gives us the opportunity of taking up the subject again and carrying it a little further. It is boldly decreed that we may already speak of a new 'Georgian' period; and we accept the licence with alacrity. The word was wanted, and it sufficiently meets our need. The editor of the volume does not use it himself with undue strictness; for, though his chosen poems have all been published within the last two years, not a few of them come from writers whose work was known and valued at a remoter period. These are included, says the editor, 'because within the chosen period their work seemed to have gained some accession of power'. The implication evidently is that for a poet to extend the limit of his power more than two years after he has begun to publish his poems is an exceptional occurrence. For our part we venture to hope that it happens more often than the editor would seem to suggest. A good many of our poets, we would fain believe, even of those who can remember the death of Queen Victoria, are still capable of developing and enriching their elderly strains. But Georgian, if we may apply the word (with a slightly different laxity) to poets whose work is characteristic of the twentieth rather than of the nineteenth century, conveniently summarizes the revival we wish to examine. Elizabethan literature, as we all know, was freely produced in the reign of James I., so it is no objection that most Georgian poetry has hitherto been written in the reign of Edward VII.

There is a general difficulty in describing and defining any sort of literary movement in this country. It is that we have no continuous orthodoxy, no central academic tradition, to give us an immediate standard of comparison. A literary movement defines itself with the definition of the yoke which it refuses: but if there is no yoke, and nothing to rebel against, this simple method is denied us. It may be pleasing to an English poet to reflect how free he is born, but his condition deprives him of the pleasures of defiance. A semblance of them he may attain, or he could at one time, by agitating the delicacy of the public. This, however, is at best an illusory excitement. A poet defies the public from the very start, by the mere act of writing poetry. No agreement, in terms relevant to the poet's case, is really discussable between them; there is no imaginable round-table where they

could meet to confer.   The only body with which an ex-
cited poet can join direct issue is a constituted liter-
ary authority, in possession of the ground which he claims.
Perhaps the post-Georgians may be granted the privilege of
such an encounter.   We have already an Academy, and the
day may come when these poets exercise a tyranny under
which they will never themselves have had the advantage of
languishing.   It will be no bad thing if they do so.   The
value of authority may be denied on other accounts, but it
is unquestionable for those who attack it.   It is so, not
only because it compels all insurgents to produce a clear
theory of their aims and objects, but also because it
makes them concentrate all their forces and use them with
the greatest possible vigour and wariness.   The only
poetic authority of any sort which has been seen in
England for nearly a hundred years - at least since the
final triumph of romanticism destroyed the last ortho-
doxy - has been (as we suggested before) the extra-
ordinary personal domination of Tennyson.   It is true
that that had no very wholesome effect on poetry, includ-
ing Tennyson's: but then his authority, precisely, was
not that of an Academy.   It was the authority of one
intensely picturesque and majestic personality - an auth-
ority, moreover, elected, for all kinds of genial but
irrelevant reasons, by popular acclaim.   That was a fine
and remarkable loyalty in its way; but we do not want a
body of Academicians reverenced by the public for their
great age and their flashing eyes.   We want an Academy
vaguely respected by the public as an official institut-
ion, and fiercely attacked by every poet (until he be-
comes a member of it) as an obstruction to all light and
liberty.   Then indeed we shall feel that poetry has
every chance in its favour.
    For the present our Georgians have to make the best of
their misfortune that nobody wishes to interfere with
them; and we, too, have to put up with the difficulty
that they cannot be defined by a common antagonism.   Yet
they do undoubtedly represent, though not a revolt, at
least a reaction from a mood which was characteristic of
poetry in its latest Victorian years.   That was, on the
whole, a pale and uncertain mood, though it produced a
small quantity of beautiful verse.   Its weakness - which
was not at all a weakness it would have been ready to ad-
mit - was its timidity in affronting experience.   It
keenly felt the failure of the cheerful mid-Victorian
individualism, but it was generally contented to sing its
blighted faith, its perished hopes, its fugitive and mean-
ingless loves.   It is easy to persuade oneself that ab-
stention of this kind is really a facing of hard facts -

that it is braver and more sensible to leave the broken
fragments where they lie than fondly to set about piec-
ing them together again. But to refuse to be comforted
is, none the less, in fact the line of least resistance;
and an art which amuses itself with isolated moments and
detached fancies is justly called decadent. The mood of
our younger poetry to-day is sufficiently remote from all
this; it is curious to think that a disdainful rejection
of philosophic consolation was at one time a character-
istic of youth. A poet who is afraid to use his brains
seems nowadays to be as rare as was a poet twenty years
ago who trusted anything but his sensibilities. There
is no danger here of aridity. Imagination is a far
robuster growth in the mind which desires to know, which
regards the world as real and discoverable, than it can
ever be in the mind which only ventures to affirm its own
nonentity. The desire, however wild its aim may be at
first, to clarify and shape experience, rather than to
sit receptively awaiting its impact, promises more for
poetry than the power of writing now and then an exquis-
ite lyric. The tendency of poetry to-day is thus al-
most exclusively towards drama, not necessarily the drama
of the stage, though it may well reach its best in that;
but the dramatic handling, in some form or other, of life
and character. It is not surprising if there is still a
good deal more promise than performance. It is an am-
bitious undertaking, and the most we can say is that
nearly all these writers are disposed for it, and that a
few of them seem to be well on their way. Their danger
is obviously that in mistrusting personal and evanescent
impressions, in shunning lyrical simplicity, their sense
of beauty may suffer and become roughened. The degener-
ation of beauty towards prettiness is not in these days
to be feared: where that happens it means that art is
travelling between narrowing walls. But the duty of
fastidiousness is both greater and much more likely to
be under-estimated when art is facing, as it assuredly is
now, towards the open, and has to choose its path from
among a hundred. The temptation is great to think that
life and strength and energy are enough, and that an art
which is conscious of enjoying these advantages had
better let itself be guided entirely by them, without
appealing to preconceived critical doctrine. Life,
unfortunately, will not submit to form on terms so easy
for the artist; and unless the Georgian poets realize
more clearly that some of them seem to have realized at
present, that formlessness means, not untrammelled
vigour, but vigour wasted and missing its mark, the best
of their promise will be unfulfilled. Their fertility

and their attack are both so remarkable that the hand of
discipline, where it has not yet been raised, will have a
difficult time of it; but it is the sort of difficulty
that many an artist has desired in vain to be confronted
with.

So much it seems possible to say, by way of general-
ization, about these poets. We are not to expect simple
music, spontaneous song, pure melody. We shall find
imaginative impressions, elaborated through harmonies
which are sometimes very striking; we shall look for
development of motive and instance, rather than for the
fleeting apparition caught in a melodious stanza. But
beyond this we cannot generalize. The differences
between them are strongly marked, and the group breaks up
as we approach it more closely. We note as curious that
from one point of view the group appears as two, both
fairly well defined. It is when we look particularly at
their style of expression. One company finds its natur-
al idiom in a direct and vernacular plainness, the other
in a riot of aureate and archaistic decoration. Both
methods are, in themselves, equally poetic and equally
treacherous. Poetry is not more in one vocabulary or
syntax than in another, and every writer makes his own as
he discovers himself and his requirements. That both
styles should appear in these poems often exaggerated and
forced, the one into an affected and self-conscious brut-
ality, the other into overwrought ornament, means no more
than that these particular writers have not all of them
completed the discovery. What is interesting is to see
in this diversity a sign that no single literary in-
fluence is dominant; with the result that, while they
agree on the whole in their attitude towards experience,
each one easily follows his own manner, undisturbed by
accidental attraction from without.

In a volume of this kind, so original and so imper-
fect, the effect is naturally a cumulative one; so that,
when we come to particularize, it is difficult to detach
names and poems which will seem to support the view
taken of them as a company. A few of them, indeed, we
may release at once, as having been invited into the com-
pany from a different era. Sir Ronald Ross came of age
too long ago; Mr Chesterton will do so when he pleases,
but whenever he does, it will be in the nineteenth cent-
ury; Mr Sturge Moore has had time for too many exten-
sions of his compass; Mr Walter de la Mare can stretch
the octave. There remain a dozen or so whom by
stricter tests we may regard as representative; and, so
far as we are able to judge, the choice of a few char-
acteristic pages from each seems to have been made with

happy judgment.   Mr Abercrombie heads the list, and it
can hardly be doubted that he would still do so if the
order were other than alphabetic.   Of all the poetic
talents which have appeared since the beginning of the
century, his is the most conspicuous union of breadth and
intensity.   He figures here with 'The Sale of St Thomas',
a piece of characterization which makes us feel, as we
note how easily the speakers shoulder their way through
such prodigality of image and ornament and packed phrase,
that we may see a re-birth of living poetic drama before
the Georgian period is much older.   There is no doubt
about the strength of this writer's sense of character;
it is proved by the fact that it is not deflected by the
extraordinary ease with which he can mass effects of
vivid colour.   If he can complete and round off a drama-
tic motive as vigorously as he can throw out a fragment-
ary sketch, we shall have from him work of the highest
kind.   Stronger, more brilliant verse than this we need
not desire:

                    A palace made of souls:-
        Ay, there's a folly for a man to dream!
        He saw a palace covering all the land,
        Big as the day itself, made of a stone
        That answered with a better gleam than glass
        To the sun's greeting, fashioned like the sound
        Of laughter copied into shining shape:
        So the king said.   And with him in the dream
        There was a voice that fleered upon the King:
        'This is the man who makes much of himself
        For filling the common eyes with palaces
        Gorgeously bragging out his royalty:
        Whereas he hath not one that seemeth not
        In work, in height, in posture on the ground,
        A hut, a peasant's dingy shed, to mine . . .'
                            And the king,
        Gloating upon the white sheen of that palace,
        And weeping like a girl ashamed, inquired,
        'What is that stone?'   And the voice answered him
        'Soul'.   'But in my palaces too', said he.
        'There should be soul built: I have driven nations,
        What with quarrying, what with craning, down
        To death, and sure their souls stay in my work'.
        And 'Mud and wattle' sneered the voice again.

This is a level of execution which is not reached by the
other Georgians.   But for tense and daring imagination
Mr Gordon Bottomley's strange visions are not less re-
markable.   The two given in this volume, 'The End of the

World' and 'Babel', are too long to quote, and they are
so closely written that they must be read entire.   They
are dramatic pictures which perhaps over-reach them-
selves in their breathless desire to make their effect.
But the pressure is from within, in the force of the
vision itself;   the thought is of the vision only, and
how to express it.   Here, again, the *phrase*, though un-
certain and imperfect, is kept in its place;   it may be
richly ornamented, but it is not used as an ornament in
itself - a distinction which gives no bad criterion for
testing the direction in which poetry of this sort is
moving.   We reach a clearer atmosphere in Mr John
Drinkwater's long and interesting poem, 'The Fires of
God', almost the only one in the book which shows a
certain degree of chastened and classical finish.   This
poem rises gradually to its climax with an orderliness
which is hardly Georgian.   The reflective matter of it
is modern enough, and it is reassuring that at least one
poet finds himself suited by the lucidity of a tradition-
al style.   The culminating song of all the 'pilgrim
souls' who challenge the silence of the skies scarcely
carries the weight thrown on it;   but a stanza of it will
show the clarity of line which is in such contrast with
most of the other poets' work:

> Wise of the great unshapen age,
> To which we move with measured tread
> All girt with passionate truth to wage
> High battle for the word unsaid,
> The song unsung, the cause unled,
> The freedom that no hope can gauge;
> Strong-armed, sure-footed, iron-willed
> We sift and weave, we break and build.

Of Mr Masefield we have only his comparatively short
poem, 'Biography'.   This, if it does not show him at
his most ambitious, shows him certainly at his least
exceptionable.   He has raised, with his better known
poems, questions of form and manner which do not meet us
here.   'Biography' is a clear and attractive series of
vignettes, rising here and there to romantic beauty, and
rendered with the masterly cleanness of style which he
can always command when he chooses.   Criticism of Mr
Masefield would be simple if his poetry were all like
this, though it doubtless becomes more interesting, now
that so much of his poetry is not like this at all.   He
represents a claim which is the antithesis to Mr Aber-
crombie's - the claim that fluent directness, constantly
dropping to a pedestrian and prosaic level, and never for

long far above it, can be made a vehicle for impressive
dramatic beauty. With his sureness of aim and his skill
in managing swift transitions, Mr Masefield is so far
well equipped for proving that it can be. The critical
question would be addressed to his creative gift, his
power of conceiving character, and it could not be summ-
arily answered in either sense. But it cannot be pur-
sued in this connexion if we are to keep within the pages
before us, though, indeed, we have now almost finished
with them. The poets whom we have not yet mentioned
could be invited separately, with hardly an exception, to
illustrate the general impression of life and reality
they have combined to give. Mr W.W. Gibson, Mr James
Stephens, and Mr E.B. Sargant, under very different
manners, have all of them the same unmistakable purpose
to touch and express genuine imaginative experience; and
there are not more than one or two in whom the purpose is
doubtful. Finally, we have Mr Rupert Brooke, who
occupies, in such a company as this, a very curious
position. He is literally the only one, so it seems,
who takes the immemorial advice to the poet - 'Fool! said
my Muse to me, look in thy heart, and write!' - exactly
as it has been understood in all ages and as Sidney him-
self understood it. Mr Brooke's work is highly unequal,
but there are here one or two lyrics of his which are not
remarkable only for the fact that they *are* lyrics. They
have not the fusion of sound and sense which makes music
of a poem; but they are written in just that emotional
simplicity which the other poets have eschewed, and
passion is to be heard in them, even if it is a little
shrill. Stanzas such as these belong to no particular
period, any more than passion does:

[Quotes 'Dust', stanzas I-III, and VI.]

'This volume is issued', says the editor's prefatory
note, 'in the belief that English poetry is now once
again putting on a new strength and beauty.' We share
the belief, we cheer the poets, and we congratulate our-
selves on the good time coming.

9. 'SOME POETS OF TO-DAY', UNSIGNED REVIEW, 'THE NATION'

8 March 1913, 934 and 936

This is likely to be by the same hand as the anonymous
review in 'The Nation' (6 July 1912) of Rupert Brooke's
'Poems' (1911). That review referred likewise to the
influence of Donne, who had taught Brooke to be 'not only
remarkably skilful, but ..... insolently skilful also'.

It is the fate of poets not yet famous to be inadequately
reviewed. Poetry is difficult to interpret - there is
that to be said on behalf of readers and reviewers, and
it is truer of the poet than of other writers that 'you
must love him ere to you he will seem worthy of your love'
A state of the poet's own mind is always the real subject
of a poem; incidents and objects are only the terms in
which it is expressed, and the completeness with which we
enter into the mind of another largely depends on our con-
fidence in the integrity of his vision and the sincerity
of his words. It is true we are trusting creatures,
some of us, and a single poem, one stanza, one thing per-
fectly expressed, is often enough to give us faith in a
poet and supply the light by which to read him, but unless
this confidence is confirmed it is apt to fade. In the
case of the famous and the dead, it has been repeatedly
confirmed, so that even when they fail we still believe
in them. The dead are oftener judged by their
successes, the living by their failures. Here lies the
new poet's great disadvantage. In his case no weakness
is condoned, and while we do not know him well enough to
expand his meaning to its full significance, his defects
must throw doubt on his merits, and his obscurities upon
the genuineness of his vision. We ignore no faults of
his as fumes of a peculiar fire; on the contrary, we
snuff them up contemptuously. 'This man a fine poet?
Just listen, then, to this!' - if you introduce a book
of new poems to anyone, that is quite likely to be the
kind of reception it will receive; and down he settles
in comfortable censoriousness to read a page or so, with
an expression on his face which says plainly, 'Shelley I
know and Keats I know, but who is this?' There is an
admissible tendency in many to believe that all really
good poets are either dead or recognised already. It is
the homage that the ordinary reader pays to genius to
believe it is extinct.

Now this anthology will do more than dozens and dozens
of reviews to show people that good poetry of the most
various kinds is being written now.   The editor has
limited his selection to two years (1911-1912);   and by
doing so he has lost poems which otherwise would have
been included;   but if his selection loses in that way,
it gains in this, that we are impressed with the amount
of original beauty which can be gleaned, not even from a
decade, but from writings almost fresh enough to be des-
cribed as recently published.

The three best known names in this anthology are
Sturge Moore, Masefield, Lascelles Abercrombie.   There
is more imaginative poetry to be found in Mr Sturge
Moore's work than in any of his contemporaries.   He is
perhaps the most *poetical* of them all in the conception
of his subjects.   He has the pure aesthetic passion.
As a craftsman he is often faulty.   There are odd wry-
nesses in his thought, his work has seldom the grace of
ease, intellectual excitement sometimes makes him over-
labour an idea;   but of modern poets he is one in whom
the passion of the artist is most intense.   Writing from
that plane, he can be amazingly unconscious of his
readers' sense of the ludicrous and indifferent to their
impatience.   Here he is represented by 'A Sicilian
Idyll'.   He writes for artists, and they are few;   but
anyone with a literary sense, though he may be jarred
occasionally by what seems an infelicitous word, can
feel the distinction of his descriptive passages.

Mr Masefield is at the present moment the most widely
read of poets;   he has succeeded in overcoming the pop-
ular prejudice that whatever brevity may be to wit, it is
certainly the soul of agreeable poetry.   As much novel-
ist as poet, he tells a story and describes character in
a masterly fashion, and he gives us poetry by the way.
Stories in verse are common in English literature, but Mr
Masefield's stories blend in an original fashion the
fascinations of poetry and prose.   In 'Enoch Arden' the
value of the characterisation is *nil*, the verbal beauty
everything;   in T.E. Brown's sketches and stories it is
only emotion and melodrama that count;   Crabbe has the
artistic equipment of a realist, and the mind of an ex-
ceedingly sensible country parson;   his beauty is the
beauty of fine, direct, compact prose;   but Mr Masefield
tells his stories with the flexible exuberance of poetry,
without the tragedy and comedy of character being lost
sight of for a moment.   'Biography' in this anthology is
a beautiful, entertaining piece of literature.

Mr Abercrombie as a poet has an astonishing power of
dramatic psychological analysis.   He is a vehement,
imaginative thinker.   If he were a race-horse he might

be described as by Browning out of Elizabethan drama.
The vigour and distinction of his phrases is a continual
delight; but the beauty his writing has for the mind is
far greater than the charm of it to the ear.   The sound
of phrases is magnificent; the rhythm of passages in-
ferior to that.   He does not harangue the reader person-
ally like Browning; he states things like an Elizabethan.
His language is not like brilliant talk; it has the
elaborated compact force of the written word.   Otherwise,
there is something Browningesque in the cumulative subt-
lety of his treatment of crucial moments, and in the free,
hurrying vigour of his descriptions.   His poem on St
Thomas's mission to India is one of the very best in this
book.   Here is a characteristic passage, but not a whit
more vigorous than many others.

> And flies! a land of flies! where the hot soil
> Foul with ceaseless decay steams into flies!
> So thick they pile themselves into the air above
> Their meal of filth, they seem like breathing heaps
> Of formless life mounded upon the earth;
> And buzzing always like the pipes and strings
> Of solemn music made for sorcerers. -
> I abhor flies, - to see them stare upon me
> Out of their little faces of gibbous eyes;
> To feel the dry cool skin of their bodies alight
> Perching upon my lips! - O yea, a dream,
> A dream of impious, obscene Satan, this
> Monstrous frenzy of life, the Indian being!

To pass now to the lesser known of Georgian poets: the
imagination of Mr Rupert Brooke is both ecstatic and
harsh.   His explosions of passion in an ether too
rarefied for common lovers' sighs, alternating with re-
coils of hatred against whatever is physically humiliat-
ing, put one in mind of Donne.   He is an intellectual
poet; bygone criticism would have dubbed him 'meta-
physical', and he would have met with readier appreciation
in the seventeenth century.
   To Mr Walter de la Mare many more readers will at any
rate immediately respond.   There is a homely, twilight
quality in the scenes he evokes.   They have the distinct-
ness, yet inconclusiveness, of the fireside reveries of
one whose head is full of old romance.   He is a senti-
mental poet, if that adjective may be used for once with-
out reproach, and the melody and movement of his verse is
familiar.   There is a tincture of Coleridge in the
temper of his imagination.   He can touch us with a
ghostly finger, and there is something Coleridgian in the
innocent epicureanism of his tenderness.

Mr James Stephens is a violent contrast. Much of this
Irish poet's sympathy leans towards the savagery, pride,
and queer grumbling bitterness of such characters as
Gorki has made disquieting, and Synge fantastic and poet-
ical. Mr Stephens belongs to the realistic side of the
Celtic movement. His first book was called 'Insurrect-
ions', and it was well named. His characteristics are a
grim poetic humour and a conception of God, the heavens
and the spheres, at once childlike and awful. In 'The
Lonely God', Jehovah walking in Eden, grieving over the
loss of Adam, recalls one of Blake's solemn, but almost
comically human, conceptions of The Ancient of Days.

> His face was sad, His hands hung slackly down
> Along His robe; too sorrowful to frown
> He paced along the grassy paths and through
> The silent trees, and where the flowers grew
> Tended by Adam. All the birds had gone
> Out to the world, and singing was not one
> To cheer the lonely God out of His grief -
> The silence broken only when a leaf
> Tapt lightly on a leaf, or when the wind,
> Slow-handed, swayed the bushes to its mind.

No poet shows to greater advantage here than Mr William
Davies. If the well-worn word 'delightful' may be
understood here in a special sense, it might be said that
Mr Davies was the most delightful of all these poets.
His writing is so unexpected and yet so natural. A
poet's style tells us how he feels, and Mr Davies's words
and images make us think two things about him; we say,
only quite a simple man would have wanted to say that,
and only a delicate mind could have found that way of
saying it. His instincts are essentially literary, but
his inspiration comes from life. We are given two
lyrics, 'Days too Short' and 'The Kingfisher'. They are
as easy and slight as a poem from an Elizabethan song-
book, but in the place of a charming convention we feel
rather the influence of a definite personality.

'The Child and the Mariner' shows him in another vein,
one in which we feel more distinctly than ever the charm
of a quaint integrity. It is a perfectly successful
revocation of people and things seen long ago with a
child's eyes.

Each poet tempts the reviewer to say something about
him; but one is impossible to omit in any review of
this book - Mr Gibson. 'The Hare' and 'Devil's Edge'
are fine poems. He combines perfectly felicitous des-
criptions of Nature, never strained, observed by an eye

which loves things as they are, with an intensity of mood,
which raises these poems to the level of admirable poetry.
The tramping wanderer's emotions, his passions, his
response to the sights and sounds of nature, have been
the inspiration of many recent poems; but they have
never made better a poem than 'The Hare'. His style is
the perfection of colloquial poetry. Mr Gordon Bottom-
ley's 'Babel' is an imposing piece of description - a
Doré picture, but translated into words with a massive
thoroughness of imagination. The anthology closes with
a dirge by Mr Robert Trevelyan, so simple that its merits
seem apprehensible at once and even uninteresting; but
read a second time, it will seem in its own style, that
of the classic tradition of avoiding emphasis and every
emotion which cannot be directly expressed, a lyric which
has the lasting charm of genuine art.

10. 'SOME RECENT POETS', EDWARD THOMAS, 'THE BOOKMAN'

March 1913, 330

_____

Edward Thomas reviews 'Georgian Poetry, 1911-1912'
(chiefly) together with 'The Poetical Works of Robert
Bridges', and books by Lascelles Abercrombie, Evelyn
Underhill, Lucy Masterman, Douglas Goldring, and
Vivian Locke Ellis.
    For a note on Edward Thomas see headnote to No. 4.

_____

Whether it is or is not a compliment to publish all the
poems, except the dramas, of the chief of living poets,
at as low a price as if he were a classic, by a happy
chance something more than a compliment is simultaneously
paid by the dedication to him, on the part of editor and
poets, of an anthology of Georgian Poetry. The poets
are Messrs Abercrombie, Bottomley, Brooke, Chesterton,
W.H. Davies, de la Mare, Drinkwater, Flecker, Gibson,
D.H. Lawrence, Masefield, Monro, Sturge Moore, Ronald
Ross, Sargant, Stephens, and R.C. Trevelyan; and if only
Mr de la Mare among the number bears any obvious relation-
ship to Mr Bridges, the dedication is the more remarkable,
as showing from how many different young men - dwelling
in how different a world from that of 'I love all

beauteous things' and 'I have loved flowers that fade' -
his loveliness, his purity and his originality command
homage.

'Georgian Poetry' contains 'beauteous things'. It in-
cludes for example long poems by Messrs Abercrombie,
Davies, Masefield, Sturge Moore, and James Stephens. It
includes the two most impressive of Mr Gordon Bottomley's
recent poems, five remarkable pieces by Mr Rupert Brooke,
and five representative poems from Mr de la Mare's
'Listeners'. Altogether it is a brilliant selection from
the poetry of 1911 and 1912. But it is less and more
than that. It excludes many poems because it aims at
showing what young men are typical and promising, what
elder men notably reflect the spirit of the moment. No-
body not jaded by excess of poetry or starved for lack of
it, will fail to see that there is such a spirit when he
meets it thus concentrated. Compare it with a similar
book of poetry from 1901 and 1902 and its novelty is
apparent. There is, by the way, no anthology of 1901 and
1902, but if it is now too late to make one, it is to be
hoped that similar volumes will henceforward be compiled
decennially or even quinquennially. If they find editors
as generous and impartial as 'E.M.' they will, like this
Georgian anthology, be valuable and delightful.

Was there ten years ago such vividness - or such hectic
and excited striving after vividness - as in Mr Aber-
crombie? In his new play - where he redresses the long-
troubled balance by putting into the mouths of fishermen
such poetry as used to be held too good for any but kings
- a man speaks of a plague thus:

> The whole earth's peoples have been fiercely caught
> Like torn small papers in a wind, in this
> Great powerful ailing.

Another speaks of a sailor:

> With the ribs of his breast crusht like a trodden
>   hamper,
> Lying three days crampt in a boat, and he for ever
>   groaning.

Ten years ago Mr Chesterton was consoling and praising
the ass by recalling the day when Christ rode one into
Jerusalem. To-day Mr Rupert Brooke sincerely and (so
far as an unbewitched landsman can judge) powerfully
endeavours to sympathise with a fish and its 'dark
ecstasies' where:

Those silent waters weave for him
A fluctuant mutable world and dim,
Where wavering masses bulge and gape . . .

Ten years ago Mr Gordon Bottomley was not picturing the
end of the world and the building of Babel in blank verse
like the quintessence of G.W. Stevens's prose.   Ten
years ago nobody knew that Mr W.H. Davies was a poet, -
not even himself.   But then he is a fortunate accident
that might have happened at any time, but did not.   Ten
years ago the surviving 'Yellow Book' men would have been
pleased with Mr D.H. Lawrence's subject, enraged with his
indifference to their execution.   Nor would they alone
have been enraged, and not only Mr Lawrence would have
given offence.   They would have contracted a chill from
so much eagerness both to come at truth and to avoid the
appearance of insincerity, the fidelity to crudest fact in
Messrs Abercrombie, Gibson and Masefield, the fidelity to
airiest fancy in Mr de la Mare, and to remotest intuition
or guessing in Mr Brooke, the mixture everywhere of what
they would have called realism and extravagance.   They
could not have endured the simplicity of Mr Abercrombie's
'Deborah' as here:

Is it only a small thing to you, this
That once was David's? . . .

or the violent subtlety of his 'Sale of St Thomas', as
here:

Gigantic thirst grieving our mouths with dust,
Scattering up against our breathing salt
Of blown dried dung, till the taste eat like fires
Of a wild vinegar into our sheathéd marrows . . .

The anthology does not include all that is typical, or
all that is best.   It excludes women altogether, and
therefore tells us nothing of Miss Underhill's spiritual
and definitely mystic lyric, of which her new book gives
many perfect examples: nor in any case could it have in-
cluded anything from Mrs C.F.G. Masterman's first book,
so gravely, courageously and widely sympathetic, so
graceful and finished in a variety of metrical forms.
Still more serious omissions are the names of Messrs
Douglas Goldring and Vivian Locke Ellis.   Mr Goldring
was perhaps not impossible ten years ago.   His book
consists of experiments in capturing the soul, or one of
the souls, of twenty or thirty London streets.   In some
he speaks of his own feeling towards them; in others he

speaks for them as if he were an inhabitant.   His
methods vary almost as much as his streets, from the
downright to the romantic, but he is invariably interest-
ing, often brilliant.

Mr Ellis published his first book eight years ago, and
though he deserved a place for every possible reason in
'Georgian Poetry', he would have stood well apart from
most of his companions, except Messrs Davies and de la
Mare.   He is conscious that the fates have confused him
with mortal questionings - the sonnet, 'In Cornwall', in
which he says so, is not his best, but is a good example
of his more purely reflective work:

[Quotes the sonnet, 'In Cornwall']

11.   HENRY NEWBOLT, 'POETRY AND DRAMA'

March 1913, 45-52

Sir Henry Newbolt (1862-1938) published his first book of
poems, 'Admirals All', in 1897, and it had by this time run
through thirty editions.   Although his own poetry was less
adventurous in form than in theme, he had recommended him-
self to younger poets, and in particular to Monro (editor
of 'Poetry and Drama': see Introduction, pp. 26-7), by
two lectures to the Royal Society of Literature to whose
newly-created Chair of Poetry he had recently been
elected.   It was Newbolt whom Monro had chosen to open
the Poetry Bookshop on 8 January of that year.

'To-day', said a lecturer ten years ago, 'to-day we have
no great novelist: will any one suggest that we have a
poet?' - and the audience echoed his contempt.   They
probably knew as well as he did that Hardy and Meredith,
William Morris and Swinburne, were not only then living,
but had already brought in the bulk of their harvest.   In
their eyes, as in the lecturer's, it all counted for noth-
ing, because it was not what they were looking for.
Dickens and Thackeray were great novelists, Tennyson and
Browning great poets: no one living resembled these,
therefore no one living was either poet or novelist.
The same argument is reported to hold good among the

savage tribes of North Africa, who will refuse all your
gold and accept only a silver dollar with the head of
Maria Theresa upon it.   The metal counts for nothing:
they know what money is - money is that which they have
seen before.

It is unfortunate that in our own country this way of
looking at things is not confined to the less civilised
tribes: it is perhaps most common among the educated and
the professed lovers of literature.   Their very educ-
ation, their very love of the beauty they know, lays the
fatal spell of habit upon them: the unfamiliar becomes
the uncomfortable, and they spend, at any rate, the
latter part of their intellectual existence in lamenting
as decadent whatever in art possesses any newness of life.
No doubt Time brings in his revenges: no doubt, as the
years go on, the saplings prove to be something more than
hazel or dog-oak.   They grow to undeniable timber and
replace the old kings of the forest.   But no one is con-
verted: their greatness is now a part of the laudable
past and is used in its turn as a standard by which to
depreciate the newer growth around them.   This perpet-
ually repeated error is a costly one.   Poets are a part
of their age: a generation that does not realise its own
literature is an unwholesome generation, an organism un-
refreshed, cut off from that renewal of the blood which
is among the first conditions of health.

How, then, is the public to be convinced?   How is the
most willing reader to discover the best poets of his own
day?   The number of those who are writing in verse is
very large and they cover an immense field of thought:
they are little talked about, and in the press they are
too often either neglected altogether or reviewed in
batches of twenty at a time, with five lines of comment
apiece, and perhaps in favourable cases a single hap-
hazard quotation.   We have well-known reviewers of
fiction, and stalls-full of dramatic critics: but what
editor would think it worth his while to keep a reviewer
on his staff who should write week by week on the whole
output of current poetry, not as an anonymous and casual
impressionist, but pledging the credit of his own name
for a serious and consistent judgment?   And perhaps for
this state of things the critics are more to blame than
the editors, for they have long been accustomed to
lighten the responsibility of praise or blame by con-
cluding with a traditional remark on the impossibility
of estimating the work of a contemporary, and the com-
fortable assurance that the ultimate verdict is for post-
erity alone to pronounce.   Hopes of the verdict of post-
erity may afford some gratification to a sanguine poet,

but how can it benefit his hungry contemporaries - the
would-be readers - to know that the food they are starv-
ing for will be adjudicated good or bad a hundred years
hence?   That verdict, moreover, of absolute good or bad,
is not the one they need.   What concerns them most is to
know, not what may be good for posterity, but what is
good for them, which is not necessarily the same thing.
The right poetry for any age is not the poetry of the
future, but the poetry of the past and the present.   A
poet writes to express himself, but he does so nearly
always with an ardent belief that he is serving his fell-
ows.   If he looks forward to a fame that shall survive
him, it cannot in reason be for his own sake, but rather
that his service may not be limited to the period of his
own generation, which perhaps has given him but a partial
and long-delayed opportunity.   What would most benefit
him and his contemporaries alike is the action and re-
action of sympathy between the living writer and his
living audience.   To secure this result what experiment
would not be worth making?

Several experiments are in fact being tried, and one
of them has already achieved a considerable amount of
success.   A certain 'E.M.' has published in the volume
which he calls 'Georgian Poetry' a selection from the work
of seventeen living poets.   The qualification for ad-
mission is that the verse chosen should have been first
published during the past two years, and that the authors
should be only such as were practically unknown two years
ago, or such as have since that time gained some access-
ion of power.   The editor believes that his collection
'may, if it is fortunate, help the lovers of poetry to
realise that we are at the beginning of another "Georgian
period" which may take rank in due time with the several
great poetic ages of the past'.   Let us grant to the
critics, if they will, that since we are only at the
beginning of the period we cannot know what rank it may
or may not take in due time.   The important point is
that E.M.'s enthusiasm is amply justified.   The book is
a striking one: it has been eagerly bought up, and I
believe that it cannot fail to astonish most of its
readers for there are probably but few who have been
carefully noting the scattered appearances which to-
gether prove the coming of a new breath of poetic
emotion.   And the reader who has no standard of condemn-
ation ready, who desires life and the movement of life
rather than a belated copy of it - he, I think, will be
not only astonished, but delighted.

Let us turn to the poets themselves: for a first
survey any order is equally good.   Mr Lascelles

Abercrombie is represented by his 'Sale of St Thomas', a
legend or morality play, put before us in a single scene
of some five hundred lines, one half of which are spoken
by Thomas himself. The story is a simple one: Thomas
is a soul of flame blown this way and that alternately
between the impulse to preach Christ among the heathen
and the even stronger impulse to draw back and take
shelter in prudence from the dangers which his too vivid
imagination presents to him. He has already turned back
from Baghdad: rather than face the desert he will go by
sea to India. The captain of the ship he is to sail in,
with his quiet humorous hints of danger, and his horrible
tales of Eastern cruelty, sets him wavering once more;
once more his own teeming imagination fills the world
with enemies and apes, and flies and fevers. Then comes
the Stranger, claims Thomas as his runaway servant, and
sells him to the captain for twenty pieces of silver.
He will go the voyage after all, in irons. His sin, so
his Master tells him, was not fear, but prudence - a more
deadly thing:

> For this refuses faith in the unknown powers
> Within man's nature: shrewdly bringeth all
> Their inspiration of strange eagerness
> To a judgment bought by safe experience;
> Narrows desire into the scope of thought.
> But it is written in the heart of man,
> Thou shalt no larger be than thy desire.
> Thou must not therefore stoop thy spirit's sight
> To pore only within the candle-gleam
> Of conscious wit and reasonable brain;
> But search into the sacred darkness lying
> Outside thy knowledge of thyself, the vast
> Measureless fate, full of the power of stars,
> The outer noiseless heavens of thy soul.

This is the moral; but, full of high imagination as the
lines are, they give no idea of the almost physical in-
tensity with which we are made to see and feel and fear
with Thomas himself, or of the delicate and humorous
skill which contrasts with these agitations the cool
worldly wisdom of the captain and the calm heavenly
wisdom of the Stranger.

Mr Gordon Bottomley contributes two pieces, both of
blank verse. The successful one is called 'The End of
the World':

> The snow had fallen many nights and days;
> The sky was come upon the earth at last.

Here, in sixty lines, is the more extended realisation of
a vision seen long ago by Mr Bridges - the vision of

> The Earth that, sleeping 'neath her frozen stole,
> Shall dream a dream, crept from the sunless pole
> Of how her end shall be.

Mr Bottomley's effect is produced by direct and literal
narrative; it passes from apprehension to terror, and
from terror to a deep pathos of human tenderness.   It is
haunting in retrospect: it revives that old panic of
childhood when the joy of the white world turned suddenly
to the thought, 'But there is too much snow; what shall
we do if there is too much? what if it should never
stop?'
     Mr Rupert Brooke has not only distinction, but a dist-
inction which is of rare interest.   He is gifted with an
intellectual curiosity and a natural and habitual intens-
ity of feeling that recall the work of Donne, and of
Donne only, among the English poets.   In some of his
poems there is the vital directness which startles one in
such a line as the famous -

> For God's sake hold your tongue and let me love.

The selection here given is not quite representative -
it does not cover the whole range - but three of the five
poems are of great beauty and originality.   In 'The Fish'
this poet has so used words as almost to endow humanity
with a new and non-human rapture of sensation.   In the
poem called 'Dining-room Tea' he has done what only the
greatest of painters succeed in doing.   First, he has
arrested, in a familiar moment, the kinematograph of eye
and brain by which life is displayed to us as an unend-
ing, unseverable tissue of everchanging action.   But he
has done more: he has not merely made his picture - a
commonplace, bright domestic interior - he has thrown
over it the light, invisible to others, of the eternal
reality lying behind the appearances of our transitory
life.   The poem called 'Dust' is a triumph of Passion
over Reason: the lovers that are so surely to be dust
shall yet, as wind-blown dust, come together again, and
bring a radiant ecstasy to other loves in other sunset
gardens.   Here, as elsewhere, Mr Brooke's bravely hope-
less philosophy is burnt up in the flame of his poetic
faith.
     Mr James Stephens is another contributor who is but
half represented here.   His own volume, 'The Hill of
Vision', opens with a 'Prelude and Song' which can only

be read - and cannot quite be read - in one breathless
rapture.   Many poems have been made about the skylark's
singing: one, at least, has described it with supreme
felicity.   Mr Stephens does not describe at all - he
sings: his song is the very song itself, the profuse
strains of unpremeditated art, joyous and clear and
fresh, a rain of melody showering from rainbow clouds.
But here, instead of this, we have a poem equally arrest-
ing but of much less certain acceptability.   'The Lonely
God' is a fine piece of criticism in the form of an epic
fragment.   It will shock; but it will shock only those
who claim for themselves and refuse to others the right
to make God in their own image.   Milton took the God of
Genesis and recreated Him as an irresponsible being with
the ideas of a Puritan politician.   Mr Stephens has
accepted the outline of the story and of the supreme
figure, but has changed the Creator's mental and moral
attributes to those demanded by a philosophy and humanity
which are of to-day.

[Quotes 'The Lonely God', stanzas II, IX and XI.]

The concluding part of this poem may be thought fantast-
ic: if so, the fantasy is such as would have seriously
pleased Coventry Patmore.   But, in any case, Poetry is
not Dogma; and this is poetry.
   Two of the longer poems in the book are autobiograph-
ical.   Mr Masefield's, which bears the title 'Biography',
is almost an essay on the subject, with poetical pass-
ages by way of illustration.   It is highly epigrammatic,
and would yield a number of striking quotations; but it
has not the qualities for which its author is best
known and admired.   Mr Drinkwater's ode 'The Fires of
God' is one of the most careful and accomplished pieces
of writing in the book: the unfortunate result is that
the thought, in so elaborate and finished a form, seems
to fail of its due impressiveness.   Mr Gibson and Mr
Sargant achieve more conviction with far less artifice.
The style of the former's gipsy romance, 'The Hare', is
a triumph of the happy-go-lucky: it gives the story
both charm and reality.   Wordsworth would have liked
this poem, in the days when he was so unpunctual for
meals, and of a mood not to mind the aversion of the
heroine's father for clergy and police.   Mr Sargant
will also please and convince those who get entangled in
his magic 'Cuckoo Wood'.   The underwood may need a
little cutting, but it is impossible to doubt that the
poet did really get inside that wood and see all the
little flying things, and the snows of the anemones, and

the shifting light and shade - and all but saw, if only
he had dared to stay, the goatfoot himself.

Mr Lawrence, it would appear, has seen him - Pan, that
is more and less than human, the divine brute, the
bringer of madness.   The poem called 'Snapdragon' is
flooded with the distress of mere animal impulse - the
man is beaten down and blinded with it, as one may be made
sightless and almost breathless by unendurable excess of
sunlight.   The reader is driven to wonder what such a
power as this will make of other scenes and less painful
emotions.   In this book the poem stands quite alone, for
the realism of Mr de la Mare is of a totally different
character.   He too conveys an extraordinarily vivid
sense of physical reality; but he conveys it, like the
Pre-Raphaelite painters, through the eyes, and mingles
with it a spiritual suggestion which makes it act like a
spell rather than a drug.   'The Sleeper' in his poem
is -

>   Fast - fast asleep; her two hands laid
>   Loose-folded on her knee,
>   So that her small unconscious face
>   Looked half unreal to be.

So fast asleep indeed that -

>   Even her hands upon her lap
>   Seemed saturate with sleep.

In the poem called 'The Listeners', which gives the name
to his latest volume, this power is turned to the uses
of romance.

>   'Is there anybody there?' said the Traveller,
>   Knocking on the moonlit door;
>   And his horse in the silence champed the grasses
>   Of the forest's ferny floor.

When the reader comes to the end of this piece it is no
longer only the bodily nerves that are awake: there is
also stirring that unexplained sense which gives such a
pleasurable shiver to those who feel it and such indig-
nant pain to the more scientific who do not.   In Mr
Chesterton's 'Song of Elf' the feeling is no longer
romantic: it reaches the point of 'sheer superstition'.

[Quotes 'The Song of Elf', concluding stanzas (VII and
                                                  VIII).]

Unfortunately this tells us very little about the writer,
and the same complaint may be made of the few lines con-
tributed by Mr Flecker and Sir Ronald Ross.   Mr Trevel-
yan, too, has only a single page, and, poignant and
sincere as the tiny stanzas are, they can only set the
reader upon inquiry.   Mr Monro's two pieces are both
pleasing, but they also are hardly representative: they
have neither the incisiveness nor the more memorable
charm which may be found in some of the short poems at
the end of his 'Before Dawn'.

There remain two poems only, and of them, for differ-
ent reasons, it is hardly necessary to speak.   'The
Child and the Mariner', by Mr Davies, is a character-
sketch;   a sketch of a figure with a kind of double rain-
bow round it, made by the light of humour in an old man's
eyes and the light of romance in a child's.   It is a
delightful piece, the best and the most personal that
Mr Davies has yet given us, and it needs only to be read.
The 'Sicilian Idyll' of Mr Sturge Moore also needs only
to be read.   It is undoubtedly the finest piece of work
in the volume, as it is by far the longest and most elab-
orate.   Strictly, it ought not to be here at all, for
Mr Sturge Moore can by no stretch be brought within the
new group of Georgian Poets.   His reputation, and much
of his finest verse, was made ten years ago.   But the
inclusion of this Idyll certainly adds to the value of
the book, for the poem throws much light on the work of
his younger contemporaries and takes none from them.

I have spoken of these poets one by one;   but what of
the whole company of them?   Is their book merely an
agreeable and various anthology, or is it something
more?   Has it the force of accumulated evidence? and,
if so, what does it prove?

To these questions two entirely opposite answers will
be given by the two classes of readers.   Those who are
accustomed to consider the poem apart from the poet, to
regard it as a work of skilled craftsmanship, an external
or decorative scheme with a possible perfection of its
own - certainly for them the collection will be merely a
collection, without any kind of unity;   a chaos, if not
a discord.   But to those who look rather to the essent-
ial elements of poetry than to its external form it will,
I think, be clear that at least three qualities are
strikingly exemplified in this book.   They may not be -
they are not - all present in all the poems;   but each
of the three is to be found in a majority of them.   The
first of these qualities is poetic imagination, the power
of the poet to grasp the things of earth and to trans-
figure them, to take the world of the senses and to re-

cast it - to send it forth glowing from the furnace of
his own heart.   This is a power which has been given
to the generations of men in very varying degrees: it
was as common in the age of Shakespeare and Lope de Vega
as it was rare in the England of the eighteenth century.
It came back with Blake and has never since entirely
failed us.   But it would be difficult to point to a time
when it has been seen more suddenly, more widely and more
strongly at work than it is at the present moment.   This,
it may be said, is merely a personal judgment, merely the
record of answering vibrations in a particular receiver.
I reply that the testing apparatus is, and must always be,
a particular one; but the actual test, though every one
can make it for himself, is not an individual one - it
lies in the comparison of the new work with those poems
which have always and by all been acknowledged as supreme
in the quality of imaginative intensity.   Let those
readers who are looking for poetical imagination look
here, and let them impose as they will the ordeal by
juxtaposition: they will not, I believe, be disappointed.
     The second quality of which I spoke is constructive
power.   It is not properly separable from the first,
being in reality included in the power of intuitive
creation.   Shapeless or incoherent poetry is simply
inferior poetry, the expression of a defective or im-
mature imagination.   But there is a degree of construct-
ive power which is needed only for poems of a certain
form and magnitude, and this may well be spoken of
separately.   It is certain that, by the lack of it, many
poems of great intensity have been rendered almost in-
effective.   Keats's 'Endymion' and George Darley's
'Nepenthe' would probably have had a different fate if
their readers had not seen that each of these poets had
to some extent failed to determine and mark out, before
the fiery process of fusion began, the lines within
which his molten metal was to run.   In the poems before
us there is no such failure.   Mr Sturge Moore has long
been recognised as a master of his favourite form of ex-
pression - the idyllic drama.   Mr Lascelles Abercrombie,
whose 'Emblems of Love' seemed to suffer from having been
written piece by piece at different dates and under
different impulses, has in the 'Sale of St Thomas' made
a garment for his spirit as perfect in outline and
fashioning as it is rich in texture.   Mr Gibson has told
his romantic story with as sure a sense of proportion as
Mr Davies has shown in his romantic portrait.   Propor-
tion has been kept too by Mr Stephens, one of the two
most impulsive poets in the company: the other, Mr
Masefield, is perhaps the only one who has not quite

realised where intuition ceased and intellect alone pro-
longed the flow.   In the shorter poems there is plenty
of freedom, some uncertainty perhaps, but no eccentricity.
    The third quality is truth of diction - an achievement
so hedged with entanglements as to seem, theoretically,
almost beyond reach for a modern poet.   The absolute im-
possibility of forgetting the richly coloured words and
haunting cadences of the past; the more absolute necess-
ity of speaking in a natural voice and in the language of
to-day; the risk of distracting or offending a hearer
whose ear is differently tuned; the increased difficulty
of dyeing speech of commoner material with deep shades of
thought, - if all this were in the poet's consciousness
at once we may be sure we should have little poetry.
Fortunately, it is hardly in his consciousness at all.
The younger poets of to-day - it follows inevitably from
their imaginative gift - have no temptation to a false
and embarrassing aesthetic.   They are not for making
something pretty, something up to the standard of the
professional patterns; they are not members of an arts-
and-crafts industrial guild.   They write as grown men
walk, each with his own unconscious gesture; and with
the same instinctive tact as the walker they vary their
pace and direction, keep their balance, and avoid coll-
isions.   In short, they express themselves, and seem to
steer without an effort between the dangers of innovation
and reminiscence.   In the whole book there are only two
disconcerting cases of resemblance: Sir Ronald Ross has
once seen Shelley plain, and Mr Masefield has bowed too
completely to the spell of Mr Bridges' 'Recollections of
Solitude'.   The rest speak in tones so natural, so
characteristic, and so flexible that the reader may
easily fail to note the degree of mastery implied.   That
eighteenth-century dodo, the pseudo-Miltonic Diction,
with its half-bred varieties, has made a long struggle
for existence, but it would seem to be extinct at last.
If it troubles us again it will not be as a thing of
life but as a triumph of some taxidermist's craft.   The
new English is to be one with life itself: to slip like
running water over rock, sand, or weed with the same
swift adaptability but with ever-varying sound.   The
secret of this adaptability is no discovery of the
Georgian Poets - it is their birthright, inherited from
those predecessors who from Wordsworth and Coleridge on-
wards have worked for the assimilation of verse to the
manner and accent of natural speech.   In recognition of
one of their more immediate benefactors they have un-
animously inscribed their volume with the name of Robert
Bridges.   Better still, they have secured the continuance
of his line.

12. 'THE GEORGIAN RENAISSANCE', D.H. LAWRENCE, 'RHYTHM'

March 1913, xvii-xx

This review was reprinted in 'Phoenix', 1936.
     D.H. Lawrence contributed to all but the third of the
Georgian anthologies (see Appendix, p. 406). For a note
on the historical context of this exuberant piece, see
Introduction, pp. 5-6; for a note on Middleton Murry's
'Rhythm' see Introduction, pp. 22-3.

'Georgian Poetry' is an anthology of verse which has been
published during the reign of our present king, George V.
It contains one poem of my own, but this fact will not,
I hope, preclude my reviewing the book.
     This collection is like a big breath taken when we are
waking up after a night of oppressive dreams. The
nihilists, the intellectual, hopeless people - Ibsen,
Flaubert, Thomas Hardy - represent the dream we are waking
from. It was a dream of demolition. Nothing was, but
was nothing. Everything was taken from us. And now our
lungs are full of new air, and our eyes see it is morning,
but we have not forgotten the terror of the night. We
dreamed we were falling through space into nothingness, and
the anguish of it leaves us rather eager.
     But we are awake again, our lungs are full of new air,
our eyes of morning. The first song is nearly a cry,
fear and the pain of remembrance sharpening away the pure
music. And that is this book.
     The last years have been years of demolition. Because
faith and belief were getting pot-bound, and the Temple
was made a place to barter sacrifices, therefore faith
and belief and the Temple must be broken. This time Art
fought the battle, rather than Science or any new
religious faction. And Art has been demolishing for us:
Nietzsche the Christian Religion as it stood, Hardy our
faith in our own endeavour, Flaubert our belief in love.
Now, for us, it is all smashed, we can see the whole
again. We were in prison, peeping at the sky through
loop-holes. The great prisoners smashed at the loop-
holes, for lying to us. And behold, out of the ruins
leaps the whole sky.
     It is we who see it and breathe in it for joy. God
is there, faith, belief, love, everything. We are drunk
with the joy of it, having got away from the fear. In

almost every poem in the book comes this note of exultat-
ion after fear, the exultation in the vast freedom, the
illimitable wealth that we have suddenly got.

> But send desire often forth to scan
> The immense night that is thy greater soul,

says Mr Abercrombie.   His deadly sin is Prudence, that
will not risk to avail itself of the new freedom.   Mr
Bottomley exults to find men for ever building religions
which yet can never compass all.

> Yet the yielding sky
> Invincible vacancy was there discovered.

Mr Rupert Brooke sees

> every glint
> Posture and jest and thought and tint
> Freed from the mask of transiency
> Triumphant in eternity,
> Immote, immortal

and this at Afternoon Tea.
   Mr John Drinkwater sings:

> We cherish every hour that strays
> Adown the cataract of days:
> We see the clear, untroubled skies,
> We see the glory of the rose -

Mr Wilfrid Gibson hears the 'terror turned to tenderness'
then

> I watched the mother sing to rest
> The baby snuggling on her breast.

And to Mr Masefield:

> When men count
> Those hours of life that were a bursting fount
> Sparkling the dusty heart with living springs,
> There seems a world, beyond our earthly things,
> Gated by golden moments.

It is all the same - hope, and religious joy.   Nothing
is really wrong.   Every new religion is a waste-product
from the last, and every religion stands for us for ever.

We love Christianity for what it has brought us, now that
we are no longer upon the cross.

The great liberation gives us an overwhelming sense of
joy, *joie d'être, joie de vivre.* This sense of exceeding
keen relish and appreciation of life makes romance.   I
think I could say every poem in the book is romantic,
tinged with a love of the marvellous, a joy of natural
things, as if the poet were a child for the first time on
the seashore, finding treasures.   'Best trust the happy
moments', says Mr Masefield, who seems nearest to the
black dream behind us.   There is Mr W.H. Davies's lovely
joy, Mr de la Mare's perfect appreciation of life at still
moments, Mr Rupert Brooke's brightness, when he 'lived
from laugh to laugh', Mr Edmund Beale Sargant's pure,
excited happiness in the woodland - it is all the same,
keen zest in life found wonderful.   In Mr Bottomley it is
the zest of activity, of hurrying, labouring men; or the
zest of the utter stillness of long snows.   It is a book-
ful of Romance that has not quite got clear of the terror
of realism.

There is no 'Carpe diem' touch.   The joy is sure and
fast.   It is not the falling rose, but the rose for ever
rising to bud and falling to fruit that gives us joy.   We
have faith in the vastness of life's wealth.   We are al-
ways rich: rich in buds and in shed blossoms.   There is
no winter that we fear.   Life is like an orange tree, al-
ways in leaf and bud, in blossom and fruit.

And we ourselves, in each of us, have everything.
Somebody said: 'The Georgian Poets are not Love Poets.
The influence of Swinburne has gone.'   But I should say
the Georgian Poets are just ripening to be love-poets.
Swinburne was no love-poet.   What are the Georgian poets,
nearly all, but just bursting into a thick blaze of
being.   They are not poets of passion, perhaps, but they
are essentially passionate poets.   The time to be im-
personal has gone.   We start from the joy we have in
being ourselves, and everything must take colour from that
joy.   It is the return of the blood, that has been held
back, as when the heart's action is arrested by fear.   Now
the warmth of blood is in everything, quick, healthy,
passionate blood.   I look at my hands as I write and know
they are mine, with red blood running its way, sleuthing
out Truth and pursuing it to eternity, and I am full of
awe for this flesh and blood that holds this pen.   Every-
thing that ever was thought and ever will be thought, lies
in this body of mine.   This flesh and blood sitting here
writing, the great impersonal flesh and blood, greater
than me, which I am proud to belong to, contains all the
future.   What is it but the quick of all growth, the seed

of all harvest, this body of mine.   And grapes and corn
and birds and rocks and visions, all are in my fingers.
I am so full of wonder at my own miracle of flesh and
blood that I could not contain myself, if I did not
remember we are all alive, have all of us living bodies.
And that is a joy greater than any dream of immortality
in the spirit, to me.   It reminds me of Rupert Brooke's
moment triumphant in its eternality;   and of Michel-
angelo, who is also the moment triumphant in its eternal-
ity;   just the opposite from Corot, who is the eternal
triumphing over the moment, at the moment, at the very
point of sweeping it into the flow.

Of all love-poets, we are the love-poets.   For our
religion is loving.   To love passionately, but completely,
is our one desire.

What is 'The Hare' but a complete love-poem, with none
of the hackneyed 'But a bitter blossom was born' about it,
nor yet the Yeats, 'Never give all the heart'.   Love is
the greatest of all things, no 'bitter-blossom' nor such
like.   It is sex-passion, so separated, in which we do
not believe.   The 'Carmen' and 'Tosca' sort of passion
is not interesting any longer, because it can't progress.
Its goal and aim is possession, whereas possession in
love is only a means to love.   And because passion can-
not go beyond possession, the passionate heroes and her-
oines - Tristans and what-not - must die.   We believe in
the love that is happy ever after, progressive as life
itself.

I worship Christ, I worship Jehovah, I worship Pan, I
worship Aphrodite.   But I do not worship hands nailed
and running with blood upon a cross, nor licentiousness,
nor lust.   I want them all, all the gods.   They are all
God.   But I must serve in real love.   If I take my
whole, passionate, spiritual and physical love to the
woman who in return loves me, that is how I serve God.
And my hymn and my game of joy is my work.   All of which
I read in the Anthology of Georgian Poetry.

13.   'AN ELIZABETHAN POET AND MODERN POETRY',
WALTER DE LA MARE, 'THE EDINBURGH REVIEW'

April 1913, 377-86

Walter de la Mare writes of Donne and 'Georgian Poetry',
the latter part of the article only being given
here.
    Walter de la Mare contributed to all five of the
Georgian anthologies (see Introduction, p.19 , and
Appendix, pp. 400-1).

To prove that English poetry, of which Donne is so idio-
syncratic an ingredient, is 'now again putting on a new
strength and beauty', that we are even perhaps at the
beginning of another great poetic age, is the aim of a
little anthology, recently published, entitled 'Georgian
Poetry'. Some day, if fate smiled kindly on the promise
of his venture, the initials of its 'onlie begetter',
E.M., may become the nucleus of as animated and academic
a controversy as has raged round those of 'William Him-
self'.   'Georgian Poetry' is a collection of verse drawn
entirely from publications of the last two years, and
presents the work of writers who, either before 1911, had
published nothing, or who have since then gained some
accession of power.   With the single exception of Mr
Sturge Moore, it excludes poets of established and in-
controvertible reputation, and it is dedicated with all
gratitude and devotion to Mr Robert Bridges.   That
titanic achievement, for instance, 'The Dynasts', is not
here!   Upwards of a hundred and seventy names are
mentioned in 'The Literary Year-Book' under the heading of
poetry.   Nor is this list exhaustive.   Such writers as
Mr Ralph Hodgson, Mr Vivian Locke Ellis, and Mr John
Freeman, were eligible for this volume , and no woman's
work is included in it.   This is only to say that E.M.
had ample forces in reserve.   A volume which comprises
thirty-six poems by seventeen poets who have published
between them fifty-five volumes of verse, should be
sufficiently representative for his purpose.
    If, however, 'Georgian Poetry' is justified of its
challenge, what does that justification imply?   English
poets do not readily marshal themselves into schools, nor
strive for anything but a personal cause.   Whence comes
this unanimous impulse to write (and to publish) poetry

in an age of journalism? Has the fountain of Hippocrene
suddenly showered wild 'drafts of spray' upon this emer-
ald isle; did Pegasus, a generation ago, venture, wildly
treading the green pastures, among the mares? If English
poetry is indeed renewing its youth, does the phenomenon
imply a promise of even wider significance: the stirring
and awakening of the whole national imagination, a widen-
ing desire to escape

> from that which sinks each individual man
> Into the common dream?

Hope may falter, though it need not sink, when it is dis-
covered that some of the poets included here must have
been practising their art under three rulers. It is nine
years since Mr Sturge Moore published that masterpiece,
'The Rout of the Amazons'. Here we have a further ex-
ample of an art never content to repeat its first
triumphs - the First Scene of the classically pure and
ripe 'Sicilian Idyll'. Mr Masefield, too, has long
since proved himself, what need not always imply a contra-
diction in terms, a 'popular poet'. What some critics
would consider the flower of his work appeared in 1902.
His 'Biography' is the last of a series of remarkably
original and vivid, but somewhat unequal narrative poems.
Mr Chesterton, still happily young in years, is old in
fame. Only to this degree is E.M.'s anthology in any
sense Victorian.
   But in any attempt to appraise this volume with the
jealous eyes of posterity not only must we be sure that
poetry distinctly of our own day is here, but some kind
of parallel is necessary. What kind of volume, for
example, would have been put together by the poets, then
under forty and over twenty, who were writing in 1611-12? -
Dekker, Browne, Donne, Carew, Beaumont, Drummond,
Heywood, Jonson, Massinger, Ford, Fletcher, Quarles -
when Shakespeare was forty-eight, Milton was three, and
Shirley, Herbert, and Herrick were still in their teens.
By 1712 the stage was dark and deserted; Pope and Gay
were thirty-four. Another crucial date - skipping the
two years of Keats's 'Poems', of 'Alastor', 'The Revolt of
Islam', 'Childe Harold', 'Christabel', and 'Kubla Khan' -
would be 1865-66, when 'Atlanta in Calydon', 'Enoch
Arden', 'Dramatis Personae', 'The Prince's Progress' were
published, when Morris, Dante Gabriel Rossetti, Dixon,
and T.E. Brown were still in their thirties, and Arnold's
'New Poems' may have been in proof. Such comparisons are
only comparisons, but as such, searching enough.
   Every age unquestionably needs and seeks its own

poetry.   And, as it has been said of man and woman,
every age has bestowed upon it the poetry it deserves -
though this is not a genial comment to make on the eight-
eenth century.   But true poetry is never the peculiar
possession of any particular race or period.   It varies
superficially and in differing environments, flags, and
is renewed;   but in essentials it does not change.   As
each new poet, then, responds to one of the rarest and
deepest of all impulses, he is bound to follow and at the
same time slightly to stray from the one clear tradition.
As rhythm is to metre, so is his divergence into origin-
ality to the poetry of his great predecessors.   In every
individual poet in this volume, as in its contents as a
whole, we must look for both of these features.   The
test, we think, is easily survived.   These poets are at
least legitimate.   A wholesome independence is manifest,
together with as wholesome an exuberance and bravado.
Their faults are the faults of youth.   They have gone
'exploring';   have chosen their own path and filled their
hands with wild flowers, many of which by noon-day will
have withered and been thrown away.   But there is no
anarchic challenge of old ideals, no obvious tendency to-
wards any particular *ism*.   The general trend of the work
is lyrical - with a dramatic undercurrent.   If Cole-
ridge's assertion, that poets of promise usually choose
themes from their own personal life, be a sound one, then
promise is here in abundance.   The range of subject is
remarkably wide.   Mr Lascelles Abercrombie, in 'The Sale
of St Thomas', pictures the saint anxiously setting forth
on his legendary mission to Melankara and King Gondophares
in world-wide search of a carpenter to build him a satanic
palace made of souls.   Mr Gordon Bottomley's poems are
entitled 'The End of the World' and 'Babel'.   Mr Flecker
contributes 'Joseph and Mary' and the pagan 'Queen's
Song';   Mr Edmund Beale Sargant, the lovely wizard,
'Cuckoo Wood'.   Mr James Stephens roars with joy with
Mad Patsy in 'The Poppy-field', and in 'The Lonely God'
returns to the Garden of Eden.   Mr Ronald Ross stands
solitary upon a peak in Darien.   Mr Wilfrid Gibson is
away in the heather under sunned and starry skies in
'The Hare'.   Mr Robert Trevelyan contributes an ex-
quisitely modulated and tender little dirge.   Mr
William Davies flits on the wings of Ariel back to
childhood and tells over again a ne'er-do-well mariner's
fabulous tales of the sea.   Mr Chesterton sings 'The
Song of Elf'.   And Mr Rupert Brooke views existence
from the 'cool, curving world' which enshrines 'The Fish',
and lives again 'an immortal moment', spent in the ex-
tremely mortal environment of 'Dining-room Tea'.

If, for all other qualities essential to lyrical poetry -
intensity of vision, imagination, architectonicé,
metrical craft, economy of means, music and finish -
'Georgian Poetry' be compared with such a volume as 'The
Oxford Book of English Verse', the ordeal is drastic but
not discouraging.   Simple, sensuous, passionate - the
old formula is unescapable.   And again, viewed roughly
as a whole, it is clear that what is more or less undilut-
edly 'Georgian' in this anthology tends less towards
simplicity than elaboration and complexity;   that it is
undeniably sensuous, though it exhibits not less clearly
symptoms of genuine 'fundamental brainwork';   and that its
passion reveals itself in a desire for beauty, and for a
truth, not objectively and consciously moral or philo-
sophic, but imaginative and creative.   Those who seek in
poetry ethical solace and edification, or demand of it a
reasoned criticism of life, are unlikely to be won over.
There is a strikingly modern, but none the less poetic,
'moral' to 'The Sale of St Thomas':

> Now, Thomas, know thy sin.   It was not fear;
> Easily may a man crouch down for fear,
> And yet rise up on firmer knees, and face
> The hailing storm of the world with graver courage.
> But prudence, prudence is the deadly sin . . .
> Keep thy desire closed in the room of light
> The labouring fires of thy mind have made,
> And thou shalt find the vision of thy spirit
> Pitifully dazzled to so shrunk a ken,
> There are no spacious puissances about it.
> But send desire often forth to scan
> The immense night which is thy greater soul;
> Knowing the possible, see thou try beyond it
> Into impossible things, unlikely ends;
> And thou shalt find thy knowledgeable desire
> Grow large as all the regions of thy soul,
> Whose firmament doth cover the whole of Being,
> And of created purpose reach the ends.

But with the exception of Mr Drinkwater, whose 'Fires
of God' is a profound questioning of heart, a lofty, some-
what too eloquent, hymn to the glory of the world, to the
courage, hope, and aspirations of humanity, the aim of
these poets is as alien from that of 'The Prelude' as it
is from that of 'Prometheus Unbound', of 'Don Juan', or
of the 'Essay on Man'.   They borrow inspiration neither
from books nor from science, unless it be the science of
psychology, or the Proceedings of the Society of Psychic-
al Research!   To express his love, desire, dream, grief

or rapture, his sense of an age-long solitude beset by a
cloud of witnesses, to bear record, if it may be for a
little longer than mortal life permits, to his ex-
perience of a strange, absorbing, baffling world, in the
briefest and loveliest terms within his power - this
alone is every true poet's aim.   He may write not always
because he can, but should write never unless he must:
Noah, after all, did not reject the twittering entreaty
of the wren when he welcomed the nightingale to the
shadowy roostings of his ark.   And since the expression
of beauty beats on the mind like a purifying flame, and
any lucid imaginative truth of presentation ever bears
hidden within it the secret of life, and kindles the
desire to possess life more abundantly, from these pages,
too, cannot be absent what it would be rather dishearten-
ing and restrictive to call their 'lesson'·

There is, at any rate, no attempt to say pretty and
acceptable things;   no bait to tickle and catch small
fry.   'Muse' and 'lyre' are left hushed and unevoked.
The love that rhymes with grove nowhere wastes its sweet-
ness.   But in its stead we have the turbulent, arrogant
rapture of Mr Brooke's 'Dust' and 'Town and Country';
the delicate and lucent visionariness of Mr Harold
Monro's 'Child of Dawn';   the dense, brooding desire that
in the broken stanzas of Mr D.H. Lawrence's 'Snapdragon'
almost dazes and nauseates the reader with its desperate,
naked excess.   Page after page of this volume will prove
that it is not an unexacting standard of thought, feel-
ing, and technique which these writers share.   In a word,
unquestionable *seriousness*, as distinguished from what an-
other generation rather solemnly and chillingly called
'high seriousness', is the sincere mark and claim of this
anthology.

It is, it may be hoped, only a fine loyalty to the
past that induces most historians of English literature
to disparage their own times.   What student of modern
criticism has not been professorially assured that poetry
nowadays is 'Every dead thing'?   A little enthusiasm for
the work of one's contemporaries does no mischief to the
secure immortals.   'Georgian Poetry', even after it has
been subjected to the discipline of a sound and conserv-
ative criticism, should at least momentarily shake the
confidence of such pessimism.

As regards individual poets, space will admit only of
the briefest comment and quotation.   Mr James Stephens
contributes two poems.   It.is the conception and atmos-
phere of 'The Lonely God', rather than its theme, which
give it strength and originality.   Mr Stephens is in-
clined to allow his Celtic imagination to run away with

him, and his verse falls occasionally into the florid and
rhetorical.   Like many a theologian before him, he has
made God in his own image.

> So Eden was deserted, and at eve
> Into the quiet place God came to grieve.

In the still twilight He paces the dews of the garden,
brooding on His might and majesty and 'solitude unspeak-
able', considering His creation - Man.   'It is not good
for man to be alone.'   In the fruition of time He fore-
sees:

> The perfect woman of his perfect race
> Shall sit beside Me in the highest place
> And be My Goddess, Queen, Companion, Wife . . .

He stoops to the beehive hut wherein Adam and Eve sit
happy and at fearful peace in each other's company,
sharing their common doom.   He takes up the dusty gar-
land with which Eve has been crowned:

> So the Mighty Guest
> Rent, took, and placed the blossoms in His breast.
> 'This', said He gently, 'I shall show My queen
> When she has grown to Me in space serene,
> And say 'Twas worn by Eve.'   So, smiling fair,
> He spread abroad His wings upon the air.

'In the Cool of the Evening' is a less anthropomorphic
pendant to the longer poem:

> I thought I heard Him calling.   Did you hear
> A sound, a little sound?   My curious ear
> Is dinned with flying noises, and the tree
> Goes - whisper, whisper, whisper silently
> Till all its whispers spread into the sound
> Of a dull roar.   Lie closer to the ground,
> The shade is deep and He may pass us by.
> We are so very small, and His great eye,
> Customed to starry majesties, may gaze
> Too wide to spy us hiding in the maze;
> Ah, misery!   the sun has not yet gone
> And we are naked: He will look upon
> Our crouching shame, may make us stand upright
> Burning in terror - O that it were night!
> He may not come ... what? listen, listen, now -
> He is here!   Lie closer ... *Adam, where art thou*?

The happiest poetry gains from its readers not only
admiration but a warm and familiar regard for its writer.
So it is with Mr Davies's work.   It is naïf and fresh
with a winning personality.   Its art seems to be (yet
how can it be?) the purest intuition.   Mr Davies loves
instinctively all simple things.   He gives us back the
eager absorbed eyes of childhood.   Birds never before in
verse seem to have hopped down from line to line;   nor
bees to have 'stood upon their heads' in pollen, nor the
moon

> behind the Clouds' dark bars,
> Searched for her stolen flocks of stars,

when we read of them all in his delightful lyrics.
Nothing is forced.   A romantic Elizabethan conceit, a
romantic credulity, slips as naturally into his speech as
does the exquisite cadence in the last two lines of his
'Kingfisher':

> It was the Rainbow gave thee birth,
> And left thee all her lovely hues;
> And, as her mother's name was Tears,
> So runs it in thy blood to choose
> For haunts the lonely pools, and keep
> In company with trees that weep.
>
> Go you and, with such glorious hues,
> Live with proud Peacocks in green parks;
> On lawns as smooth as shining glass,
> Let every feather show its marks;
> Get thee on boughs and clap thy wings
> Before the windows of proud kings.
>
> Nay, lovely Bird, thou art not vain;
> Thou has no proud, ambitious mind;
> I also love a quiet place
> That's green, away from all mankind;
> A lonely pool, and let a tree
> Sigh with her bosom over me.

Mr Gibson owes nothing to Crabbe or to Goldsmith, but
shares their sympathy with those who (like poets) do hard
work for small pay.   He never rants;   he puts bare
things barely.   His verse is supple;   its ease, the out-
come of craft and labour.   'The Hare' is full of light,
movement, and abandon;   though its supernatural element
is symbolically a little over-ingenious, 'Geraniums' is
the shortest, but not least characteristic, of his poems

here.   'Broken with lust and drink, blear-eyed and ill',
an old woman comes nodding from under her dark arch to
sell a nosegay for a night's lodging.   And this is how
Mr Gibson escapes a facile moral:

> And yet to-morrow will these blooms be dead
> With all their lively beauty; and to-morrow
> May end the light lusts and the heavy sorrow
> Of that old body with the nodding head.
> The last oath muttered, the last pint drained deep,
> She'll sink, as Cleopatra sank, to sleep;
> Nor need to barter blossoms for a bed.

Reference has already been made to Mr Abercombie's 'Sale
of St Thomas'.   Flaubert's St Anthony himself never woke
from a dream of more fabulous and sinister bizarrerie,
nor Mandeville imagined more exotic marvels, nor Purchas's
pilgrims explored a stranger world than are described in
this poem.   The verse blazes with radiance, jets, leaps,
dins, insinuates with every turn and twist of the narrative.
Quaking with the 'huddled man' upon the quay, the reader
listens to the cynical Captain's recital of the terror
and cruelties that await his timid hyper-imaginative
passenger's entry into unknown India, with its flies and
apes, its gongs, horns, and enormities.   The verse
breaks into the wildest fantasy.   With a sardonic
humour the poet gloats over the pictures that at the same
time appal and enthral him; yet he never loses his
grasp.   The poem is admirably constructed and kept in
tone, and comes to a dramatic and serene conclusion.
    There are many influences perceptible in this volume;
but that of Donne - Donne in his headlong, rebellious
youth - is traceable only in the work of Mr Rupert
Brooke.   He is more self-centred than the rest, more
analytical and intellectual.   He is also more impatient
of tradition, defiant of the dictates of poetic Grundy-
ism.   His verse keeps unusually close to actual exper-
ience and is yet imaginatively in focus.   He rails at
dull sublunary 'fools', and, like Mr Abercrombie, cannot
resist the fascination of what repels him.   He is at
once the youngest and the most promising of his cont-
emporaries.   And his are among the curiously few love-
poems in the collection.   The following extract is from
the poem entitled 'Dust':

> When the white flame in us is gone,
> And we that lost the world's delight
> Stiffen in darkness, left alone
> To crumble in our separate night;

When your swift hair is quiet in death,
And through the lips corruption thrust
Has stilled the labour of my breath -
When we are dust, when we are dust! -

Not dead, not undesirous yet,
Still sentient, still unsatisfied,
We'll ride the air, and shine, and flit,
Around the places where we died,

And dance as dust before the sun,
And light of foot, and unconfined,
Hurry from road to road, and run
About the errands of the wind.

And every mote, on earth or air,
Will speed and gleam, down later days,
And like a secret pilgrim fare
By eager and invisible ways.

Nor ever rest, nor ever lie,
Till, beyond thinking, out of view,
One mote of all the dust that's I
Shall meet one atom that was you.

There remains Mr Gordon Bottomley to be mentioned.
Quiet as swiftly falling, drifting, thickening snow is the
verse that depicts the cold, dark 'End of the World',
etched in with little familiar pictures of life amidst
its desolation:

The dawn now seemed neglected in the grey
Where mountains were unbuilt, and shadowless trees
Rootlessly paused or hung upon the air . . .

A gigantic phantom figure strides out of sight,

But if he seemed too tall to be a man
It was that men had been so long unseen,
Or shapes loom larger through a moving snow.

Night darkens and darkens; earth and air congeal.

The air was crumbling. There was no more sky.

And at last Death himself, flaked with the same dazzling
whiteness, enters where love and fear sit half insanely
awaiting the end:

> She said 'O, do not sleep,
> Heart, heart of mine, keep near me.   No, no;   sleep,
> I will not lift his fallen, quiet eyelids,
> Although I know he would awaken then -
> He closed them thus but now of his own will.
> He can stay with me while I do not lift them.'

It is a poem that absorbs and haunts the imagination.
Like 'Babel', where, daring the solitudes of heaven,

> Man with his bricks was building, building yet,
> Where dawn and midnight mingled and woke no birds,

where Nimroud stands up 'conceiving he shall live to
conquer 'god', and men's tongues crumble into the in-
articulate, it transports consciousness clean out of the
tangible world.   It is the poetry of magic and strange-
ness;   indefinable, inexplicable;   the farthest venture
beyond the confines of time and space recorded in the
pages of 'E.M.'s' anthology.

14.   J. LHONEUX, 'LA MEUSE'

21 April 1913, 1

Excerpts from an article in the Belgian newspaper,
'La Meuse'.
    This cross-Channel greeting is sufficient a curiosity
to justify its inclusion here (see Introduction, pp. 25
and 34).   It would be a reasonable conjecture to connect
the Belgian interest with Monro's Belgian upbringing.
The original cutting is among the Marsh papers now in the
Berg Collection.   I am indebted to my colleague, Mr John
Barwood, for his help in translating it.

The most serious and perceptive study of very recent
French poetry that I know appeared last year in a special
issue of 'The Poetry Review'.   In it F.S. Flint devoted
several pages to French poetry from 1885.   He saw a
revival dating from 1900, and reviewed in turn Henri
Ghéon and 'free verse', Jean Royère and 'neo-Mallarmism',
L'Abbaye, Henri-Martin Barzun, and, in short, each

individual poet and each of even the least important
contemporary groups.   His numerous quotations made the
issue a true anthology.

It is from this conscientious work that I first learned
of the existence of a group of young English poets who,
though free and independent, were none the less concerned
to keep in touch with the aspirations of poets in France
and elsewhere.   That this should be so is a complete
refutation of the charge of English insularity in poetry,
just as we have seen it refuted also in the theatre and
in the novel.

'The Poetry Review' lasted only one year (1912):   I do
not have all the issues to hand, but its contents in-
cluded a special number on women poets, another on
American poetry, and another on the mystics.   The editor
had not finished his task at the end of the year, but he
was so hampered by his directors that he founded 'Poetry
and Drama', a most important quarterly periodical, which
seems to be the organ of a whole generation of young
English poets.

A real impression had to be made to prove to the
British public - and to those foreigners who take an
interest in English letters - that this generation of
young poets had truly enriched the artistic heritage of
England.   They had to identify themselves with a
renaissance in English poetry dating from the reign of
King George.

To this end that same group which supports 'Poetry and
Drama' has produced an anthology of seventeen English
poets each of whom had either published nothing before
1911 or had achieved recognition only in the last two
years.   And the result has been admirable, for the
collection, 'Georgian Poetry, 1911-1912', after public-
ation in December 1912, went into a second edition in
January, a third in February and a fourth in March, a
fifth being now in preparation.

What is curious is the review which 'Poetry and Drama'
devotes to the anthology over whose compilation it did,
after all, preside.

The beginning of the piece is pithy and worth quoting:
it is moreover from the authoritative pen of Henry
Newbolt.

[Quotes opening paragraph of No. 9.]

But what does this collection show us that is new?

Certainly it establishes the existence in England of a
plethora of original and talented poets.   So well has
the public appreciated this that the book has enjoyed
exceptional success.

[The writer then gives his own - not Newbolt's - synopsis
of 'The Sale of St Thomas', translating a different
passage from it.   Without anywhere explaining his
apparent surprise that 'Poetry and Drama' should have
printed this review, he concludes:]

I shall return to this interesting publication, and to
the young generation of English poets.   What I have said
about them will, I hope, suffice to show that they
deserve our attention, and are worthy of our interest.

15.   'THE POETRY OF ROBERT BRIDGES', JOHN BAILEY,
'QUARTERLY REVIEW'

July 1913, 231-2

These opening paragraphs from an article on the poet to
whom 'Georgian Poetry, 1911-1922' was dedicated are
revealing of the poetic background.   In a passage
immediately following that given, John Bailey refers to
the recent death of Alfred Austin, and suggests Bridges
as successor to the laureateship (see also Introduction,
p. 26).
    John Bailey (1864-1931) was chairman (1912-15) and
president (1925-6) of the English Association, Clark
lecturer at Cambridge (1921) and Taylorian lecturer at
Oxford (1926).   Among his books are 'Poets and Poetry'
(1911), 'Dr Johnson and his Circle' (1913), 'The
Continuity of Letters' (1923), and 'Shakespeare' (1929).

One of the pleasantest features in the intellectual
landscape of the moment is unquestionably the revival of
poetry.   Not that anyone who knew anything at all about
poetry could suppose it would really die.   It has had
too many deaths, followed by too many resurrections, for
that.   We are now grown older and wiser than the people
who, in the age of Spenser and the Elizabethan drama,
declared poetry to be useless and provoked Sidney to
write the 'Apology', without which their very existence
would be forgotten;   or than Peacock, who, in the age of
Wordsworth, Keats and Shelley, asserted that poetry was
obsolete and absurd, and had the same good fortune as his

obscurer predecessors by provoking a reply from Shelley
which has saved his attack from total oblivion.   All such
fears have now passed away for ever from the minds of
intelligent people.   Criticism, which has often injured
poetry, has now done for it the supreme service of showing
the essential eternity of its nature.   It has taught us
to see in poetry the highest and most permanently satisfy-
ing of all interpretations of life, a thing which has the
potentiality of being as many-coloured, as transcendental,
as infinite and therefore as immortal as life itself.   So
long as man lives he will have an ear, a mind, an imagin-
ation and a spirit;   and all four, especially if, as we
may hope, they gradually develop in power, will more and
more claim poetry as the only food which they can partake
in common, and in the strength of which they realise their
unity in themselves and their hold on ultimate and
immutable truth.

This being so, believers in poetry were not likely to
be led away by the voices which, after the deaths of
Browning, Tennyson and Swinburne, proclaimed that English
poetry was dead in their graves.   Nor are they likely to
be taken by surprise by the present revival.   This, like
everything else in a democratic age, seems at present to
be more remarkable for extent and size than for distinct-
ion.   But we need not quarrel with that.   The thing is
genuine;   the stuff is honest poetic material, not
shoddy;   and if some of the treatment tends at present to
give us a kind of rhetorical realism in place of that
musical and imaginative interpretation of life which is
poetry, that is not unnatural in an age dominated by
melodramatic journalism;   and will pass away as those who
practise it learn its emptiness by experience.   Even if
these defects were more marked than they are, they would
afford no reason for failing to rejoice in the fact that
poetry now makes monthly magazines go into second
editions;   that it has established a book-shop of its own,
selling nothing but its own wares, a thing probably un-
known before on this, hitherto, mainly prosaic earth;
that it has issued a volume of 'Georgian Poetry' which
includes nothing published before the accession of George
V;   finally that it has now established a quarterly
review devoted solely to poetry and the discussion of
poetry.   All these things are of the best omen;   they
mean that the young poets believe in themselves and have
found a public which believes in them too.

But in poetry, as in life itself, there are no
absolutely new departures.   The new which is to live is
rooted in the old and knows that it is.   So these young
poets - and it is not the least interesting fact about

them - have dedicated their volume, not to some
revolutionary critic who flatters them by saying that
they are the people and that wisdom was born with them,
but to the most scholarly of English poets, to the
intensely Etonian and Oxonian Robert Bridges.   In him
they rightly recognise the greatest living master of
their art in this country, and at his feet they lay their
work, an offering which does as much honour to them as to
him.   Mr Bridges has been as careful, not to say perverse,
in avoiding fame as other men are in seeking it: but even
he must, we should suppose, take some pleasure in this
striking tribute from his young fellow-craftsmen, poets
so unlike him, and yet so like in that likeness which
obliterates all unlikeness, in the sincere love and
earnest practice of the greatest of the arts.

16.   A PETRARCHAN SONNET, BERNARD HOLLAND,
'THE SPECTATOR'

19 July 1913, 99

Like the reviewer in 'The Times Literary Supplement'
(No. 8), but more nostalgically, the poet looks back to
'the extraordinary personal domination of Tennyson'.
Many of the Georgians saw themselves in reaction against
Tennyson: cf. Brooke's parody of 'Ulysses' in 'A Letter
to a Live Poet' and of 'In Memoriam' in 'Heaven' ('The
Poetical Works of Rupert Brooke', 1946, 87 and 35).   The
'weird Georgian ways' and 'subtle Georgian lays' serve
as a historical reminder of the seeming strength of that
reaction as perceived by a contemporary.
    Bernard Holland has published 'Verse' (1912), a
collection of his poems containing a number of sonnets,
as well as poems addressed to Henry Newbolt, J.K.
Stephen, and Mary Coleridge.

    Friend, born with me in full Victorian days,
    When Palmerston proud-voiced our glorious State,
    And Tennyson was England's Laureate,
    Now that, alas! your life and mine decays,
    And Time, dread chess-player, is threatening mate,
    We, undelighting in weird Georgian ways,
    Uncomprehending subtle Georgian lays,
    In our old fashion feel and meditate,

For us Romance and Beauty perish not:
Sir Galahad yet rides through forests dim,
The pale maid, dying, floats to Camelot,
The happy princess o'er the world's blue rim
Follows her lover;   Freedom on the height
Chants, all the same, her great immortal hymn.

'Georgian Poetry 1913-1915'

Published November 1915
'In Memoriam
R.B.
J.E.F.'

[Rupert Brooke, James Elroy Flecker]

Prefatory note

The object of 'Georgian Poetry 1911-1912' was to give a
convenient survey of the work published within two years
by some poets of the newer generation.   The book was
welcomed;   and perhaps, even in a time like this, those
whom it interested may care to have a corresponding
volume for the three years which have since passed.

Two of the poets - I think the youngest, and certainly
not the least gifted - are dead.   Rupert Brooke, who
seemed to have everything that is worth having, died last
April in the service of his country.   James Elroy
Flecker, to whom life and death were less generous, died
in January after a long and disabling illness.

A few of the contributors to the former volume are not
represented in this one, either because they have pub-
lished nothing which comes within its scope, or because
they belong in fact to an earlier poetic generation, and
their inclusion must be allowed to have been an anach-
ronism.   Two names are added.

The alphabetical arrangement of the writers has been
modified in order to recognize the honour which Mr
Gordon Bottomley has done to the book by allowing his
play to be first published here.

October 1915   E.M.

121

17.   'THE YOUNG POETS', UNSIGNED REVIEW,
'THE TIMES LITERARY SUPPLEMENT'

9 December 1915, 447

Unsigned review of 'Georgian Poetry, 1913-1915' and
'Poems of To-Day - An anthology'.   (The final paragraph,
on 'Poems of To-Day', has been omitted.)
   The two verse plays which begin and end 'Georgian
Poetry, 1913-1915', Bottomley's 'King Lear's Wife' and
Abercrombie's 'The End of the World', attracted much of
the critical attention (see Introduction, pp. 9-10).
Abercrombie's play had first appeared in early 1914 in
the second issue of 'New Numbers', and provoked D.H.
Lawrence to write to Marsh:

>   I hate and detest his ridiculous imitation yokels and
>   all the silly hash of his bucolics;   I loathe his
>   rather nasty efforts at cruelty, like the wrapping of
>   frogs in paper and putting them for cartwheels to
>   crush .....   What is the matter with the man?
>   There's something wrong with his soul.

   ['The Letters of D.H. Lawrence', ed. Aldous Huxley,
   1932, 194.]

When Bottomley's play was produced at the Birmingham Rep.
(25 September 1915), the censor refused to allow inclus-
ion of the corpse-washer's song, the third verse of
which is quoted in the following review and the first
and second verses in No. 19.   Marsh, who admired both
plays and told Brooke that Bottomley's was 'the one
really great literary event' of the year, found these
two reviews the most distressing.   In its style and its
opinions (for example, the remarks on ugliness) the
review suggests the hand of Gosse.

There has been lately a general desire to encourage our
young poets by praising them and even by buying them.
We have all discovered at last that the romantic move-
ment is over, and that no young poet who has anything in
him can belong to it.   The time has come for free
experiment in poetry, and we must not expect to find in
it the accustomed beauties of the past.   Out attitude
towards it has suddenly become as expectant and as

liberal as our attitude to modern painting.   In both
cases the old masters are dead, and we do not want the
work of the young to remind us of them.   The very title
'Georgian Poetry' insists upon the fact.   It is no
longer Victorian poetry, and Swinburne is an old master
to it.

We hope very much that this new interest will not die
away, that the young poets will continue to be young, and
that the enthusiasms of the young critics will not stiffen
into prejudice.   For criticism has also its part to play.
It must not only encourage but must be on the look-out
for dangers, for mechanical reactions against the fashions
of the past and for imitation of the fashions of the
present.   We insist upon this now because we see signs
of mechanical reaction in the two longest poems in this
volume of Georgian poetry - the play by Mr Gordon
Bottomley with which it begins and the play by Mr
Lascelles Abercrombie with which it ends.   We have en-
joyed reading both, but in each we enjoyed the last half
less than the first.   In each we became aware of a con-
vention as the theme worked itself out - or rather a
convention which bound it and prevented it from working
itself out freely.

Mr Bottomley's play is called 'King Lear's Wife', and
it deals with the disreputable past of King Lear when his
wife was dying and Cordelia was a child.   Mr Aber-
crombie's play is about modern rustics.   It is called
'The End of the World': a dowser comes into a public
house in a valley deep in the country and tells the men
drinking there that a comet already blazing in the sky
is about to destroy the earth.   They are gradually
wrought upon to believe this; and the play shows us the
effect of this belief upon them and then the effect of
their sudden recovery from it.

We do not know whether Mr Bottomley supposes his Lear
to be the same person as Shakespeare's Lear, only
younger; or whether he meant to conceive a different
Lear altogether.   Nor, does it matter much, except that
the use of Shakespeare's characters may puzzle and
irritate the reader.   But certainly his Lear is not
Shakespeare's, and no suffering could change him into
Shakespeare's.   He is merely a selfish and lustful
brute, who takes his wife's maid on his knee whilst his
wife is dying of a broken heart, and who, when Goneril
murders the maid, does not care, because the maid is
proved unfaithful to him.   Goneril and her mother are
savages, but capable of savage affection.   Lear is
capable of nothing, except lust and pride, and Cordelia
is a spoilt child.   Regan does not appear, but Goneril
draws her character for us:

Does Regan worship anywhere at dawn?
The sweaty half-clad cook-maids render lard
Out in the scullery, after pig-killing,
And Regan sidles among their greasy skirts,
Smeary and hot as they, for craps to suck.

In fact, the world of this play is like the world which
Shakespeare's Lear sees in his madness and Edgar in his
pretended madness.   Now undoubtedly there are unpleasant
people and horrible things in the real world, but we feel
that there is too much method in Mr Bottomley's madness.
He is out to write a new kind of poetry, a poetry which is
not romantic.   He is not going to get a cheap effect,
like Tennyson in the 'Idylls of the King', by drawing
blameless prigs.   But he does get a cheap effect by the
opposite method.   At first we are interested in the
setting out of his theme and in his considerable power of
expressing himself.   We wait to see what he has to say.
But gradually we discover that he only says the same
things about his characters over and over again and with
increasing violence.   He draws ugliness, as the Victor-
ians drew beauty, for the sake of the ugliness, as if it
were interesting in itself quite apart from what is made
of it.   This is mere reaction from the notion that
beauty is interesting in itself;   and his King Lear is no
more interesting, no more alive and growing than Tenny-
son's King Arthur.   He is rigid and unreal in his own
conventional baseness as King Arthur in his conventional
loftiness.
     But Mr Bottomley shows what he could do, if he would
stop reacting, with his character of Goneril.   Goneril
is a fierce huntress, cruel but not base, and only cruel
like a fine beast of prey.   She has some love for her
mother;   she is capable of growth one way or another,
though not of growth into Shakespeare's Goneril.   But
Mr Bottomley's Lear is not capable of growth at all.   He
is merely and irretrievably damned;   and the whole play
is a play of damned souls, ending with the ugly song of
the old woman who comes to lay out King Lear's wife:

The louse made off unhappy and wet -
Ahumm, Ahumm, Ahee -
He's looking for us, the little pet;
So haste, for her chin's to tie up yet,
And let us be gone with what we can get -
Her ring for thee, her gown for Bet,
Her pocket turned out for me.

This atmosphere of general damnation is not new in
English literature.   We find it in Elizabethan drama-
tists like Cyril Tourneur, and it may thrill you if you
can believe in it.   We cannot.   It seems to us to be
merely a mechanical development of something altogether
outside the experience of the writer.   We do not say
that he has designs on us, but we feel that he has had
designs upon himself - that he has tried to impose upon
himself a conception of mankind which is not really his,
for the purposes of his art.   The result is violence,
but a violence as conventional as the Victorian sweetness.
    Mr Abercrombie works much more within his own ex-
perience, and his characters are more like real people;
but he too develops his theme mechanically.   He is
determined above all things not to be sentimental.   Not
one of his rustics shall show a glimmer of decent feeling,
and they too become rigid in their conventional baseness.
The life given to them at first by the author's command
of racy and pithy speech dies out of them, until they all
seem puppets condemned to dance for ever the same igno-
minious dance to the cold laughter of the audience.
    Where both writers' characters are unlike human beings
is in this - that they do not even value anything decent.
The fear of sentimentality has gone so far that these
poets are determined to eliminate it even from their
characters.   But human beings are always and inevitably
sentimental until they reach a height of nobility in
which they can do without the help of sentimentality.
Mr Bottomley and Mr Abercrombie talk scandal about human
nature, but it is not plausible scandal.   They have the
air of telling home truths, but they are falsehoods as
conventional as those of the 'Idylls of the King',   It
is a pity, because the execution of both plays,
especially of Mr Abercrombie's, is still vigorous with the
energy of youth.   It is the conception in each case
which seems to be stale;   and it is none the less stale
because it has a modern exasperation and violence in it.
Remember how modern, how exasperated, and how violent
were the conceptions of Byron in all his romantic tales
about men of one virtue and a thousand crimes.   You may
go one better, or worse, and represent men of no
virtues and no power of rising even to the height of
crimes;   and yet in a few years you will seem as romantic-
ally unreal as Byron himself.   That is the fate from
which we hope the new poetry will preserve itself;   and
we speak of the defects more than of the merits of these
two plays, because these defects seem to us to threaten
that fate.

The same volume contains Mr Hodgson's 'Bull', which, we
are sure, will never grow stale.   It is not a pleasant
subject, and Mr Hodgson does not attempt to prettify it,
but he talks no scandal about bull-nature.   He treats it
seriously, and it seems to be a poem about a bull written
by a bull with the gift of poetry, not by a poet who has
developed hostile observation for the purposes of his art.
There are two kinds of morbidity in art - the morbidity
which the artist cannot help, which he is even unconscious
of, and the morbidity which he encourages in himself so
that he may be spurred on to write by the very exasper-
ation of it.   This second kind is dangerous to art it-
self, as the effective anger of the partisan is dangerous
to truth.   We see something of it in Mr D.H. Lawrence's
'Cruelty and Love'.   The woman in that poem is morbid,
and her morbidity seems to be exaggerated by the poet so
that he may do something new in poetry.   The worst of
such novelties is that they so soon seem old.   But in
another poem, 'Meeting Among the Mountains', if there is
morbidity, if there is an excessive sense of pain in mere
existence, it is natural and not encouraged; and here the
expression of it is also natural and beautiful and does
not provoke us to revolt.

> Against the hard and pale blue evening sky
> The mountain's new-dropped summer snow is clear,
> Glistening in steadfast stillness; like transcendent
> Clean pain sending on us a chill down here.

Mr Lawrence seems to welcome pain as if he might at least
discover something of the mystery of things in it, as if,
because it is so disconcerting, it must mean more than
pleasure.   He is bewildered by the mixture of good and
evil in life; and so was Rupert Brooke, only to a more
smiling scepticism.   One sees him in most of his poetry
resolved not to give his heart away, not to let himself
go, as if he were afraid that the universe with all its
beauty might play a practical joke upon him and behind it
all there might be nothing.   If there is a joke he would
be in it, one of the laughers, not one of the laughed at;
and yet he would laugh with passion and beauty and with a
sense of all that ought to be, not with the Cockney
laughter of one who is not deceived because he sees and
feels nothing.   One can see that theories of immortality
haunted him, and yet he mocked at them because he could
not conceive of the richness of life, which is life it-
self, without matter and the individuality of matter.   In
'The Great Lover' he tells us of all the things that he
loved, making a vivid catalogue of them with the natural

virtuosity of youth.   They are all things with the
delight and character of matter in them:

> White plates and cups, clean gleaming,
> Ringed with blue lines;   and feathery, faery dust;
> Wet roofs, beneath the lamp-light;   the strong crust
> Of friendly bread;   and many-tasting food;
> Rainbows;   and the blue bitter smoke of wood;
> And radiant raindrops couching in cool flowers;
> And flowers themselves, that sway through sunny
>   hours,
> Dreaming of moths that drink them under the moon;
> Then, the cool kindliness of sheets, that soon
> Smooth away trouble;   and the rough male kiss
> Of blankets;   grainy wood;   live hair that is
> Shining and free;   blue-massing clouds;   the keen
> Unpassioned beauty of a great machine.

His complaint against them all is that they will desert
him when he dies.

> Oh, never a doubt but, somewhere, I shall wake,
> And give what's left of love again, and make
> New friends, now strangers, . . .
>   But the best I've known
> Stays here, and changes, breaks, grows old, is blown
> About the winds of the world, and fades from brains
> Of living men, and dies.   Nothing remains.

What troubled him, in fact, was the destructibility of
form and all that form means.   It was not enough that
spirit should be immortal;   and in another poem, 'Tiare
Tahiti', he mocks at the conception of an utterly im-
material immortality, in which we shall have to pretend
to be satisfied with the abstract.

> How shall we wind these wreaths of ours,
> Where there are neither heads nor flowers?
> Oh, Heaven's Heaven! - but we'll be missing
> The palms, and sunlight, and the south;
> And there's an end, I think, of kissing,
> When our mouths are one with Mouth.

In all this verse there is the insecurity of emotion
that comes of scepticism.   Philosophy hurts the poet who
is intrigued with it, because it empties life of all its
rich content.   Of all poets only Shelley could be in
love with abstractions as if they were women: and he
also could love women as if they were abstractions.

A difficulty in front of the new poetry, if the poets are
to get all their intellect into it, if they are not to
sacrifice reality at all to their art, is the reconciling
of the abstract with the concrete, the turning of sceptic-
ism into a new faith.   Some of them, such as Mr W.H.
Davies and Mr James Stephens, seem to be simple for the
purposes of their art, as if they had warned their intell-
ect off like a mischievous child that might trouble their
inspiration.   They are charming, no doubt, but simpler,
one feels, than anyone has a right to be nowadays.   What
a passion of thought, an almost theological passion and
dogmatism, is hidden in the simplicity of Blake.   Phrases
that are purely beautiful to us meant Heaven knows what to
him, and that is why they have such depth of sound and
shapeliness of form.   Their simplicity is not thought-
lessness, but philosophy heightened into faith; and the
effort of our new poetry, if it is not to grow quickly
old, must be to turn philosophy into faith and so into
music.

18.   'THE GEORGIANS', UNSIGNED REVIEW, 'THE NATION'

11 December 1915, 394, 396, 398

The judgment that the second anthology 'is not so salient
an achievement as its predecessor' has not been supported
by later critical opinions, which are almost unanimous in
finding it the best of the series.   This was the first
review to suggest Squire's inclusion.   It is interesting
to note the entirely different basis for objections to
Abercrombie and Bottomley.

The first Georgian book of verse had, we believe, a
success quite incommensurate with the accepted opinions as
to modern indifference towards other than fashionable
poetry - a success on something of the same scale as the
collected edition of Francis Thompson.   And, in spite of
a tendency towards patchiness and indiscriminate ad-
mission, the Poetry Bookshop thoroughly deserved it.   Now
we have another instalment, comprising a selection of
poetry written during the last two years, and containing
two fresh names - Mr Francis Ledwidge and Mr Ralph

Hodgson. These, alas! supply a gap; James Flecker and
Rupert Brooke having died within recent memory.

It is, of course, one of the most difficult things in
the world to review an honestly and devotedly ambitious
contemporary anthology. The literary record of this
generation is such that one is only too glad to see it,
and so to subordinate the critical temper to the mood of
appreciation. These poets are nearly all young men, and
few of them have suffered the mildew of commercial popular-
ity. Their office is only to their Muse and their in-
clinations and endeavours to their work - an attitude
which, in our opinion, spells salvation in any potential
revival of literature. And a volume which throws so
wide a net is bound to have its catch of trout and
minnows, of genuine and mediocre verse. For all that, it
is not so salient an achievement as its predecessor. That
is not altogether the fault of the Poetry Bookshop. To
fill nearly 250 pages, and at the same time fetch a com-
pass of only two years, is to put a premium on quantitat-
ive rather than qualitative poetry. And the publishers
are under a disability for which the times more than they
are responsible. It is one of the most curious feat-
ures of our generation that the young authors open their
career with a good book and pursue it with a number of
imitations. Their inspiration, that is to say, has not
enough body in it to carry them over their first and
lavish venture. Rupert Brooke and Mr de la Mare are ex-
amples. Brooke, we think, never realized the exuberant
promise of his early poems, in which there was certainly
'poetry enough for anything'. His process was a gradual
loss in objectivity. Great poetry, that is to say uni-
versal poetry, cannot be achieved without an impersonal
quality. The poet's personality is not so much lost as
merged in the objective reality of his vision. And
Brooke's growth was equivalent to the development of
self-consciousness. His eye steadily receded from the
object and turned inwards upon itself. For instance, in
this volume (we quote from 'Tiare Tahiti'):

> Taū here, Mamua,
> Crown the hair and come away!
> Hear the calling of the moon,
> And the whispering scents that stray
> About the idle warm lagoon.
> Hasten, hand in human hand,
> Down the dark, the flowered way,
> Along the whiteness of the sand,
> And in the water's soft caress,
> Wash the mind of foolishness.

This and the others, all collected from '1914 and Other Poems', are a cabinet of all the talents, but just because of that emphasis upon self-conscious expression, re-strained from discovery beyond.   And the same, though in a less degree, is true of Mr de la Mare.   All but one of his poems represented here are reprinted from 'Peacock Pie'. But their virtue is many leagues from that of 'Poems' (1906) and 'The Listeners'.   There was a quite incomparable subtlety of rhythm and elfin magic in 'The Listeners', nearer perhaps to Coleridge at his best than any other English poet since.   But in these poems, crystalline and delicate as they are, Mr de la Mare is living on his past. The quality of strangeness, which, in his supple metres, was the most natural thing in the world, has become purely fantastic - fantastic, so to speak, in the air, a part seductively but none the less artificially breaking off from the whole.   Yet another instance is Mr Stephens, five of whose poems are selected from 'Songs from the Clay'.   Mr Stephens really deserves his fall from poetic grace, because he has treated his Muse so cavalier-ly.   His verse is no longer a severe emotional discipline, but a plaything, an idle bauble.   Place this kind of jingle:

> I was singing all the time,
> Just as prettily as he,
> About the dew upon the lawn
> And the wind upon the lea;
> So I didn't listen to him
> And he sang upon a tree.

- beside the lean, insurgent passion, the dramatic pungency, the direct originality of 'Insurrections' (1909). It is to make a poppet of an athlete.

For all these disadvantages, the Bookshop should have been more judicious in its selection.   Why is not Mr Squire included?   His 'The Three Hills' was published in 1913, and so is within the boundaries of choice.   The book is, we grant, decidedly unequal in merit, but at least one poem, 'Antinomies on a Railway Station', which has a genuine metaphysical rapture, ought to have been included, and a poem of something of the same calibre, 'In a Restaurant', and, we believe, of later date, would have been a Castor to Pollux.   Then Mr Davies, being perhaps our best purely lyrical poet, should have appeared in full dress.   Instead, it is rather in shirt-sleeves and dressing-gown.   Of the eight poems reprinted here, six are from 'The Bird of Paradise' and two from 'Foliage', in our opinion a greatly superior volume.   And

the only two which represent Mr Davies at his best and
most unified are 'The Hawk' and 'Thunderstorms'. But
what of the almost Shakespearean concept of 'Dreams of
the Sea' in 'Foliage':

> Thou knowest the way to tame the wildest life,
> Thou knowest the way to bend the great and proud;
> I think of that Armada, whose puffed sails,
> Greedy and large, came swallowing every cloud.
>
> But I have seen the sea-boy, young and drownded,
> Lying on shore, and by thy cruel hand,
> A seaweed beard was on his tender chin,
> His heaven-blue eyes were filled with common sand.
>
> And yet, for all, I yearn, for thee again,
> To sail once more upon thy fickle flood;
> I'll hear thy waves wash under my death-bed,
> Thy salt is lodged forever in my blood.

And 'Plants and Men', in 'The Bird of Paradise', which, if
more tenuous in thought and expression, is highly charact-
eristic of Mr Davies's translucent manner, more finely so
than 'A Fleeting Passion' and 'The Bird of Paradise'.
But where we are chiefly at odds with the editor is in
the inclusion of Mr Gordon Bottomley's and Mr Aber-
crombie's poetic dramas. A predominantly lyrical anth-
ology like this is not the place for them. Their
poetic excellence is not such as to warrant such a large
grant of space, as they impair the unity of the volume.
Mr Bottomley's 'King Lear's Wife' has a certain distinct-
ion and felicity of phrasing. But Lear's intrigue with
the waiting woman Gormflaith over his wife Hygd's death-
bed, and Goneril's murder of her do not fit the essent-
ial dignity of poetic tragedy. And Mr Abercrombie's
'The End of the World' is too wilfully anachronistic in
its language, too undramatic in its theme, and too
laboured and nebulous in its execution for the achieve-
ment of its artistic purpose. We firmly hold, besides,
that the poetic drama (that is to say, the *heroic* drama)
is only suited to the heroic ages. Poetic drama must,
by its very nature, be an exercise nowadays. The
appropriate figures have become a faded memory, and there
is no modern storehouse of material upon which the poetic
dramatist can draw. One has only to look at the poetic
tragedies of Dryden, Nicholas Rowe, Addison, etc., in a
quintessentially unheroic age, to see a parallel. The
historical spirit obtrudes disastrously upon the poetic.
Aristotle was right when he laid it down that to make a

heroic drama, you want a Gulliver in conflict with Lilli-
putians, and brought to his fall by an error, omission,
or even accident.   In that sense, 'Samson Agonistes' is
the authentic poetic drama.

But to return to our lyricists.   Flecker is a little
disappointing.   'The Old Ships' has a sumptuously deco-
rative effect, without being merely a mosaic.   But the
others (from 'The Golden Journey to Samarkand') are too
elaborately coloured and patterned.   They are like the
waving of many-coloured scarves.   And there is nothing
here to equal the magnificent impulse and quite extra-
ordinary versification of 'The War-Song of the Saracens'.
Mr Drinkwater, again, writes not poetry, but descriptive
rhetoric.   He is like an energetic swimmer, caught in an
irresistible current, and struggling painfully but vainly
to reach the coveted shore - poetic imagination.   Mr
Ledwidge, one of the new-comers, has a pleasant, if
rather slender, oaten pipe.   Mr Lawrence's sombre
numbers prove him a unique artist of sensation, but
hardly of the transfigured poetic mood.   But, to our
mind, the pearl of all the poems in the book is Mr Ralph
Hodgson's 'The Song of Honour' reprinted from one of the
'Flying Fame' broadsides.   Mr Hodgson did not appear in
the former volume.   We have little hesitation in hailing
this poem as a work of exquisite imagination, profound
feeling, and first-hand inspiration.   It possesses just
that element of spiritual insight which distinguishes the
great poem and transforms it into a universal, inevitable
entity.   Its music is exactly matched to its feeling,
its thought to its expression.   And beyond this harmony,
just that impalpable, serene consciousness that makes the
mysterious truth of poetry.   We can only quote a stanza
or two:

[Quotes 'The Song of Honour', stanzas V, VII and VIII.]

If Mr Hodgson can develop a promise so radiant as this,
he has a great future before him.

19.   'BOOKS IN GENERAL', J.C. SQUIRE, 'THE NEW STATESMAN'

25 December 1915, 281

J.C. Squire, under the pseudonym 'Solomon Eagle',
continued the assault on the two verse plays, especially
on Bottomley's.   Robert H. Ross gives an interesting
selection from the letters of loyal Georgians to their
editor ('The Georgian Revolt', 155-8), Gibson quoting
Brooke's opinion that 'Squire didn't know a poem when he
saw it', and Abercrombie and Bottomley defending their
plays.   Marsh tried to convert Squire, who replied that
'Unhappily, we shall have to agree to differ'.   For a
recent defence of 'King Lear's Wife', see Christopher
Hassall, 'Edward Marsh', 378.   For a note on Squire, see
Introduction, pp. 21-2, and Appendix, p. 415.

It used frequently to be remarked that the public did not
want anthologies of contemporary work.   The obvious
answer to that was that such anthologies were almost al-
ways bad, and that in refusing to touch them the public
showed an amount of good sense with which, failing this
demonstration, one would not have credited it.   How
false was the assumption underlying the generalisation is
shown by the great success of 'Georgian Poetry, 1911-12'.
This collection of poems by a number of the younger
writers appeared only two years ago, and most of its
short life has been spent in the atmosphere of war.
Nevertheless it is now in its thirteenth edition.   Its
editor, therefore - a very devoted and self-effacing
editor - had some grounds for his feeling that a second
volume might be acceptable, even at a time so generally
unfavourable to publishing and the meditative kind of
reading as the present.   So 'Georgian Poetry, 1913-14'
(Poetry Bookshop, 3s. 6d. net), has appeared.
     As a body the shorter poems in the book are fully equal
to those in its predecessor.   It contains, in fact, more
good ones than that did, if, perhaps, fewer first-rate
ones.   Four or five of Mr Davies's lyrics, Mr de la Mare's
'Music', Mr Lawrence's 'Service of All the Dead', and Mr
Hodgson's 'The Bull', for example, are all remarkable
poems;   and there is a perfect selection from the later
work of Rupert Brooke and J.E. Flecker.   But the volume
suffers rather by the comparative weakness of two long
plays that fill a great deal of the space: Mr Bottomley's

- that is to say, Mr Gordon Bottomley's - 'King Lear's
Wife', and Mr Lascelles Abercrombie's 'The End of the
World'.   Mr Abercrombie's subject - the reception in a
secluded village of the news (it proves false) that the
world is coming at once into fatal collision with a comet
- has possibilities enough.   One sees what he wanted to
show: scales dropping from men's eyes, the shams and
hypocrisies of some shrivelling in the fire, the re-
straints of others breaking down, and the awful pageant of
the 'end of all things' going on in the background.   There
are one or two good spots in the play.   In one passage
Mr Abercrombie, like Vine, sees the moon in a new light;
in another, where Sollers runs amok in the bar-parlour,
there is some really dramatic writing.   But most of it,
in spite of the laboured strain and tensity of the
writing, is lifeless.   The play by Mr Gordon Bottomley -
whose lyrics in the first Georgian book had a strangely
original beauty - is very much superior.   For one thing
it is well-made and even actable;   for another the lan-
guage has a peculiar, clean, hard bite;   for another there
are frequent little flashes of sight and insight which
show an original and unconventional mind at work.   But
the 'incidental beauties' are not sufficiently numerous to
veil the poverty of the main conception and the wrong-
headedness of the general treatment.   The poet is per-
fectly entitled to write a play which begins with King
Lear's wife slowly dying, whilst the King in the death-
chamber dandles the nurse upon his knee;   which con-
tinues with the death of the Queen and the murder of the
nurse by Goneril, a sort of blend of Boadicea and
Artemis;   and which ends with the corpse-washer laying
out the Queen to the tune of a song about a louse com-
pelled to migrate from a body which had long given him a
comfortable home.   But Mr Bottomley lays it on too
thick;   his characters have no complexity, and one feels
about the horror, not that it is a natural and inevitable
growth, but that he is *putting* it there all the time.   As
for the Song of the Louse, I cannot help saying that -
though nobody but a good poet gone wrong could have
written it - it strikes me, like the Song of the Flea in
'Faust', as comic and not at all grim.   It begins:

A louse crept out of my lady's shift -
Ahumm, Ahumm, Ahee -
Crying 'Oi! Oi!   We are turned adrift;
The lady's bosom is cold and stiffed,
And her arm-pit's cold for me.'

'The lady's linen's no longer neat' -
Ahumm, Ahumm, Ahee -
'Her savour is neither warm nor sweet;
It's close for two in a winding sheet,
And lice are too good for worms to eat;
So here's no place for me.' . . .

I do not hold up my hands in protest against the morbid-
ity of this or any such stuff.   The way it takes me is
that I automatically compose a rollicking tune to it and
go about singing it.   And the play as a whole affects me
in much the same manner: one feels that the best comment
on it would be provided by, say, the Lord Winterton we
used to know, or a Cockney soldier: ' 'Ere, cheese it!'
   There is in places a curious similarity between the
writing of several of these poets who are sick of stale
beauties and clutching at the ugly and the grotesque.
One of Mr Abercrombie's characters remembers how

                              When I was young
   My mother would catch us frogs and set them down,
   Lapt in a screw of paper, in the ruts,
   And carts going by would quash 'em

- a bucolic pastime that has somehow escaped the notice
of Mr Masefield;   and for a new image of the world's end
Mr Abercrombie speaks of life

   All blocht out by a brutal thrust of fire
   Like a midge that a clumsy thumb squashes and smears.

Mr Gibson, in a poem which shows distinct traces of Mr
Abercrombie's influence, describes camels:

                        Only think
   Of camels long enough and you'ld go mad -
   With all their humps and lumps;   their knobbly knees,
   Splay feet, and straddle legs;   their sagging necks,
   Flat flanks, and scraggy tails and monstrous teeth.

And Mr John Drinkwater elaborates a rather good descript-
ion of a toad:

                        A queer
   Puff-bellied toad, with eyes that always stared
   Sidelong at heaven and saw no heaven there,
   Weak-hammed, and with a throttle somehow twisted
   Beyond full wholesome draughts of air, and skin
   Of wrinkled lips, the only zest or will
   The little flashing tongue searching the leaves.

Anything is better than chrysolites and roses, but an un-
conventionally ugly image is not necessarily illuminating,
and descriptions of grotesques and gargoyles have their
limitations like other descriptions.   One hopes that the
poetical pursuit of insects and batrachians will not
become a habit.

It is an exciting enterprise, and it is to be hoped
that the editor, 'E.M.', will go on with it.   If he pub-
lishes his volumes every two years, the quality of them
may vary through no fault of his, but he will do great
service in securing the most vital contemporary verse
rapid access to its public.   The scheme rather reminds
one of the eighteenth-century Miscellanies - Dryden's
(Tonson's), Dodsley's, Percy's, and so on - in which much
of the best verse of the Queen Anne and early Hanoverian
poets was either reprinted or appeared for the first time.
'Georgian Poetry' cannot hope to be completely infallible
or comprehensive: everyone will feel that he could
repair a few errors of either sort.   But anyone who
might take the two volumes together and try, with poems
omitted from them and written by young men during the
period covered, to make a single other volume as good as
either would find all his work cut out.

20.   'GEORGIAN POETRY, 1913-1915', UNSIGNED REVIEW,
'THE SPECTATOR'

5 February 1916, 190-1

By John St Loe Strachey (1860-1927), editor and propriet-
or of 'The Spectator' until his retirement in 1925.   His
books include 'Problems and Perils of Socialism' and 'The
Practical Wisdom of the Bible' (1908), and 'Economics of
the Hour' (1923).

Fifteen years were to pass before 'a new Pope', Roy
Campbell, was to write his 'Georgiad' (see Introduction,
p. 29), and Campbell's message was not quite that in-
dicated by Pope's couplet quoted here.   Bottomley, with
only a fortnight to go to his forty-second birthday, was
hardly a young man.   'King Lear's Wife' had been pub-
lished in the previous year with four earlier plays (one
dating from 1902), and he had by this time published
three other books.

We congratulate 'E.M.' on having given us a continuation
volume of his original anthology of Georgian poetry,
published some four years ago. The first volume dealt
with the poetry of 1911-1912. The present one includes
three years - i.e., 1913-1915. Two of the poets whose
work is represented in this volume are dead - Rupert
Brooke, who gave his life for his country, and James Elroy
Flecker, who died 'after a long and disabling illness'.
  We do not wish to be hypercritical in dealing with
Georgian any more than with any other class of poetry.
But no one could read the very accomplished verse which
fills the present volume, and indeed fills the air - it is
very seldom now that verse which gets any publicity lacks
accomplishment - without being aware that the general
characteristic of the verse is a certain forcing of the
note. By this we do not mean, of course, that every one
of the singers tries to scream, or, in the words of a
Victorian poet, 'cracks a weak voice to too lofty a tune',
but rather that whatever mood he assumes, whether melan-
cholic or robustious, is pushed to the extreme point.
There is a feverish anxiety at all costs not to be common-
place. Virgil was said to have disdained to say a plain
thing in a plain way. If the Georgian poet wants to say
a plain thing, he takes care to say it with an emphatic
baldness and crudity which not only hit you in the eye,
but lay you flat. Quarles told the poets of his time
who dealt with sacred things to 'screw their divine theor-
bos six notes higher'. The Georgian poet, instead of
screwing his divine theorbo up, is very apt to unscrew it,
and so to reach either a kind of simpering simplicity or
sophistical squalor which smells of the lamp rather than
of the real slum. Indeed, if a new Pope were to arise
to pillory in a new 'Dunciad' our Georgian poets, he might
tell them that they -

    Re-write the thrice re-written, strive to say
    Some older nothing in some newer way.

If allowance is made for the objection we have just de-
scribed, it must be admitted that there is a great deal
of conscious art and of high poetic intention in much of
the Georgian verse. Even if the note is forced, the
singer makes an appeal to ear and mind which is often
extraordinarily attractive. Take, for example, Mr
Gordon Bottomley's play, 'King Lear's Wife', which stands
first in the volume before us. King Lear, like the
heroes of many squalid dramas in real life, is represent-
ed as falling in love with his wife's nurse. Again, as
often happens in such cases, he has trouble with his

daughters and with the family physician. Many readers
will think that Mr Bottomley's King Lear is very unlike
Shakespeare's, but if we are to suppose that Lear really
played in early life the part assigned to him here, one
is quite pleased to think that he was punished later on.
In spite, however, of what looks as if it were going to
be a burlesque setting, there is some really very power-
ful and very harmonious poetry developed in the telling of
the story. Take, for example, the Physician's speech and
the King's answer:

[Quotes third speech of Physician and Lear's reply:
29 lines.]

We shall not quote examples of the love-making, squalid
and robustious, for it is both, between Lear and Gorm-
flaith, the Queen's nurse. But a word must be said
about the wild beauty of some of Goneril's speeches.
Goneril is represented here as a wayward early British
'Diane Chasseresse'. She comes in in her hunting dress,
fresh from the chase, 'her kirtle caught up in her girdle
and a light spear over her shoulder'. She is, say the
stage directions, which are of the conventional modern
type, a 'girl just turning to womanhood, proud in her
poise, swift and cold, an almost gleaming presence, a
virgin huntress'. Here is part of her conversation with
her mother, in which she describes a dream:

[Quotes Goneril's third speech: 22 lines.]

We wonder whether Mr Bottomley is a young man. If he is,
he ought some day to do very fine work. May we give him
a piece of advice, which, even if he rejects it, he will,
we feel sure, understand? It may be conveyed in a story
of a house-painter, who practised with great success the
noble Early Victorian art of producing grained oak panel-
ling out of painted deal. He complained that the trouble
with the young hands was that they would put too many
knots into their work, and so spoil the effect. 'King
Lear's Wife' is almost all knots.
    Of Mr Masefield we shall say nothing now, because we
naturally prefer to deal with his work separately rather
than in an anthology of minor poets. Rupert Brooke's
verse has already been written about at length. Still,
we must make an exception here, and quote the very
striking sonnet entitled 'Suggested by Some of the Pro-
ceedings of the Society for Psychical Research':

[Quotes Rupert Brooke's sonnet.]

Very admirable are some of Mr Walter de la Mare's
children's poems.   The best, however, are too long for
complete quotation, and do not lend themselves to ex-
cision.   An interesting poem is Mr Harold Monro's 'Milk
for the Cat'.   But though interesting, it is disappoint-
ing.   It tantalizes and is intolerable.   It is a piece
of very clever but amorphous and rhetorical realism.   What
a world of difference there is between it and Gray's 'Ode
on a Favourite Cat, Drowned in a Tub of Gold Fishes'!   Mr
Monro will of course think us mad when we say that the
necessity for making this unfavourable comparison is due
to the fact that he has not moralized his lay.   Yet,
strange as it may seem to him, that is our deliberate
opinion.   You cannot really sustain interest in anything
unless it has a moral and a motive, whether good, bad, or
indifferent.   The path which lands you in a ploughed
field, peters out, and leaves you there, is never so int-
eresting as the path which links lane to lane, or village
to village, and however much it strays by field and wood-
land, down and heath, brings you somewhere at last.
    This has necessarily been a review unjust to individ-
uals.   The truth is, there is enough material in the
volume for half-a-dozen reviews of three columns each.
All we have been able to do is to sample the work of one
or two poets.   Considering the book once more as a whole,
we say deliberately that all who care for the future of
English poetry - we hope there are a great many people
who care a very great deal about it - should certainly
read and consider 'Georgian Poetry', and thereby learn
something of the goals upon which our younger poets are
now fixing their eyes.   Possibly when the war is over
there will be new starts made by many of them.   Anyway,
here is a means for gauging the waters in the reservoirs
as they stood in 1913, 1914, and 1915.

21.   'THE NEW POETRY', ARTHUR WAUGH, 'QUARTERLY REVIEW'

October 1916, 365-86

Arthur Waugh reviews 'Georgian Poetry, 1911-1912' and
Georgian Poetry, 1913-1915' with Ezra Pound's 'The
Catholic Anthology, 1914-1915' in the 'Quarterly Review'
(reprinted in 'Tradition and Change', 1919, 9-39).
    It is interesting to find the first two Georgian

anthologies here bracketed with Pound's 'Catholic
Anthology' and discussed as 'the new rebellion' (see
Introduction, p. 2).   Further, that most conservative
of critics, Arthur Waugh, describes Pound as one of the
champions of the Georgians.

The story that Waugh likened Pound and Eliot to 'drunk-
en helots' is a misrepresentation of his warning to the
Georgians contained in the final paragraph of this review.
Pound was responsible for the misrepresentation in 'The
Egoist', June 1917, and Eliot repeated it in 'The Use of
Poetry', 1933, 72.

Arthur Waugh (1866-1943) won the Newdigate English
verse prize in 1888, was a literary journalist, and liter-
ary adviser to Kegan Paul & Co. Ltd., and managing direct-
or and for ten years chairman of the publishers, Chapman &
Hall.   He wrote literary studies of Tennyson and Brown-
ing, and edited many authors, including Dickens, Milton,
Tennyson, Arnold, Lamb, and Herbert.   His autobiography,
'One Man's Road', was published in 1931.   He was the
father of Alec (see No. 62) and Evelyn Waugh.

The difficulty which has always beset criticism in its
attempts to arrive at a satisfactory definition of the
word Poetry is by no means confined to the elusive nature
of the art itself.   For not only is the art of Poetry so
sensitive and subtle as to escape again and again from
the process of analysis, but the very standards by which
it is controlled are continually changing, and the
artist's own conception of his business is in a state of
perpetual transition.   Religion, philosophy, imagination,
fancy, rebellion, and reaction - these, and many other
elements in human thought, have left their impress upon
the poetic tradition;   and the function of criticism, as
each new generation breaks with some established canon,
has been more and more to hold to what is best in trad-
ition, to test new movements in the light of that best,
and yet to keep an open mind towards innovations, and to
welcome any change, however revolutionary, that is cal-
culated to enlarge the field of poetic vision and act-
ivity.   This last function is the hardest of all the
tasks that criticism is called upon to undertake;   but
the more intelligently the critic embraces it, the better
will he fulfil his responsibilities.   The history of lit-
erature has proved with weary iteration that the worst and
most retarding fault that criticism can commit is the tend-
ency to doubt every new movement, and to challenge and
defy methods whose novelty may indeed be disconcerting,
and yet may contain the germ of artistic emancipation and
enlightenment.

It behoves the critic, therefore, to walk warily among new
movements, without losing touch with the permanent laws of
his craft;   and, to guide him amid all minor differences
of period and taste, there will be found certain main con-
ceptions of the poetic art, which have stood fast in the
face of change and revolution.   Pre-eminent among these,
the very charter of Poetry itself, is the conception that
poetry consists in the imputation of universality to the
individual idea and impulse;   and conversely in the inter-
pretation of the individual impulse in the light of
universal truth.   The personal quality of the emotion or
impulse expressed has been always regarded as essential,
because it is only through personality that the artist can
make his appeal.   But the individual personality ac-
quires acceptance precisely as it relates itself to the
universal heart of the world.   When we read a poem, or a
passage in a poem, and exclaim instinctively: 'That is
true.   I never thought it before, but now it is said, I
recognise it as true, and as so well said that it is never
likely to be said better':   when, in short, we find our-
selves face to face with an eternal idea expressed in
flawless language, we acknowledge instinctively that we
are in the presence of poetry of the essential classic
order, against which time and the ebbing tide of taste are
powerless.   But there must be this complete fusion of
thought with expression.   The qualities of form, beauty,
and music, which tradition has accepted as inseparable
from poetry, remain inseparable from it to-day.   Without
the universal, living idea, embodying itself in personal
experience, you may have agreeable, charming verse, but
you cannot have poetry.   And, with equal emphasis,
unless the idea is clothed in language that fits, em-
bodies it, and gives it poetic currency, you may have
rhetoric and eloquence, but you will not and cannot have
poetry.   For poetry so indissolubly blends the universal
and the personal that idea, image, expression, and symbol
are indistinguishable from one another in the perfected
harmony of their union.

These considerations (trite enough, perhaps, in them-
selves) would appear to be worth recalling at the present
time, since there is evidently some danger of their being
forgotten in the indefatigable search for novelty and
sensation which, after vexing the field of the English
novel with varying fortunes, has recently attacked the
poet's art as well.   We have been passing through a
period of intellectual transition and readjustment.   The
stirring and revolutionary movements which convulsed the
Victorian era have exhausted themselves;   the world of
ideas has grown stagnant;   and the art of poetry has made

but little recognisable advance for a period of some-
thing like twenty years.   And now we are suddenly con-
fronted by a new movement, on whose behalf the claim
is made that 'English poetry is once again putting on
a new strength and beauty', so that 'we are at the
beginning of another Georgian period which may take
rank in due time with the several great poetic ages of
the past'.   These are proud words; and one of the
most conspicuous revolutionists of the new school has
elsewhere defined the movement with which he is ident-
ified in no uncertain terms.   'Our aim', he says, 'is
natural speech, the language as spoken.   We desire the
words of poetry to follow the natural order.   We would
write nothing that we might not say actually in life -
under emotion.'   It is, perhaps, not surprising to
learn, as we do in the same context, that the herald of
this new standard of poetry has 'degrees of antipathy
and even contempt for Milton and Victorianism and the
softness of the nineties' ('The Poems of Lionel Johnson'.
With an Introduction by Ezra Pound, Elkin Mathews); and,
though it is improbable that his contempt for what he
describes as 'the Miltonian quagmire' would be endorsed
by many of the other champions of Georgian Poetry, it is
at least certain that the atmosphere of all the three
volumes cited at the head of this article is an atmos-
phere of empirical rebellion.   Since, moreover, this
atmosphere of rebellion is introduced with a confidence
quite gloriously cocksure, it may not be without value to
consider the claims of these young innovators, and to
estimate the effect which their influence seems likely to
exercise upon English poetry in the immediate future.   It
is evident that such influence is by no means negligible,
for the first anthology of Georgian Poetry is already in
a twelfth impression, and many of the names that decorate
it are among the most enthusiastically acclaimed of the
younger generation.   But, before we consider their per-
formance in detail, a few reflections upon the art which
they practise may help us to appreciate the precise
standard of poetry to which their workmanship and
spiritual outlook conform.

   Poetry, it will be generally conceded, even by the most
enterprising claimant for plain speaking in common
speech, must work in one or other, or in all combined, of
three different media - ideas, emotions, and moods.   When
poetry was defined as 'a criticism of life', the framer
of the definition had in mind chiefly the poetry of
ideas; when it is described as 'emotion remembered in
tranquillity', the description is directed chiefly to
emotional poetry; and when we are told, as we often are

nowadays, that the sincere reproduction of a moment's
spiritual experience is the proper concern of the poetic
art, this third and final definition applies almost ex-
clusively to the poetry which seeks to reproduce the
writer's passing mood without any reference to its truth
or value. The highest order of poetry will be found,
under analysis, to combine elements from each of these
three classes; for the emotion, without which poetry is
barren, contains in itself an indirect reference to the
mood in which it is evoked, while the poet proceeds from
the registration of the emotion to test it by the stand-
ard of the universal idea. But it must never be for-
gotten that the idea is the germ of the poem; that the
truth and universality of the idea is the test of the
poem's quality; and that, as poetry recedes from the
region of ideas into that of emotions, and sinks still
further from emotions into moods, it retires more and
more from that high vantage ground from whose summit the
classic poetry of the ages overlooks the manifold activ-
ity of the world. From the idea to the emotion, and
from the emotion to the mood, is a downward path, separ-
ating poetry from its high, universal significance, and
bringing it step by step nearer to a condition of an-
archy, in which every individual's claim is paramount,
where art can represent nothing permanent, since nothing
permanent or stable exists within its survey to be
represented.

Now a careful examination of these two volumes of
Georgian poetry seems to suggest that during the last ten
years or so English poetry has been approaching a cond-
ition of poetic liberty and licence which threatens, not
only to submerge old standards altogether, but, if per-
severed in to its logical limits, to hand over the sens-
itive art of verse to a general process of literary dem-
ocratisation. For some time before this movement took
shape, the powers of reaction had been at work upon
English poetry. The Pre-Raphaelite movement, for ex-
ample, was in itself a reaction. It found the soulful
earnestness of the Victorians quietly sinking into a sort
of dogmatic philosophy. Science, religion, doubt, and
faith had apparently taken the Muses' Hill by storm; and
a way of escape was sought into the dreams of the past,
by reviving ideals and standards of a simpler and a more
artistically-minded world. The step from such a mood to
one of general discontent with all surviving traditions
was but a short one; and the next step after that is in-
evitably the complete abandonment of tradition and stan-
dard alike. 'We write nothing that we might not speak',
proclaims the new rebellion in effect: 'we draw the

thing as we see it for the God of things as they are.
Every aspect of life shall be the subject of our art, and
what we see we will describe in the language which we use
every day. The result shall be the New Poetry, the vital
expression of a new race.'

To such a manifesto, even before its artistic achieve-
ments come to be examined, there is one preliminary reply.
It is indeed true that the artificer may put whatever he
sees into his melting-pot, but it by no means follows that
he will get a work of art out of his mould. It may be
arguable that the poet should shovel the language of the
mining-camp into his lyrics, but it is more than doubtful
whether poetry will emerge. Force may emerge, vigour may
emerge, an impressive and vital kind of rhetoric may take
form from the composition; but poetry is something more
than these. Poetry must possess beauty; beauty is the
essence of its being; and it has never been the general
experience that the language of the common crowd possesses
either beauty or authority. When poetry proposes to con-
fine itself to the commercial counters of speech, the
first thing we should expect would be a failure in dignity
and charm. When it sets itself to break loose from the
traditions of structure and harmony, the next inevitable
consequence would be the wastage of form and melody. And,
emphatically enough, the very first impression with which
the reader of these volumes of Georgian poetry is
assailed is an impression of a fitful lack of dignity, and
a recurrent tendency to neglect the claims of form and
structure, which continually distract the reader's atten-
tion from his author's meaning, by thrusting into the
foreground a sense of the unrestrained and even violent
fashion in which that meaning is striving to get itself
expressed. That the form of expression has crude energy,
rising at intervals into power, we do not dispute; but it
is emphatically the sort of energy that has not hitherto
been associated with the methods and aims of poetry.

The blank verse of Mr Wilfrid Wilson Gibson, for ex-
ample, has evidently thrown aside in weariness the golden
foot-rule of the Augustans:

For sure enough the camel's old evil incarnate! . . .
The only moments I've lived my life to the full
And that live again in remembrance unfaded are those
When I've seen life compact in some perfect body . . .

It would be amusing to hear Dr Johnson's comments upon
this turbulent kind of prosody. Such liberties with his
favourite ten-syllabled line might well 'perturbate his
paradisal state', torturing it into one of fuliginous

thunderstorm.   But Mr Lascelles Abercrombie's blank verse
is yet more rough and unmelodious:

> Anger was smarting in my eyes like grit.
> O the fine earth and fine all for nothing!
> Mazed I walkt, seeing and smelling and hearing:
> The meadowlands all shining fearfully gold, -
> Cruel as fire the sight of them toucht my mind;
> Breathing was all a honeytaste of clover
> And bean flowers: I would have rather had it
> Carrion, or the stink of smouldering brimstone.

Now, it is evident that the writer who sets down such un-
metrical lines as these is writing in deliberate defiance
of metrical tradition.   No man, possessed by the impulse
to express himself in verse, was ever the victim of so bad
an ear as to believe that

> O the fine earth and fine all for nothing!

is a reasonable line of blank-verse as it was understood
by the classicists.   But Mr Abercrombie would very
properly reply that he is not writing for the classicists
at all, but for the young bloods of the twentieth cen-
tury, and that he chooses to write like this for the sake
of avoiding monotony and of achieving sudden and vigorous
effect.   But, as a matter of fact, is the effect really
heightened by this kind of incoherent violence?   Is it
not rather true that the description in the first passage
quoted above is so confused and involved that the lines
must be read twice before they take hold upon the imagin-
ation, and that even then the final impression left by
them is one of an imperfect and unfinished draft?   Vehe-
mence without corresponding effect is nothing worth; it
resembles the volubility of an unpractised orator, and
the taint of undisciplined experiment too frequently
affects and mars Mr Abercrombie's workmanship.   His
'Sale of St Thomas' has a fine imaginative idea at the
heart of it; it is, in fact, one of the few poems in the
collection which deal with an idea of permanent signifi-
cance and original force.   St Thomas is conceived as torn
asunder between a divine impulse to carry on the work of
his Master and a restraining prudence which perpetually
retards his mission by suggesting the risks and perils of
the enterprise.   Finally the Master reappears and sells
St Thomas into bondage.   For fear, He says, is a venial
failing,

> But prudence, prudence is the deadly sin,
> And one that groweth deep into a life
> With hardening roots that clutch about the breast.
> For this refuses faith in the unknown powers
> Within man's nature;   shrewdly bringeth all
> Their inspiration of strange eagerness
> To a judgment bought by safe experience;   ·
> Narrows desire into the scope of thought.

Here is a fine animating theme for poetry;   and one well
suited to a muse bent upon new adventure;   but throughout
the poem, as even more noticeably in his breathless, ex-
clamatory drama 'The End of the World', the poet appears
to have hurled himself into the effort of creation
before properly digesting his material, and to be content
to accept as finished work what ought to have been rec-
ognised as the first rough notes, or 'trial balance' of
his composition.   He is so eager to be trying conclus-
ions with the new idea that he exhausts himself in a
single flight, and never advances beyond the initial
phases of the experiment.

This restlessness seems to be growing upon the poet,
for his earlier work showed imagination much more satis-
factorily at one with its material.   His *vers libre*,
which is now often crude and shapeless, had at first a
genuine justification, in its courageous attempt to break
free once and for all from the mild fluidity of the
Tennysonian euphuists.   He introduced a degree of elast-
icity and variety into the metre which was stimulating to
the ear, while the eye was continually fed by rich and
clustered imagery:

> The world's a flame of the unquenching fire,
> An upward-rapturing unhindered flame,
> Singing a golden praise that it can be,
> One of the joys of God the eternal fire.
> But than this soaring nature, this green flame,
> Largely exulting, not knowing how to cringe,
> God's joy, there are things even sacreder,
> Words: they are messengers from out God's heart,
> Intimate with him;   through his deed they go,
> This passion of him called the world, approving
> All of fierce gladness in it, bidding leap
> To a yet higher rapture ere it sink.

And again, in the lyric metre of the choruses in 'Pere-
grinus' there was a haunting beauty, which appears too
rarely in his later work:

Little flames, merry flames, modest low chucklings,
This is but maidenly pretence of shyness;
Little flames, happy flames, what are these secrets
You so modestly whisper one another?
Do we not know your golden desires,
And the brave way you tower into lust
Mightily shameless?
Why do you inly skulk among the timber?
Stand up, yellow flames, take the joy given you;
Resins and spunkwood, faggots and turpentine,
A deal of spices, a great cost of benzoin,
Everything proper for your riot, O flames.

It is a great pity that a sort of impulsive impatience
should mar such genuine ability, but it is difficult to
resist the impression that Mr Abercrombie is in danger of
accepting everything that occurs spasmodically to his
fancy as the finished product of a meditative art.

Something of the same haste and impatient negligence
of technique disfigures the work of Mr Walter de la Mare,
who aims at a simpler form of fantasy than Mr Aber-
crombie, only again and again to spoil a dainty fancy by
wayward affectations and clumsy inversions:

Three jolly Farmers
Once bet a pound
Each dance the others would
Off the ground.
Out of their coats
They slipped right soon,
And neat and nicesome
Put each his shoon.

An onomatopoeic measure like this, chosen to reproduce
the spirit of the dance, is absolutely ruined by such
tortured phrases as weigh down the third, seventh, and
eighth lines of this opening, and the same fault crops up
all through the piece. And in 'Melmillo' a gossamer
imagination is marred by similar clumsiness of touch:

Three and thirty birds there stood
In an elder in a wood;
Called Melmillo - flew off three,
Leaving thirty in the tree;
Called Melmillo - nine now gone,
And the boughs held twenty-one;
Called Melmillo - and eighteen
Left but three to nod and preen;
Called Melmillo - three - two - one -
Now of birds were feathers none.

Here again the awkwardness of inversion, and the conse-
quent suggestion of artificiality, go a long way to
dispel the dainty and sincere simplicity of the picture.
     But the champion of the new impressionism in poetry
may reasonably rejoin that the very object to which these
young writers are bending their energies is nothing less
than emancipation from the metrical trammels of the past;
that what they particularly desire is freedom of method
allied to freedom of thought; and that their workmanship
can only be judged in connection with the ideas which it
embodies.   This is true enough;   all artistic technique
must be largely controlled by the subject it portrays.
We do not expect Caliban to discuss Setebos in the sub-
lime language of the Deity, musing upon the perfected
beauty of Eden.   But dramatic propriety is one thing,
and lyrical poetry is quite another.   The question is,
whether lyric verse can possibly 'take rank with the sev-
eral great poetic ages of the past', unless thought and
expression combine to produce a thing of beauty, recog-
nisable as beautiful by any sensitive taste, and contain-
ing at the heart's core that inevitable quality of the
universal which will be found to distinguish all the
poetry that endures.   There are certain poems in the
collection to which it is possible to ascribe without
hesitation this high and inalienable privilege, and it is
no slight vindication of the standards of the past that
they are all poems conceived and executed in the soundest
tradition of fine workmanship.
     Let us take, for instance, Mr Sturge Moore's
'Sicilian Idyll', which is not only the most striking
poem in the earlier volume, but may be said to present,
in an allegory, the complete philosophy of the poetic
movement which it adorns.   An aged couple in a Sicilian
village are immersed in the mild atmosphere of repose and
acquiescence which middle-age brings to those who have
escaped from the disturbing passions of youth.   Damon
with his wine-bowl and his gossip, and Cydilla with her
ball of worsted and nimble fingers, are content enough in
their backwater of life.   Only one anxiety troubles
them.   Their son Delphis has broken loose from their un-
eventful home, and gone out into the world in a mist of
rebellion and adventure, to warm both hands before the
fire of life.   What has befallen him by the way?   The
shadow of that anxiety is always over the old people.
One day Damon meets his son again.   He has become tutor
to a young lad, and his imagination is aflame with the
delight of moulding an impressionable soul to his own
pattern.   The very ecstasy of creation inspires him;
and then suddenly another man crosses his path, a

creature of low instincts and animal impulses, who in-
flames the boy's mind with unclean fancies and seems
likely in a moment to ruin the work of Delphis's long-
cherished ambition.   Then Delphis in his turn has to
learn the lesson of the world's progress.   Youth will
not stay for the word of experience;   the call of the
wild tempts every new generation to its disaster.   So
Delphis, enraged with civilisation, takes the solitary
way:

> A vagabond I shall be as the moon is.
> The sun, the waves, the winds, all birds, all beasts
> Are ever on the move, and take what comes;
> They are not parasites like plants and men
> Rooted in that which fed them yesterday....
>
> Free minds must bargain with each greedy moment
> And seize the most that lies to hand at once.
> Ye are too old to understand my words;
> I yet have youth enough, and can escape
> From that which sucks each individual man
> Into the common dream.

What is this but the perfect apologia for the wandering
life of an art which makes no compromise with tradition,
an apologia expressed in language of great force, sin-
cerity, and persuaveness?
     But the apologia is double-edged.   For the wanderer
goes his way, drifting without purpose upon a rudderless
course, while the little citadel of civilisation stands
firm, because man is a social being, and it is through
the self-sacrifice of the individual that the life of
each generation is made easier than the last.   And so,
after Delphis has raved himself out of sight, the last
word is with the old parents, as they gather up the
worsted and the knitting, and trot off in search of their
son's pupil 'to offer their poor service in his stead'.

> We must be doing something, for I feel
> We both shall drown our hearts with time to spare.

Man cannot live for himself alone;   his past and present
must control the laws for his future.   Nor can the
artist separate himself from the traditions of his art,
and start afresh upon a new programme with each new gen-
eration.   The continuity of life and of art is alike un-
broken;   there is nothing really new nor isolated under
the sun.

But Mr Sturge Moore has disappeared from the later volume
of Georgian Poetry, whether because, as the editor says
of absent contributors, he has 'published nothing which
comes within its scope', or because he 'belongs in fact to
an earlier poetic generation, and his inclusion must be
allowed to have been an anachronism', we are not told.   In
any case the absence of his restrained and eloquent verse
is a distinct loss to the later collection;   and it is a
further, and a very real misfortune to the movement as a
whole, that two of its most gifted and promising leaders
have been removed during the last year by the untimely
stroke of death.   In James Elroy Flecker and Rupert
Brooke we gladly recognise two other poets of indisputable
and glowing promise, whose influence upon their contempor-
aries might possibly have had the most salutary and form-
ative results.   Without them much that is left of the
movement fades into a feverish confusion of experiment;
but one of these two possessed intuitively, and the other
was on the point of acquiring by experience, just that
quality of artistic self-control which would save them
from the excesses with which they were surrounded, and
leaven the modern movement as a whole with a powerful
leaven of beauty and spirituality.   Flecker, indeed, had
little to connect him with rebellious modernity.   He in-
dulged in no half-fledged experiments, and made no
attempt to shock his readers' susceptibilities.   His
passion was chiefly for the old - old ships, old build-
ings, old legends, and old loyalties;   and he sang their
praise in haunting melodies which recalled the immemorial
music of the old, unchangeable sea:

> Evening on the olden, the golden sea of Wales,
> When the first star shivers and the last wave pales:
> O evening dreams!
> There's a house that Britons walked in, long ago,
> Where now the springs of ocean fall and flow,
> And the dead robed in red and sea-lilies overhead
> Sway when the long winds blow.
>
> Sleep not, my country;   though night is here, afar
> Your children of the morning are clamorous for war:
> Fire in the night, O dreams!
> Though she send you as she sent you, long ago,
> South to desert, east to ocean, west to snow,
> West of these out to seas colder than the Hebrides
>   I must go
> Where the fleet of stars is anchored, and the young
>   Star-captains glow.

Such melody and such imagery as this are in the true
succession; they owe nothing to any passing fashion.
But Rupert Brooke was essentially in the heart of the new
movement; and his earlier work was not immune from its
shortcomings both of taste and of faulty selection.   He
was obsessed by the modern melancholy.   Fired by that
love of English life and English scenery which is the
hall-mark of the public school and University man, bubb-
ling over with delight in life and love and sweet compan-
ionship, he could nevertheless rarely escape, even for an
hour, from all the depressing conviction of the transient
quality of all beauty and all human enjoyment, even
indeed of love itself.

      Magnificently unprepared
      For the long littleness of life,

he had scarcely raised its goblet to his lips, before he
saw the wine turn to poison in the cup.   Bright eyes,
gold hair, red lips - all would be dust in a few years,
blown upon the wind in solitary, loveless pilgrimage.

      And every mote, on earth or air,
      Will speed and gleam, down later days,
      And like a secret pilgrim fare
      By eager and invisible ways,

      Nor ever rest, nor ever lie,
      Till, beyond thinking, out of view,
      One mote of all the dust that's I
      Shall meet one atom that was you.

And then, perhaps, would be granted to the dead passion
its one faint hope of immortality, that the flame of re-
united love should strike into the heart of some pair of
living lovers, rapt out of themselves into an unfamiliar
ecstasy:

      And they will know - poor fools, they'll know! -
      One moment, what it is to love.

The dread of the loss of individuality burned into the
soul of this eager individualist, until the horror of
Nirvana almost consumed his power of expression.

      Oh, Heaven's Heaven! - but we'll be missing
      The palms, and sunlight, and the south;
      And there's an end, I think, of kissing
      When our mouths are one with Mouth . . .

That last line, with its taint of inherent ugliness, an
ugliness which becomes almost vulgar, is unfortunately
characteristic of the worst side of Rupert Brooke, the
itch to say a thing in such an arresting fashion as to
shock the literary purist into attention even against his
will.   There are too many such blots upon his poetry.

> Here, where love's stuff is body, arm and side
> Are stabbing-sweet 'gainst chair and lamp and wall.
> In every touch more intimate meanings hide;
> And flaming brains are the white heart of all.

This is not poetry at all;   once more we are confronted
with the failure of a vehemence that loses itself in
words.   So too in the interminable list of material com-
forts which he loved (and Brooke never quite knew when to
stop, when his imagination had started upon a mental cat-
alogue), he exhausts and irritates the fancy with the
suggestion of a cloistered, almost an epicurean, self-
consciousness.   Individualism indeed ran riot in his
temperament;   but, when the call came to make the sup-
reme sacrifice, he learnt in a sudden flash of relevat-
ion, what so many of his comrades had learnt by degrees
upon the hard stones of experience, that individuality is
only given to man in order that he may devote it to the
service of his generation.

[Quotes the sonnet, 'Peace'.]

So invigorating, and so transcendently sincere, is this
return of the poet upon the self-centred dreams of youth,
with their vain regrets for the passage of beauty, that
we may be excused for believing that, had Rupert Brooke
survived the war, its cleansing fire would have lighted
him to achievements both in life and poetry far greater
than had yet been dreamed of by a philosophy so dis-
illusioned and so disintegrate.   *Dis aliter visum*: (1)
and now this bright young harbinger of beaconing poss-
ibilities sleeps by the Aegean sea:

> A dust whom England bore, shaped, made aware,
> Gave, once, her flowers to love, her ways to roam,
> A body of England's, breathing English air,
> Washed by the rivers, blest by suns of home.

And in his grave rest, beyond doubt, the highest expect-
ations of the poetic movement which he seemed destined in
the very hour of his death, to turn into richer and more
profitable channels.

The gulf which separates these three poets from the
larger body of the New Poetry may, perhaps, be bridged by
Mr John Drinkwater, who in a well-conceived and finely-
written idyll gives expression to yet one more allegory
of the artistic life. 'The Carver in Stone' indeed is
easily referable to the sister art of poetry.   It tells
of a sculptor, patient and idealistic, who was engaged,
with a host of his fellow-workmen, to decorate the frieze
of a great temple.   They set to work to embody the forms
of local deities, tiger, owl, bull, leopard, ram, camel,
lizard, and the rest, and carved them, as the crowd pre-
ferred to find them, without life or vital meaning.   The
solitary artist, on the other hand, threw all his ener-
gies into the sculpture of an eagle, that spread

> Wide pinions on a cloudless ground of heaven,
> Glad with the heart's high courage of that dawn
> Moving upon the ploughlands newly sown,
> Dead stone the rest. He looked, and knew it so.

The crowd, however, looked with other eyes.   The king
and his counsellors flocked to inspect the work, and
praised the lean, dull animals of the field.   Only one
critic noticed the eagle at all, and he would have pre-
ferred a swan.   So the lonely artist left popularity to
the others, and begged to be allowed to decorate the
panels in the clerestory, unseen because nc one would
ever trouble to climb the winding stair.   There he
carved a great, squatting toad, the emblem of the crowd's
'emphatic warrant,' and surrounded it with the other
types of the people's gods, wonderfully interpreted now
in the light of their own ugliness - cruelty, fear, and
servile toil.   The temple was finished, and nobody
climbed the stair to see his panels between the high win-
dows.   But he looked in solitude and contentment

> Again upon his work, and knew it good,
> Smiled on his toad, passed down the stair unseen,
> And sang across the teeming meadows home.

It would not be just to carry the comparison too far; for
the fault of the New Poetry is certainly not that it lacks
life, like the heavy images of the people's gods in the
poem, but rather, and principally, that it lacks beauty
and spirituality.   Life it has in abundance, the fierce,
feverish life of a mind that has not yet established its
relations with its environment, and is perpetually launch-
ing excursions into new territory, without consolidating
the ground that it has won.   It is the life, in fact, of

experiments and moods; and the poetry in which it issues
is precisely that poetry of the mood and of the emotion,
which we have already defined as lacking the sound found-
ations and universal significance of the poetry of ideas.
The general atmosphere is that of a world in which there
is no prevailing current of ideas, no pervading intellect-
ual stimulus, and from which the natural refuge is found
in the exaggeration of trivial incidents into some sort of
symbolic relation with big movements, and in the accept-
ance of individual whims and wayward fancies in the place
of firm philosophic ideals.

Symbolism plays an inevitable part in such a movement;
and the readiness with which symbolism runs to seed always
renders it a dangerous ally of poetry. For when it gets
out of hand, it is apt to trail off into a sort of en-
tanglement of its own elaboration, growing by self-
indulgence.   The prolixity of the author's fancy dulls
the edge of the animating idea; and this is the very
foible in which the imagery of the New Poetry loses it-
self again and again.   It gets hold of a half-developed
idea, and elaborates it out of all proportion and perspect-
ive.   'The Hare', by Mr Wilfrid Gibson, a fine poem in
many respects, nevertheless labours under this disadvant-
age.   In the hunted eyes of the hare the rustic sports-
man realises something of the shy apprehension of woman-
hood, a shyness which maternity and its consolations
alone have the power to dispel.   The image and the idea
are true, but the poet proceeds to decorate them with all
the circumstances of venery - first the pursuit of the
hare, then the pursuit of the woman, and then the two
pursuits merged symbolically into one; until the whole
thing is so overclouded by half-realised metaphor that the
main idea fades out of sight.

This fault strikes one the more strangely in Mr
Gibson's work, since his particular strength lies at the
other extreme of quality.   Swift vividness of impression
is the essence of his art, and none among the younger
writers has a surer gift for seizing upon the elements of
a scene or incident and presenting them arrestingly to the
imagination.   The brief, eager little poems, which he has
devoted to events and impressions of the present war, fur-
nish characteristic illustrations of his talent in this
respect; and it is curious to find, as occasionally hap-
pens in his longer flights, that his touch is capable of
faltering into indecision.   But, when the artist breaks
free of restraining standards, it is no uncommon exper-
ience that he should lose a sense of selection also.   The
very vividness of his insight tempts him to multiply im-
pressions, until they overcrowd the picture and obliterate

its purpose.   This is one of the most insidious dangers
of realism;   and there are occasions when an even more
perilous boundary gets crossed, in the poet's effort to be
original and arresting at any cost.
    The two pieces by Mr D.H. Lawrence, which bear the
names 'The Snapdragon' and 'Love and Cruelty', might well
serve as cautionary examples of realism running riot in
verse.   Both deal with the sudden submergence of judgment
and self-restraint in the clutch of gross physical passion,
and both use symbols from the natural world to illustrate
a degree of self-abandonment which is so invertebrate as
to be practically abnormal.   The sinister power of the
impression is not to be denied;   but it bears no sort of
affinity to poetry.   It is in both cases an experiment
in perverted symbolism, casting a sombre shadow upon the
wholesome impulses of passion and of natural sexual
attraction.
    Realism, however, is no rarity among the younger poets;
and the lack of restraint which stimulates their frequent
and irrelevant prolixity inspires them no less in the
choice of subjects and of methods so coarse as inevitably
to repel the clear, bright atmosphere of poetry altogether.
Mr John Masefield, no doubt, has done something to set the
fashion, although he is only inadequately represented in
these pages.   But Mr Masefield's moral narratives in
verse have a powerful sense of virility behind them;   and
two of them, 'The Everlasting Mercy' and 'The Widow in the
Bye Street', whatever may be thought of their violence of
taste and diction, are at any rate highly impressive hom-
ilies in metre, filled to the brim with a glowing passion
for morality.   Mr Masefield, moreover, is full of the true
stuff of poetry, and, when he is once at work by the
countryside or on his even more familiar ocean, the splen-
dour and variety of his imagery are impeccable.   His real-
ism also is invariably in the dramatic vein.   If he is
coarse, he takes his colour from the theme;   directly the
theme rises in the spiritual scale, the poet's inspirat-
ion rises with it to heights that not infrequently border
on sublimity.   The same is true of Mr Ralph Hodgson, who
completely justifies the rather sombre realism of 'The
Bull' by the intense pathos and sincerity of its human
allegory.   Strength of this sort, even if it broadens
down into crudity, is in direct harmony with its subject;
the dramatic situation requires it, and its final effect
appears artistically inevitable.
    The realism of Mr Lawrence and of Mr William Davies is
of an entirely different order.   Here, as in certain iso-
lated passages in Rupert Brooke's work, individualism
bursts its bounds, and elevates a merely animal instinct

into that higher region of ideas to which, of course,
animal instinct has always been recognised as a congen-
ital foe.   And the result, as in 'The Bird of Paradise',
is sheer ugliness, an ugliness which does grave injustice
to the true spirit of beauty which fills Mr Davies's past-
oral poems with sunshine and the scent of flowers in a
spring breeze.   It is strange, at first sight, that such
aberrations of taste should exist side by side with so
much natural beauty; but they are evidently a common
defect of the New Poetry, and would appear to have their
root in the defiance, and consequent loss, of authority
which attends all efforts to democratise society and art.

   This failing is painfully evident in one of the finest
and most impressive poems in either volume, the noble
'King Lear's Wife' of Mr Gordon Bottomley.   Here, in a
strongly-knit, vigorous, dramatic fragment, we are given
a sort of prelude to Shakespeare's tragedy, and that a
prelude which serves very reasonably to explain the in-
human treatment meted out to their father by Goneril and
Regan at a later stage of his history.   The Lear of this
fragment is still a man in his prime, lusty and lustful,
with a sickly dying wife who has long since ceased to
satisfy his uxorious demands.   Goneril is just emerging
into womanhood - a huntress maid; Cordelia is a pratt-
ling nursery child; Regan hangs about the kitchen for
scraps.   Upon Goneril falls the horror of relevation,
for, as her mother lies dying in the great bed, she sees
her father toying in the shadow with her mother's maid,
who is already destined by the doting Lear to be the
moribund wife's successor, while all the time the wanton
is carrying on an intrigue with a younger man in the
King's retinue.   The honour of the house is in Goneril's
hand, and she stabs her father's paramour to death,return-
ing with the blood upon her hands, to point the moral of
a woman's intuition:

   I do not understand how men can govern,
   Use craft and exercise the duty of cunning,
   Anticipate treason, treachery meet with treachery,
   And yet believe a woman because she looks
   Straight in their eyes with mournful, trustful gaze,
   And lips like innocence, all gentleness.
   Your Gormflaith could not answer a woman's eyes.
   I did not need to read her in a letter;
   I am not woman yet, but I can feel
   What untruths are instinctive in my kind,
   And how some men desire deceit from us.

So far the drama, though not without a certain pagan
brutality, is four-square within the containing walls of
poetry - a fine and living piece of literature. How,
then, comes it that on the very last page Mr Bottomley
should be willing to dissipate the final effect of a
powerful scene by introducing into the death-chamber two'
prattling beldames, who, coming to lay the dead woman out,
croon over her body a squalid ballad about a louse, and
plunge the episode into a conclusion of intolerable
bathos? It is in precisely the same spirit that Mr
William Davies paints a richly picturesque portrait of an
old seagoing salt, whose memory was packed with the rough
stuff of romance, and then tears the picture to pieces in
a colophon,

'A damn bad sailor and a landshark too,
No good in port or out' - my granddad said.

The disillusionment of such a finish is complete; it is
like a child destroying its sand-castle in a fit of pet-
ulance. And the motive is very much the same in both
cases, for it has its origin in a freakish desire to
shock.
Cleverness is, indeed, the pitfall of the New Poetry.
There is no question about the ingenuity with which its
varying moods are exploited, its elaborate symbolism
evolved, and its sudden, disconcerting effects exploded
upon the imagination. Swift, brilliant images break
into the field of vision, scatter like rockets, and leave
a trail of flying fire behind. But the general impress-
ion is momentary; there are moods and emotions, but no
steady current of ideas behind them. Further, in their
determination to surprise and even to puzzle at all costs,
these young poets are continually forgetting that the
first essence of poetry is beauty; and that, however
much you may have observed the world around you, it is
impossible to translate your observation into poetry,
without the intervention of the spirit of beauty, control-
ling the vision, and reanimating the idea.
The temptations of cleverness may be insistent, but its
risks are equally great: how great indeed will, perhaps,
be best indicated by the example of the 'Catholic Anthol-
ogy', which apparently represents the very newest of all
the new poetic movements of the day. This strange
little volume bears upon its cover a geometrical device,
suggesting that the material within holds the same rel-
ation to the art of poetry as the work of the Cubist
school holds to the art of painting and design. The
product of the volume is mainly American in origin, only

one or two of the contributors being of indisputably
English birth.   But it appears here under the auspices
of a house associated with some of the best poetry of the
younger generation, and is prefaced by a short lyric by
Mr W.B. Yeats, in which that honoured representative of a
very different school of inspiration makes bitter fun of
scholars and critics, who

>   Edit and annotate the lines
>   That young men, tossing on their beds,
>   Rhymed out in love's despair
>   To flatter beauty's ignorant ear.

The reader will not have penetrated far beyond this warn-
ing notice before he finds himself in the very stronghold
of literary rebellion, if not of anarchy.   Mr Orrick
Johns may be allowed to speak for his colleagues, as well
as for himself:

>   This is the song of youth,
>   This is the cause of myself;
>   I knew my father well and he was a fool,
>   Therefore will I have my own foot in the path before
>   I take a step;
>   I will go only into new lands,
>   And I will walk on no plank-walks.
>   The horses of my family are wind-broken,
>   And the dogs are old,
>   And the guns rust;
>   I will make me a new bow from an ash-tree,
>   And cut up the homestead into arrows.

And Mr Ezra Pound takes up the parable in turn, in the
same wooden prose, cut into battens:

>   Come, my songs, let us express our baser passions.
>   Let us express our envy for the man with a steady job
>   and no worry about the future.
>   You are very idle, my songs,
>   I fear you will come to a bad end.
>   You stand about the streets.   You loiter at the
>   corners and bus-stops,
>   You do next to nothing at all.
>   You do not even express our inner nobility,
>   You will come to a very bad end.
>   And I?   I have gone half cracked.

It is not for his audience to contradict the poet, who
for once may be allowed to pronounce his own literary

epitaph.   But this, it is to be noted, is the 'poetry'
that was to say nothing that might not be said 'actually
in life - under emotion', the sort of emotion that
settles down into the banality of a premature decrepit-
ude:

> I grow old ...   I grow old ...
> I shall wear the bottoms of my trousers rolled.
> Shall I part my hair behind?   Do I dare to eat a
>   peach?
> I shall wear white flannel trousers, and walk upon
>   the beach.
> I have heard the mermaids singing each to each.
> I do not think that they will sing to me.

Here, surely, is the reduction to absurdity of that
school of literary licence which, beginning with the
declaration

> I knew my father well and he was a fool,

naturally proceeds to the convenient assumption that
everything which seemed wise and true to the father must
inevitably be false and foolish to the son.   Yet if the
fruits of emancipation are to be recognised in the un-
metrical, incoherent banalities of these literary
'Cubists', the state of Poetry is indeed threatened with
anarchy which will end in something worse even than 'red
ruin and the breaking up of laws'·   From such a cata-
strophe the humour, commonsense, and artistic judgment of
the best of the new 'Georgians' will assuredly save their
generation;   nevertheless, a hint of warning may not be
altogether out of place.   It was a classic custom in the
family hall, when the feast was at its height, to display
a drunken slave among the sons of the household, to the
end that they, being ashamed at the ignominious folly of
his gesticulations, might determine never to be tempted
into such a pitable condition themselves.   The custom
had its advantages;   for the wisdom of the younger gener-
ation was found to be fostered more surely by a single
example than by a world of homily and precept.

Note

1   Fate decreed otherwise.

22.   'SOME POETS OF TODAY', S.P.B. MAIS,
'THE NINETEENTH CENTURY'

November 1916, 1008-22

This article was reprinted as 'Some Modern Poets' in
'From Shakespeare to O. Henry', 1917, 59-80.
   S.P.B. Mais (1885-1975) was a public schoolmaster who
turned author, lecturer and free-lance journalist.   When
T.S. Eliot described 'Wheels' as 'a more serious book'
than 'Georgian Poetry', he said it was 'not Mr S.P.B.
Mais's sort of poetry at all;   these are not the good boys
of the Sixth Form' (No. 30).   When Mais wrote the follow-
ing article he was teaching at Sherborne, where Arthur
Waugh (No. 21) had been at school, and his elder son,
Alec (No. 62), was then a pupil.   Alec Waugh writes of
him in 'The Loom of Youth' (1917) as 'Ferrers':

   only the Army and Matriculation classes had the
   tremendous advantages of doing English with him.
   Most of Ferrers's time was wasted in attempts to drive
   home mathematical theories into the dense brains of
   a lower school set.

   As to his influence in the school there could be no
   two opinions .....   It would be difficult to over-
   estimate the good Ferrers did at Fernhurst
   [Sherborne].   From afar Gordon [Waugh] worshipped
   him.   ['The Loom of Youth', 205-6.   See also pp. 240,
   285 and, for a glimpse of the Poetry Bookshop 'as a dim
   chapel, where the echoes of the world were lost', 287.]

'The Loom of Youth' caused so much resentment that both
Alec and his publisher father were asked to resign from
the Shirburnian Society, and Evelyn Waugh was sent to
Lancing.   Mais's second novel, 'Interlude' (1917),
described the school so closely that he too was obliged
to resign from the staff (see his autobiography, 'All the
Days of My Life', 1937, 68, in which however he wrote
generously about Sherborne, and 'A Public School in War-
time', 1916).   For publication in book form he wrote a
sequel to 'Some Modern Poets', 'More Modern Poets', in
which he quoted poems from three of his former pupils,
including Alec Waugh (pp. 117-28), and J.R. Ackerley
(pp. 109-12):   see No. 45.
   S.P.B. Mais published school textbooks, novels,
essays, and numerous travel books.

When Mr Marsh first collected the poems most represent-
ative of his age in 1912 he kindly provided the critic
with a beacon-light by quoting the following passage from
Lord Dunsany:

> Of all materials for labour, dreams are the hardest;
> and the artificer in ideas is the chief of workers, who
> out of nothing will make a piece of work that may stop
> a child from crying or lead nations to higher things.
> For what is it to be a poet? It is to see at a
> glance the glory of the world, to see beauty in all its
> forms and manifestations, to feel ugliness like a pain,
> to resent the wrongs of others as bitterly as one's
> own, to know mankind as others know single men, to know
> nature as botanists know a flower, to be thought a fool,
> to hear at moments the clear voice of God.

This brave venture appeared just at a time when there was
literally no sale whatever for poetry, when Richard
Middleton was driven to commit suicide because he could
make no headway in an age given over to materialism.   It
seemed that so far as the general public was concerned
poetry was at its nadir; the poet was, in Dunsany's
words, truly thought to be a fool; yet Mr Marsh persisted,
and, as we now know, took the tide on its turn; by May
1914 this slender volume had gone into its tenth edition:
poetry had come into its own again.
    Cambridge published its own productions in verse,
Oxford followed suit; quite normal citizens waited im-
patiently for fresh issues of 'New Numbers', so that they
might glut themselves with the poetry of Wilfrid Gibson,
Lascelles Abercrombie, and John Drinkwater; where
previously John Masefield alone had been able to create a
public for his long narrative poems, now every new poet
had a following, a coterie of devoted adherents.   Then
the War came, and with it the inevitable reaction.   A
writer of doggerel in one of the halfpenny papers welcomed
a new age of action which should cause us to turn aside
from this foolish cult of reading and making poetry; Mr
Birrell publicly announced that it would be as well to
give poetry the 'go-by' until after the War; publishers
found that money lay in war-books; only in 'The Times' did
the dying Muse dare to assert herself, and there rarely
with distinction; silence would have been a sweeter swan-
song; but with the passage of days the public became dis-
contented with 'Secrets of the Prussian Court': they longed
for some seductive writer who would carry them away from
the War and lure them back to an age when we were obsessed
by less weighty problems, back to a time when destruction

was not the world's united aim.   Reprints of the great
masterpieces began to sell again;   the modern novelist
returned to his old successful niche;   and now there has
come about a reaction even against the six-shilling novel.
Poetry which but a little time ago was shunned by every
canny publisher is now being sought by them eagerly;   it
is not really easy to discover why.

Most of us can, of course, understand the reason for
Rupert Brooke's enormous success;   he stood alone, above
his age, as one who expressed finally all its aims and
aspirations.   Everything about him attracted something
in each of us;   his brilliant intellect captivated some,
his ruthless realism others, his sense of beauty ensnared
the most perhaps, but his poetry lives as the epitome of
all our cravings and our strange perplexities;   we are
like blind children in the dark, and we cling to a
slightly stronger brother who can yet, for all that, give
voice to our agony:

> Who want and know not what we want and cry
> With crooked mouths for Heaven and throw it by.

There is no doubt, too, that the manner of his death en-
ticed the great public to start buying and even reading
his work.   But though he is the greatest, he is certain-
ly not the only poet whose works are selling.   We hear
that John Oxenham's 'Bees in Amber' and 'All's Well' have
quite outstripped his novels in circulation, that Miss
McLeod's 'Songs to Save a Soul' are having an immense
vogue, that Miss Elinor Jenkins has her thousands of
readers;   all our public and secondary school boys and
girls are reading with great keenness that splendid
collection of contemporary poetry brought out by Messrs
Sidgwick and Jackson at the instigation of the English
Association, entitled 'Poems of To-day'.   To these we have
now to add daily the songs of dead heroes of the type of
Charles Sorley, Colwyn Phillips, Evan Morgan, and count-
less others.

All these are signs that there is a very sure renasc-
ence of poetry in our midst, and it is worth trying to
find out what are the leading principles of its pioneers
and whether it is likely to be ephemeral or lasting.

We expect to find (and are not disappointed) all the
best traits and most characteristic results in Mr Marsh's
second volume of 'Georgian Poetry', which contains all the
work written between 1913 and 1915 which he was allowed
to reproduce and at the same time thought worthy of in-
clusion.   Taken in conjunction with his volume of three
years earlier the contrast is in some ways amazing.

Most of the present-day critics are loud in their prot-
estations against this new school: they say that in their
passionate revolt against the romantic movement they are
rapidly working into a groove of mechanical reaction;
that there is a danger lest their convention become only
a worse convention than that of the Victorians who drew
beauty for its own sake as if it were interesting quite
apart from what is made of it; worse in that the young
poet now draws ugliness for its own sake though it
neither points a moral nor adorns a tale.

This seems to be the one handle which the critic turns
unceasingly: Rupert Brooke was attacked for his realism
in 'Jealousy', 'Menelaus and Helen', 'A Channel Passage',
and innumerable other poems.   Even those who professed
themselves among his most fervid admirers exclaimed that
they could not bear the introduction of words like 'dirty'
and 'blear-eyed' into the middle of poems otherwise
beautiful.   What such people fail to realise is that in
his search for beauty the true poet must occasionally
find himself confronted by ugliness; he refuses to shut
his eyes to it; he knows it to be monstrous, unreason-
able, and yet almost a commonplace to less sensitive,
saner minds who can accustom themselves to the monstrous
and gradually become blind to it, in direct proportion as
they become blind to the beauty all around them; fear-
lessly he sets out to correlate it with his other vision,
and the result is to alienate men and women of weaker
stomachs who imagine that he dabbles in uncleanness
because he likes it.

In the first, and in some ways the greatest, poem in
this new volume, 'King Lear's Wife', Gordon Bottomley
has given such critics ground for complaint which they
have not been slow to take.

What right, they ask, has a poet to deduce that Lear
in his earlier life was wanton, callous to and neglect-
ful of his wife, making mistresses of her maidens?

They declare that this is a play of great beauty,
spoilt by hideous touches, notably by lyrics about lice,
which have nothing to do with the great Shakespearean
tragedy.   In point of fact, anyone who has for years
been troubled by the earlier play will recognise at once
how much the new one clears up the ground.   It is im-
possible to re-read 'King Lear' after finishing 'King
Lear's Wife' without noticing again and again points that
used to puzzle the imagination, now made perfectly plain.
Why did the old King, in his madness, burst forth into
that frenzied speech about adultery?   There was method
in his madness: there always is in Shakespeare's madness.
'This is not altogether fool, my Lord.'   His mind casts

back to some episode in his earlier days, to Gormflaith:

> Open your window when the moon is dead,
> And I will come again.
> The men say everywhere that you are faithless,
> The women say your face is a false face
> And your eyes shifty eyes.   Ah, but I love you,
>   Gormflaith.

The following passage sheds an entirely new light on the
relationship existing between Cordelia and her much older
sisters:

> Because a woman gives herself for ever,
> Cordeil the useless had to be conceived
> To keep her father from another woman.

Does it not help us in our differentiation between
Goneril and Regan that Goneril is here shown firm, wary,
swift and secret, the virgin huntress, harsh in her purity,
one lustful to kill but one who would kill cleanly, full
of contempt for her sister:

> Does Regan worship anywhere at dawn?
> The sweaty, half-clad cook-maids render lard
> Out in the scullery, after pig-killing,
> And Regan sidles among their greasy skirts,
> Smeary and hot as they, for craps to suck ...

She kills her father's mistress and so obtains an ascend-
ancy over him which she never after loses: 'I thought she
had been broken long ago', says Lear in his last speech.
'She must be wedded and broken; I cannot do it.'   What a
blaze of sudden light this throws on Goneril as we have
known her only in her later days.   We gained some insight
into Mr Gordon Bottomley's poetic vision in the earlier
volume, but in 'King Lear's Wife' he may, without hyperbole,
be said to have arrived.   Mr Marsh is not wrong when he
speaks of the honour which the author has done to the book
by allowing his play to be published for the first time
there.   All readers at once feel impatient on coming to
the end that they cannot at once rush out and see it acted.
     The quiet sadness of the neglected dying queen, the
savagery of Lear, the freshness of the cold Goneril, the
tragedy of Cordeil, the lullaby with which Hygd is hushed
to sleep:

> The owlets in roof holes Can sing for themselves;
> The smallest brown squirrel Both scampers and delves;
> But a baby does nothing - She never knows how -
> She must hark to her mother Who sings to her now;

the love-making of Gormflaith:

> It is a lonely thing to love a king,
> Life holds no more than this for me: this is my hour;

her singing in the garden:

> If you have a mind to kiss me,
> You shall kiss me in the dark:
> Yet rehearse, or you might miss me -
> Make my mouth your noontide mark:

these are only a few among the gems in the play that make
it stand out from contemporary plays of a like kind.
    No one would deny that there are ugly things here and
there, just as there are ugly things in life, but certain-
ly beauty predominates.   Goneril's worship on the hills
at dawn, raising up her 'shining hand in cold stern ador-
ation Even as the first great gleam went up the sky, '
her lament over the body of her mother:

> This is not death: death could not be like this ...
> I did not know death could come all at once.
> Come back: come back; the things I have not done
> Beat in upon my brain from every side ...
> If I could have you now I could act well ...
> My inward life, deeds that you have not known,
> I burn to tell you in a sudden dread
> That now your ghost discovers them in me:

all these are beautiful, beautiful not with an exotic
richness that hides its meaning under a magic rhythm, but
beautiful with the inevitable simplicity of the Anglo-
Saxon, monosyllabic yet haunting.   It is their very
directness, their terse, uncompromising, actual, every-
day speech that first attracts us in all these new writers.
Mr Bottomley does not strive to heighten his effect by the
introduction of the quaint or the remote: he is almost
Blake-like in his choice of phrases.   The result is that
he has written a play which will remain in the memory (in
spite of the weak machinery of the laying-out women which
we could well have spared) as long as any we have ever
read.   It is a fine achievement; not the least fine part
of its great attraction lying in that direct, straight-

forward simplicity, which is the keynote to the whole
volume.

Rupert Brooke occupies the second place of honour, and
we are here given valuable glimpses of his later develop-
ment.

In 'Tiare Tahiti' we find him rebelling once more
against the Paradise of the Wise: he is so much in love
with material beauty, 'Miri's laugh, Teipo's feet, and
the hands of Matua, Mamua, your lovelier head ...' that
he cannot reconcile himself to the idea that in another
life there might be richness of life without matter and
the individuality of matter:

> How shall we wind these wreaths of ours,
> Where there are neither heads nor flowers?

'There's little comfort in the wise', he concludes.   To
accentuate this point further we have here included 'The
Great Lover', in which the poet shows us his overpowering
passion for the beauty of the ordinary things of life:

> White plates and cups, clean-gleaming,
> Ringed with blue lines ... new-peeled sticks
> And shining pools on grass.

His great regret is that they cannot accompany him into
the life hereafter.   His scintillating wit is shown by
the inclusion of 'Heaven', in which the poet frames a
religion and a view of the Beyond for fish: a poem
compact of bitter, caustic irony relieved by an exquisite
humour.   One war sonnet and two more on the subject of
the after-life complete the extracts from the greatest
poet of our time: they are certainly representative, and
ought to drive anyone who has not yet read all Brooke's
work (if any such exist) to remedy this deficiency.   He
who has given expression to all the insatiable yearnings
of his age deserves not only its gratitude but its un-
dying love.

Mr William H. Davies is one of those contributors
whose work seems to me to have deteriorated with the
passing years: he is still the singer of the hedgerows:

> And I'll be dreaming of green lanes,
> Where little things with beating hearts
> Hold shining eyes between the leaves,
> Till men with horses pass, and carts.

He is just as charming and as naïvely simple as he used
to be, but there seems to be nothing behind it all; it

is beautiful but flimsy: it seems almost at times as if
he had exhausted his theme: only in

    Sweet Stay-at-Home, sweet Well-content,
    Sweet Stay-at-Home, sweet Love-one-place,

does the richness of the lilt satisfy us, and we are con-
tent for the moment to be without that philosophy which we
now all demand from those who would inspire us.

Mr Walter de la Mare is still master of that fairy
language that captivated us so surely in the previous
volume.   None of us has forgotten the charm of

    'Is there anybody there?' said the Traveller,
    Knocking on the moonlit door.

It is not likely that we shall soon forget 'The Mocking
Fairy' in the new volume:

    'Won't you look out of your window, Mrs Gill?'
    Quoth the Fairy, nidding, nodding, in the garden;

nor the delicate, fantastic joy in 'Off the Ground':

    Three jolly Farmers
    Once bet a pound
    Each dance the others would
    Off the ground....
    One - Two - Three!
    And away they go,
    Not too fast,
    And not too slow;

of their progress through

    Withy - Wellover -
    Wassop - Wo ...

until at last they reach the great green sea: whereupon
Farmer Turvey joins the mermaids and wins the bet.   Mr de
la Mare seems to make poetry for the pure delight of
rhyming, for the sheer ecstasy of hearing words bubble
like a mountain burn: the irresponsibility of childhood,
infant's happy laughter - these are the things that his
poetry brings back to us: we forget the scheme and order
of life, its myriad perplexities; we are content simply
to sit spell-bound and listen; here at least is happiness
of a sort.

John Drinkwater is a poet of very brilliant calibre.

He has certainly never before risen to the height that he
reaches in 'The Carver in Stone' of this volume: here
one may read exactly what is the impelling force that
guides the young genius of to-day: this Carver with eyes

> Grey, like the drift of twitch-fires blown in June,
> That, without fearing, searched if any wrong
> Might threaten from your heart,

is 'Every-poet' of the Georgian age: he is talking of
himself:

> Slowly out of the dark confusion, spread
> By life's innumerable venturings
> Over his brain, he would triumph into the light
> Of one clear mood, unblemished of the blind
> Legions of errant thought that cried about
> His rapt seclusion ...

Here we find ourselves again in the atmosphere of Rupert
Brooke: the sense of adventure, the sense of an eternal
yearning after self-expression, the brave attempt to
leave something behind us which will last long enough to
show those who shall come after that in spite of multi-
tudinous futilities there is much fine stuff inter-
mingled with the dross of the world if we could only see
it and transmute it into real metal: but the Carver can-
not bear the travesties which pass for sound workmanship
with the crowd:

> Figures of habit driven on the stone
> By chisels governed by no heat of the brain
> But drudges of hand that moved by easy rule.
> Proudly recorded mood was none, no thought
> Plucked from the dark battalions of the mind
> And throned in everlasting sight.

Worst of all are the critics, wise

> With words, weary of custom, and eyes askew
> That watched their neighbour face for any news
> Of the best way of judgment, till, each sure
> None would determine with authority,
> All spoke in prudent praise.

Sickened by the inanity of the judges, when he is bidden
to re-shape his chosen god along the walls of the temple
together with all his fellow-craftsmen, he seizes on the
idea of carving a queer, puff-bellied toad, with eyes

that always stared sidelong at heaven and saw no heaven
there;   this toad seemed to him to stand for an emblem of
his kings and priests;   he loathed the false work of his
colleagues that passed for true and so determined that
his truth should not be doomed to march among this false-
hood to the ages.   So he chose a secluded spot and there
fashioned his toad: and round it his people's gods,
tigers, bats and owls ... 'all signs of sightless thought
adventuring the host that is mere spirit';   his leopard
became 'fear in flight before accusing faith', his bull
bore 'the burden of the patient of the earth'.

> And other than the gods he made.   The stalks
> Of bluebells heavy with the news of spring, ...
> And all were deftly ordered, duly set ...
> Till on the wall, out of the sullen stone,
> A glory blazed, his vision manifest,
> His wonder captive.   And he was content.

In this poem we are made to feel all the wild unsatisfied
longings of the would-be creator, the ecstatic joy of him
who builds for eternity, the paean of triumph of the man
who has risen superior to all the little empty world of
critics and out of the crucible of his mind has formed
and perfected solid, substantial, lasting beauty.   It
stands as the victorious anthem of the poet of our era
whose hand has found at last something worthy to do and
is doing it with all his power, knowing full well that
he is building for eternity and in the serenity of his
might content with that.
    No more shall we hear the cry of the restless spirit
of Brooke, no more will the sweet, exotic flavour of
Flecker's Eastern poems lull our senses in these volumes:
of these two we take our farewell here, and deep indeed
is our regret.   Widely differing as these poets were,
they both attracted much the same lovers.   Who could
resist the metre of 'Yasmin'?

> But when the silver dove descends I find the little
>   flower of friends
> Whose very name that sweetly ends I say when I have
>   said, Yasmin.

Though perhaps it sounds a grotesque simile, the triple
rhyme in this metre strikes exactly the same chord as is
struck by the noise of a railway engine when it is start-
ing out of a station: it is attractive, though somehow
it ought to be ugly.   We hear the throb of the engine
again in 'The Gates of Damascus':

> The dragon-green, the luminous, the dark, the
>   serpent-haunted sea,
> The snow-besprinkled wine of earth, the white-
>   and-blue-flower foaming sea.

Unlike most of his school, Flecker relies for effect on
strange words and Oriental names; there is more of Keats
in his beauty than in most of his younger contemporaries.
As a master of metre and lyrical expression he stood high
among his companions, as can be seen in 'The Dying
Patriot':

> Noon strikes on England, noon on Oxford town,
> Beauty she was statue cold - there's blood upon her
>   gown;
> Noon of my dreams, O noon!
> Proud and goodly kings had built her, long ago,
> With her towers and tombs and statues all arow,
> With her fair and floral air and the love that lingers
>   there,
> And the streets where the great men go!

No more beautiful poem has been written since the War
began.   And now he can sing to us no more.   One more
apostle of beauty is lost to us just when we needed him
most.
   No one who had read 'The Hare' of Wilfrid Gibson in
1912 doubted but that he had a rare gift of dramatic
musical self-expression, but in 'Hoops' he has outgrown
any puerilities of which he might then have been just-
ifiably accused.   Here again we have the passionate
love of beauty, this time beauty of form, as desired by
a mis-stitched, gnarled, crooked stableman and odd-job
man attached to a travelling circus:

> I've always worshipped the body, all my life -
> The body, quick with the perfect health which is
>   beauty,
> Lively, lissom, alert ...
> The living God made manifest in man.

   Wilfrid Gibson seems to owe something of his easy coll-
oquial style in verse to Masefield's longer narrative
poems; he seems - alone in this book - to be carrying on
that tradition which threatened to become an obsession
amongst our poetasters before the War.   But Wilfrid
Gibson has something to say; he does 'see beauty in all
its forms and manifestations', he certainly does, more
almost than all the others, 'feel ugliness like a pain';

though he does not shut his eyes to it, as all those who have read his short volume of War poems know.

Ralph Hodgson is a newcomer: and all true lovers of poetry will welcome him with open arms: for he has come to stay.   'Time, you old gypsy man', we regret to see is not included in this volume: but that, after all, is obtainable in 'Poems of To-day'. We certainly could not spare either of the two of his poems which are included. Many people prefer 'The Bull' to anything in the book. It is a wonderful piece of realism; the beauty and horror of the jungle permeate every line: the whole poem is throbbing with life: it reads almost, as someone has said, as if it were written by one bull about another: we seem actually to see him,

> Standing with his head hung down
> In a stupor, dreaming things;
> Green savannas, jungles brown,
> Battlefields and bellowings,
> Bulls undone and lions dead
> And vultures flapping overhead.
> Dreaming things: of days he spent
> With his mother gaunt and lean
> In the valley warm and green,
> Full of baby wonderment
> Blinking out of silly eyes
> At a hundred mysteries.

... and now he is deserted, dying ... and has to turn

> From his visionary herds
> And his splendid yesterday,
> Turns to meet the loathly birds
> Flocking round him from the skies,
> Waiting for the flesh that dies.

Ralph Hodgson more than fulfils Lord Dunsany's definition of a poet, for he does more than know mankind as others know single men, he seems to know the world of beasts better than most of us know single men.

But there are sure to be some to whom this poem will come as a *tour de force*: they will acknowledge its beauty of finish, the perfect workmanship that went to the making of it, but they will deny that such a subject is the end and aim of poetry.   Let such readers turn to 'The Song of Honour'; there will they find a universal hymn of thankfulness from all the world that should be sung on the hill-tops by every lover of Nature; it is the hosanna of all created things:

The song of each and all who gaze
On Beauty in her naked blaze,
Or see her dimly in a haze....
The song of all not wholly dark,
Not wholly sunk in stupor stark
Too deep for groping Heaven.

All the songs that ever man sang are grouped together
here and poured out in one glorious medley, the song of
every singing bird, of poets, painters, wise men, beggars,
of men who face a hopeless hill with sparkling and delight,
of sailors, fighters, lovers, of men whose love of mother-
land is like a dog's for one dear hand, sole, selfless,
boundless, blind:

The song of men all sorts and kinds,
As many tempers, moods and minds
As leaves are on a tree.

It places Mr Hodgson among those rare singers who uplift
us and put new courage in our hearts by reason of their
sublime joyfulness; we forget the real genius of his
lyricism in the sheer unreasoning abandon of his theme.
He makes us too want to cry out with thankfulness for
being alive.
    Mr D.H. Lawrence is a poet of rigidity: some years ago
he wrote some beautiful verses on 'A Schoolmaster'; since
then he has been cursed with an obsession of sex which has
threatened to destroy his equipoise; he still achieves
beauty at intervals, but there is an undercurrent of mor-
bidity which disturbs the whole true current of his art.
You see it most plainly here in 'Cruelty and Love': some-
how he always leaves us with a sense that Lust is at the
back of both his Cruelty and his Love: it is too fleshly
altogether: 'He caresses my mouth with his fingers,
smelling grim Of the rabbit's fur.'   The girl talks of
her lover 'nosing like a stoat Who sniffs with joy before
he drinks the blood'.   It isn't that it is not nice; it
is much worse than that: it is not artistically true.
That such things happen in isolated cases does not justify
a man portraying it as if it were a universal tendency
among lovers: it is the more distressing because in Mr
Lawrence we have a great novelist and a real poet losing
himself in the meshes of a foolish obsession.
    Mr Francis Ledwidge is the other newcomer: he sings
sweetly, cleanly and surely on 'A Rainy Day in April'.
He is the singer of the open fields and may (we hope he
will) carry on the tradition of the Mr Davies we used to
know.

The only selection from Mr Masefield is not really
typical of the last two years' work done by him, but it
was the only one at the disposal of the Editor.   Probably
all of us would have preferred 'August 1914' to 'The
Wanderer'.   Still, in some sense, the poem only goes to
prove more conclusively than ever how radically wrong are
those critics who imagine that these realist poets of ours
are not just as desperately serious in their search for
beauty as the most romantic amongst us.

The theme of the poem is the same as that which runs
through nearly all Mr Masefield's poetry - the power of
beauty, the blindness of fate:

Blind pieces in a mighty game we swing:
Life's battle is a conquest for the strong;
The meaning shows in the defeated thing.

There is the same true workmanship and perfect execution
that characterises most of his work, but in some ways he
seems outside the scope of this book;   probably it is
because we were reading his 'Poems and Ballads' twelve
years ago, and all these other men are more or less new
to us.   One of the few precious cameos of a trifling
nature which this book contains is called 'Milk for the
Cat', by Harold Monro;   it is rather open to question
whether such a poem is quite worthy of inclusion: it is
certainly a miracle of description, but it is, after all,
a fantastic trifle, and as such seems to quite a
number of people to be out of place.   On the other hand,
the theme of 'Children of Love' (the infant Christ and
the child Cupid) is most delicately handled, and is one
of the many really beautifully conceived ideas in the
volume.

The criticism which we applied to Mr W.H. Davies
applies almost equally to Mr James Stephens;   we all
went into rhapsodies over 'The Crock of Gold' and over
parts of 'Here are Ladies', but his art was too precious
to be roughly handled;   somehow he seems to have lost for
the moment his faery touch, his glorious sense of humour;
much the same has happened to his verse: there was in-
finitely more real poetry in his contribution to the 1912
volume than there can be said to be in the present one;
he has melody and facility;   he is in touch with Nature
himself, but he is unable to make us realise quite how
Nature affects him;   his simplicity makes the poverty
underlying his words more than ever evident: there is
not enough reality to make us love him, probably because
we in our overburdened lives have somehow got past that
childish ingenuousness and cannot tolerate it any longer;

so many of us have had to grow up in the last two or
three years.

The volume ends, as it begins, with a play: Mr
Lascelles Abercrombie's 'The End of the World'.   Let it
be granted at once that there will be endless discussions
as to which is the greater of the two, Mr Bottomley's or
Mr Abercrombie's; for the moment it is sufficient to say
that they are both good enough to make us glad to live in
an age both great and courageous enough to produce them.

The plot of 'The End of the World' is quite simple.
The scene is an ale-house kitchen; a stranger comes in
full of news to the assembled drinkers, news which they
attempt to drag from him by various means.   He tries to
convey to them his state of mind:

> I wonder, did you ever hate to feel
> The earth so fine and splendid?

They come to the conclusion that he is mad:

> Yes, I was mad, and crying mad, to see
> The earth so fine, fine all for nothing;

he then opens the door and shows them a comet in the sky;
he says that that means the end of the world; they are
about to be burnt up:

> And time shall brush the fields as visibly
> As a rough hand brushes against the nap
> Of gleaming cloth - killing the season's colour ...
> And sailors panting on their warping decks
> Will watch the sea steam like broth about them.

The publican wishes he had his old wife with him:

> This would have suited her.
> 'I do like things to happen!' she would say,
> Never shindy enough for her; and now
> She's gone, and can't be seeing this!

Each man takes the news differently, and calls down the
derision of the dowser on their original scepticism:

> Ay, you begin to feel it now, I think;
>   ...   But Life, ...
> Life with her skill of a.million years' perfection, ...
> Of sunlight, and of clouds about the moon,
> Spring lighting her daffodils...
> And mountains sitting in their purple clothes -
> O life I am thinking of, life the wonder,
> All blotcht out by a brutal thrust of fire
> Like a midge that a clumsy thumb squashes and smears.

Huff the farmer seizes the occasion to gloat over the
faithlessness of his wife: now at least he will see
vengeance.   The man with whom his wife ran away comes in,
and Huff attempts to make him cower, but to no purpose,
and the curtain rings down on Act I, leaving the dowser
alone bemoaning the intolerable waste of beauty that all
this scorching of the world will bring about.

On the rise of the curtain for the second and last Act
we see Sollers, the wainwright, wrecking the ale-house
room in a frenzy of apprehension; the publican comes in
weeping, 'I've seen the moon; it has nigh broke my
heart ... I never before so noted her.'   Beauty at last
is beginning to mean something to him now that it is all
about to be smashed up and ruined.   Merrick, the smith,
begins to achieve a philosophy; he begins to find a
meaning in the life which is just slipping past him:

> You know, this is much more than being happy.
> 'Tis hunger of some power in you, that lives
> On your heart's welcome for all sorts of luck,
> But always looks beyond you for its meaning. ...
> The world was always looking to use its life
> In some great handsome way at last.   And now -
> We are just fooled ...   I've had my turn.
> The world may be for the sake of naught at last,
> But it has been for my sake: I've had that.

Huff comes in, moody, unable to find comfort in the ven-
geance he thought to obtain from the panic-stricken evil-
doers: his good, straight life has been like that of a
crawling caterpillar ... he thinks of a day long past in
Droitwich where he saw women half-naked cooking brine ...
he could have been daring once but missed his chance:
suddenly Shale, his wife's lover, comes in and implores
Huff to take his wife back: Warp, the molecatcher, enters
during the scene that follows and tells them that there is
nothing to fear: the comet is going away from them:
Huff's ricks are alight, certainly, but there is to be no
end of the world - yet.

Mrs Huff turns both from her lover and her husband:

> They thinking I'ld be near one or the other
> After this night.

We are left with Vine moaning:

> But is it certain there'll be nothing smasht?
> Not even a house knockt roaring down in crumbles?
> - And I did think, I'ld open my wife's mouth
> With envy of the dreadful things I'd seen!

There is no doubt about the fascination of the play: it
holds the reader's attention throughout: there is not a
false note from beginning to end.   It contains all the
philosophy of the younger school: the unending search
after beauty, the refusal to shut the eyes to ugliness
and dirt, the endeavour to find a meaning in life, the
determination to live life to the full and to enjoy.   At
all costs they strive to avoid sentimentality: these
country folk in 'The End of the World' really love: they
may be coarse: they certainly have their tragedies, but
they are human.   We seem to know them through and
through: we certainly sympathise with their trials and
resent their wrongs as bitterly as we do our own.

This noble volume is intensely typical of the age:
everything is tentative, experimental: we are no longer
satisfied with the old gods, the old ideals: we set out
to prove all things and get most horribly hurt in doing
it; but life becomes much more of an adventure: we are
at least brave enough to cut ourselves adrift from the
old, safe, enclosed harbourage: we make many and gross
mistakes, but we do achieve something: we begin to
learn for ourselves what life really means and are not
content to let our elders tell us what they think it
ought to mean.

It means beauty to start with: and that is an almost
new thought: at any rate beauty has to be found by each
individual soul at the cost of much sorrow of heart and
much unfortunate experience with the ugly: it means
love, which is not so easily to be found as our fore-
fathers seem to have thought: we are not to be put off
with shams ... it means courage, and courage is not to
be cultivated in safety, in an armchair: we have to cut
adrift, away from convention and laws made for a milk-
livered generation.   'Georgian Poetry 1913-1915' is a
brave book: it is the standard of revolt of the younger,
braver souls among us, and we who are apt at times to
acquiesce because it is easier, owe much to a book which
strengthens and fortifies our resolution just when we
show signs of wavering.   Our poets are our real national
leaders; they alone can express all those desires which
we feel but are unable to articulate; if our poets are
false to us then indeed are we decadent: from 1913 to
1915 at any rate we may be thankful that they have led us
fearlessly, put fresh vitality and renewed energy into
our hopes, and helped us once more to try to wrest life's
secret from her.

23.   'GEORGIAN BARDS AND VICTORIAN REVIEWERS', 'PUNCH'

15 November 1916, 353

Unsigned parody of Byron's 'English Bards, and Scotch
Reviewers' (1809).
   It may seem strange after the passage of years to hear
the spirits of Browning, Swinburne, Tennyson, and Rossetti
invoked to hurl curses on the 'Georgy-Porgians', and to
deny them - 'if only for two days' - their contemporary
acclaim.   So many talented versifiers have contributed
to 'Punch' that it would perhaps be foolish to try to
assign these lines to any one of them;   but Edmund Gosse,
who was also a poet, was to comment a year later on the
absence of 'the influence of Tennyson, Browning, Swin-
burne and Rossetti' (No. 26).

Some of our Georgians view the old Victorians
Just as so many pre-historic Saurians
Whose skeletons, most formidably gaunt,
The draughtiest courts of our Museums haunt.
I sometimes wonder, were the tables turned
And the Victorian idols (lately burned)
Restored in their full vigour to our view,
What would they say about the Georgian crew?
Can't you imagine ROBERT, nobly harsh,
Comparing poets of the Lakes and Marsh;
Or ALGERNON, hurling corrosive curses
At the new metreless and rhymeless verses;
Or ALFRED, in a later 'Locksley Hall',
Scourging the Realists who rave and squall;
Or DANTE GABRIEL writing Limericks
Upon our literary Cubists' tricks?
It wouldn't *all* be censure - that I'll swear,
For men of genius sometimes have a *flair*,
And BROWNING spotted talent ev'rywhere.
But it might do the Georgy-Porgians good
To hear their strident claims for once withstood,
And go without - if only for two days -
Their usual diet of 'the pap of praise'.

24.   J.C. SQUIRE, 'THE NEW STATESMAN'

31 March 1917, 617

'Solomon Eagle' (J.C. Squire) reviews 'An Annual of New
Poetry' in 'The New Statesman'·

   The resemblance of R.C. Trevelyan's 'An Annual of New
Poetry' to 'Georgian Poetry' was noted by a number of
reviewers (see also 'The Times Literary Supplement', 29
March 1917, 151).   Squire's unfavourable comparison of
it with the Georgian anthologies should be read both for
its comments on some of the common contributors and its
welcome of 'Edward Eastaway' (Edward Thomas) who was not
included in the Marsh anthologies (see headnote to No. 4).
The remarks about Thomas's friend, Robert Frost, are the
more unfortunate.

   For a note on R.C. Trevelyan see Appendix, p. 415.

The first issue of 'An Annual of New Poetry' has just been
published at 5s. net by Constable's.   The contributors
are Gordon Bottomley, W.H. Davies, John Drinkwater,
Edward Eastaway, Robert Frost, W.W. Gibson, T. Sturge
Moore, and R.C. Trevelyan.   Most of these writers have
contributed to the two books of 'Georgian Poetry', which
will, presumably, be followed by a third and a fourth;
and one's first thought is that the overlapping will be
inconvenient unless the rate at which good new verse is
produced is speeded up.   After reading the volume, how-
ever, one feels that the editor of the Georgian books has
not lost much by missing the chance of publishing in his
miscellany the works now presented to the public.

   Several of the authors represented have done good work,
and will again.   But neither Mr Gordon Bottomley nor Mr
Davies is at his best here, and Mr Sturge Moore's 'Micah',
though in places it has the vividness and the grave music
characteristic of his verse, is not, to put it bluntly,
uniformly interesting.   The best of Mr Bottomley's lyrics
is 'The Ploughman', in which he reflects on the number of
times he has seen the ploughman, on the fell, leaving
'man's tide-mark' on ridge after ridge and turning 'the
hard grey soil to brown'·   But certain stanzas about the
passage of time cannot but remind one that the same thing
has been very much better done in the Shropshire Lad's
poem about the cherry trees.   Mr R.C. Trevelyan's Indian
mythological play 'The Pearl Tree', on the other hand, is

one of the best things of his that I have seen.   All
sorts of things can be said against it.   The language is
thin, and the rhythms commonplace; but the author has
seen very clearly the things he is describing, and his
very indifference to the details of craftsmanship allows
him to move rapidly with his 'story'.   He has a vigorous
imagination, but lacks artistic gifts which are possessed
by many people with no imaginations at all.
    Mr Gibson, Mr Drinkwater, and Mr Frost, I admit, I
never have liked; and like here less than ever.   Mr
Gibson habitually writes prose-sketches in verse.   They
are the sort of prose-sketches that weekly papers used to
print before the war.   You take a pathetic figure,
usually a poor old man (the Lloyd George of the Old Age
Pensions period would have been a good hand at this), and
describe his poverty, his grey hairs, his loneliness and
his memories of sweeter things.   I don't suggest that
this kind of subject is outside the artist's province; I
merely suggest that there is almost a formula for doing
it, and that in any case it might as well be done in prose
as in the sort of banal foot-rule verse Mr Gibson does it
in.   One of his present batch of novelettes has an odd
scene.   A (poor old) man goes to a peer's country house
to mend the china, is received by the butler, and is in-
formed that his lordship 'won't require no more crocks
riveted or mended till the war is over' - which sentence,
though you may not think it, is a passage of 'rhymed
verse', and illustrates perfectly the way in which this
author habitually misplaces his accents.   The scene does
not appear to me, in any of its details, very convincing,
even in war-time.   Mr Drinkwater's verse, like Mr
Gibson's, shows him to be a good man, a sensitive man, and
an idealist; but he is usually an uninspired and un-
inspiring poet.   He can give his work a certain polish;
but you might as well have honest deal as pitchpine.   As
for Mr Robert Frost, one really must protest against this
effort to impose dull American poets upon us when we can
produce such people so easily ourselves.   I have no room
here to print one of his poems at length; I don't know
that I should do so even if I had.   His defects include
almost every possible defect except obscurity; but, in a
poem at all events, intelligibility is a poor substitute
for intelligence.
    The one poet whose contributions make this book really
worth having is Mr Edward Eastaway.   This name is a
pseudonym; I happen to be aware that it conceals the
identity of a man who has written large numbers of prose-
works; but as it appears to be his wish to remain pseud-
onymous, I leave it for someone else to strip off the

disguise. One's knowledge did not prepossess one in favour of his poetry; one did not think that a real gift for verse could remain so long unexploited without becoming atrophied. But the unlikely has happened; and his poems are better than his prose, good though some of this has been. There are not enough of them here to give an exact notion of his power and his limitations. But 'The Wood', 'Aspens', 'The Brook', 'Wind and Mist', and 'For These' would, by themselves, be enough to show that he is worth fifty Frosts. His verse does not sing, and it never shouts; yet the absence of music in the words is compensated for by a sort of music of the mind. He seizes a moment's mood, and gives it with all the circumstances that lead to it and the ripples it leaves behind it; and if you find his moods monotonous he gives his answer in the last stanza of 'Aspens':

> All day and night, save winter, every weather,
> Above the inn, the smithy and the shop,
> The aspens at the cross-roads talk together
> Of rain, until their last leaves fall from the top.
>
> Out of the blacksmith's cavern comes the ringing
> Of hammer, shoe and anvil; out of the inn
> The clink, the hum, the roar, the random singing,
> The sounds that for these fifty years have been.
>
> Whatever wind blows, while they and I have leaves
> We cannot other than an aspen be
> That ceaselessly, unreasonably grieves,
> Or so men think who like a different tree.

One of the best of his poems is 'Wind and Mist', in which a man describes a house that he used to occupy on the edge of the downs, and on winter days it was like being on a cliff's edge above a gulf of mist. I hear that the author (who is now in the army in France) intends shortly to issue a volume of his own. If they are as interesting as those given here they will give him his place among contemporary poets at once.

25. 'REFLECTIONS ON CONTEMPORARY POETRY', T.S. E[LIOT].,
'THE EGOIST'

September 1917, 118-19

_____

T.S. Eliot reflects on Wordsworth, the Georgians and
Harold Monro in particular in 'The Egoist'.
    It is with regret that the original versions of T.S.
Eliot's two articles in 'The Egoist' (see also No. 30)
have been omitted.   Unfortunately, Mrs Eliot, who is
collecting her late husband's early reviews, has felt
unable to allow their prior republication here.   Their
importance to the Georgian debate will be evident even
from the lame paraphrases which replace them.   Copies of
'The Egoist', either in the original or in the six-volume
reprint by the Kraus Reprint Corporation of New York, are,
however, widely available.
    T.S. Eliot (1888-1965) had recently succeeded Richard
Aldington as assistant editor of 'The Egoist' (see Intro-
duction, pp. 32 and 33).   The immediate occasion for
his first article was the publication of Harold Monro's
'Strange Meetings' (1917), although he does not refer to
the book until the final paragraph.

_____

Contemporary verse in trying to escape the rhetorical and
to recover the accents of speech has concentrated on the
trivial and accidental.   Eliot distinguishes 'American'
and 'English' currents in this tendency.   Whereas the
American (perhaps influenced by the Russian novel) is pre-
occupied with the accidental, the English (which is
insular and borrows little from abroad) is preoccupied
with the trivial: 'The Georgian poets insist upon the
English countryside, and are even positively patriotic'.
Thus they turn to the common object, 'animal or flower or
hearthrug', in the mood, not of Dostoevsky, but of Words-
worth.   Whereas Donne expresses a definitely human
emotion in his 'subtle wreath of hair' and the 'bracelet
of bright hair about the bone', preserving the balance
between the feeling and the material symbol, Wordsworth's
'meanest flower that blows' emphasizes the importance of
the flower for its own sake.
    Likewise with the Georgians emotion is derived from the
object, and 'must either be vague (as in Wordsworth) or,
if more definite, pleasing.'   Eliot remarks on the fre-
quency with which the word 'little' appears in contemporary

verse, giving instances from Brooke ('Grantchester' and
'Heaven'), James Stephens ('The Snare'), Monro ('Milk for
the Cat'), and Ralph Hodgson ('The Bull'), all but the
first of these from the second Georgian anthology.
(Richard Aldington was to take up this cue: 'The Georg-
ians were regional in their outlook and in love with
littleness.   They took a little trip for a little week-
end to a little cottage where they wrote a little poem on
a little theme': 'Life for Life's Sake', 1941, 110.)
Eliot then quotes eight lines from W.H. Davies's 'A Great
Time' (also from this anthology), and finds it a typical
and 'most charming' example of the type.   Both this poem
and Davies's 'The Kingfisher' are related to Wordsworth.
But Georgian love of nature is less vague than Words-
worth's, and has less philosophy behind it; the Georgian
has often more in common with Stevenson.   Eliot shows
how 'the modern poet, when he diverts his attention from
birds, fields, and villages, is subject to lapses of
rhetoric from which Wordsworth ..... is comparatively
free'.   Brooke again provides an example.   In 'The Fish'
after 'a number of lines which show a really amazing fel-
icity and command of language', he descends to:

   O world of lips, O world of laughter,
   Where hope is fleet and thought flies after ... -

'retrieved happily by another fine passage at the end.'
   Monro's vocabulary is 'less rich, less astonishing'
than Brooke's, but also less rhetorical.   He is less
literary, less the Little-Englander than other Georgians.
His 'consistent effort has been to express the strangeness
of familiar objects and "meetings"'.   Eliot concludes:
'Perhaps it is one sign of ..... weakness that I cannot
select any poems from this book as of particular excell-
ence; but the book as a whole makes a more complete im-
pression than any but a very few of recent years.'

26.   'SOME SOLDIER POETS', EDMUND GOSSE,
'THE EDINBURGH REVIEW'

October 1917, 296-316

Edmund Gosse reviews seven books of war poems.
   Although not strictly a review of 'Georgian Poetry' as

such, the opening paragraphs survey the Georgian scene,
and five of the poets noticed (Brooke, Baring, Nichols,
Graves, Sassoon) were contributors to the anthologies.
Paragraphs on Lord Desborough's memorial volume to his
son, Julian Grenfell, who wrote 'Into Battle' on hearing
of Brooke's death, and on E. Wyndham Tennant's 'Worple
Flat and Other Poems', have been omitted.

While noting 'some evidence of a Rupert Brooke legend
in the process of formation', and warning of its danger
in misinterpreting Brooke's mind and character, Gosse in
some part contributes to that legend.   Contemporaries
seemed unable to write about Brooke without reference to
'gold', whether of hair or poetry.   Even his friend
Lascelles Abercrombie concluded an article on 'The War
and the Poets':   ' ..... with Rupert Brooke's sonnets, we
may say that no other war in our whole history has been
instantly transmuted into poetry of purer gold' ('Quart-
erly Review', October 1915, 414).

Charles Hamilton Sorley (1895-1915), who is referred
to in the penultimate paragraph, was thought by Masefield
(and by others since) the most promising of the war poets.
A Marlburian like Sassoon, he enlisted in the Suffolk
Regiment in August 1914, and was promoted captain two
months before his death on 13 October 1915 during the
Battle of Loos.   His 'Marlborough and Other Poems' (1916)
and his 'Letters' (1919) were edited by his father, who
was Professor of Philosophy at Cambridge.   (See John H.
Johnson, 'English Poetry of the First World War', 1964,
53-70.)

For a note on Edmund Gosse see headnote to No. 7.
See also Introduction, pp. 13-14.

The two years which preceded the outbreak of the war were
marked in this country by a revival of public interest in
the art of poetry.   To this movement coherence was given
and organisation introduced by Mr Edward Marsh's now-
famous volume entitled 'Georgian Poetry'.   The effect of
this collection - for it is hardly correct to call it an
anthology - of the best poems written by the youngest
poets since 1911 was two-fold: it acquainted readers
with work few had the 'leisure or the zeal to investig-
ate', and it brought the writers themselves together in
a corporate and selected relation.   I do not recollect
that this had been done - except prematurely and part-
ially by 'The Germ' of 1850 - since the 'England's Parnas-
sus' and 'England's Helicon' of 1600.   In point of fact
the only real precursor of Mr Marsh's venture in our whole

literature is the 'Songs and Sonnettes' of 1557, commonly
known as 'Tottel's Miscellany'.   Tottel brought together,
for the first time, the lyrics of Wyatt, Surrey, Church-
yard, Vaux, and Bryan, exactly as Mr Marsh called public
attention to Rupert Brooke, James Elroy Flecker and the
rest of the Georgians, and he thereby fixed the names of
those poets, as Mr Marsh has fixed those of our youngest
fledglings, on the roll of English literature.

The general tone of the latest poetry, up to the
moment of the outbreak of hostilities, was pensive;
instinct with natural piety, given somewhat in excess to
description of landscape, tender in feeling, essentially
unaggressive except towards the clergy and towards other
versifiers of an earlier generation.   There was absolute-
ly not a trace in any one of the young poets of that arro-
gance and vociferous defiance which marked German verse
during the same years.   These English shepherds might hit
at their elders with their staves, but they had turned
their swords into pruning-hooks and had no scabbards to
rattle.   This is a point which might have attracted
notice, if we had not all been too drowsy in the lap of
our imperial prosperity to observe the signs of the times
in Berlin.   Why did no one call our attention to the
beating of the big drum which was going on so briskly on
the Teutonic Parnassus?   At all events, there was no echo
of such a noise in the 'chambers of imagery' which con-
tained Mr Gordon Bottomley, or in Mr W.H. Davies's wander-
ing 'songs of joy', or on 'the great hills and solemn
chanting seas' where Mr John Drinkwater waited for the
advent of beauty.   And the guns of August 1914 found Mr
W.W. Gibson encompassed by 'one dim, blue infinity of
starry peace'.   There is a sort of German 'Georgian Poets'
in existence;   in time to come a comparison of its pages
with those of Mr Marsh may throw a side-light on the
question, Who prepared the War?

The youngest poets were more completely taken by sur-
prise in August 1914 than their elders.   The earliest
expressions of lyric military feeling came from veteran
voices.   It was only proper that the earliest of all
should be the Poet Laureate's address to England, ending
with the prophecy:

　　Much suffering shall cleanse thee!
　　But thou through the flood
　　Shalt win to Salvation,
　　To Beauty through blood.

As sensation, however, followed sensation in those first
terrific and bewildering weeks, much was happening that

called forth with the utmost exuberance the primal
emotions of mankind;   there was full occasion for

>   exultations, agonies,
>   And love, and man's unconquerable mind.

By September, a full chorus was vocal, led by our national
veteran, Mr Thomas Hardy, with his 'Song of the Soldiers':

> What of the faith and fire within us,
> Men who march away
> Ere the barn-cocks say
> Night is growing gray,
>
> To hazards whence no tears can win us;
> What of the faith and fire within us,
> Men who march away?

Already, before the close of the autumn of 1914, four or
five anthologies of war-poems were in the press, and the
desire of the general public to be fed with patriotic and
emotional verse was manifested in unmistakable ways.   We
had been accustomed for some time past to the issue of a
multitude of little pamphlets of verse, often very care-
fully written, and these the critics had treated with an
indulgence which would have whitened the hair of the
stern reviewers of forty years ago.   The youthful poets,
almost a trade-union in themselves, protected one another
by their sedulous generosity.   It was very unusual to
see anything criticised, much less 'slated';   the balms
of praise were poured over every rising head, and im-
mortalities were predicted by the dozen.   Yet, as a rule,
the sale of these little poetic pamphlets had been small,
and they had been read only by those who had a definite
object in doing so.
The immediate success of the anthologies, however,
proved that the war had aroused in a new public an ear
for contemporary verse, an attention anxious to be stirred
or soothed by the assiduous company of poets who had been
ripening their talents in a little clan.   These had now
an eager world ready to listen to them.   The result had
been surprising;   we may even, without exaggeration, call
it unparalleled.   There has never before, in the world's
history, been an epoch which has tolerated and even wel-
comed such a flood of verse as has been poured forth over
Great Britain during the last three years.   These years
have seen the publication, as I am credibly informed, of
more than five hundred volumes of new and original poetry.
It would be the silliest complaisance to pretend that all
of this, or much of it, or any but a very little of it,

has been of permanent value.   Much of it is windy and
superficial, striving in wild vague terms to express
great agitations which are obscurely felt by the poet.
There was too much of the bathos of rhetoric, especially
at first;   too much addressing the German as 'thou fell,
bloody brute', and the like, which broke no bones and
took no trenches.

When once it was understood that, as a cancelled line
in Tennyson's 'Maud' has it,

The long, long canker of peace was over and done,

the sentiments of indignation and horror made themselves
felt with considerable vivacity.   In this direction,
however, none of the youngest poets approached Sir Owen
Seaman in the vigour of their invective.   Most of them
seemed to be overpowered by the political situation, and
few could free themselves from their inured pacific
habit of speech.   Even when they wrote of Belgium, the
Muse seemed rather to weep than to curse.   Looking back
to the winter of 1914, it is almost pathetic to observe
how difficult it was for our easy-going British bards to
hate the Germans.   There was a good deal of ineffective
violence, and considerable misuse of technical terms,
caused, in many cases, by a too hasty reference to news-
paper reports of gallantry under danger, in the course
of which the more or less obscure verbiage of military
science was picturesquely and inaccurately employed.   As
the slightly censorious reader looks back upon these
poems of the beginning of the war, he cannot resist a
certain impatience.   In the first place, there is a
family likeness which makes it impossible to distinguish
one writer from another, and there is a tendency to a
smug approval of British prejudice, and to a horrible
confidence in England's power of 'muddling through',
which look rather ghastly in the light of the autumn of
1917.

There was, however, a new spirit presently apparent,
and a much healthier one.   The bards became soldiers,
and in crossing over to France and Flanders, each had
packed his flute in his kit.   They began to send home
verses in which they translated into music their actual
experiences and their authentic emotions.   We found our-
selves listening to young men who had something new, and
what was better, something noble to say to us, and we
returned to the national spirit which inspired the
Chansons de Geste in the eleventh century.   To the
spirit - but not in the least to the form, since it is
curious that the war-poetry of 1914-17 is, even in the

most skilful hands, poetry on a small scale.   The two
greatest of the primal species of verse, the Epic and the
Ode, have been entirely neglected, except, as will later
be observed, in one notable instance by Major Maurice
Baring.   As a rule, the poets have constrained them-
selves to observe the discipline of a rather confined
lyrical analysis in forms of the simplest character.
Although particular examples have shown a rare felicity
of touch, and although the sincerity of the reflection
has in many cases hit upon very happy forms of expression,
it is impossible to overlook the general monotony.   There
used to be a story that the Japanese Government sent a
committee of its best art-critics to study the relative
merits of the modern European painters, and that they
returned with the bewildered statement that they could
make no report, because all European pictures were ex-
actly alike.   A student from Patagonia might conceivably
argue that he could discover no difference whatever
between our various poets of the war.

This would be unjust, but it is perhaps not unfair to
suggest that the determined resistance to all restraint,
which has marked the latest school, is not really favour-
able to individuality.   There has been a very general,
almost a universal tendency to throw off the shackles of
poetic form.   It has been supposed that by abandoning
the normal restraints or artificialities, of metre and
rhyme, a greater directness and fidelity would be
secured.   Of course, if an intensified journalistic im-
pression is all that is desired, 'prose cut up into
lengths' is the readiest by-way to effect.   But if the
poets desire - and they all do desire - to speak to ages
yet unborn, they should not forget that all the exper-
ience of history goes to prove discipline not unfavour-
able to poetic sincerity, while, on the other hand, the
absence of all restraint is fatal to it.   Inspiration
does not willingly attend upon flagging metre and dis-
cordant rhyme, and never in the whole choral progress
from Pindar down to Swinburne has a great master been
found who did not exult in the stubbornness of 'dancing
words and speaking strings', or who did not find his joy
in reducing them to harmony.   The artist who avoids all
difficulties may be pleased with the rapidity of his
effect, but he will have the vexation of finding his succ-
ess an ephemeral one.   The old advice to the poet, in
preparing the rich chariot of the Muse, still holds good:

Let the postillion, Nature, mount, but let
The coachman, Art, be set.

Too many of our recent rebellious bards fancy that the
coach will drive itself, if only the post-boy sticks his
heels hard into Pegasus.

It is not, however, the object of this essay to review
all the poetry which has been written about the war, not
even that part of it which has owed its existence to the
strong feeling of non-combatants at home.   We rather
propose to fix our attention on what has been written by
the young soldiers themselves in their beautiful gall-
antry, verse which comes to us hallowed by the glorious
effort of battle, and in too many poignant cases by the
ultimate sacrifice of life itself.   The poet achieves
his highest meed of contemporary glory, if

> some brave young man's untimely fate
> In words worth dying for he celebrate,

and when he is himself a young man striving for the same
deathless honour on the same field of blood it is diff-
icult to conceive of circumstances more poignant than
those which surround his effort.   On many of these poets
a death of the highest nobility has set the seal of eter-
nal life.   They were simple and passionate, radiant and
calm, they fought for their country, and they have enter-
ed into glory.   This alone might be enough to say in
their praise, but star differeth from star in brightness,
and from the constellation we propose to select half a
dozen of the clearest luminaries.   What is said in hon-
est praise of these may be said, with due modification,
of many others who miss merely the polish of their
accomplishment.   It is perhaps worth noticing, in pass-
ing, that most of the poets are men of university train-
ing, and that certain literary strains are common to the
rank and file of them.   The influence of Tennyson,
Browning, Swinburne, and Rossetti is almost entirely ab-
sent.   The only one of the great Victorians whom they
seem to have read is Matthew Arnold, but it is impossible
to help observing that the 'Shropshire Lad' of Mr A.E.
Housman has been in the tunic-pocket of every one of
them.   Among the English poets of the past it is mainly
the so-called 'metaphysical' writers in the seventeenth
century whom they have studied;   Donne seems to have been
a favourite with them all, and Vaughan and Traherne are
not far behind.

The spontaneous instinct of readers has taken the name
of Rupert Brooke to illustrate the poetic spirit of the
great war in a superlative degree.   His posthumous vol-
ume, brought out in May 1915, a few weeks after his death,
has enjoyed a success which is greater, perhaps, than

that of all the other poems of the war put together. He
has become a sort of symbol, even a sort of fetish, and
he is to English sentiment what Charles Péguy is to France,
an oriflamme of the chivalry of his country. It is
curious, in this connection, that neither Péguy nor Brooke
had the opportunity of fighting much in the cause; they
fell, as it seemed for the moment, obscurely; Rupert
Brooke was a pawn in the dark and dolorous flight from
Antwerp. An officer at last, he died in the Aegean,
between Egypt and Gallipoli, having never seen a Turkish
enemy. So Péguy faded out of sight on the very opening
day of the battle of the Marne, yet each of these young
men was immediately perceived to have embodied the gall-
antry of his country. The extraordinary popularity of
Rupert Brooke is due to the excellence of his verse, to
the tact with which it was presented to the public, but
also to a vague perception of his representative nature.
He was the finest specimen of a certain type produced at
the universities, and then sacrificed to our national
necessity.

It is needless to describe the verses of Rupert
Brooke, which have attained a circulation which any poet
might envy. They are comprised in two slender volumes,
that above mentioned, and one of 1911, published while he
was still at Cambridge. He was born in 1887, and when
he died off Skyros, in circumstances of the most roman-
tic pathos, he had not completed his twenty-eighth year.
He was, unlike the majority of his contemporaries, a
meticulous and reserved writer, little inclined to be
pleased with his work, and cautious to avoid the snare of
improvisation. Hence, though he lived to be older than
did Keats or Fergusson, he left a very slender garland of
verse behind him, in which there is scarcely a petal
which is not of some permanent value. For instance, in
the volume of 1911 we found not a few pieces which then
seemed crude in taste and petulant in temper; but even
these now illustrate a most interesting character of
which time has rounded the angles, and we would not have
otherwise what illustrates so luminously - and so divert-
ingly - that precious object, the mind of Rupert Brooke.

Yet there is a danger that this mind and character may
be misinterpreted, even by those who contemplate the
poet's memory with idolatry. There is some evidence of a
Rupert Brooke legend in the process of formation, which
deserves to be guarded against not less jealously than the
R.L. Stevenson legend of a few years ago. We know that
for some people gold and lilies are not properly honoured
until they are gilded and painted. Rupert Brooke was far
from being either a plaster saint or a vivid public

witness.   He was neither a trumpet nor a torch.   He
lives in the memory of those who knew him as a smiling
and attentive spectator, eager to watch every flourish of
the pageantry of life.   Existence was a wonderful har-
mony to Rupert Brooke, who was determined to lose no tone
of it by making too much noise himself.   In company he
was not a great talker, but loved to listen, with spark-
ling deference, to people less gifted than himself if
only they had experience to impart.   He lived in a fas-
cinated state, bewitched with wonder and appreciation.
His very fine appearance, which seemed to glow with dorm-
ant vitality, his beautiful manners, the quickness of his
intelligence, his humour, were combined under the spell
of a curious magnetism, difficult to analyse.   When he
entered a room, he seemed to bring sunshine with him, al-
though he was usually rather silent, and pointedly im-
mobile.   I do not think it would be easy to recollect
any utterance of his which was very remarkable, but all
he said and did added to the harmonious, ardent, and
simple effect.
    There is very little of the poetry of Rupert Brooke
which can be definitely identified with the war.   The
last six months of his life, spent in conditions for
which nothing in his previous existence in Cambridge or
Berlin, in Grantchester or Tahiti, had in the least pre-
pared him, were devoted - for we must not say wasted - to
breaking up the *cliché* of civilised habits.   But of this
harassed time there remain to us the five immortal
Sonnets, which form the crown of Rupert Brooke's verse,
and his principal legacy to English literature.   Our
record would be imperfect without the citation of one,
perhaps the least hackneyed of these:

[Quotes the third of them, 'The Dead'.]

If the fortune of his country had not disturbed his
plans, it is more than probable that Rupert Brooke would
have become an enlightened and enthusiastic professor .....
    The ancient mystery of verse is so deeply based on
tradition that it is not surprising that all the strange
contrivances of twentieth-century warfare have been
found too crabbed for our poets to use.   When great
Marlborough, as Addison puts it, 'examin'd all the
dreadful scenes of war' at Blenheim, he was really in
closer touch with Marathon than with the tanks and gas of
Ypres.   But there is one military implement so beautiful
in itself, and so magical in the nature of its service,
that it is bound to conquer a place in poetry.   The air-
machine, to quote 'The Campaign' once more, 'rides in the

whirlwind and directs the storm.'   But the poets are
still shy of it.   In French it has, we believe, inspired
but one good poem, the 'Plus haut toujours!' of Jean
Allard-Méeus, a hymn of real aerial majesty.   In English
Major Maurice Baring's ode 'In Memoriam: A.H.' is
equally unique, and, in its complete diversity from
Allard-Méeus's rhapsody, suggests that the aeroplane has a
wide field before it in the realms of imaginative writing.
Major Baring's subject is the death of Auberon Herbert,
Lord Lucas, who was killed on the 3rd of November 1916.
This distinguished young statesman and soldier had just
been promoted, after a career of prolonged gallantry in
the air, and would have flown no more, if he had returned
in safety on that fatal day.
    Major Baring has long been known as an excellent
composer of sonnets and other short pieces.   But 'In
Memoriam: A.H.' lifts him to a position among our living
poets to which he had hardly a pretension.   In a long
irregular threnody or funeral ode, the great technical
difficulty is to support lyrical emotion throughout.   No
form of verse is more liable to lapses of dignity, to dull
and flagging passages.   Even Dryden in 'Anne Killigrew',
even Coleridge in the 'Departing Year', have not been able
to avoid those languors.   Many poets attempt to escape
them by a use of swollen and pompous language.   We will
not say that Major Baring has been universally successful,
where the success of the great masters is only relative,
but he has produced a poem of great beauty and originality,
which interprets an emotion and illustrates an incident
the poignancy of which could scarcely be exaggerated.   We
have no hesitation in saying that 'A.H.' is one of the few
durable contributions to the literature of the present war.
    It is difficult to quote effectively from a poem which
is constructed with great care on a complicated plan, but
a fragment of Major Baring's elegy may lead readers to the
original:

> God, Who had made you valiant, strong and swift,
> And maimed you with a bullet long ago,
> And cleft your riotous ardour with a rift,
> And checked your youth's tumultuous overflow,
> Gave back your youth to you,
> And packed in moments rare and few
> Achievements manifold
> And happiness untold,
> And bade you spring to Death as to a bride,
> In manhood's ripeness, power and pride,
> And on your sandals the strong wings of youth.

There is no rhetoric here, no empty piling up of fine
words; it is a closely followed study in poetical bio-
graphy .....
     So lately as June of the present year there was pub-
lished a volume which is in several ways the most puzzling
and the most interesting of all that lie upon our table
to-day.   This is the 'Ardours and Endurances' of Lieut.
Robert Nichols.   We know nothing of the author save what
we learn from his writings, that he is very young, that he
went out from Oxford early in the war, that he was fight-
ing in Flanders before the end of 1914, that he was
wounded, perhaps at Loos, in 1915, and that he has been
long in hospital.   We add the hope, which nothing which
we have seen printed belies, that he is still alive and on
the road to recovery.   Before 'Ardours and Endurances'
reached us, we had met with 'Invocation', a smaller volume
published by Lieut. Nichols in December 1915.   There has
rarely been a more radical change in the character of an
artist than is displayed by a comparison of these two coll-
ections.   'Invocation', in which the war takes a small
and unconvincing place, is creditable, though rather un-
certain, in workmanship, and displays a tendency towards
experiment in rich fancy and vague ornament.   In 'Ardours
and Endurances' the same accents are scarcely to be de-
tected; the pleasant boy has grown into a war-worn man;
while the mastery over the material of poetic art has be-
come so remarkable as to make the epithet 'promising'
otiose.   There is no 'promise' here; there is high
performance.
     Alone among the poets before us, Lieut. Nichols has
set down a reasoned sequence of war impressions.   The
opening third of his book, and by far its most interest-
ing section, consists of a cycle of pieces in which the
personal experience of fighting is minutely reported,
stage by stage.   We have 'The Summons', the reluctant
but unhesitating answer to the call in England, the break-
up of plans; then the farewell to home, 'the place of
comfort'.   'The Approach', in three successive lyrics,
describes the arrival at the Front.   'Battle', in eleven
sections, reproduces the mental and physical phenomena of
the attack.   'The Dead', in four instalments, tells the
tale of grief.   'The Aftermath', with extraordinary
skill, records in eight stages the gradual recovery of
nerve-power after the shattering emotions of the fight.
The first section of 'Battle', as being shorter than the
rest, may be quoted in full as an example of Lieut.
Nichols's method:

[Quotes 'Battle', stanzas I-V.]

This is painfully vivid, but it is far exceeded in
poignancy by what follows.   Indeed it would be difficult
to find in all literature, from the wail of David over
Jonathan downward, such an expression of the hopeless
longing for an irrecoverable presence as informs the
broken melodies, the stanzas which are like sobs, of the
fifth section of 'Ardours and Endurances':

> In a far field, away from England, lies
> A Boy I friended with a care like love;
> All day the wide earth aches, the cold wind cries,
> The melancholy clouds drive on above.
>
> There, separate from him by a little span,
> Two eagle cousins, generous, reckless, free,
> Two Grenfells, lie, and my Boy is made man,
> One with these elder knights of chivalry.

It is difficult to qualify, it seems almost indelicate to
intrude upon, such passionate grief.   These poems form a
revelation of the agony of a spirit of superabundant re-
finement and native sensuousness suddenly stunned, and as
it were momentarily petrified, by horrible spiritual
anguish.   If the strain were not relieved by the final
numbers of 'Aftermath', where the pain of the soul is
abated, and where the poet, scarred and shattered, but
'free at last', snaps the chain of despair, these poems
would be positively intolerable.
    In the closeness of his analysis and in the accurate
heaping up of exact and pregnant observations, Lieut.
Nichols comes closer than any other of these English poets
to the best of the French paladins, of whom we wrote
in the last number of this '[Edinburgh] Review'.   One
peculiarity which he shares with them is his seriousness:
there is no trace in him of the English cheerfulness and
levity.   Most of our war-writers are incorrigible Mark
Tapleys.   But Lieut. Nichols, even when he uses colloqu-
ial phrases - and he introduces them with great effect -
never smiles.   He is most unlike the French, on the other
hand, in his general attitude towards the war.   He has no
military enthusiasm, no aspiration after *gloire*.   Indeed,
the most curious feature of his poetry is that its range
is concentrated on the few yards about the trench in which
he stands.   He seems to have no national view of the pur-
pose of the war, no enthusiasm for the cause, no anger
against the enemy.   There is no mention of the Germans
from beginning to end;   the poet does not seem to know of
their existence.   His experiences, his agonies, his des-
pair, are what a purely natural phenomenon, such as the

eruption of a volcano or the chaos of an earthquake,
might cause. We might read his poems over and over
again without forming the slightest idea of what all the
distress was about, or who was guilty, or what was being
defended. This is a mark of great artistic sincerity;
but it also points to a certain moral narrowness.
Lieut. Robert Nichols' 'endurances' are magnificently
described, but we are left in the dark regarding his
'ardours'. We are sure of one thing, however, that none
of us may guess what such a talent, in one still so young,
may have in store for us; and we may hope for broader
views expressed in no less burning accents.

There could hardly be a more vivid contrast than
exists between the melancholy passion of Lieut. Nichols
and the fantastic high spirits of Captain Robert Graves.
He again is evidently a very young man, who was but
yesteryear a jolly boy at the Charterhouse. He has
always meant to be a poet; he is not one of those who
have been driven into verse by the strenuous emotion of
the war. In some diverting prefatory lines to 'Over the
Brazier' he gives us a picture of the nursery-scene when
a bright green-covered book bewitched him by its 'metre
twisting like a chain of daisies, with great big splendid
words'. He has still a wholesome hunger for splendid
words; he has kept more deliberately than most of his
compeers a poetical vocation steadily before him. He
has his moments of dejection when the first battle faces
him:

> Here's an end to my art!
> I must die and I know it,
> With battle-murder at my heart -
> Sad death for a poet!
>
> Oh, my songs never sung,
> And my plays to darkness blown!
> I am still so young, so young,
> And life was my own.

But this mood soon passes, and is merged in the humor-
istic and fantastic elation characteristic of this buoy-
ant writer, whose whim it is to meet the tragedy not
mournfully but boisterously. Where by most of the
soldier-bards the subjective manner is a little over-
done, it is impossible not to welcome so objective a
writer as Captain Graves, from whose observations of the
battle of La Bassée we quote an episode:

[Quotes 'The Dead Fox Hunter', stanzas I-IV.]

We have an idea that this is a gallant poem which English-
men will not allow to be forgotten. The great quality of
Captain Graves's verse at present is its elated vivacity,
which neither fire, nor pain, nor grief can long subdue.
Acutely sensitive to all these depressing elements, his
animal spirits lift him like an aeroplane, and he is
above us in a moment, soaring through clouds of nonsense
under a sky of unmuffled gaiety. In our old literature,
of which he is plainly a student, he has found a neglected
author who is wholly to his taste. This is Skelton,
Henry VIII's Rabelaisian laureate. Captain Graves
imitates, with a great deal of bravado, those breathless
absurdities, 'The Tunning of Elinore Rummyng' and 'Colin
Clout'. He likes rough metre, bad rhymes and squalid
images: we suspect him of an inclination to be rude to
his immediate predecessors. But his extreme modernness
- 'Life is a cliché - I would find a gesture of my own' -
is, in the case of so lively a songster, an evidence of
vitality. He promises a new volume, to be called
'Fairies and Fusiliers', and it will be looked forward to
with anticipation.

All these poets seem to be drawn into relation to one
another. Robert Graves and Siegfried Sassoon are both
Fusiliers, and they publish a *stichomythia* (1) 'on Non-
sense', just as Cowley and Crashaw did 'on Hope' two
centuries and a half ago. Lieut. Sassoon's own volume
is later than those which we have hitherto examined, and
bears a somewhat different character. The gallantry of
1915 and the optimism of 1916 have passed away, and in
Lieut. Sassoon's poems their place is taken by a sense of
intolerable weariness and impatience: 'How long, O Lord,
how long?' The name-piece of the volume, and perhaps
its first in execution, is a monologue by an ignorant and
shrewd old huntsman, who looks back over his life with
philosophy and regret. Like Captain Graves, he is
haunted with the idea that there must be fox-hounds in
Heaven. All Lieut. Sassoon's poems about horses and
hunting and country life generally betray his tastes and
habits. This particular poem hardly touches on the war,
but those which follow are absorbed by the ugliness, lass-
itude, and horror of fighting. Lieut. Sassoon's verse is
not sufficiently alive to the importance of always hitting
upon the best and only word. He is essentially a satir-
ist, and sometimes a very bold one, as in 'The Hero',
where the death of a soldier is announced home in 'gall-
ant lies', so that his mother brags to her neighbours of
the courage of her dead son. At the close of all this
pious make-believe, the Colonel

> thought how 'Jack,' cold-footed, useless swine,
> Had panicked down the trench that night the mine
> Went up at Wicked Corner; how he's tried
> To get sent home; and how, at last, he died,
> Blown to small bits;

or, again, as in 'Blighters', where the sentimentality of
London is contrasted with the reality in Flanders:

> The House is crammed: tier beyond tier they grin
> And cackle at the Show, while prancing ranks
> Of harlots shrill the chorus, drunk with din;
> 'We're sure the Kaiser loves the dear old Tanks!'
>
> I'd like to see a Tank come down the stalls,
> Lurching to rag-time tunes, or 'Home, sweet Home!' -
> And there'd be no more jokes in Music-halls
> To mock the riddled corpses round Bapaume.

It is this note of bitter anger, miles away from the
serenity of Rupert Brooke, the lion-heart of Julian
Grenfell, the mournful passion of Robert Nichols, which
differentiates Lieut. Sassoon from his fellows. They
accept the war, with gallantry or with resignation; he
detests it with wrathful impatience. He has much to
learn as an artist, for his diction is often hard, and he
does not always remember that Horace, 'when he writ on
vulgar subjects, yet writ not vulgarly'. But he has
force, sincerity, and a line of his own in thought and
fancy. A considerable section of his poetry is
occupied with studies of men he has observed at the
Front, a subaltern, a private of the Lancashires, con-
scripts, the dress of a battle-field, the one-legged man
('Thank God, they had to amputate!'), the sniper who goes
crazy - savage, disconcerting silhouettes drawn roughly
against a lurid background.
    The bitterness of Lieut. Sassoon is not cynical, it is
the rage of disenchantment, the violence of a young man
eager to pursue other aims, who, finding the age out of
joint, resents being called upon to help to mend it. His
temper is not altogether to be applauded, for such senti-
ments must tend to relax the effort of the struggle, yet
they can hardly be reproved when conducted with so much
honesty and courage. Lieut. Sassoon, who, as we learn,
has twice been severely wounded and has been in the very
furnace of the fighting, has reflected, more perhaps than
his fellow-singers, about the causes and conditions of
the war. He may not always have thought correctly, nor
have recorded his impressions with proper circumspection,
but his honesty must be respectfully acknowledged.

We have now called attention to those soldier-writers of
verse who, in our judgment, have expressed themselves
with most originality during the present war.   There is
a temptation to continue the inquiry, and to expatiate on
others of only less merit and promise.   Much could be
said of Charles Hamilton Sorley, who gave evidence of
precocious literary talent, though less, we think, in
verse, since the unmistakable singing faculty is absent
in 'Marlborough' (Cambridge University Press, 1916), than
in prose, a form in which he already excelled.   Sorley
must have shown military gifts as well as a fine courage,
for when he was killed in action in October 1915, al-
though he was but twenty years of age, he had been pro-
moted captain.   In the universal sorrow, few figures
awaken more regret than his. .....
There can be no healthy criticism where the principle
of selection is neglected, and we regret that patriotism
or indulgence tempts so many of those who speak of the
war-poets of the day to plaster them with indiscriminate
praise.   We have spoken here of a few, in whose honour
even a little excess of laudation may not be out of
place.   But these are the exceptions, in a mass of
standardised poetry made to pattern, loosely versified,
excellent in sentiment, uniformly meditative, and entire-
ly without individual character.   The reviewers who
applaud all these ephemeral efforts with a like acclaim,
and who say that there are hundreds of poets now writing
who equal if they do not excel the great masters of the
past, talk nonsense; they talk nonsense, and they know
it.   They lavish their flatteries in order to widen the
circle of their audience.   They are like the prophets of
Samaria, who declared good unto the King of Israel with
one mouth: and we need a Micaiah to clear the scene of
all such flatulent Zedekiahs.   It is not true that the
poets of the youngest generation are a myriad Shelleys
and Burnses and Bérangers rolled into one.   But it is
true that they carry on the great tradition of poetry
with enthusiasm, and a few of them with high accomplish-
ment.

Note

1 *Stichomythia* = dialogue in alternate lines of verse,
   as in Greek plays.

'Georgian Poetry 1916-1917'

Published November 1917
'To Edmund Gosse'

Prefatory note

This third book of 'Georgian Poetry' carries to the end
of a seventh year the presentation of chosen examples
from the work of contemporary poets belonging to the
younger generation.   Of the eighteen writers included,
nine appear in the series for the first time.   The
representation of the older inhabitants has in most cases
been restricted in order to allow full space for the new-
comers; and the alphabetical order of the names has been
reversed, so as to bring more of these into prominence
than would otherwise have been done.

September 1917   E.M.

27. 'GEORGIAN POETRY', EDWARD SHANKS, 'THE NEW STATESMAN'

22 December 1917, 280

Shanks was under some difficulty in writing this review,
as Robert H. Ross has noted.   Neither Squire nor Freeman,
his colleagues on 'The New Statesman', felt they could
review an anthology to which they had contributed.
Squire wrote to Marsh: 'It is obviously impossible for
me to puff G.P. myself this time, but I tried to do my

bit beforehand'.   In reply to a letter from Marsh ex-
pressing mild disagreement with those parts of the review
which had found fault with his flock, Shanks wrote:

> it is really rather absurd to criticize such a book
> at all.   No doubt you could be as destructive about
> it as any reviewer.   We ought to recognize your diff-
> iculties more.   My chief difficulty, of course, was
> that I was forbidden to say anything about Squire.
> [Letters quoted in Robert H. Ross, 'The Georgian
> Revolt', 1967, 181.]

Shanks is right in noting 'a distinct impression of
battle', but wrong in attributing it only to three new-
comers, Sassoon, Nichols and Graves.   Gibson's three
battle songs, in that they are sung by one of E.M.'s
'older inhabitants', point more strikingly the change of
mood.   Although the poems by Sassoon are more restrained
than some in 'The Old Huntsman' [1917] and Marsh would
never have printed Graves's 'A Dead Boche', his choice of
'They' and 'It's a Queer time' says something for his
editorial breadth and discernment.
    For a note on Edward Shanks see Appendix, p. 414.
See also No. 63.

The new volume of 'Georgian Poetry' makes something of a
break in the continuity of the series;   and it should
effectually dispel an idea, which is still prevalent in
some quarters, that it is no more than the expression of
a single school or group or even clique.   The absence of
Brooke and Flecker would, of course, have been in itself
enough to have changed the appearance and modified the
atmosphere of the collection.   The first volume of the
series coincided with the beginnings of their reputations;
the second emphasized the posthumous growth of their
fame;   and in the general mind the term 'Georgian Poetry'
was particularly associated with these two writers.   But
there are other gaps.   Mr Lascelles Abercrombie has been
silent for the last two years;   and Francis Ledwidge is
omitted, presumably because his last book was not thought
to have reached the level of his first.   It may cause
some surprise to find that Mr D.H. Lawrence is missing as
well;   but it may be guessed that either his versificat-
ion or his psychology has at last become too much for his
editor.   Against these, no fewer than nine names appear
for the first time;   and I should imagine that the
average age of the eighteen poets included is perceptibly
lower than it was in 1915 or 1912.

The nine new writers are as follows: W.J. Turner,
J.C. Squire, Siegfried Sassoon, I. Rosenberg, Robert
Nichols, Robert Graves, John Freeman, Maurice Baring and
Herbert Asquith.   By a quaint device, the alphabetical
order is inverted, so that the new entrants enter in the
order stated.   This has been done, according to the
editor, so as to bring more of the novices into promin-
ence than would otherwise have been the case.   But the
inversion does no more than bring five new-comers into
the first half of the book instead of four, and actually
ends with two instead of with one.   It would have been
better, if it was really thought necessary to take any
steps at all, to have printed all the new-comers at the
beginning and let alphabetical order go hang.

We can all of us, of course, shout resentfully that
So-and-so has been omitted and that So-and-so has been
included.   Remonstrances in this key lie among the
common expectations of the anthologist; but they are
rarely very helpful to him or very enlightening to his
public and may be passed over on the present occasion.
It will be more profitable to take the book as it is.
But it is difficult to say how far it represents in any
intelligible way the trend of English poetry during the
last two years.   This question depends very much on the
answer to another question, whether during this time
English poetry has shown itself as developing any
particular trend.   Certainly, on a first reading, the
book communicates a distinct impression of battle, murder
and sudden death.   Mr Sassoon writes:

> Robert, there's a war in France,
> Everywhere men bang and blunder,
> Sweat and swear, and worship Chance,
> Creep and blink through cannon thunder.

And Mr Nichols writes:

> Ha! ha! Bunched figures waiting.
> Revolver levelled quick!
> Flick! Flick!
> Red as blood.
> Germans.   Germans.
> Good! O good!
> Cool madness.

And Mr Graves writes, somehow more convincingly:

One moment you'll be crouching at your gun,
Traversing, mowing heaps down half in fun;
The next, you choke and clutch at your right breast -
No time to think - leave all- and off you go ...
To Treasure Island where the Spice winds blow,
To lovely groves of mango, quince and lime -
Breathe no good-bye, but ho, for the Red West!
It's a queer time.

But a closer examination reveals the fact that this im-
pression is derived almost wholly from Mr Sassoon, Mr
Nichols and Mr Graves, and does not give a complete or a
correct notion even of them.   The military inspiration
in the book, apart from the special emphasis put upon it
by these three writers, is really very slight;   and there
is nothing to prove that the war has yet had any serious
effect on the development of English poetry.   It exists
in the work of some of these writers as a thing which
happens to have happened to them, just as they might have
been by chance in a railway accident and have written
about it.

    When the true influence of the war appears, as it may
very well yet do, it will appear in a much subtler and
more powerful manner.   It will determine not so much the
matter as the manner and the tone and the atmosphere of
our poetry.   Meanwhile the better-founded impression
which is derived from a second and closer examination of
the present volume shows that modern inspiration has not
altered appreciably since 1912;   and the new-comers to
the gathering have as much in common with the original
contributors as the originals have in common among them-
selves.   They show, that is to say, curiosity, restless-
ness, impatience, a determination to be honest and to see
clearly and to avoid the use of subjects and diction
which appear suitable only because they have been used
before.   These are large and vague phrases, but there is
no closer formula which will embrace the modern movement.
The important point is that no formula could be devised
which would include the older contributors to these
anthologies and exclude the new entrants.

    The editor's decision to cut down the space allowed to
the older inhabitants in order to make room for the new
can be defended on obvious grounds;   but its results are
sometimes unhappy.   It is a little absurd, for example,
to give Mr de la Mare six pages against the seventeen
allotted to Mr Robert Nichols.   During the last two
years or so, Mr de la Mare, though without any revolut-
ionary change of heart, has so developed as almost to
have become a new poet;   and the progress he has thus

made is really vastly more interesting than the whole
appearance of Mr Nichols.   Mr W.H. Davies is not ashamed
to sing the same song a hundred times over; and the four
pieces by him given here represent him adequately, being
just such excellent pieces as he has always written.   But
Mr de la Mare has been growing enormously and has entered
on a new stage of the utmost possible interest, of which
the four pieces here chosen only give a very imperfect
notion.   One of them, 'The Scribe', indicates briefly
his new greatness of conception; but the others, though
beautiful, are less remarkable.

Of the new-comers, Mr John Freeman has been the long-
est before the public and should really have been in-
cluded in the 1912 volume.   Tardy justice is done to him
now by the allocation of twelve pages to a really excell-
ent selection from his poems.   His talent is strange,
difficult and aloof; and it is not always easy to be
sure whether he is in trouble with his metres or can hear
rhythms which are not perceptible to the ordinary ear.
But, however this may be, he has a marvellous command of
landscape and atmosphere, and can make an unreal scene
vivid in a few abrupt touches, as in the first verse of
'Stone Trees':

> Last night a sword-light in the sky
> Flashed a swift terror on the dark.
> In that sharp light the fields did lie
> Naked and stone-like; each tree stood
> Like a tranced woman, bound and stark.
> Far off the wood
> With darkness ridged the riven dark.

Mr W.J. Turner, who is equal with him in obscurity, will
be a very fine poet when he has attained a sufficient
control of his medium.   At present he is too impatient
always to write well or to make himself clear; but he
has access to a whole range of subjects and sensations
which are entirely new and entirely his own.   Of his six
pieces here, there is only one, 'Ecstasy', which one
could think of as having possibly been written by another
poet; and this does not mean that 'Ecstasy' is imitative.
The themes of the other five would, in all probability,
never have occurred to anyone else.   Perhaps the best of
them is 'Magic', which begins:

> I love a still conservatory
> That's full of giant, breathless palms,
> Azaleas, clematis and vines,
> Whose quietness great Trees becalms,
> Filling the air with foliage,
> A curved and dreamy statuary.

What is valuable in Mr Turner is the suggestion his work
conveys that E.M. was not mistaken when, in 1912, he
detected signs of a new effort in English poetry.   The
new effort is still working and Mr Turner contributes to
it; his curiosity, restlessness and impatience are the
qualities of his older colleagues.

It is impossible, of course, in any reasonable space
to give a full description of a book containing extracts
from the work of eighteen poets, nearly all of whom
deserve detailed discussion.   But a few more points may
be mentioned briefly in conclusion.   The selection from
Mr Ralph Hodgson is, perhaps, the most inadequate thing
in the book.   Of his three pieces, 'The Gypsy Girl' is
good, but the others are below his usual standard.   It
is true that his finest poems were published too early
for this collection and that two of them appeared in the
1915; but that most exquisite poem, 'The Bride', was
available for this and is almost on a level with 'The
Bull' and 'The Song of Honour'.   Mr Harold Monro, who
ought not to have been in the 1912 volume at all, but who
underwent a cataclysmic change of heart in time for 1915,
continues to deserve his place and is well represented.
Mr James Stephens has been overtaken by a disastrous
facility and his talent is for the time obscured.   It is
all very well for him to

Sing that Peg
Has an egg, egg, egg,

but the song is hardly in the Georgian key.   Mr Mase-
field contributes sonnets and other poems about Beauty
and such things; but the best sonnet on Beauty in his
last volume is not here.   Mr Gordon Bottomley's three
pieces are graceful, but not likely to attract so much
attention as 'King Lear's Wife' two years ago.   Mr
Maurice Baring's one beautiful poem is somewhat out of
the picture.   The other good pieces in the book point
forward and the bad pieces nowhere; but Mr Baring seems
to point backwards, having recaptured the sweetness of a
former age.   Mr Herbert Asquith's 'The Volunteer' is
already well known.   Mr I. Rosenberg and Mr John
Drinkwater also ran.

28.   'GEORGIAN POETRY', UNSIGNED REVIEW, 'THE TIMES
LITERARY SUPPLEMENT'

27 December 1917, 646

'Even from the viewpoint of the conservative "Times
Literary Supplement" the volume appeared too traditional,
too conservative' (Robert H. Ross, 'The Georgian Revolt',
1967, 180).   It is interesting to compare the review
with the shorter notice of 'Wheels' appearing in the same
issue (p. 646), of which this is the opening paragraph:

> This hardly carries on the promise, and indeed the
> performance, which the nine writers who contribute to
> it showed in the first 'Cycle', reviewed by us a year
> ago.   The dissatisfaction with things in general which
> many of them then showed continues, but it has grown
> more tenuous.   None of them *sing*;   most of them are
> far too much inclined to stand outside the scene of
> life, grumble and make faces, and roll big words in
> their mouths.   Even when they rise to something like
> poetry they are content, like so many of the new
> school, especially if they are *vers libristes*, to
> confine their efforts to descriptive details - giving
> by catalogue pictures which the true poet flashes into
> three or four lines - or to elaborate analysis of a
> moment's personal sensations.   They do not, in fact,
> hear the echoes of greater spiritual movements;   their
> method is static, not dynamic.

If this, the third, book of 'Georgian Poetry' selected
by E.M. be representative, there is nothing in the poetry
of our young writers to alarm or distress the most conser-
vative.   Not only youth, but example and, more than
either, new conditions of life might offer them the excuse
for impatient rejection of the established and for the
playing of all sorts of pranks in the effort to get ex-
pression for their youth and their strange and violent
being.   And what they are found for the most part to be
doing is pouring their new wine into the old bottles;
or - to use a more homely and perhaps more 'Georgian'
simile - thrusting their proud young feet into old boots,
and finding them good to march or to dance in.   Now, when
the old civilization is passing, or has passed, and not
even our poets - our seers - can tell us what sort of
order, if any, is to follow the ruin, our young singers,
most of them roughly torn from the old decent ways and

thrown willy-nilly into a welter of dirt and death, sing
out their hearts to us; and sing them by the old means of
stanza and metre and rhyme.   They often make the old means
look new; but the old means abide.   Where, in the rest-
lessness that heralded the war, strange experiments were
tried and the old means were contemptuously or angrily
thrown away, the new conditions, enforcing sincerity, have
maintained the old ways.   Poetic form (as the word used
to be understood before Whitman broke fence) is discovered
to be something other than the self-imposed difficulties
of a game - a game of 'patience', as it were, which leads
nowhere except to the pleasure of 'getting it out'.   If
these young poets write in metre and rhyme and shape, it
is because they want to, because expression urges them to
form.   And it is mighty comforting - in these days when
the spirit is hungry for any scrap of permanence and con-
tinuity - to see the old friendly boots shaping themselves
thus kindly to the proud young feet.
   Of the eighteen poets in this volume one or two, no
doubt, belong to the old world before the war.   Mr Mase-
field is one of them.   But it is not without signific-
ance that Mr Masefield, in his most recent volume, was
found to be expressing his reveries on life and on him-
self in the sonnet - and the Shakespearian sonnet, which
is, for English people, older than the Petrarchan, since
'The House of Life', and nothing older than that, is the
true source of suggestion of all modern English Petrar-
chan sonnets.   In giving five sonnets and only two other
lyric poems from 'Lollingdon Downs', the editor has not
done the best for Mr Masefield; and (let us hasten to
admit it, since it goes against our point) the Shakes-
pearian sonnet is not a form in which he moves easily.

   Ah, we are neither heaven nor earth, but men;
   Something that uses and despises both,
   That takes its earth's contentment in the pen,
   That sees the world's injustice and is wroth,
   And flinging off youth's happy promise, flies
   Up to some breach, despising earthly things,
   And, in contempt of hell and heaven, dies
   Rather than bear some yoke of priests or kings.
   Our joys are not of heaven nor earth, but man's,
   A woman's beauty, or a child's delight,
   The trembling blood when the discoverer scans
   The sought-for world, the guessed-at satellite;
   The ringing scene, the stone at point to blush
   For unborn men to look at and say 'Hush'.

The first ten lines (but for that 'in the pen') are beautiful and true.   But the last four, dressing up in phrases exploration, astronomy, acting, and sculpture .and sculpture by Bernini or Canova at their worst ;   the forced rhymes, the feeble close seem to concentrate all the faults besetting Mr Masefield in particular, and in general all poets who use established forms.   We have ventured to take Mr Masefield for an object-lesson, because his reputation is higher and wider spread than that of any other poet in the book;   and, if this select- ion is unfair to him, his admirers know where they can find this passionate servant of beauty at his best.

Then there is Mr John Drinkwater, with his charming, graceful, accomplished little impressions of quiet old country scenes;   and one poem, 'Reciprocity', which we quote, partly for its own sake and partly because it bears on something that will come leter:

> I do not think that skies and meadows are
> Moral, or that the fixture of a star
> Comes of a quiet spirit, or that trees
> Have wisdom in their windless silences.
> Yet these are things invested in my mood
> With constancy, and peace, and fortitude,
> That in my troubled season I can cry
> Upon the wide composure of the sky,
> And envy fields, and wish that I might be
> As little daunted as a star or tree.

There is Mr Walter de la Mare, with four poems, each full of that peculiar spirit which we should like to describe as intimate remoteness - a strangeness which, partly by his exquisite use of detail, partly by the insidiousness of his delicate and beautiful art, he persuades us is not strange, but a part of ourselves.   There is no other poet living who could be at once so playful, so minute,   and so profound as Mr de la Mare in 'The Scribe':

[Quotes 'The Scribe', both stanzas.]

The book gives, too, well-chosen things from Mr W.H. Davies (including that absolutely Daviesian poem, 'The White Cascade');   from Mr Harold Monro, with his affect- ionate susceptibility to the character of common things, whether natural or made with hands;   and Mr James Stephens, who, for all his quick fancy, is perhaps rather a vivid recorder in verse than a poet.   But these are all singers who can, so to speak, look after themselves;   and curiosity pushes one past them to the newer names.

We quoted, against our own interest, a sonnet by Mr
Masefield.   A few lines from Mr Robert Nichols's 'The
Assault' will restore the balance:

> Blindness a moment.   Sick,
> There the men are!
> Bayonets ready: click!
> Time goes quick;
> A stumbled prayer . . . somehow a blazing star
> In a blue night . . . where?
> Again prayer.
> The tongue trips.   Start:
> How's time?   Soon now.   Two minutes or less .
> The gun's fury mounting higher . . .
> Their utmost.   I lift a silent hand.   Unseen I bless
> Those hearts will follow me.
> And beautifully,
> Now beautifully my will grips,
> Soul calm and round and filmed and white!

Something of the kind was bound, no doubt, to be written;
and we can only be glad that it has been written so well.
Admiration of the men who do these things pleads import-
unately for such expression of their feelings, but the
case must go against it.   We think only: What a brill-
iant fellow is this war correspondent! and wonder why he
has troubled to make rhymes.   If we want to hear the war
in poetry we must turn on to Mr Robert Nichols's
'Fulfilment':

> Was there love once?   I have forgotten her.
> Was there grief once?   grief yet is mine.
> Other loves I have, men rough, but men who stir
> More grief, more joy, than love of thee and thine.
>
> Faces cheerful, full of whimsical mirth,
> Lined by the wind, burned by the sun;
> Bodies enraptured by the abounding earth,
> As whose children we are brethren: one.
>
> At any moment may descend hot death
> To shatter limbs! pulp, tear, blast
> Beloved soldiers who love rough life and breath
> Not less for dying faithful to the last.
>
> O the fading eyes, the grimed face turned bony,
> Open mouth gushing, fallen head,
> Lessening pressure of a hand shrunk, clammed, and
>   stony!
> O sudden spasm, release of the dead!

Was there love once?   I have forgotten her,
Was there grief once? grief yet is mine.
O loved, living, dying, heroic soldier,
All, all, my joy, my grief, my love, are thine!

That is 'Georgian' enough in its vocabulary, its rhythm,
its actuality.   It does not dress things up; it uses
form as it will.   But form it has; and, being so
sincere, so direct, so Georgian as it is, it is at once
more interesting to the student of poetry and more poet-
ically beautiful than many true and beautiful but less
intensely realized things from 'A Faun's Holiday', of
which this volume gives perhaps too many.

   We turn to Mr Siegfried Sassoon, and having enjoyed
his boyish, vivid letter in verse to Mr Robert Graves,
blunder, we might almost say into a steel trap.   It is
called 'The Kiss'; and this is what it says:

To these I turn, in these I trust;
Brother Lead and Sister Steel.
To his blind power I make appeal;
I guard her beauty clean from rust.

He spins and burns and loves the air,
And splits a skull to win my praise;
But up the nobly marching days
She glitters naked, cold and fair.

Sweet Sister, grant your soldier this:
That in good fury he may feel
The body where he sets his heel
Quail from your downward darting kiss.

Well!   'Hyperion' is written in the metre of 'An Essay
on Man', and 'Love in the Valley' in the metre of 'The
King was in his counting-house'; but when the metre of
'In Memoriam' may be used thus - and used, we feel, not
with deliberate, cold purpose, but with an instinctive
sense of rightness - the notion that any form of poetry
can become outworn seems absurd.   Mr Sassoon is, in
general, a more ebullient poet than here; and we should
like to quote - not his more realistic and dashing, or
more elaborately 'creepy' poems, but the brave, flowing
'To Victory', with its weariness, its regret, its home-
sickness, and its high pride, musically suggesting both
flying banners and long sighs.   But others wait their
turn.

There is Mr Wilfrid Wilson Gibson, a poet who has made
experiments (as another W.W. made them) in natural
diction, but who is most natural when he is most sincere.
To many readers Mr Gibson's 'Lament' will seem the most
desired poem in this volume.   It says for us all, in the
very words that we wanted, what we have all been trying
to say:

We who are left, how shall we look again
Happily on the sun, or feel the rain
Without remembering how they who went
Ungrudgingly and spent
Their lives for us loved, too, the sun and rain?

A bird among the rain-wet lilac sings -
But we, how shall we turn to little things
And listen to the birds and winds and streams
Made holy by their dreams,
Nor feel the heart-break in the heart of things?

The artfulness of it - with the repetition, for instance,
of 'rain' and 'things', to express how sorrow winds back
upon itself - only becomes apparent after the truth and
beauty of the poem have got home;   and then we think, not
how clever of the poet to use this form, but how faith-
fully this form has fixed his meaning.
    Mr W.J. Turner, with his perhaps overready response
to the thrilling touch of strange names, his riotous
imagination, not always concentrated on the object as it
is in his beautiful poem 'Ecstasy', about the marble
frieze;   Mr Gordon Bottomley, a skilful craftsman in
verse;   gallant Mr Robert Graves, with his hearty chants
of the war, his beautiful poem, 'Not Dead', on his friend
David, which was quoted in these columns only a week or
two ago;   Mr Maurice Baring's long, ornate, and thought-
ful memorial poem to Lord Lucas;   and Herbert Asquith's
fine thought on 'The Volunteer', the city clerk who went
'to join the men of Agincourt' - in all these Georgian
poetry proves its worth.   The book gives also Mr Ralph
Hodgson's 'The Gipsy Girl', with the blinding flash of
its conclusion:

A man came up, too loose of tongue,
And said no good to her;
She did not blush as Saxons do,
Or turn upon the cur;

She fawned and whined 'Sweet gentleman,
A penny for three tries!'
- But oh, the den of wild things in
The darkness of her eyes!

We have still left, however, two poets who seem a little
taller than the general.   One of them is Mr John
Freeman, the other is Mr J.C. Squire.   Mr Freeman is at
once the most ambitious and the most wilful artist of the
set, and his thought and emotions are the most difficult
to share.   He suffers, perhaps, from excessive choice-
ness;   is so much afraid of the commonplace that he
prefers even the appearance of individuality which can be
gained by wilful carelessness.   'November Skies' would
be a beautiful poem but for a caprice in rhyming and
order which cannot, in the case of so strong an artist as
this, be put down to ignorance or lack of ear.   He is at
his most masterful in 'Discovery', which, indeed, is the
key to his poetic practice:

>   All this was hers - yet all this had not been
>   Except 'twas seen.
>   It was my eyes, Beauty, that made thee bright;
>   My ears that heard, the blood leaping in my veins,
>   The vehemence of transfiguring thought -
>   Not lights and shadows, birds, grasses and rains -
>   That made thy wonders wonderful.

True;   but not, in the end, a sufficient excuse for Mr
Freeman's tyranny over the means of poetic beauty.   He
is at his best in the long poem, 'The Pigeons', where his
realization of the story of two children frozen to death
has been passionate enough to carry him out of his curio-
sity and self-consciousness:

>   Under the roof the air and water froze,
>   And no smoke from the gaping chimney rose.
>   The silver frost upon the window pane
>   Flowered and branched each starving night anew,
>   And stranger, lovelier, and crueller grew;
>   Pouring her silver that cold silver through,
>   The moon made all the dim flower bright again.

Lovely, cruel, cold: the poem forces these upon us as
relentlessly as the frost which killed the birds and the
children.   And with subtle art Mr Freeman, after melting
suddenly into pitiful indignation at this cruel scheme of
things, freezes us again at the close.   He has written
the poem because he was haunted with the idea, 'So men
are driven to things they hate to do'.   There may be
more wrestling yet between Mr Freeman's self-
consciousness and his feeling, but when they make friends
he will write fine poetry.

Mr Squire is well known as a parodist of the first
order;   fairly well known as a satirist with courage
equal to his deftness.   The poem called 'The Lily of
Malud' shows another side to his talent.   'From Poe
through "The Revenge"' might tick it off;   and, like most
ticking off, would misrepresent it.

> The Lily of Malud is born in secret mud,
> It is breathed like a word in a little dark ravine
> Where no bird was ever heard and no beast was ever
>   seen,
> And the leaves are never stirred by the panther's
>   velvet sheen.
>
> It blooms once a year in summer moonlight,
> In a valley of dark fear full of pale moonlight;
> It blooms once a year, and dies in a night,
> And its petals disappear with the dawn's first light;
> And when that night has come, black small-breasted
>   maids;
> With ecstatic terror dumb, steal fawn-like through
>   the shades
> To watch, hour by hour, the unfolding of the flower.

The poem goes on to describe the night's doings, the
opening of the lily, and the return of the maids.   It
may seem a mere fancy, but in its fancy it holds fast
that moment in the lives of all after which nothing is
the same again.   Lightly, as if the poet were letting
anything pass through his brain that would, yet with a
security that reveals concentration and choice, it draws
us into wonder;   and, technically, it is a good example
of Georgian freedom controlled by the poet's own sense of
point and beauty.   Another poem full of imagination is
'A House';   but, arresting and vivid though it be, it is
to a great extent mere display.   We feel it to be all
about nothing, because houses do not as a matter of fact
bear with tempests, or outface awful unconjectured myst-
eries.   Mr Squire certainly in one verse guards against
our mistaking him to suppose that they do, but the bal-
ance is not even.   Mr Drinkwater's 'Reciprocity', which
we have quoted, holds the needed truth.   And perhaps be-
cause Mr Squire is here building on a false foundation,
his superstructure has obvious faults and passages of
ugliness.   In his lines 'To a Bull-dog', on the other
hand - a memorial poem to a soldier killed in war - there
is not a false note.   Homely in detail, as free-and-easy
as could be in movement and diction, the poem is a work
of true emotion.

      And, when mankind is dead and the world cold,
      Poetry's immortality will pass,

sings Mr Gordon Bottomley.   To read this volume of
'Georgian Poetry', knowing that it contains only a few
poems from a few of the younger poets of the day, is to
be encouraged and comforted in woeful times.   They do
not turn their backs on the tradition, these young poets,
most of whom are living lives that no poet lived before.
They take up their heritage, as an heir takes his estate,
and make what changes they will.   But poetry goes on;
and, with poetry, all that poetry stands for.

29.   HOLBROOK JACKSON, 'TO-DAY'

January 1918, 197-8

'Along such friendly bypaths we have found it exceedingly
pleasant to stray': that would seem the keynote of
Holbrook Jackson's review, as it was typical of much
contemporary response.
      Holbrook Jackson (1874-1948), who briefly partnered
Orage on 'The New Age' (see Introduction, pp. 20-1), edited
'To-Day' from 1917 to 1923.   He wrote studies of Shaw,
William Morris and William Caxton, and many other books.
'Dreamer of Dreams', a series of studies of a group of
nineteenth-century idealists, was published two months
before his death.

It is too often taken for granted that great poetry is
produced only in the great days - the 'periods' that are
noted and labelled in handbooks of literature written by
analytical and sometimes uninspiring professors.   There
are, of course, decades or lustrums when the arts seem to
flourish with exceptional and sudden vigour and names are
made that will ring through history; but it is quite un-
fair and uncritical to neglect the interspaces.   Wise
anthologists know that these spaces are full of flowers,
and that fame does not always come at a bound.   In
poesy, the quality of the work in recent years has been
proved by the series of 'Georgian Poetry' selections, the
third of which is before us - an admirable and successful

effort to preserve in more permanent form the best work -
and often the great work - of the younger generation of
poets.   This volume is of interest, in many ways, apart
from the principal path of art; it provides, for example,
an illuminating study in contrasts.   What finer foil for
Robert Nichols's staccato war-impression 'The Assault'
than Harold Monro's wonderful, quiet, creepy mood entitled
'Every Thing'?   And what more fascinating than to compare
the manner in which a similar subject is treated by
Herbert Asquith in 'The Volunteer', and by J.C. Squire in
the lines 'To a Bulldog'?   Along such friendly bypaths
we have found it exceedingly pleasant to stray, while
still bearing in mind the main fact - that in this and the
two preceding companion volumes we possess the most rep-
resentative selection of modern verse that it is possible
to obtain.   In spite of all personal preferences - and
no anthology ever yet succeeded in perfectly satisfying
every reader - we find nothing here that should have been
omitted, although, with others, we may turn the pages in
an occasional search for something else which we should
be loath to miss, naturally!
   Eighteen writers are represented, some of them bearing
names familiar to readers of 'To-Day'; nine of these
appear for the first time in this series, and the wisdom
of the editors [sic] is well shown in their decision to
allot more space to new-comers.   The book is an example
of skilful choice and thoughtful, critical appreciation.

30.   'VERSE PLEASANT AND UNPLEASANT', T.S. ELIOT,
'THE EGOIST'

March 1918, 43-4

_____

'Apteryx' [T.S. Eliot] reviews 'Georgian Poetry, 1916-
1917' and 'Wheels, a Second Cycle'.
   For the regrettable necessity of paraphrasing Eliot's
article, see headnote to No. 25.
   Eliot takes here a more critical look at Georgian
'pleasantness'.   Robert H. Ross comments fairly:

   It is unfortunate that Eliot chose to distort one of
   the secondary qualities of 'Georgian Poetry' I and II
   under the pretext of reviewing volume III.   The
   charge of 'pleasantness' is far more easily supportable

against volumes I and II than against III .....
'Georgian Poetry' III was precisely the one volume in
the series in which 'pleasantness' was at a minimum.
It is difficult to understand what Eliot found either
'insidiously didactic' and 'Wordsworthian', or
'decorative, playful' and 'minor-Keatsian' in Sassoon's
war poem, 'They' ..... or in Graves's 'It's a Queer
Time'; or Nichols's 'Assault' ..... The charge of
'caressing all they touched' might have set well
against only one of the major groups of poets in
'Georgian Poetry' III: the Squire - Turner - Freeman
school. But curiously Eliot saw fit specifically to
exempt the archetypal poem of that group from his
strictures. '"The Lily of Malud"', he concludes, 'is
an original and rather impressive poem which deserves
better company.' [Robert H. Ross, 'The Georgian
Revolt', 1967, 182-3.]

In the following (April) issue of 'The Egoist' Eliot
was to return to the attack on neo-romanticism: 'Keats,
Shelley and Wordsworth punish us from their graves with
the annual scourge of the Georgian anthology'.
It is happy to recall that Eliot was present at the
small dinner party in honour of Marsh's eightieth birth-
day. Although neither he nor Christopher Hassall kept a
record of his speech, Hassall writes:

the general drift was to the effect that for some time
people had regarded the two of them almost as antagon-
ists. And yet they had both worked to the same end -
each in his own way. 'Schools' and fashions might
give rise to heated differences of opinion, but they
came and went, while Poetry remained. The only real
distinction was 'good' and 'bad' verse. They both
knew the 'good' when they saw it, each in his own as-
pect of poetry, so that all along, above any contro-
versy there may have been, they had, in fact, been
colleagues in one cause. 'I salute you', he said,
'and drink your health'. ['Edward Marsh: a Bio-
graphy', 1959, 672-3.]

Why Eliot should have chosen as a pseudonym the Greek
name (meaning 'without wing') for the kiwi, the New
Zealand bird which 'lies during the day in holes in the
ground, or at the foot of trees, and comes out in the twi-
light' ('Chambers's Encyclopaedia'), is puzzling. Could
it have been in reaction against the Georgian lark or the
more exotic aviary of the Sitwells? For a note on Eliot
and 'The Egoist' see Introduction, p. 33.

Writing clearly from his own experience, Eliot speaks of
the poet's need to 'cross himself with the best verse of
other languages and the best prose of all languages'.
Georgian poetry, on the contrary, is inbred.   He finds
exceptions in the third Georgian anthology, notably
Squire's long poem (see Robert H. Ross's comments quoted
above).   He also allows some differences between the
contributors.   But nearly all of them have in common the
quality of 'pleasantness'.   Of this there are two
varieties: the Wordsworthian ('a rainbow and a cuckoo's
song') and the decorative, minor-Keatsian ('too happy,
happy brook').   'In either variety, the Georgians caress
everything they touch .....'   There is incidentally
another variety of the pleasant: the unpleasant (see
Rupert Brooke on sea-sickness).

Eliot cannot see the resemblance to Tennyson which,
apparently, 'people often remark' in Georgian poetry
(many of the Georgians were, of course, consciously re-
acting against Tennyson).   He does not 'care to pose as
a champion of Tennyson', but he was careful in his syntax,
and his adjectives had definite meaning.   Moreover he
had a brain and it saved him from triviality: James
Stephens (Eliot runs together couplets from 'Westland Row'
and 'Check') takes a trivial subject ponderously.   There
are passing comments on Sassoon, Turner ('not very happy
in his adjectives'), Squire, Nichols, Graves ('a hale and
hearty daintiness'), Gibson, Baring and Asquith (each of
whom employs the word 'oriflamme'), Drinkwater (who says
'Hist!') and Freeman.

'Wheels', Eliot continues, 'is a more serious book'
(David Daiches was to write: '"Wheels" presents the
Waste Land in cap and bells':   'Poetry and the Modern
World', Chicago, 1940, 87).   'The book ..... has a
dilettante effect, refreshing after the schoolroom', and
its contributors are aware of literature in other
languages.   They have 'extracted the juice' from Verlaine
and Laforgue, but they need Catullus, Homer, Heine and
Gautier.   Eliot concludes his article with six para-
graphs, in note form and smaller print, commenting on the
contributions to 'Wheels' of Osbert Sitwell, Aldous
Huxley, Sacheverell Sitwell, Iris Tree, Edith Sitwell, and
Helen Rootham.

'Georgian Poetry 1918-1919'

Published November 1919
'To Thomas Hardy'

Prefatory note

This is the fourth volume of the present series.   I hope
it may be thought to show that what for want of a better
word is called Peace has not interfered with the writing
of good poetry.
    Five authors appear for the first time, and to one of
them I have an apology to make.   The poem called 'The
Temple', which was published in 'The Westminster Gazette'
last year, is here printed without the permission of the
writer, whom I have tried in vain to trace.   I can only
ask him to accept my admiration as an excuse.

September 1919   E.M.

31.   'MODERN POETRY AND MODERN SOCIETY', UNSIGNED ARTICLE,
'THE ATHENAEUM'

16 May 1919, 325-6

This unsigned attack on the Georgians in particular and
the whole anthological hierarchy, which appeared as lead-
ing article in 'The Athenaeum', was almost certainly by
the magazine's editor, J. Middleton Murry.

Murry's was one of the first assaults on the anthology
movement which had built up increasingly as other editors
followed Marsh's successful example.   One of the earliest
and closest rivals had been R.C. Trevelyan's 'Annual of
New Poetry', whose resemblance to 'Georgian Poetry' was
noted by several reviewers (see No. 24);   for later rivals
see Nos 34, 56 and 57.   Murry's case is a fair one:
anthologies can encourage a taste for anthologies, and
can influence poets to write the sort of poems acceptable
in them.   In a letter to 'The Times Literary Supple-
ment' (24 November 1921, 746), T.S. Eliot proposed that
poets should take a stand against the system: 'The work
of any poet who has already published a book of verse is
likely to be more damaged than aided by anthologies'.
Robert Graves joined in the correspondence: 'A poet who
once gets marked by the reviewers with the ranch-brand of
the anthology in which he first appears is thereafter
made to suffer for the failings of the other weaker mem-
bers of the herd, with whom he may have nothing in
common' ('The Times Literary Supplement', 1 December
1921, 789).   This consideration, however, did not
prevent Graves's contributing to the fifth Georgian anth-
ology.   (See also Robert Graves and Laura Riding, 'A
Pamphlet Against Anthologies', 1928.)
For a note on Murry and his editorial career see
Introduction, pp. 22-4.

For some few years past England has been the theatre of
a strange comedy - a 'boom' in poetry.   Poetry has been
almost as fashionable as war-work, and perhaps the
interest in it has been almost as external.   Ladies with
independent incomes and advanced drawing-rooms have com-
peted for the condescension of poets not averse to recit-
ing their own compositions.   The poetical tea has run
the _thé dansant_ close in social estimation.
The immediate cause of this curious phenomenon is
pretty well-known.   The publication of the anthology of
'Georgian Poetry' a year before the war marks the begin-
ning of a trajectory of which the downward curve has per-
haps already begun.   'Georgian Poetry' was cheap;   it
was fairly comprehensive.   It gave the purchaser the
right to claim at least a nodding acquaintance with a
dozen poets whom he had not the energy or the inclination
to unearth singly.   Thus it became a sort of easy guide
to polite conversation.   You could choose one of the
batch at random and maintain your choice against all
comers.   In a company of a dozen ladies each could

manifest the individuality of her intellectual interests
with a delightfully small expenditure of intellectual
effort.   To pursue our simile of a trajectory, the cannon-
ball was well designed, after a pattern calculated to re-
duce friction to a minimum.   If only it could be ejected
with a fair amount of force from a considerable elevation,
an unusual flight was assured.   Happily, these other con-
ditions were satisfied.   The social elevation was consid-
erable.   It was, indeed, (for poetry) almost dizzy.

No wonder, then, that the flight seemed miraculous.
Even without the tragic accident of Rupert Brooke's death
at that phase in his experience of war when the intellect
had not yet begun to rebel against the instinct's enthus-
iasm, - even without the glamour of this heroic sacrifice,
the large course of the movement was already secure.   But
Brooke's death had incalculable consequences.   Up to that
moment the new popularity of poetry had only, as it were,
a government backing.   Brooke, becoming a national hero,
covered with his mantle of stars all his poetical compan-
ions;   they became participants in a national movement.
The general public is not to be expected to distinguish
between contemporary poets.   At a liberal estimate the
number of persons who can do that with a rough accuracy
is at no time more than a few hundreds.   The fact that
the Georgians had as little in common as an average dozen
jurymen did not detract from their homogeneity for the
purposes of the social psyche.   It was not this or that
contemporary poet who had been assigned to the national
Pantheon.   Contemporary poetry itself had suffered apo-
theosis.

So it was that the interest in modern poetry taken by
what is more narrowly called 'society' was more than sim-
ilar to its interest in war-work.   The two interests in-
sensibly merged into one another.   The cult of poetry
had a vague patriotic justification.   To entertain a
poet to tea was a slightly more exotic variation on enter-
taining a wounded soldier.   The consequences of the coin-
cidence were portentous.   The production of poetry in-
creased as the production of war-material.   Publishers
who had for years past refused to touch a verse by an un-
known writer suddenly discovered that their lists were
commercially incomplete without four or five books of
poetry.   Anthology followed anthology.   It is said with
authority that the demand has for some months past been
abating.   If this is so, it would be of interest to de-
termine more exactly the point at which the ebb began.
The inexperienced observer would probably select the date
of the armistice;   the older hand, for reasons which he
himself might find it hard to put on paper, would more

likely choose Christmas, 1917, the date when Mr Asquith's
Government was displaced by that of Mr Lloyd George.
    It is, however, sufficient for our immediate purposes
to establish that the boom has been, and that it is now on
the decline.   We have an excuse and an opportunity for
attempting to appraise the effects of this surprising con-
jecture of social sentiment and poetical production.
First of all, it must be steadily borne in mind that the
conjecture is surprising.   One has continually to bear in
mind the attitude of the educated public to the outburst
of poetry a century ago to realize that the social atten-
tion to young poets which has now become a commonplace is
a very odd phenomenon indeed.   We believe that the first
edition of five hundred copies of Keats's 1821 volume was
not sold out until nearly thirty years after his death.
Modern poets in their twenties, who even on a generous
estimate are not quite of Keats's quality, have no diff-
iculty in disposing of as many editions as there are years
since they left their schools.   The situation is singular
enough to deserve more than a perfunctory examination.
    If we regard the 'boom' as already on the decline and
consider first its effects, we are led to pronounce that
the most obvious of these is that young poetry is
rangé. (1)   It has been an establishment of its own.
Before the 'boom' took place, the Poet Laureate was our
single poetical institution, about which were grouped one
or two potential Poets Laureate.   After the 'boom' we
observe a certain displacement in the heavens.   'Georgian
Poetry' is a new fixed star, nebular perhaps in structure,
but with a cumulative brightness sufficient to outshine
the old and familiar constellation.   There is no reason
to suppose that it will not be as regular in its annual
orbit as any charted luminary.   Round it revolve, with
the laudable periodicity of true satellites, lesser anth-
ologies, which hardly need to be enumerated.   The whole,
with its perturbations and aberrations, its wheels within
wheels, has the characteristics of a system;   and this
system is now a familiar feature of the intellectual
heavens.
    From this the remote, dispassionate astronomer is led
to a second observation: that the stability and brill-
iance of this new system mainly depend upon its nebular
structure.   It is based upon anthologies.   They alone
can have the necessary regularity;   they alone (for
reasons which we have already explained) can exert the
necessary attraction, stars that nobody looks at being of
course celestial nonentities.   This anthological basis of
the system has, however, an important consequence.   An
anthology demands, if not minor poets, minor poetry.   An

anthology that recreates itself annually demands the
habit of minor poetry in its component minds.   And even
a poet who is potentially major cannot form the habit of
minor poetry without running a grave risk of becoming a
minor poet.

A further observation follows.   The poets upon whom
this inexorable anthological law is exercised are, by
hypothesis, young poets.   Yet precisely in youth is this
habit of minor poetry most dangerous.   Youth is the time
for a poet to try every potentiality he has.   He can only
do this, as they say, by 'stretching himself'.   Youth
does not beat Milton by trying to write a better sonnet
than 'To Cyriack Skinner'; but youth, by trying to beat
'Paradise Lost', may achieve not a fine, not a more
beautiful, but a more important poem than 'Lycidas'.   Or,
at least, youth may gain an inkling of the way to such an
achievement.   But by the self-chosen groove of minor
poetry, youth, like a marble on a toy bagatelle board,
rolls assuredly to nothing but a *trompe l'oeil* perfection.
That this is, in fact, its gentle destination is shown
most forcibly by the visible and astonishing excellence
of Mr Hardy's later poems.   Beside these, the gems of a
Georgian anthology are manifestly paste.   They have no
substance.   You feel that a brass pin applied to the back
of them would be enough to destroy their glitter for ever.
On Mr Hardy's poems the keenest and most toughened knife
blade would break.

Mr Hardy is a man of indubitable genius.   It is, we
willingly admit, unfair to pit him against Georgian or
post-Georgian.   But that is not our intention.   What is,
or what should be, disquieting is that Mr Hardy, whether
perforce or by inclination, was during the greater part of
his life only occasionally a poet.   His years of plenty
were devoted to the composition of the Wessex novels.   The
great and, in outward form, minor poetry of his later
years is not the logical culmination of a lifetime de-
voted to the practice of minor poetry - if it were, it
would be something very different - but the consequence of
the habit of large design and stubborn accomplishment in
the novel form.   He has acquired the capacity of long
breath and great effort.   His lyrics display no facile or
beautiful adaptation of content to form.   The content is
tremendous; it is, we feel, compelled into the form by a
mind which has learned to make language obey its purposes.
This is the constructive secret of real poetry.   It can
never be acquired by the practice of minor poetry; it is
therefore, profoundly rebellious to the constraint of the
anthological law.

So we may conclude that the effects of the poetical
'boom' upon poetry are likely to be unfortunate to the
poets involved in it.   We may also conclude that contem-
porary poets have their salvation in their own hands.
They must break up the anthological system in which their
comfortable revolutions are at present pursued.   They
must shoot off into the invisible unknown upon preposter-
ous epic paths; there they may find at last an orbit of
their own and may display a brilliance which, though it
may take years to be discovered, will certainly not be
nebular.   On the other hand, they may be dissipated into
a pinch of stellar dust descending unnoticed through the
atmosphere.   That is the risk when you challenge immort-
ality; but not to have taken it is to be for a poet a
very clayey soul indeed.   Finally, there is a possibility
- remote and unlikely indeed but still a possibility -
that the poet of our day is already completely outside the
anthological system, preoccupied, obscure, invisible
through the telescope of the modern Maecenas, which is
perhaps, after all, not so very powerful.

Note

1 Steady.

32. UNSIGNED REVIEW, 'THE LONDON MERCURY'

December 1919, 201-5

The anonymous author of this review of 'Georgian Poetry,
1918-1919' suggests in the second and final paragraphs
the movement towards a coterie which Murry had attacked
(No. 31) and was to attack again (No. 34).

The new collection of 'Georgian Poetry' contains specimens
of the work of nineteen poets, fourteen of whom have
appeared in one or more of the previous volumes of the
series, while five are represented for the first time.
The fourteen are Mr Lascelles Abercrombie, Mr Gordon
Bottomley, Mr W.H. Davies, Mr Walter de la Mare, Mr John
Drinkwater, Mr John Freeman, Mr W.W. Gibson, Mr Robert

Graves, Mr D.H. Lawrence, Mr Harold Monro, Mr Robert
Nichols, Mr Siegfried Sassoon, Mr J.C. Squire and Mr W.J.
Turner.   The five are Mr Francis Brett Young, Mr Thomas
Moult, Mr J.D.C. Pellow, Mr Edward Shanks, and Mrs
Fredegond Shove.   On account of their editorial connect-
ion with 'The London Mercury', the contributions of Mr
Squire and Mr Shanks will not receive further mention in
this notice.

'I hope', observes E.M. in his preface, 'that [the
present volume] may be thought to show that what for want
of a better word is called Peace has not interfered with
the writing of good poetry.'   Certainly many critics
have supposed that war was the prime generator of what
they admit to be a new movement in poetry.   But the
anthologist's hope is justified, on *a priori* grounds at
least, by the fact that the movement began, however tent-
atively, before the late war.   The first collection of
'Georgian Poetry' appeared in 1912, when the title ex-
pressed an act of faith, based on an act of divination,
which has since been confirmed.   A comparison of the four
members of the series suggests that what, for want of a
better word, has received this name, is still in a state
of slow development towards a certain community of spirit
and attitude, which does not however connote any uniform-
ity of style.   In the third volume the nebula appeared
to be taking shape, and in the fourth the process has ad-
vanced a stage.   E.M. may be issuing the fourteenth
before that shape can be accurately defined and described.
The curve has not been drawn far back enough for us to say
what course it will trace;   but there is already enough
of it to look like a curve and not merely like a wavy
line.

That remote first volume, which was of course a symptom
and a rallying-point of the new tendencies, not their
origin, seems now to have been somewhat chaotic and lack-
ing in direction.   It included such older poets as Mr
G.K. Chesterton, Mr Sturge Moore, and Sir Ronald Ross;
and some of those who appear to-day the most character-
istic had not then shown themselves.   At that time the
most powerful tendency seemed to be leading towards the
realism, sometimes informed with a conscious brutality,
of Mr Masefield, Mr Gibson, and Mr Abercrombie.   In 1919
this sort is fully represented only by Mr Abercrombie's
'Witchcraft: New Style', a poem principally in dialogue
which is realistic in method, if its conception has a
fairy-tale brutality about it.   Such lines as the follow-
ing are in a familiar style:

> A little brisk grey slattern of a woman,
> Pattering along in her loose-heel'd clogs,
> Push't the brass-barr'd door of a public-house;
> The spring went hard against her; hand and knee
> Shoved their weak best. As the door poised ajar,
> Hullabaloo of talking men burst out,
> A pouring babble of inflamed palaver.

In spite of their vividness and exactitude, they make us
think of a good passage of prose slightly spoiled. Mr
Gibson has not continued in the vein, and is confined here
to a few momentary impressions, mostly in the sonnet form.

But if we dismiss this tendency from those we imply
when we speak of 'Georgian' poetry, if we admit too that
Mr W.H. Davies is often not characteristic but a poet who
might have appeared at almost any time (as, in another way,
is Mr John Drinkwater), what are we to take for our defin-
ition? If we are ever to devise one, we must somehow re-
concile and bring under one heading a bundle of qualities,
which seem to have but little in common when they are sep-
arately described. Yet that there is some common term,
some central motive, is suggested by the fact that the
pieces in this book which may be thought to be on a lower
level than the rest, those by Mr Moult and Mrs Shove, are
yet not wholly out of place. These writers have been
touched in some degree by the spirit of the time, which
manifests itself with more power and originality in poets
so diverse as Mr de la Mare, Mr Sassoon, and Mr Turner.
But it is likely that for some time we shall have to con-
tent ourselves with such vague recognitions of spirit,
without attempting to be more precise in definition.

We must at all events include Mr Monro's curious and
good poem, 'Man Carrying Bale', which by its title gives
a faint suggestion of some sorts of modern painting, and
is actuated by the same desire, to flash suddenly a light
on a familiar thing from an unfamiliar angle:

> The tough hand closes gently on the load;
> Out of the mind, a voice
> Calls 'Lift!' and the arms, remembering well their work,
> Lengthen and pause for help.
> Then a slow ripple flows from head to foot
> While all the muscles call to one another:
> 'Lift!' and the bulging bale
> Floats like a butterfly in June.

With this may be associated Mr Davies's remarkable piece,
'A Child's Pet':

[Quotes 'A Child's Pet', all five stanzas.]

Yet of how different a quality is the whole admirable selection of eight poems from Mr de la Mare, to illustrate which we quote the exquisite 'Fare Well':

[Quotes 'Fare Well', all three stanzas.]

We come again upon another manner in the poems of Mr Robert Nichols.   Here an inadequate passage from a long and very lovely piece called 'The Sprig of Lime' will serve to suggest his qualities:

> Sweet lime that often at the height of noon
> Diffusing dizzy fragrance from your boughs,
> Tasselled with blossoms more innumerable
> Than the black bees, the uproar of whose toil
> Filled your green vaults, winning such metheglyn. (1)
> As clouds their sappy cells, distil, as once
> Ye used, your sunniest emanations
> Towards the window where a woman kneels -
> She who within that room in childish hours
> Lay through the lasting murmur of blanch'd noon
> Behind the sultry blind, now full, now flat,
> Drinking anew of every odorous breath,
> Supremely happy in her ignorance
> Of Time that hastens hourly and of Death
> Who need not haste.

These poems are not realism, but passages of reality imaginatively seized and transfigured by passion;   and the same description may be applied to a number of pieces in this book as different from these as these are from one another.   If we attempt to map out the whole achievement and promise which the book represents, we must refer to the originality and beauty of rhythm displayed by Mr John Freeman in such a poem as 'The Alde', which begins

> How near I walked to Love,
> How long, I cannot tell.
> I was like the Alde that flows
> Quietly through green level lands,
> So quietly, it knows
> Their shape, their greenness and their shadows well;
> And then undreamingly for miles it goes
> And silently, beside the sea.

We must refer also to Mr W.J. Turner's noble and largely
conceived, if a little chaotic, poem 'Death'; and to Mr
Sassoon's extraordinarily economical and finished pictures
of impressions at the front and in England.   There is
moreover Mr Brett Young's graceful and delicate talent.

If we say that in all these it is possible to perceive
reality imaginatively seized and transfigured by passion,
even if we add a general curiosity to penetrate behind
the appearances of things to their substance, we say no
more than we ought to say of any poetry which we are dis-
posed to praise.   Perhaps if we could say much more we
should distinguish the literature with which we are deal-
ing as one which has forsaken the proper traditions of the
art for qualities of a merely temporary interest.   It is
not necessarily the business of new poets to discover new
objects for poetry; it is their business to bring to bear
on the old objects their own new personalities and what-
ever has accrued both to the language and to general human
experience.   We are of opinion that the 'Georgian' poets
are doing this; and though to give them that title still
requires something of an act of faith, it is one much
easier to make than it was seven years ago.

The survival of the word as the name of a period is,
of course, not yet assured.   Many of these writers are
still extremely young.   Some of them will develop in ways
which cannot yet be foreseen.   Mr Nichols and Mr Turner,
both of them capable of grandiose conceptions and engaged
in making a style to sustain them, will very likely att-
empt the drama, where an empty throne is waiting.   Mr de
la Mare, who is probably the oldest of the distinctively
Georgian writers, grows every year deeper and solider,
and it is impossible to say what will become of him.   Mr
Robert Graves is producing a body of work almost every
line of which is as sweet and sound as a nut, and is an
influence against the obscurity from which a good many of
his contemporaries suffer.   The author of 'A Ballad of
Nursery Rhyme', which begins:

> Strawberries that in gardens grow
> Are plump and juicy fine,
> But sweeter far as wise men know
> Spring from the woodland vine.
>
> No need for bowl or silver spoon,
> Sugar or spice or cream,
> Has the wild berry plucked in June
> Beside the trickling stream,

may perhaps have done a service by writing these lines at
the same time as Mr Turner was writing such a fine but
involved stanza as this from 'Death':

> That sound rings down the years - I hear it yet -
> All earthly life's a winding funeral -
> And though I never wept,
> But into the dark coach stept,
> Dreaming by night to answer the blood's sweet call,
> She who stood there, high-breasted, with small, wise
>   lips,
> And gave me wine to drink and bread to eat,
> Has not more steadfast feet,
> But fades from my arms as fade from mariners' eyes
> The sea's most beauteous ships.

And others no doubt will appear who are now no more
thought of than were Mr Nichols or Mr Graves or Mr Turner
in 1912.

At least this movement - we do not use the word in the
sense of 'organised movement' or 'school' - has had the
luck of early recognition and careful fostering.   There
are faults to be found with this as with the three earl-
ier volumes of the series, but, in a world which has
produced no faultless anthology, we ought not to expect
the first to be a collection of contemporary verse.   No
one will be able to look through the book without object-
ions rising to his lips.   Every reader will want this or
that poet omitted, this or that included.   There are few
readers of anthologies who do not find, on mature consid-
eration, that they could have done the work better them-
selves, and this would be just if, in fact, anthologists
worked only for themselves.   But to E.M. we must assign
the credit of having carried through an exceedingly diff-
icult task with as few mistakes as could be thought poss-
ible.   He has the extra distinction of having foreseen
seven years ago the beginning of a 'liveliness' which has
justified him by enduring until at this moment it shows
no signs of recession.   He would be no doubt the last
person to claim the invention, or even the discovery, of
the 'Georgian' movement.   But he might reasonably
claim, and, if he does not, the honour must be thrust
upon him, to have provided it with a means of growing
naturally and without undue extravagance.

Note

1   'A spiced or medicated variety of mead, originally
    peculiar to Wales'. 'O.E.D.'

33. UNSIGNED REVIEW BY J.C. SQUIRE, 'THE NEW STATESMAN'

22 November 1919, 224 and 226

It is interesting to establish from a file copy Squire's
authorship of this review. His support of the Squire-
archy (himself, of course, excepted) is understandable;
that 'one misses Mr Ralph Hodgson and Mr Masefield' can
only mean, for him, that they are missing, for he ad-
mired neither. But what is particularly significant is
the praise of Walter de la Mare, together with his comm-
ent that 'the weaker of the poets ..... shows traces of
the influence of the others'. Only a fortnight later
Middleton Murry was to show (see No. 34) that Squire had
been as guilty as anyone in 'the sincerest form of
flattery' of one of de la Mare's poems.
For a note on Squire see Appendix, p. 415.

It is seven years since the first Georgian Poetry book
appeared. It contained a selection from poems pub-
lished in the years 1911-1912. Its success was immed-
iate, and the editor, who preferred to disguise himself
- if disguise it can be called - under the initials of
'E.M.', was emboldened to publish a second volume, for
1913-1915, and a third for 1916-1917. These three vol-
umes are now in their thirteenth, twelfth and eleventh
thousands respectively. The enterprise is established
on a solid basis; it has been proved both that there is
a demand for an anthology of current production and that
the public is satisfied that 'E.M.' is the man to make it.
No justification is needed, therefore, for continuing it;
indeed, it is difficult to imagine an excuse for stopping
it. So long as good poetry is being written so freely
as it is at present this miscellany - reminiscent of
Tonson's systematic undertaking and the more sporadic
Elizabethan 'posies' - should endure; and the fourth
volume, published this week, comes as an expected thing,
which will in due time be succeeded by a fifth and sixth.
A considerable change has come over the list of con-
tents since seven years ago. The first Georgian Book
did contain in Rupert Brooke, J.E. Flecker and Walter de
la Mare three poets whom to-day we recognise as having
been, however indefinably, in the van of the contemporary
movement. But there was no detectable tendency in the
volume as a whole, or indeed in its next successor.

Several poets, rather casually chosen from the elder gen-
eration, were included; and even the younger poets in
these volumes differed greatly in outlook and method.   If
they did, they did; the object of the anthologist was to
collect the best recent verse, irrespective of substance
or style; and that was his proper object.   But the int-
eresting thing, to a close student of the series, is that
as time has passed the volumes - therein presumably, and
we think certainly, reflecting the movement of the time -
have become increasingly homogeneous.   Of almost all the
poems of the third volume it could be said that they
would not have been written precisely thus at any other
time; and we can already feel, though only a later gen-
eration will be able precisely to analyse, elements
which almost all their authors have in common.   The
editor has not confined himself to one of several
equally intelligent and competent groups; his admissions
are far more open to criticism than his exclusions;
there are streams of feeling and habits of mind, as there
are modes of expression, which are characteristic of al-
most all the poets of this generation who are worth
noticing.

The third volume made something of a sensation owing
to the inclusion of a large body of satirical or realist-
ic war-poetry by Messrs Nichols, Graves and Sassoon.
There is no such arresting section in the present volume,
which reflects the war not at all, and is very largely
concerned with the English landscape.   Fourteen poets
who were in previous volumes (one misses Mr Ralph Hodg-
son and Mr Masefield) are here, and there are five new-
comers: Francis Brett Young, Thomas Moult, J.D.C.
Pellow, Edward Shanks and Fredegond Shove.   To say that
the quality of the newer, or of the older, poets is uni-
formly good would be to 'employ the language of exagger-
ation'.   But it is significant that the weaker of the
poets included show traces of the influence of the
others; and that some of those - rather tedious realists
originally - who are veterans in the series have now cast
off their old habits and become guilty of the sincerest
form of flattery.

The most conspicuous figure - if, possibly, not the
most influential - in the whole series is Mr Walter de la
Mare.   Mr de la Mare has set his generation high stand-
ards of sincerity in conception and conscientiousness in
execution; and his example has been more powerful than a
hundred essays in bringing writers back to the truth that
poetry is 'the rhythmic creation of beauty'.   There is
nothing narrowly constricting in that old definition; it
insists, not upon a limited range of objects, but upon a

genuinely poetic mood.   If poetry is to be created, the
poet must be moved and not merely interested, he must
respond to something beautiful in the object, whether the
object be a rose, a dunghill, or even Evil itself.   When
this truth is lost sight of we get at best a series of
interesting statements and at worst a series of dull ones.
Mr de la Mare has never written a poem, good or bad,
which was not the work of a poet;   and, in the process of
time, he has steadily matured.   Those who read his
'Listeners' and 'Arabia' when they first appeared must
have thought that subtlety of execution, as they must
have thought that magic of vision, could no further go;
but he has bettered those poems, and bettered them in
verses less obviously elaborate.   And an intellectual,
and a spiritual, almost, religious, element have stolen
into his work of recent years.   These are not repres-
ented in the selection here printed but it would be diff-
icult to find eight short poems of our own or any other
time more uniformly lovely.   'The Sunken Garden' and
'The Three Strangers' have a grave beauty, a completeness,
an effortless exactitude, which excel anything that Mr de
la Mare has previously done;   and 'Fare Well', if it has
not these qualities in so high a degree, expresses a pro-
found and simple emotion with exquisite spontaneity:

[Quotes 'Fare Well', all three stanzas.]

Here, and in the specifically religious poem, 'The
Scribe', we find what suffices the poet as a creed.   And
it is not far from being the creed of most of the contri-
butors to the volume.   They are, most of them and most
of their time, content to express the simpler emotions;
they look at beauty in man and in the physical world
gratefully, with an intense love bound up with, born of,
the sense of transience.   All sorts of good poems are
not in the book, but one sort is here in abundance, the
poem of landscape looked upon not with the mere careful
eye but with emotion.   Even those poems which are love
poems are dominated by landscape or images drawn from it.
Among the best are several of Mr John Freeman's;   'The
Alde', for instance, and 'The Wakers':

> The joyous morning ran and kissed the grass
> And drew his fingers through her sleeping hair,
> And cried, 'Before thy flowers are well awake
> Rise, and the lingering darkness from thee shake.
>
> 'Before the daisy and the sorrel buy
> Their brightness back from that close-folding night,
> Come, and the shadows from thy bosom shake,
> Awake from thy thick sleep, awake, awake!'

Mr Brett-Young's remarkably beautiful and personal poems
are equally steeped in English country.   His longest
poems are his best;   these are pure nature-poetry;   and is
it arguable that even his charming 'Song' is a nature
poem?

> Why have you stolen my delight
> In all the golden shows of Spring
> When every cherry-tree is white
> And in the limes the thrushes sing,
>
> O fickler than the April day,
> O brighter than the golden broom,
> O blither than the thrushes' lay,
> O whiter than the cherry-bloom,
>
> O sweeter than all things that blow . . .
> Why have you only left for me
> The broom, the cherry's crown of snow,
> And thrushes in the linden-tree?

The lady is subsidiary, we feel; but she couldn't mind.
Mr Nichols, relating a human tragedy, and very poignantly,
has as the centre of his picture not the dying man but the
lime-tree;   the latest poems of Mr Sassoon show a tendency
in the same direction;   in the religious poem of Mr J.D.C.
Pellow (his single and admirable specimen here) the temple
is the wood and trees the fellow-worshippers.   Mr Shanks's
'Night-Piece', 'The Glowworm', 'A Hollow Elm', and some of
Mr Turner's work (though his vision is peculiar) show
similar preoccupations;   and the striking thing is that
though most of the poems in the book are 'ordinary' in
form and plain in language, and though their subjects have
been familiar from the dawn of time, nevertheless, since
they are honestly written, the contemporary influences
come imperceptibly in;   scarcely a poem in the volume
could have been written in any other age.
     To praise or to stigmatise particular poems in this
short space would be invidious.   One can only conclude by
saying that Mr Turner in his long poem 'Death' reaches a
height he has not previously reached, though he still
allows himself unnecessary awkwardnesses and obscurities;
that Mr Davies still pipes his familiar tune as sweetly as
ever;   that Mr Bottomley seems to have been unproductive
of late;   that Mr Graves is turning into an excellent
writer of short songs and dialogues in antique modes;   and
that Mr Monro's entry is the best that has come from him.
Twenty years hence both the importance of this verse and
its characteristics will be more easily estimated.

34. 'THE CONDITION OF ENGLISH POETRY', J. MIDDLETON
MURRY, 'THE ATHENAEUM'

5 December 1919, 1283-5

Murry's biographer, F.A. Lea, suggests that this article
was 'mainly responsible for his reputation at that time -
a reputation that was a mystery to himself' ('The Life of
John Middleton Murry', 1959, 68).   He quotes from a
letter of Murry's to Katherine Mansfield (29 October
1919): 'There's no doubt it's a fight to finish between
us and them: them is the "Georgians" *en masse*.   It's a
queer feeling I begin to have now: that we're making
literary history' (ibid., 69).   Murry's attack was a
turning point: 'From this moment', writes Christopher
Hassall, 'E.M.'s anthologies ceased to hold their position
as the acknowledged vehicle for the best in contemporary
verse' ('Edward Marsh: A Biography', 1959, 474).   Murry
wrote to Marsh:

> Now, Eddie, I want you to believe this of me.
> Nothing in my literary career has given me greater
> pain than being compelled to fight against you.   I
> want you to believe that I hold you one of the kindest
> friends I have ever had; that it is an agony (no less)
> to me to be driven to fight one of whom all personal
> memories are fragrant with generosity and loving-
> kindness.   [Hassall, op. cit., 475.]

After more than half a century one can be impressed by
the modernity of Murry's criticism, the closeness of his
critical method in contrast to the belles-lettres of his
time.   Some of his points were to be developed by later
writers in their attacks on the Georgians.   It is well to
remember the context in which Murry makes them: he is re-
viewing the fourth anthology, not its predecessors.
   For a note on Murry see Introduction, pp.22-4.   See
also No. 31.

Shall we, or shall we not, be serious?   To be serious
nowadays is to be ill-mannered, and what, murmurs the
cynic, does it matter?   We have our opinion; we know
that there is a good deal of good poetry in the Georgian
book, a little in 'Wheels'.   We know that there is much
bad poetry in the Georgian book, and less in 'Wheels'.

We know that there is one poem in 'Wheels' beside the
intense and sombre imagination of which even the good
poetry of the Georgian book pales for a moment.   We
think we know more than this.   What does it matter?
Pick out the good things, and let the rest go.

And yet, somehow, this question of modern English
poetry has become important for us, as important as the
war, important in the same way as the war.   We can even
analogize.   'Georgian Poetry' is like the Coalition
Government;   'Wheels' is like the Radical opposition.
Out of the one there issues an indefinable odour of comp-
lacent sanctity, an unctuous redolence of *union sacrée*;
(1)   out of the other, some acidulation of perversity.
In the coalition poets we find the larger number of good
men, and the larger number of bad ones;   in the opposit-
ion poets we find no bad ones with the coalition badness,
no good ones with the coalition goodness, but in a single
case a touch of the apocalyptic, intransigent, passionate
honesty that is the mark of the martyr of art or life.

On both sides we have the corporate and the individual
flavour;   on both sides we have those individuals-by-
courtesy whose flavour is almost wholly corporate;   on
both sides the corporate flavour is one that we find
intensely disagreeable.   In the coalition we find it
noxious, in the opposition no worse than irritating.   No
doubt this is because we recognize a tendency to take the
coalition seriously, while the opposition is held to be
ridiculous.   But both the coalition and the opposition -
we use both terms in their corporate sense - are unmist-
akably the product of the present age.   In that sense
they are truly representative, and complementary each to
the other;   they are a fair sample of the goodness and
badness of the literary epoch in which we live;   they are
still more remarkable as an index of the complete confus-
ion of aesthetic values that prevails to-day.

The corporate flavour of the coalition is a false sim-
plicity.   Of the nineteen poets who compose it there are
certain individuals whom we except absolutely from this
condemnation, Mr de la Mare, Mr Davies and Mr Lawrence;
there are others who are more or less exempt from it, Mr
Abercrombie, Mr Sassoon, Mrs Shove, Mr Nichols and Mr
Moult;   and among the rest there are varying degrees of
saturation.   This false simplicity can be quite subtle.
It is compounded of worship of trees and birds and cont-
emporary poets in about equal proportions;   it is sicklied
over with at times quite a perceptible varnish of modern-
ity, and at other times with what looks to be technical
skill, but generally proves to be a fairly clumsy remini-
scence of somebody else's technical skill.   The negative

qualities of this *simplesse* (2) are, however, the most
obvious; the poems imbued with it are devoid of any
emotional significance whatever.   If they have an idea
it leaves you with the queer feeling that it is not an
idea at all, that it has been defaced, worn smooth by the
rippling of innumerable minds.   Then, spread in a lumin-
ous haze over these compounded elements, is a fundamental
right-mindedness; you feel, somehow, that they might have
been very wicked, and yet they are very good.   There is
nothing disturbing about them; *ils peuvent être mis dans
toutes les mains*, (3) they are kind, generous, even
noble.   They sympathize with animate and inanimate
nature.   They have shining foreheads with big bumps of
benevolence, like Flora Casby's father, and one inclines
to believe that their eyes must be frequently filmed with
an honest tear, if only because their vision is blurred.
They are fond of lists of names which never suggest
things; they are sparing of similes.   If they use them
they are careful to see they are not too definite, for a
definite simile makes havoc of their constructions, by
applying a certain test of reality.
     But it is impossible to be serious about them.   The
more stupid of them supply the matter for a good laugh;
the more clever the stuff of a more recondite amazement.
What *is* one to do when Mr Monro apostrophizes Gravity in
such words as these?

     By leave of you he places stone on stone;
     He scatters seed: you are at once the prop
     Among the long roots of his fragile crop.
     You manufacture for him, and insure
     House, harvest, implement and furniture,
     And hold them all secure.

We are not surprised to learn further that

     I rest my body on your grass,
     And let my brain repose in you.

All that remains to be said is that Mr Monro is fond of
dogs ('Can you smell the rose?' he says to Dog: 'Ah
no!'), and inclined to fish - both of which are Georgian
inclinations.
     Then there is Mr Drinkwater with the enthusiasm of the
just man for moonlit apples - 'moon-washed apples of
wonder' - and the righteous man's sense of robust rhythm
in this chorus from 'Lincoln':

You who know the tenderness
Of old men at eve-tide,
Coming from the hedgerows,
Coming from the plough,
And the wandering caress
Of winds upon the woodside,
When the crying yaffle goes
Underneath the bough.

Mr Drinkwater, though he cannot write good doggerel, is a
very good man.   In this poem he refers to the Sermon on
the Mount as 'the words of light From the mountainway.'
Mr Squire, who is an infinitely more able writer,
would make an excellent subject for a critical investig-
ation into false simplicity.   He would repay a very close
analysis, for he may deceive the elect in the same way as,
we suppose, he deceives himself.   Unfortunately we
cannot afford the space for the investigation.   His poem
'Rivers' is a very remarkable example of the *faux bon*. (4)
Those who are curious of these things should read the poem
and then read Mr Walter de la Mare's 'Arabia' (in 'The
Listeners').   They will find that not only the idea is
derivative, but the rhythmical treatment also, and they
will see how commonplace and coarse Mr de la Mare's ex-
quisite technique may become in the hands of even a
first-rate ability.   We may add that Mr Squire is an
amateur of nature -

And, skimming, forktailed in the evening air,
When man first was were not the martens there? -

and a lover of dogs.
Mr Shanks, Mr W.J. Turner and Mr Freeman belong to the
same order.   They have considerable technical accom-
plishment of the straightforward kind - and no emotional
content.   One can find examples of the disastrous simile
in them all.   They are all in their degree pseudo-
naïves.   Mr Turner wonders in this way:

It is strange that a little mud
Should echo with sounds, syllables, and letters,
Should rise up and call a mountain Popocatapetl,
And a green-leafed wood Oleander.

Of course Mr Turner does not really wonder;   those four
lines are proof positive of that.   But what matters is
not so much the intrinsic value of the gift as the kindly
thought which prompted the giver.   Mr Shanks's speciality
is beauty.   He is also an amateur of nature.   He bids
us: 'Hear the loud night-jar spin his pleasant note '.

Of course Mr Shanks cannot have really heard a night-jar.
His description is proof of that.   But again, it was a
kindly thought.   Mr Freeman is, like Mr Squire, a more
interesting case, deserving detailed analysis.   For the
moment we can only recommend a comparison of his first and
second poems in this book with 'Sabrina Fair' and 'Love in
a Valley' respectively.

It is only when we are confronted with the strange
blend of technical skill and an emotional void that we
begin to hunt for reminiscences.   Reminiscences are no
danger to the real poet.   He is the splendid borrower who
lends a new significance to that which he takes.   He in-
corporates his borrowing in the new thing which he creates;
it has its being there and there alone.   One can see the
process in the one fine poem in 'Wheels', Mr Wilfrid
Owen's 'Strange Meeting':

[Quotes 'Strange Meeting', lines 1 to 15.]

The poem which begins with these lines is, we believe, the
finest in these two books, both in intention and achieve-
ment.   Yet no one can mistake its source.   It comes,
almost bodily, from the revised Induction to 'Hyperion'.
The sombre imagination, the sombre rhythm is that of the
dying Keats;   the creative impulse is that of Keats.

  None can usurp this height, return'd that shade,
  But those to whom the miseries of the world
  Are misery, and will not let them rest.

That is true, word by word and line by line, of Wilfrid
Owen's 'Strange Meeting'.   It touches great poetry by
more than the fringe;   even in its technique there is the
hand of the master to be.   Those monosyllabic assonances
are the discovery of genius.   We are persuaded that this
poem by a boy with the certainty of death in his heart,
like his great forerunner, is the most magnificent ex-
pression of the emotional significance of the war that has
yet been achieved by English poetry.   By including it in
his book, the editor of 'Wheels' has done a great service
to English letters.

Extravagant words, it may be thought.   We appeal to
the documents.   Read 'Georgian Poetry' and read 'Strange
Meeting'.   Compare Wilfrid Owen's poem with the very
finest things in the Georgian book - Mr Davies's 'Lovely
Dames', or Mr de la Mare's 'The Tryst', or 'Fare Well',
or the twenty opening lines of Mr Abercrombie's disapp-
ointing poem.   You will not find those beautiful poems
less beautiful than they are;   but you will find in

'Strange Meeting' an awe, an immensity, an adequacy to
that which has been most profound in the experience of a
generation.   You will, finally, have the standard that
has been lost, and the losing of which makes the
fatras (5) of a book like 'Georgian Poetry' possible,
restored to you.   You will remember three forgotten
things - that poetry is rooted in emotion, and that it
grows by the mastery of emotion, and that its signific-
ance finally depends upon the quality and comprehensive-
ness of the emotion.   You will recognize that the tricks
of the trade have never been and never will be discovered
by which ability can conjure emptiness into meaning.

It seems hardly worth while to return to 'Wheels'.
Once the argument has been pitched on the plane of
'Strange Meeting', the rest of the contents of the book
become irrelevant.   But for the sake of symmetry we will
characterize the corporate flavour of the opposition as
false sophistication.   There are the same contemporary
reminiscences.   Compare Mr Osbert Sitwell's 'English
Gothic' with Mr T.S. Eliot's 'Sweeney';   and you will
detect a simple mind persuading itself that it has to
deal with the emotions of a complex one.   The spectacle
is almost as amusing as that of the similar process in
the Georgian book.   Nevertheless, in general, the
affected sophistication here is, as we have said, merely
irritating;   while the affected simplicity of the coal-
ition is positively noxious.   Miss Edith Sitwell's del-
iberate painted toys are a great deal better than painted
canvas trees and fields, masquerading as real ones.   In
the poems of Miss Iris Tree a perplexed emotion manages
to make its way through a chaotic technique.   She rep-
resents the solid impulse which lies behind the oppos-
ition in general.   This impulse she describes, though
she is very, very far from making poetry of it, in these
not uninteresting verses:

But since we are mere children of this age,
And must in curious ways discover salvation
I will not quit my muddled generation,
But ever plead for Beauty in this rage.

Although I know that Nature's bounty yields
Unto simplicity a beautiful content,
Only when battle breaks me and my strength is spent
Will I give back my body to the fields.

There is the opposition.   Against the righteous man, the
mauvais sujet. (6)   We sympathize with the *mauvais sujet*.
If he is persistent and laborious enough, he may achieve

poetry. But he must travel alone. In order to be
loyal to your age you must make up your mind what your
age is. To be muddled yourself is not loyalty, but
treachery, even to a muddled generation.

Notes

1 Sacred compact.
2 False simplicity.
3 They can be handed to everyone.
4 Counterfeit.
5 Hotch-potch.
6 Black sheep.

35. 'GEORGIAN POETRY: NEW STYLE', UNSIGNED REVIEW,
'THE TIMES LITERARY SUPPLEMENT'

11 December 1919, 738

Appearing less than a week after Murry's, this article
must have come as further discouragement to Marsh: note
especially the last sentence of its penultimate para-
graph.

The idea of these anthologies was excellent, success has
proved the need for them, and our gratitude is due to the
editor. The title more and more sits like a man's hat
on a boy's head, for it might easily cover much that
there has never been any intention of including: besides,
the character of the collection has altered slowly till
this last volume is least like the first; in fact, quite
different. Long poems are fewer and shorter, and the
bulk of the contents has acquired a strong family like-
ness. The original group of authors was more varied in
aim and achievement. This may be no reproach to the
editor; two of the most promising of that group are dead;
others are middle-aged, others have become too well known
for space in a collection limited as this is to be fairly
assigned to them; those who have filled these places have
perhaps necessitated this slighter and more ornamental
character. The original purpose is, however, still ful-
filled; doubtless this volume, like its predecessors,

will form and focus taste, being a little raft in the
chaotic wreckage of English literary effort that strews
the Actual Sea; it holds together and tends in one
direction.

It is possible, and may be gracious, to illustrate
this change from the work of those authors who can be
most highly praised.   In 1912 the alphabet seemed well
inspired, as it placed Mr Abercrombie first with 'The
Sale of St Thomas', one of the finest, if not the finest,
poem of an equal length produced of recent years.   This
year he once more opens the volume with 'Witchcraft: New
Style'.   Alas! its effect on the imagination resembles
that of a clumsy lie on the intellect: unconvinced, you
blush for the author; yet the writing is not careless,
the invention is still abundant and bold, only both seem
forced and vain.   There is no real effect of a woman's
attraction on an infatuated man, neither is it an apt
symbol for it; you turn away wounded instead of grateful.
It was a happy thought in the 1913-15 volume to relegate
Mr Abercrombie's unequal 'End of the World' to the end of
that volume so as to open with Mr Gordon Bottomley's 'King
Lear's Wife'.   This year, instead of a puissant and poet-
ically conceived tragedy, we have from him a short blank
verse piece which never quite flows or carries us away.
It fails in the manner opposite to Mr Abercrombie's being
more poetical by intention and suggestion than in effect.

Mr Davies is delightful, quaint, refreshing, and quite
equal to his past in these eight little poems.   You read
them over and over, listening to their beauty, and then
after a while a stanza drops out here or there and you
find them yet more perfect.

Not for her beauty will I praise the moon,
But that she lights thy purer face and throat;
The only praise I'll give the nightingale
Is that she draws from thee a richer note.

For, blinded with thy beauty, I am filled,
Like Saul of Tarsus, with a greater light;
When he had heard that warning voice in Heaven,
And lost his eyes to find a deeper sight.

The notion that this needed neither introduction nor epil-
ogue is surely no mere individual's whimsy.   Is it not
better without even those provided by Mr Davies?   By the
like process 'Birds' becomes three instead of five
stanzas, the second, third, and fifth; and 'The Bell',
which has only two, rings clearer when the last is over-
looked.   Mr Walter de la Mare has a delicate genius that

sets you thinking of Maeterlinck.   It is tempting to
account for the abundant production and popularity of the
Belgian poet as resulting from the better focused intell-
ectual life that prevails on the Continent, and the some-
what pinched and cloistered seclusion that saddens consid-
eration of Mr de la Mare's relation to the world as due to
that English diffidence in praising our own that afflicts
our finer minds and is so unhappily reinforced by the al-
most animal indifference to mental refinement which char-
acterizes our great public.   Yet perhaps all is not loss
save for that public, for Mr de la Mare is united to his
warmest admirers and has never betrayed them in a way that
some lovers of Maeterlinck would perhaps envy.

For one reason or another neither Mr Davies nor Mr de
la Mare has launched a big venture;   they content their
Muses with tiny poems, which not infrequently might be yet
further reduced by concentration, and Mr Drinkwater has
turned to prose in order to address a duller public.
Poetical minds would seem to pause and shrink from the
highest themes and grandest forms, or having essayed them
to retreat to lower ground, and the cause may lie not only
with each poet, but in the lack of spiritual direction of
a nation that turns upon itself, leaderless, discontented
and half-hearted.   Yet perhaps this is nothing but the
trough between the waves, and another and higher crest of
poetical and political power may be rolling towards us.
Or it may be that poets are little affected by the course
of events and become what they are by reacting against
their social surroundings, and that this slackwater in
both synchronizes fortuitously.

> May sudden justice overtake
> And snap the froward pen,
> That old and palsied poets shake
> Against the minds of men;
>
> Blasphemers trusting to hold caught
> In far-flung webs of ink
> The utmost ends of human thought,
> Till nothing's left to think.

The young naturally blame their predecessors;   it is the
unpardonable foible of age to 'take for granted' and treat
'as settled'·   Those archly indignant stanzas are from
one of the happiest poems in this book, by one of the
youngest contributors, Captain Robert Graves.   Neverthe-
less, it is not only among the elder and more accomplished
that we find 'the sound is forced, the notes are few'·
A striking feature is the growth and spread of ingenious

poetry of the type of Edgar Allan Poe's.   Now we know
how uncongenial his environment was to his genius.   The
focus of this tendency is at the end of the volume in the
work of Mr J.C. Squire and Mr W.J. Turner, but it is more
or less present elsewhere in Mr Edward Shanks, Mr Harold
Monro, and others;   it even has affinities with Mr de la
Mare's methods.

Some simple mood, perception, or admitted truth is
taken and deliberately elaborated until it seems portent-
ous;   the means employed are tireless repetition, as in
'The Bells', cascading catalogues of nouns and adject-
ives, and often a repeated reference to secret knowledge
or a world known only to the poet, as in 'Ulalume', 'The
City in the Sea', 'Dreamland', or 'The Raven'.   Mr
Squire's 'Rivers' proceeds coldly and steadily upon these
lines and rarely attains any felicity;   but his 'Birds'
is a success, and perhaps the most interesting and
original poem in the whole volume: it is finely proport-
ioned and well written.   Mr Turner is more musical in
phrase and rhythm, but the process lies as nakedly in his
'Talking with Soldiers', 'Princesses', and 'Death'.
There is no reason to suppose that these young men know
as much about the process as Poe did;   they are probably
almost unconscious of it;   and in each of them it is
allied with different gifts - in Mr Shanks's 'Fête
Galante' with perhaps deeper aesthetic emotion but less
intellectual power, hence its less clear progress and
confused design.   Swinburne in such a poem as 'Before the
Mirror' carries the process on to the heights of the inev-
itable by the impetus of his genius.   The tendency occurs
perhaps when the intellect seizes the bridle over soon.
'Before the Mirror' offers hardly anything for brains to
grip, hence its escape from the effect of a foregone con-
clusion.   Have these poets not been content to await the
visit of the Muse but risen to meet her halfway?   and is
that why she teases them by making her call so formal?
These processes are economical, they save time and labour;
but if effect is more easily come by, it defeats itself
and is found out and staled as quickly.   Inevitable
poetry is also inexplicable, a miracle like life in an egg,
that hatches out in the mind to endless wonder and delight.

The waste of gift and labour saddens a critic who
broods over the vast surplus of lyrics produced, which
attract, promise, but fail to fulfil.   How few capture
memory, live on, and can be trusted not to grow stale!
Have the minds that produce this waste, though truly
gifted and moved, not been related to a sufficiently wide
realm of imagination (for actual experience is of little
use until it has become imaginary), so that their

creations lack an appropriate atmosphere and background?
This book is crammed with zestful eloquence about land-
scapes, birds (especially blackbirds and night-jars),
gold flowers and gold light, flames of passion, young
women, and even the small literary bravery of approaches
to the particularities of female anatomy.   But 'the
sound is forced'.   This sparkling flood of choice and
careful speech has no background, or suggests a common-
place one from which it is a vain effort to fly.   Perhaps
in a hundred years' time an atmosphere will have risen out
of memoirs and letters to enfold some of these raw poets,
and will preserve alive, over and above a few master-
pieces, some weaker work as is the case today for Words-
worth, Keats and Shelley.   Arnold, Rossetti, Browning and
Tennyson have as yet no stable background of this kind, no
depth of atmosphere in which to breathe immortality;   for
it is not mere anecdotes, and appreciation of foibles that
creates it, but a comprehension of the springs of inspir-
ation deep down in the character which holds respect and
admiration, though leaving us free to acknowledge fault
and absurdity and even vulgarity and dullness on the sur-
face.   We are still too distant from such disinterested
nonchalance to appraise these poets, most of us champion
some of them and neglect others for accidental and person-
al reasons.   One of the most foreboding facts about
'Georgian Poetry' is its acceptance as representing the
best contemporary opinion;   and yet is it not a narrow
selection from the work published since 1911 with a grow-
ing family likeness to mark it off?
    Several poems not referred to above deserve special
commendation.   'A man dreams that he is the Creator', by
Mrs Fredegond Shove, who is the first poetess to appear
in these anthologies.   One wonders why.   Hers is a
happy talent with a novel quaintness.   Quaintness seems
to be rising in poetical estimation, as in the time of
Sir Thomas Browne and Andrew Marvell.   Mr Monro's
'Gravity', which amusedly confuses Newton's law with God,
unites this tendency with the ingenious process.   Mr
Robert Nichols's 'Sprig of Lime' is almost a success;   it
convinces you that the incident really occurred, which if
it did not is a considerable feat;   but his appreciation
of its beauty leads to a feverish eloquence which troubles
the surface of the deeper mood on which the poem rests.
Captain Siegfried Sassoon's 'Sick Leave' and 'Banishment'
are also noteworthy for profound and convincing emotion.
Mr Marsh is besides to be congratulated on having un-
earthed a charming little psalm by a poet of whom he tells
us that he knows nothing but the name appended to it,
J.D.C. Pellow -

The worshipping trees arise and run,
With never a swerve, towards the sun;
So may my soul's desire
Turn to its central fire.

With single aim they seek the light,
And scarce a twig in all their height
Breaks out until the head
In glory is outspread.

36. A. WILLIAMS-ELLIS, 'THE SPECTATOR'

31 January 1920, 143-4

Unsigned review by A. Williams-Ellis of 'The Georgian
Poetry Book [sic], 1918-1919'.
    In a perverse piece of chop-logic, F.R. Leavis was to
write: 'The Georgian movement may fairly be considered
as a "movement", since it can be considered as little
else' ('New Bearings in English Poetry', 1932, 62).
Amabel Williams-Ellis speaks of a movement, and whether
or not she intends it in the same sense as the author of
No. 32, she does not 'use the word advisedly in inverted
commas' as Monro in his letter to Marsh (No. 61).
    Lady Williams-Ellis (b. 1894) is the daughter of J. St
Loe Strachey (see No. 20), and wife of Clough Williams-
Ellis, architect of Portmeirion.   Her father was editor
of 'The Spectator' of which she was literary editor
(1922-3).   She is the author of many books, including a
psychological study, 'The Tragedy of John Ruskin', and
'An Anatomy of Poetry' (1922).

In his prefatory note to the fourth volume of 'The
Georgian Poetry Book' 'E.M.' remarks that he hopes the
collection will prove that 'what for want of a better word
is called "peace" has not interfered with the writing of
good poetry'.   Of this fact we have now seen enough of
the new writers' 'peace poetry' to be completely satisfied
Indeed, in many of the soldier poets, peace, which has
brought them time and leisure of mind to digest, amend,
and heighten their work, has wrought a very great improve-
ment.   For example, in the 1916-1917 'Georgian Poetry

Book' Mr Robert Nichols was represented, among other war
poems, by 'The Assault', in which occur such lines as:

    Revolver levelled quick!
    Flick! Flick!

'The Assault' moved the civilian reader and disturbed him,
much as would have a photograph of men going over the top;
but in 'The Sprig of Lime' and 'Seventeen', which are his
two long poems this year, he reaches a far higher platform
in his ascent of Parnassus.   'The Sprig of Lime' is an
exceedingly beautiful reflective poem.   It is an account
of a death-bed:

[Quotes 'The Sprig of Lime', section 1.]

In 'Seventeen' there is an account of a squirrel.   The
creature

    Whisked himself out of sight, and reappeared
    Leering about the bole of a young beech;
    And every time she thought to corner him
    He scrambled round on little scratchy hands.

Peace has hardly changed Mr Sassoon at all as he is
represented here, though we believe that in 'Picture Show'
a different aspect of his Muse is apparent.   'Banishment',
a poem obviously autobiographical, and that most beautiful
lyric, 'Everyone Sang', are undoubtedly the two best poems
of his in this collection.
    Mr Shanks's 'Fête Galante, or The Triumph of Love', is
a longish poem of quite extraordinary and peculiar attr-
activeness.   It is an essay in the manner of Fragonard,
though there is none of the Frenchman's hard luxuriance,
but instead, with all the delightful frippery, a melan-
choly charm.   'Fête Galante' and a Fragonard engraving
would indeed exemplify very well the eternal difference of
outlook between a Latin and a Northern genius.   We can
imagine that Russian dancers, set the theme, would have
caught Mr Shanks's mood.
    Alas that Mr Squire's 'You are my sky' has not been
included!   His beautiful poem 'Rivers' is, as ever, most
delightful reading.   Much of Mr Squire's poetry is in a
way like the strange verses of Mr Turner.   That is to say
that it does not yield up its fragrance to a hasty reader.
Mr Turner's curious 'Talking with Soldiers' and 'Silence'
are not particularly attractive at first reading, but at
third and fourth perusal it is not improbable that they
may seem some of the best work in the book.

Mr Harold Monro's 'Dog' is a cunning piece of realism.
It is an account of the emotions of a dog going for a
walk, and an extremely artful piece of work.   The most
confirmed romanticist must admit that realism executed
with such skill is likely to disturb all his pet theories
of aesthetics.   'Man Carrying a Bale' is another essay
ostensibly in the same manner.   The romanticist can, how-
ever, console himself by the reflection that here the
realism is only apparent, and the poem reaches a far
higher level than in 'Dog', where it is essential.

Mr Robert Graves's verses have all a charming air of
insouciance.   His 'Nursery Rhymes' is delightful.   His
rather Pre-Raphaelite 'The Cupboard' is also most success-
ful.

Mr de la Mare and Mr W.H. Davies are both represented
by some most enjoyable *vers de société*. (1)   The second
verse of Mr Davies's 'On Hearing Mrs Woodhouse Play the
Harpsichord' is peculiarly happy:

So, lady, I would never dare
To hear your music ev'ry day;
With those great bursts that send my nerves
In waves to pound my heart away;
And those small notes that run like mice
Bewitched by light;   else on those keys -
My tombs of song - you should engrave:
'My music, stronger than his own,
Has made this poet my dumb slave.'

Perhaps the most agreeable of Mr de la Mare's poems is the
light poem called 'The Veil', which has a delicate
elegance.

Mrs Shove's and Mr Moult's poems do not seem particular-
ly attractive.   Perhaps 'E.M.' has seen other instances
of the work of these poets which for some reason or other
could not be included in the collection, and then could
not resist the temptation, ever present to beguile the
anthologist, to put in one poem because he has liked some-
thing quite different by the same author.

The reader may ask: 'Does "Georgian Poetry, 1918-1919"
give a true and comprehensive view of the new movement?
Can the "true believer" take it up and give it to his
friend and say: "There is the gist of the whole matter.
You may know from this what I am talking about when I say
the golden age has come again"?'   Probably only a very
amiable enthusiast could say that, for we all of us have
our predilections, and we would, all of us in certain
particulars have made a different selection.   But on the
whole the missionary of the new movement can safely use it

as a shibboleth.   If his would-be convert cannot at
once gather from this volume that something new is astir
in the world, then the doom laid upon him by Apollo is
that he give up reading poetry altogether and devote him-
self to fret-saw work for the future.

Note

1   Occasional pieces.

37.   'REPRESENTATIVE ANTHOLOGIES', NEVILLE CARDUS,
'VOICES'

February 1920, 36-9

Neville Cardus reviews 'Georgian Poetry, 1918-1919' and
William Kean Seymour (ed.), 'A Miscellany of Poetry',
1919.
    'Voices', a conservative magazine of the arts,
appeared from 1919 till 1921 at approximately monthly
intervals, under the editorship of Thomas Moult who con-
tributed to the fourth Georgian anthology (see Appendix,
p. 409).   The editor has evidently 'forbidden' the
reviewer to comment on his contribution to the two anth-
ologies, which does not prevent an implied tribute.
    Neville Cardus (1889-1975) was better known for his
long career as music critic and writer on cricket in
'The (Manchester) Guardian'.

We can gather a good idea from these two books of the
condition of England in the affairs of poetry at the
present time.   It is obviously a healthy condition.   One
may well doubt, in fact, whether poetry in this country
has been in the vigorous way that it is just now since
Elizabethan times.   Not that we are overrun with great
poets - they are the exception, not the rule, even in
these books.   The fine thing about our present-day
verse is less a matter of achievement than one of taste,
especially in the case of their most capable editors,
'E.M.' and Mr Seymour - the latter himself a poet.
Taste is not the final word ...   One means a sense of
poetical fitness, the instinct which leads a writer to

choose the subjects suited to verse, and to use words only
in the order that makes for a suggestion, at least, of
poetry as distinguished from the merely prosaic.   To make
my notion the clearer, let me say that the reader, glancing
through 'Georgian Poetry, 1918-19', or 'A Miscellany of
Poetry', 1919, would get a considerable shock were he to
come upon lines like these of Wordsworth's:

> . . . a household tub, like one of those
> Which women use to wash their clothes;

or these of Tennyson's:

> Comrades leave me here a little while, as yet 'tis
>   early morn,
> Leave me here and when you want me blow upon the
>   bugle horn.

Our young men have a finer critical sense than to commit
errors of taste in this egregious way.   If, indeed, a
critical sense and good taste were sufficient in them-
selves to make a poet, then poets would be two a penny
nowadays.   Unfortunately rather rarer qualities are
needed.   The critical sense may prevent a man from
making a fool of himself, but also it puts a bit into the
mouth of his Pegasus.   Who risks not the ridiculous may
miss the sublime.   Nearly every contribution to these
books strikes one as having been written by poets of dis-
cretion.   They will only venture for the most part into
the realms of common experience;   there is little enough
indication that poetry is being conceived of as an
immense adventure.   The choice of language, as well as
the choice of theme, is invariably meticulous.   Mr
Chesterton has told us that every young man begins to
write poetry as though he were a thousand years old, and
'Georgian Poetry', in particular, reminds one of this.
There is Mr J.C. Squire, for instance.   He is probably
not quite a young man, as the calendar goes, yet who but a
'twentieth century young man' ever wrote verses like that
beginning

> Within mankind's duration, so they say,
> Khephren and Ninus lived but yesterday.
> Asia had no name till man was old
> And long had learned the use of iron and gold;
> And aeons had passed, when the first corn was planted,
> Since first the use of syllables was granted - ?

Here we have that tendency to play with an idea in a
purely intellectual way, with the result that though such
poets are often simple enough they are seldom passionate
or beautiful.   Again let us look at Mr Siegfried
Sassoon's 'Thrushes':

> Tossed on the glittering air they soar and skim,
> Whose voices make the emptiness of light
> A windy palace.   Quavering from the brim
> Of dawn, and bold with song at edge of night,
> They clutch their leafy pinnacles and sing
> Scornful of man, and from his toils aloof
> Whose heart's a haunted woodland whispering;
> Whose thoughts return on tempest-baffled wing;
> Who hears the cry of God in everything,
> And storms the gates of nothingness for proof.

The poetry gets dissipated at the beginning of the sixth
line, simply because the poet's vision and the emotion
which it has evoked lose their intensity - either through
the lack of a really powerful impulse or more likely be-
cause Mr Sassoon's habit of generalising in quasi-
philosophical terms was too strong.   Thrushes are not
'scornful of man', and the poet who has been so finely
moved by thrushes as to conceive them making 'the empti-
ness of light a windy palace' ought to have no use for a
poor intellectual conceit like that.   I would have liked
to show here how Mr Thomas Moult, who is represented in
both these volumes, has succeeded where, though not in
perfect things like 'Everyone Sang', Mr Sassoon has
failed, but I am forbidden .....   Mr Drinkwater has
verses in both anthologies which are interesting and
beautiful in a middle-aged way.   It is poetry though
that lies a little too near the conventional aspect of
things.   It is dreadfully sane.   I cannot for the life
of me understand the impulse which drives a man to write
verse which merely articulates the sentiments of average
suburbanism.   There was never a greater fallacy in the
world than that a poet must express the thought and
emotion of the plain man.   Milton's reach was beyond the
common scope, so was Browning's, Meredith's, Keats's.
Theirs is a world remote from the day's usage simply be-
cause it is ideal, and it is only to be entered after a
considerable purging of the flesh.   Mr F.V. Branford is
not always articulate, but he is at least beating his
wings against the bars.   Not for him the stucco house and
its tidy garden - to change the metaphor.   He handles
language like a lord of it.   In his finest work - not
included in 'A Miscellany' - he can handle words so that

they suggest, as no poet has suggested before, a sense of
depth, altitude and of distance, making a new sublimity
out of the sky's windy spaces.   Mr Golding's 'Shepherd
Singing Ragtime', in the 'Miscellany', has a big-throated
melody that reminds us of the essential Golding - a poet,
who when he likes, can sing as lovely a music as anybody
making poetry to-day.   He is in love with rhythms and
images.   Miss Stuart reveals a similar love in the fine
examples of her work in Mr Seymour's book.   Mr W.J.
Turner has a poem in 'Georgian Poetry' which begins -

> The mind of the people is like mud,
> From which arise strange and beautiful things,
> But mud is none the less mud ...

which would seem to show that even an acute critical
sense is not necessarily sufficient to prevent a man from
getting rather comic in poetry now and then.
     Only on a detailed analysis of these books, though,
does one grow a little captious.   The sights, sounds, and
smells of the English countryside are often in the verses
(as Mr Graves's delicious 'Ballad of Nursery Rhyme'), ex-
perienced and felt with sensitiveness and charm.   In
addition there is individuality, especially in the in-
stances of Mr Davies, Mr de la Mare, and Mr Lawrence -
those contributions must not be dwelt upon in an essay
intentionally devoted to the newer comers.   All in all,
these qualities have hardly been excelled in our poetry in
any other age.

38.   'A POET'S EXPERIMENT IN CANDID CRITICISM', SIEGFRIED
SASSOON, 'THE NEW YORK TIMES'

29 February 1920, Book Section, 2

Sassoon's review of the 1918-19 volume was one of the few
notices of 'Georgian Poetry' to appear in the USA: see
Introduction, p. 34.   Robert Graves had written to Marsh:
'"It's a very arboreal book", said Bob Nichols to me, and
I remarked on the apparent instability of all the elms as
contrasted with the enormous vitality of the nightingales'
(quoted in Christopher Hassall, 'Edward Marsh: A
Biography', 1959, 473).
     For a note on Sassoon see Appendix, pp. 413-14.

When William James was seeking a moral equivalent for war
he suggested a few perilous occupations in which the
young man power of this earth might exhaust its heroic
energy and zest for adventure.   Potential Major Generals
and probable privates were to become volunteers for a
strong selection of life risking enterprises (which were
to be at the same time physically formidable, commercially
constructive and morally magnanimous).

Can any form of spontaneous ink-spilling be reckoned
among proposed substitutes for the blood-shedding which
has so recently provided our civilization with spiritual
uplift?   Can a plain fountain pen be mightier than a
short magazine-loading Lee-Enfield rifle?

I had not considered this problem until I was asked to
write a signed review of 'Gerogian Poetry'.   But when
confronted by this blameless British anthology I find that
I am personally acquainted with all except four of the
nineteen contributors: several of them are my intimate
friends, and I am myself one of the contributors.

Could any reviewer's task be more hazardous - morally?

Nevertheless, in approaching the affair I am consoled
by the hope that my review may be an obscure but unden-
iable landmark in the history of log-rolling.

I do not know any authoritative definition of that pro-
vocative verb, but on turning to a 'Thesaurus of English
Words and Phrases' one discovers 'log-roll' significantly
associated with such nouns as 'co-operation', 'alliance',
and 'collusion'.   The word 'criticism' does not appear on
the same page at all.   Now, my brief but lurid exper-
iences of journalism and the literary life have led me to
suppose that, were the secret history of any poetic move-
ment to be written, the verse-builders might be rather
heavily implicated in the 'log-rolling' revelations.

> Wandering by lone sea-breakers,
> And roaming by desolate streams

may be an essential part of the 'music-makers'' career,
but the poetic mind can likewise turn toward the more
homely attractions of the 15 per cent. royalty, and a man
who is capable of the most crocus-crowded lyrics may yet
be a qualified chartered accountant.

From dead, symbolic logs one turns easily to the living
Georgians, several of whom are heavily compromised with
various trees.   In fact, a cursory glance might lead one
to suppose that this is a tree-anthology.   If I were in a
more enthusiastic mood I might affirm that Francis Brett
Young's 'The Leaning Elm', which concludes

> This maim'd tree
> May stand in leaf when I have ceased to be.

is a perfect peach of a poem.   Or that Edward Shanks's
'A Hollow Elm' is the finest tribute to a tree since the
revival of half-timbered domestic architecture.

> What hast thou not withstood,
> Tempest-despising tree?

he begins; while John Freeman carries on the story with

> The wind has thrown
> The boldest of trees down. . .
>
> It was the wind
> So furious and blind . . .
> Against this lonely elm
> Thrust all his strength to maim and overwhelm.

While J.D.C. Pellow (I suspect him of being a beech-lover)
writes:

> How strong each pillared trunk; the bark
> That covers them, how smooth; and hark,
> The sweet and gentle voice
> With which the leaves rejoice!

But Thomas Moult plumps for the oak: it is a positive
relief to find him amiably paying his respects to that
monarch of the glade.

> Beyond the garden heavy oaks are buoyant on the meadows,
> Their rugged bark
> No longer rough,
> But chastened and refinéd in the glowing eyes of Love.

Moult's exact meaning is not easy to ascertain: but he
meant well, I am sure.   After all, one can have too much
of a good elm!   Robert Nichols, in a poem called 'The
Sprig of Lime', adds to the fine excess of this exhibition
of delight in sylvan specimens:

> Sweet lime that often at the height of noon,
> Diffusing dizzy fragrance from your boughs,
> Tasselled with blossoms more innumerable
> Than the black bees, the uproar of whose toil
> Filled your green vaults.

Having let down this ultra-vegetated back-cloth, I must
now confess to my audience that I do not wish to dissuade
any one from purchasing the book (after all, I do get a
small percentage of the profits).   But (apart from the
appeal I have made to students of botany - a comparatively
small and specialized class) I can claim, so far, to have
achieved a strictly noncommercial attitude toward 'a vol-
ume which contains some excellent poetry'.   (Publisher
will please note the quotable phrase.)   If I appear
henceforth to be slightly biased in favor of the book, it
must be remembered that English writers almost invariably
come to America in order to boost (1) their own books,
(2) those of their friends and (3), if necessary, those
written by American authors who are being more than
usually kind to them.   This peculiarity is probably due
to the fact that the English live on a small island where
there are not enough people to buy their books.   To
return to 'Georgian Poetry':   it will be noticed that
Ralph Hodgson and John Masefield are absentees.   Hodgson
has published nothing since 1917, and Masefield has re-
served his power for one long verse-narrative, 'Reynard
the Fox', which every one is reading and no one can help
admiring;   for it is a glorious poem of the English
countryside.
     But W.H. Davies and Walter de la Mare are here, with
eight poems apiece, and their work is as beautiful as ever
it was.
     This is a specimen of Davies:

[Quotes 'When Yon Full Moon', stanzas I-III.]

     And this is 'The Linnet', by de la Mare:

[Quotes 'The Linnet', all 16 lines.]

     Among the others, it is good to see the name of D.H.
Lawrence, although he contributes but one poem, 'Seven
Seals', a magnificent thing, worthy of his wild, unhappy
genius.   In addition to those already mentioned, the
volume contains representative selections from the recent
verse of Lascelles Abercrombie, Gordon Bottomley, John
Drinkwater, Wilfred Gibson, Robert Graves, Harold Monro,
F. Shove, J.C. Squire and W. J. Turner.   Nothing that I
can say about them will either increase or diminish their
future output, so I am keeping my comments on their work
for a less conspicuous occasion.   What we need most is a
modern equivalent for Shakespeare.   'Georgian Poetry' has
failed to provide it.
     But it's not a bad book, on the whole.

39.   'GORGEOUS POETRY', A. WILLIAMS-ELLIS,
'THE SPECTATOR'

13 November 1920, 641-2

Unsigned review by A. Williams-Ellis of J.B. M[orton].'s
'Gorgeous Poetry, 1911-1920'.
    J.B. Morton (b. 1893), 'Beachcomber' of the 'Daily
Express' 1924-1975, is a less skilful parodist than E.V.
Knox (see 'Parodies Regained', 1921, and 'These Liberties',
1923) or J.C. Squire (see 'Tricks of the Trade', 1917).
Although 'Gorgeous Poetry' (1920) was not widely noticed,
and many of its shafts were directed at poets to the left
of the Georgians, this short review makes Max Beerbohm's
fair point about 'sincerest flattery'.
    Morton's collected verse, 'The Dancing Cabman', was
published in 1938.
    For a note on Lady Williams-Ellis see headnote to
No. 36.

'Gorgeous Poetry' is an admirable book of parodies
printed and arranged in such a way that it cannot fail to
bring the 'Georgian' anthologies to the mind of the
reader.   The game of trying to discover which writer
each poem is intended to parody is here most amusing, a
good many of them being elusive and difficult to fix.
On the whole, the author, J.B.M., seems to find the
Sitwells most attractive, one parody entitled 'Nocturne'
beginning:

    Two policemen
    On point duty
    In the
    Pentonville Road
    Heard a rumpus.

He is also very happy with Mr Sassoon and Mr Chesterton.

[Quotes twelve lines in parody of Sassoon and eight lines
 in parody of Chesterton.]

The Irish school, Mr Waley's Translations from the Chinese,
the disciples of Rabindranath Tagore, and Mr Robert
Graves are all equally successfully dealt with, but, in
spite of the reactionary preface, J.B.M. feels just as

strongly on the subject of what we might call the Classic-
al Inadequate School.   Witness the following:

    The blackbird's gay November song
    And the primroses scattered far
    Fill all the sky with lutes and bells
    From star to frosty star.
    Beside the pond the pipit cries,
    The heather's all abloom,
    The winter sun among the sedge
    Weaves and unweaves its loom.

There is still, bulk for bulk, three times as much of this
kind of poetry written as of the more modern sort.   We
are glad that J.B.M. has included it in his reprobation.
    It is encouraging to see that the new school of poetry
is breeding a likely school of parody and satire.   No
Government can exist without an Opposition.   Poets fall
into absurdities unless they are criticized, and of all
criticism the parody is perhaps the most effective and the
least offensive.   It is like the parable in the world of
ethics - it does not rouse a spirit of opposition in the
individual criticized.   The study it shows of the poet's
work even turns it into a kind of wry compliment.   We can
accept its hints without loss of *amour-propre*. (1)   Many
of us dislike being told that we are getting fat, but few
of us are so ill-tempered that we should frown at the dis-
torting glass that tells us so with disarming exagger-
ation.

Note

1   Self-respect.

40.   'WEARY VERSE', AMY LOWELL, 'THE DIAL'

1920, 424-31

This review was reprinted in 'Poetry and Poets' (New
York), 1930, 123-36.
    Amy Lowell (1874-1925), the American poet, was one of
the contributors to 'The Egoist' and to Pound's anthology,
'Des Imagistes' (1914), and herself edited three Imagist
anthologies (she had met Pound in England, and so

thoroughly took over the movement that he renamed it
'Amygism').   She published many books of her own poems
and several collections of essays, and completed just
before her death a long biography of Keats.   Her account
of a visit to the Poetry Bookshop where she 'listened to
Mr Rupert Brooke whispering his poems' (Brooke had called
on her in Boston) was published in the 'Little Review'
(September 1914, 6), and provoked an angry letter from
Monro.   Peace was made by kind words in a later issue
(May 1915, 19-22):   see Joy Grant, 'Harold Monro and the
Poetry Bookshop', 1967, 85-6.

It is a profound labour to read this book.   Not because,
let me hastily say, there is nothing good in it, but
because it is all so dreadfully tired.
   Is this the exhaustion of the war, or is it the debil-
ity of an old habit of mind deprived of the stimulus of a
new inspiration?   It is an interesting question, for the
fatigue is undeniable.   Here are nineteen poets, in the
heyday of their creating years, and scarcely one of them
seems to have energy enough to see personally or forge a
manner out of his own, natural speech.   They are all
respectable poets, each knows his trade and can turn out
good enough verse on an old model, but how strangely one
man's contribution dovetails into the next man's!   This
is happily not true of all, but it is true of the major-
ity.   Try it - for instance, who wrote this

   But this shall be the end of my delight:
   That you, my lovely one, may stoop and see
   Your image in the mirrored beauty there.

And did the same man write this?

   And Cleopatra's eyes, that hour they shone
   The brighter for a pearl she drank to prove
   How poor it was compared to her rich love:
   But when I look on thee, love, thou dost give
   Substance to those fine ghosts, and make them live.

Is this he again, or another?

   Thy hand my hand,
   Thine eyes my eyes,
   All of thee
   Caught and confused with me:
   My hand thy hand,

My eyes thine eyes,
All of me
Sunken and discovered anew in thee.

And who is responsible for this?

Dear Love, whose strength no pedantry can stir,
Whether in thine iron enemies,
Or in thine own strayed follower
Bemused with subtleties and sophistries,
Now dost thou rule the garden...

If the reader will play fairly and guess a bit, I
think he will find himself sufficiently bewildered.   The
answer to the riddle is purely arbitrary.   The book says
that Francis Brett Young is the author of the first
quotation and the other names, in order, read: W.H.
Davies, John Freeman, and Edward Shanks.   But, for all we
can see to the contrary, the names might be jumbled about
in any order without causing the slightest confusion in
style or attitude.
    The reason is quite plain, Mr Young, Mr Davies, Mr
Freeman, Mr Shanks are merely taking the place of our old
friends Brown, Jones, and Robinson, or, to telescope the
whole after the manner of a composite photograph, we
might name them collectively John Doe.   In other words,
these gentlemen are not writing at all, it is their
poetic ancestors who are writing, they have made them-
selves ouija boards for the recrudescence of a dead song.
    There are notable exceptions to this, I am glad to
say, and I shall come to them later, but on the whole,
the book seems pale and spectre-like, haunted by the
ghosts of England's vanished bards.
    There is really no excuse for this, for even if these
English poets choose to ignore the fresh vigour of
American poetry, they have Masefield in England, and
Ralph Hodgson, and Aldington, and Sassoon.   It is stuff
and nonsense to try and raise such echoes into the
dignity of a poetic creed as Mr Squire and Mr Shanks are
constantly trying to do.   All literature is against them;
good poets are not echoes, and never were, and that is the
long and the short of it.   I am told that Mr T.S. Eliot
is having a great influence in England and, although I am
not a complete admirer of Mr Eliot's style, I can well
believe that he is needed in a country where Mr Young
stalks abroad mellifluously bemoaning the duress of poet-
hood in such a new and striking phrase as: 'Whither, O, my
sweet mistress, must I follow thee?'   His own words,
farther on in the same poem, are more than portrait;   they

are prophecy: 'The pillared halls of sleep echoed my
ghostly tread'.
    He is a wonder, this Mr Young, I can hardly tear my-
self away from him. What a memory he has, to be sure.
Where have we read:

> With all the joy of Spring
> And morning in her eyes - ?

It is foolish to ask where; it would be much more sensible
to put it 'where not'. Certainly Mr Young challenges the
spectres right smartly. He speaks of 'snow upon the
blast' of the 'livery of death'; his moon is quite com-
fortably 'hornéd', with the accent all nicely printed over
the last syllable. But let us give him his due, his
cacophony is original. Read this aloud:

> The frozen fallows glow, the black trees shaken
> In a clear flood of sunlight vibrating awaken.

But we must not leave Mr Young alone in a glorious iso-
lation; that would be to do him too much honour, for does
not Mr Davies speak of 'Yon full moon', and Mr Abercrombie
complacently watch while 'The sun drew off at last his
piercing fires'; even Mr Gibson, who is usually above
such diction, permits himself to call the sea 'the change-
less deep'.
    One could go on poking fun forever - there is matter
for it - but the thing is not funny; on the contrary, it
is desperately sad. They want to be poets so much, these
young men. They know they have something to say, they
feel it doubtless, but they are like men uttering words in
a dream; in the cold light of day, it comes perilously
near nonsense, because it is nonsense to repeat by rote a
thing which does not express one's thoughts. There is
atrophy here; this stale stuff is not merely stale, it is
pathological. We know what these young men want to say;
the strong spirits among them have told us: they want to
say how deeply they love England, how much the English
countryside (the most beautiful countryside in the world)
means to them; they detest war, and long for the past
which cannot come back, and they hope fiercely for a
future which, if they can, they will see to it shall be
better. But the power to set down all this has been
weakened by strain. They have not the energy to see
personally, or speak with their own voices. The will to
do so is strong; the nervous strength necessary for the
task (and it requires much) is lacking.
    The English countryside is here, but in all the old

tones and colours.   Surely never book was so swayed over
by the branches of trees.   Nightingales and thrushes
abound, but seldom does the poet get them alive on the
page; he loves them, but he slays them, and more's the
pity.
     This is not always true.   Mr Drinkwater's 'Chorus from
"Lincoln"' is very England, although not quite so fine as
his 'In Lady Street', which is not in this volume, and so
is Mr de la Mare's 'Sunken Garden', and Mr Monro's 'Dog'
is fully successful.   Even Mr Davies gets himself some-
times, since he can write:

     Blink with the blind bats' wings, and heaven's bright face
     Twitch with the stars that shine in thousands there.

Mr Davies tries to be himself, and it is unfortunate that
we often wish he would not.   When he describes a lark as
'raving' above the clouds, we feel that his vocabulary is
unwarrantably scanty, and it is nonsense to speak of the
'merry sound of moths' bumping on a ceiling.   'Merry' -
watching the tortured struggles of the poor things to get
out - merry!   He tells us that he is the 'dumb slave' of
a lady who brings 'great bursts' of music out of a harpsi-
chord; 'deaf' I think should be the word, for I doubt if
even a Liszt could force that frail and delicate instru-
ment to 'great bursts'.   Or, perish the thought, was the
lady really playing a piano, and did Mr Davies merely
think 'harpsichord' more poetical?
     Yes, they do try, but often only to make a mess of it.
When the nightingale does not sing, Mr Nichols observes,
'Nor has the moon yet touched the brown bird's throat',
which is mighty fine writing of a kind usually found in
'Parlour Albums' and 'Gems from the Poets for Every Day in
the Year'.   Mr Nichols has been reading the dictionary,
his boughs are 'labyrinthine   the blossom of a lime tree
is a 'hispid star of citron bloom   and 'sigils' are
burned into his heart and face.   A sort of passion for
the archaic seems to have got hold of him, we have 'flitt-
est, profferest, blowest, renewest', all in four lines.
Most of these poets love 'thees' and 'thous', that horr-
ible second person which everyday speech has happily got
rid of.   But Mr Nichols is a good poet, only he does not
hold himself up.   To speak of the trunk of a tree as
'splitting into massy limbs' is excellent, but he spoils
it by having the branches 'bowered in foliage', and yet
the man is often full of insight.   Of a squirrel, he can
say: 'He scrambled round on little scratchy hands', and
what could be finer than the 'peaked and gleaming face' of
the dying man in 'The Sprig of Lime'.   That whole poem

touches a very high mark, and sets Mr Nichols quite apart
from the John Does.

As one glances through the four volumes of 'Georgian
Poetry', one cannot help wondering on what principle they
are edited.   Scarcely on that of presenting all the best
poetry of the moment, it would seem, since Richard Alding-
ton, F.S. Flint, the Sitwells, and Anna Wickham have never
been included.   Mr James Stephens, who had been in from
the beginning, has vanished, which is a great loss;   and
Mr Hodgson, who appeared in the second and third issues,
has also gone.   It is understandable why Mr Chesterton,
as belonging to an older group, has left, but Mr Mase-
field, by all the laws of literary relationship, should
surely have remained.   Is the editor, Mr Marsh, sole
arbiter, and if so, why?   When former contributors dis-
appear, do they remove themselves, or are they assisted to
depart?   And again, in either case, why?

It is horrible to reflect on the power of an editor.
Poets, at the mercy of editorial selection, may well
tremble, reflecting on the fate of the Dutch painter Ver-
meer, who vanished for nearly three hundred years from the
knowledge of men because a contemporary writer with whom
he was so ill-advised as to quarrel omitted him from a
list of painters which was destined to become the text-
book of future generations.

Mr Marsh edits with well-defined prejudices, evidently,
but, on the whole, he has accomplished much, for he has
brought the authors of his anthologies a wide publicity.
For those who go out, others come in.   Mr Graves, and Mr
Sassoon, who, with Mr Squire, appeared first in the 1916-
17 anthology, are the chiefs of the newcomers.   The most
powerful poem in the book is Mr Sassoon's 'Repression of
War Experience'.   The war made Mr Sassoon a poet.   He
needed to be torn and shaken by a great emotion;   he has
found this emotion in his detestation of war.   Nothing
stronger than these poems, which are the outgrowth of his
suffering, has been written in England since the war
'stopped our clocks'.   It would be hard to make a select-
ion of them, and really it does not matter;   one side of a
heart is a good deal like the other side provided it be a
real flesh and blood heart.   In this case it is, and
wherever you take it, you get the same sensation.   There
is no rhetoric here, we are not treated to erudite ex-
pressions nor literary artifices, and for that reason
these poems, and 'Repression' especially, come perilously
near to being great.   I say 'perilously', for what is Mr
Sassoon going to do now?   When was 'Everyone Sang'
written?   Perhaps that points a new departure.

Mr Sassoon and Mr Graves feel so much that they can

afford to joke about it. Mr Sassoon's joking is a shade
more bitter, more ironical. For instance, 'What Does It
Matter?' is a trifle harder and heavier than Mr Graves's
'It's a Queer Time', which unfortunately is not in this
volume. Neither is 'I Wonder What It Feels Like to be
Drowned'. But one cannot have all a man's collected
works in an anthology, and we have got that fine thing,
'A Frosty Night', and the possibly even finer 'The Cup-
board'. Mr Graves is that delightful being among poets,
a *faux naïf*. (1) He runs his ballad forms hard but so
far they do not fade upon the palate.

Miss Shove is a notable addition to this year's anth-
ology. She has originality and a saving sense of the
grotesque and macabre. 'The New Ghost' is excellent.

Of the original contributors, Mr Abercrombie's poetry
is always a strange mixture of the quick and the dead.
He builds live tales on a pattern of rusty pins. The
result is according as one feels about the vexed question
of subject and treatment. I confess that I find Mr
Abercrombie worthy of respect, but dull.

Mr Davies has ardent admirers, and I am quite aware
that my making him sit as part portrait for the highly
estimable John Doe will probably cause much offence. If
only Mr Davies would always write poems like 'A Child's
Pet', would always keep to such natural speech as that in
the first four lines of 'England', I would readily sub-
tract him from the sum total of my composite hero. But
Mr Davies has read books, and they have remained in his
mind alien and undigested. Therefore he must give his
quota to John Doe, and I regretfully beg his pardon.

Mr de la Mare is scarcely at his best in this volume,
although 'The Sunken Garden' is very charming. But I
cannot forgive him his last line with the false rhyme.
False rhyming is often a most happy device, but scarcely
here, where there have been no other such rhymes in the
poem, and for the last line - particularly when he had a
perfect rhyme in his adjective! Clearly the sound did
not trouble Mr de la Mare's ear, but it teases mine
horribly.

Mr Drinkwater is a poet who must be read in a certain
mood. His poems do not yield all their fragrance if they
are hastily approached or violently attempted. They grow
on the reader as of something becoming conscious. They
seem extraordinarily simple, by every preconceived canon
they should be dull, and behold, they are neither the one
nor the other. The best of them, that is, and two of the
best are here: 'Moonlit Apples' and 'Habitation', while
'Chorus from "Lincoln"', the first half especially, is
nearly as good. What is Mr Drinkwater's charm? how does

he escape the sensation of echo, considering that he
chooses to write in a traditional mode?   To analyse it
with any care would take up too much space here;   in
brief, I think it lies in his utter abandonment to his
poem, in his complete sincerity in regard to it, in his
straightforward, unselfconscious love of what he is
writing about.   He is a quiet poet, he keeps his drama
for his plays, but his dramatic sense has taught him the
secret of creating atmosphere.   'Moonlit Apples' is
beautifully moony.   But this simplicity and this atmos-
phere are not accidental;   they are built up with deli-
cate touch after touch throughout the poem.   One could
wish that 'In Lady Street' had been included and 'South-
ampton Bells' left out, but, on the whole, his selection
is one of the best in the book.

Mr Gibson's 'Cakewalk' is a good poem, and so is the
first stanza of 'Parrots';   the latter is a complete poem
by itself;   the second stanza adds nothing, it even de-
tracts appreciably.   Why must Mr Gibson bring in his
heart?   the Parrots did so well without it.

Mr Lawrence's 'Seven Seals' is in his most mystical
and passionate vein.   The poem is serious and exalted,
but it is a pity that it should be his only contribution;
it would stand better were it companioned.   As a poet,
Mr Lawrence is rising in stature year by year;   his last
volume, 'Bay', is the best book of poetry, pure poetry,
that he has written, although it does not reach the
startling human poignance of 'Look! We Have Come
Through'.   It is unfair to Mr Lawrence to be represented
by one poem;   the editor should take heed and give us
more of him in future.

Mr Monro improves steadily.   I have already mentioned
his beautiful and exceedingly satisfactory 'Dog'.   I wish
I had space to quote it.   It is not only good poetry, but
good dog.   Mr Monro's work is gaining in muscle.   Beauty
it has often had, but now there is a firm structure under
the beauty - see, for instance, 'Man Carrying Bale'.
'The Nightingale Near the House' was a bold challenge to
Fate, but Mr Monro has come through fairly successfully.
His nightingale lives and sings, and not too reminiscent-
ly, which is much for a modern nightingale to do.

For the newer men, Mr Squire is a clever fellow.   His
criticisms, even if one disagree with them, are always
interesting.   His poetry is clever too, and that is not
so useful an attribute in poetry.   But he has done some
good things.   'August Moon', with its marvellous des-
cription of moonlight on water, is not here (really we
must quarrel with the editor for leaving it out) but an-
other of his best things, the 'Sonnet', is.   Few modern

sonnets are as good as this;   the last two lines are mag-
nificent.   'Rivers' begins well, with an original and
fluctuating rhythm which gives the lapsing and flowing of
a river to a remarkable degree, and the slight change
between the first and second stanza is well conceived.
But then he becomes tangled in his own creation, the metre
stiffens into a convention, becomes hard, unimaginative,
and cold, and the poem loses itself in a long and rather
stupid catalogue.
   Mr Turner, who appears for the second time, has a nice
little quality - he has his own turns, and a very pleasant
whimsical touch:

   The thronged, massed, crowded multitude of leaves
   Hung like dumb tongues that loll and gasp for air

gives an effect we have all seen, most vividly.   'Tink-
ling like polished tin' has the thin sharpness of tone of
a small stream, and 'old wives cried their wares, like
queer day owls' is very nice.   'Silence' is a good poem,
but the best of those here is 'Talking With Soldiers',
with its refrain 'the mind of the people is like mud', and
then the dreaming iridescence.
   Of the remaining poets - but why catalogue the virtues
or record the faults of John Doe?

Note

1 One who achieves simplicity by artifice.

41. 'THE GROUP SYSTEM IN POETRY':   UNSIGNED ARTICLE,
'THE SATURDAY REVIEW'

29 January 1921, 86-7

'The appearance of yet another anthology', 'Cambridge
Poets, 1914-20', leads the anonymous author to reflect.
   This not very distinguished article should be read in
the context of Murry's (No. 27) and the other references
mentioned in the headnote to it.

The appearance of yet another anthology has led us to re-
flect not so much on its merits, which are inconsiderable,
as upon the application of the principle of mass-
production to verse.   The group system out of which this
tendency has developed, as such is neither new nor in it-
self undesirable.   The world's literature is starred with
groups, whether they chose their own names, like the poets
of the Pleiad, or were presented with them, like the Mer-
maid and Lake Schools.   Such association has the great
merit of bringing criticism to bear by those best qualif-
ied to use it, while adding the glow of praise and compan-
ionship to those in need of it.   The course of the true
lover of letters is rougher even than that of a woman.
The public is indifferent, established writers critical,
and publishers shy.   It is natural that the newcomers
should band themselves for a common attack on all three.
     But the brigading of talent has its dangers.   It is
true that the ways leading to Parnassus are hard to the
feet, and that they are littered with the dead of spirit-
ual adventure.   But it is equally true that those who
have attained the highest peak have climbed, often in
failure, alone.   The severe judgment, whether of Euterpe
or her sisters, is not affected by the applause attending
the climber.   Indeed, it may well be supposed that these
ladies are deaf to noise as exquisitely sensitive to
music.   For them a little creepy shape limping out of
the shadows may be the hero coming home, while the brass
bands are soundlessly performing the dirge of the con-
queror whom they celebrate.   And meanwhile, the first,
true to his own vision, plods higher and higher.   The
second more and more turns his face to the pleasant and
populous plains, and in due course, as new bands and new
populations take the place of the old, is forgotten.
     In recent years we have witnessed a paroxysm of assoc-
iation.   The impetus had its origin in a protest against
the decay of poetry.   With the death of Swinburne's
powers it seemed that English poetry died.   There was a
long and barren period fitfully illuminated by the torch
of Stephen Phillips.   But apart from the glow-worm rad-
iance, and from what was whispered over the seas from
Ireland, silence and dark descended.
     The age of gold had yielded, it was supposed, to the
age of prose, when Mr Marsh changed all that.   Out of his
head - fully armed - emerged suddenly upon an intimidated
world the Georgians.   The little mud-coloured collection
had ended and begun a period.   Verse through this gentle
channel began to struggle out to sea.
     Mr Marsh had done much, when another patron of verse -
second only to him in influence - came to the aid of the

poets.   The Great War seconded his efforts - 'after us',
said the War to Mr Marsh, 'the deluge of poetry'.   In-
deed, so complete was the association of these two forces
that those who search for the authorship of the war may
be inclined to suspect Mr Marsh.   On this we pronounce
no opinion, merely observing that if Mr Marsh did, in
order to give fuller scope to poetry, create the war, he
must have subsequently regretted his action.   For Wil-
helm is not the only monarch that has been deposed.
Other and more sinister rulers in the land of post-war
poetry have appeared, and each, like Mr Marsh, with a
court fully equipped, and disputing with acerbity the
right to exist of all the others.

Let us for a moment glance at the groups.   We have
had Mr Ezra Pound and his Imagists.   Those writers saw
through the Georgians.   They were not to be ensnared by
rhyme, or what had previously been known as rhythm.

One or at most two thoughts linked to a cadence was
their battle cry.   It might well have fallen upon an un-
receptive world but for the group system.   Mr Pound,
however, looked after the pennies of his group, realising
that only thus would the Pounds look after themselves.
The shrill voices raised in chorus attracted attention,
and thus, while each individual member of the band might
sing flat or sharp, have a cracked voice or a stringless
fiddle, the total volume of sound commanded respect.
The Amalgamated Society of Imagists registered itself as
a trade union, and, having laid down its rules, provided
publicity as one of the benefits of membership.   And one
result is that a poet like Mr Flint is now finding it
hard to prove that his merits are his own (which they
are), and not a section in the Imagist system of manu-
facture ultimately to be assembled for the production of
the finished article by Mr Pound.

But the Georgians have not remained idle under this
attack.   Mr Marsh has picked up the gauntlet, and prod-
uced a counter-group.   In this he has had the formidable
assistance of Mr Squire.   They began with the war-poets.
One after another some brilliant boy in the presence of
death sent out a brief challenge to the old assailant.
These challenges were carefully collected, and in the
place left vacant by Rupert Brooke stepped Messrs. Sass-
oon, Graves and Nichols, and a host of others who died,
not only that England, but that poetry might live.   So
far as the collection of individual verse was concerned,
death imposed a unity which Mr Squire and Mr Marsh could
not mar.   But as the first glow wore off, it was seen
that the surviving figures were perhaps hardly of the
substance to stand alone.   A new group of Georgians

emerged, but these were perhaps more fully to be described as Lloyd-Georgians, in that they woke every day to find themselves famous, and were quite unable to conjecture how the Press discovered all these things.   Each of them was for all, and all for each, so that some day the printers of the next anthology will mix the type and each author's name will be affixed to the work of another, and nobody - neither author nor public - will know.

Meanwhile Mr Davison has rushed in with his anthology. The fear that here was yet a new group is allayed by an examination of Mr Davison's own poems.   He belongs, we are happy to assure the curious, to the Squirearchy. This Cambridge Anthology is, as it were, a by-product using up some of the fragments not required for the main business of production.   This explains why the intrusion of new authors is permitted.   They are not Georgians - Miss Harrison, Mr Le Maitre, Fredegond Shove and the rest - but probationers in the preparatory school which Mr Davison, with his wealth of experience and in virtue of his advanced age, is well equipped to conduct.   He is a merciless master.   All passion, all individuality go, save where the women 'D' and Miss Shove will indicate in spite of their cool pedagogue, that even at Cambridge there are hearts to be hurt.   Meantime, the central assembling factory is amassing material, and it may be that, when Mr Davison recommends one of his pupils for promotion, they may be admitted to the smoothly running shop where they will be worked into the finished Georgian article, and accorded all the advantages of being ab- sorbed into a powerful combine, with its admirable system of publicity.

Nor do we exhaust the centres of self-appreciation with these.   Are we to forget 'Coterie', 'Voices', and 'Wheels'?   We are not, at any rate, not if the capable editors of these publications can prevent it.   But in each of these groups, and so far as they are separable, there is the same instinct of self-protection.

These are all good trade unionists, rightly contempt- uous of the unorganized.   They recognize, with some pet- ulance, other unions, but for the unattached they have no mercy.   And rightly so.   If single poets - for example, Mr Binyon - are to take huge tracts of Parnassus, what is left for the groups?   The grim shadow of under- employment, even of unemployment, is always present to them.   In combining they have grasped the spirit of the age.

Posterity may, perhaps, not be so sure that this is the best spirit in which to preserve poetry.   But the groups don't care.   'Posterity', they say; 'Nonsense! We are posterity.'

'Georgian Poetry 1920-1922'

Published November 1922
'To Alice Meynell'

Prefatory note

When the fourth volume of this series was published three
years ago, many of the critics who had up till then, as
Horace Walpole said of God, been the dearest creatures in
the world to me·, took another turn.   Not only did they
very properly disapprove my choice of poems: they went
on to write as if the Editor of 'Georgian Poetry' were a
kind of public functionary, like the President of the
Royal Academy;   and they asked - again, on this assumpt-
ion, very properly - who was E.M. that he should bestow
and withhold crowns and sceptres, and decide that this or
that poet was or was not to count.

   This, in the words of Pirate Smee, was *a kind of a
compliment*, but it was also, to quote the same hero,
galling;   and I have wished for an opportunity of dis-
owning the pretension which I found attributed to me of
setting up as a pundit, or a pontiff, or a Petronius
Arbiter;   for I have neither the sure taste, nor the ex-
haustive reading, nor the ample leisure which would be
necessary in any such role.

   The origin of these books, which is set forth in the
memoir of Rupert Brooke, was simple and humble.   I found,
ten years ago, that there were a number of writers doing
work which appeared to me extremely good, but which was
narrowly known;   and I thought that anyone, however un-
professional and meagrely gifted, who presented a con-
spectus of it in a challenging and manageable form might
be doing a good turn both to the poets and to the reading
public.   So, I think I may claim, it proved to be.   The

first volume seemed to supply a want.   It was eagerly
bought;   the continuation of the affair was at once taken
so much for granted as to be almost unavoidable;   and
there has been no break in the demand for the successive
books.   If they have won for themselves any position,
there is no possible reason except the pleasure they have
given.

Having entered upon a course of disclamation, I should
like to make a mild protest against a further charge that
'Georgian Poetry' has merely encouraged a small clique of
mutually indistinguishable poetasters to abound in their
own and each other's sense or nonsense.   It is natural
that the poets of a generation should have points in
common;   but to my fond eye those who have graced these
collections look as diverse as sheep to their shepherd, or
the members of a Chinese family to their uncle;   and if
there is an allegation which I would *deny with both hands,*
it is this: that an insipid sameness is the chief char-
acteristic of an anthology which offers - to name almost
at random seven only out of forty (oh ominous academic
number!) - the work of Messrs Abercrombie, Davies, de la
Mare, Graves, Lawrence, Nichols and Squire.

The ideal 'Georgian Poetry' - a book which would err
neither by omission nor by inclusion, and would contain
the best, and only the best poems of the best, and only
the best poets of the day - could only be achieved, if at
all, by dint of a Royal Commission.   The present volume
is nothing of the kind.

I may add one word bearing on my aim in selection.
Much admired modern work seems to me, in its lack of in-
spiration and its disregard of form, like gravy imitating
lava.   Its upholders may retort that much of the work
which I prefer seems to them, in its lack of inspiration
and its comparative finish, like tapioca imitating pearls.
Either view - possibly both - may be right.   I will only
say that with an occasional exception for some piece of
rebelliousness or even levity which may have taken my
fancy, I have tried to choose no verse but such as in
Wordsworth's phrase

The high and tender Muses shall accept
With gracious smile, deliberately pleased.

July 1922   E.M.

42.   'EDDIE MARSH', 'THE CLUBMAN'S TALK OF THE TOWN',
'PALL MALL AND GLOBE'

1 December 1922, 8

The following piece is offered, not for literary distinct-
ion, but as typical of the journalistic tattle which
greeted each new anthology on its publication.   The des-
cription of Eddie Marsh as 'one of the best-known of our
literary dilettanti', a first-nighter to boot, and the
epithets attached to some of the poems - 'sheer beauty',
'a gem', 'full of charm' - serve as prelude to those later
judgments of Georgianism in decline which can be seen as
reactions against such unserious, popular acceptance.

(A single example of this *genre* should suffice;   but,
among those omitted, a review by 'D' in 'The Daily
Despatch' (Manchester), 22 December 1922, 3, likewise
refers to that first-nighter, Eddie Marsh, and adds for
good measure that Miss Victoria Sackville-West is 'the
"kidlet" of an old-time *cause célèbre*, who has fully
deserved her inclusion ..... in this selection of the
cream of modern poetic thought'.   D.H. Lawrence's
'single effort' ('Snake') is 'an extraordinary bit of
vers libre of a laboured realism that quite misses fire'.)

The fifth book of 'Georgian Poetry, 1920-22' has just
issued from the Poetry Bookshop, and in an introductory
note the editor, 'E.M.', deals faithfully with his
critics.

'E.M.', of course, is Eddie Marsh, one of the best-
known of our literary dilettanti.

Mr Marsh, who was Mr Winston Churchill's secretary
during the war, is a persona grata in literary circles and
is a confirmed first-nighter.

In his series of 'Georgian Poetry' Mr Marsh has done
the younger poets of the day great service, and has also
conferred a boon upon lovers of poetry by bringing to-
gether much of the best verse of the time.

Not all, of course, and this has been charged against
him as a literary crime by certain of his critics.

There never was, and never will be a perfect anthology,
and, that anyone should blame 'E.M.' for not producing
one is, perhaps, the highest compliment that could be paid
him.

Tastes differ and omissions are always easy to discover
in such collections.

The fact remains, however, that 'Georgian Poetry'
covers a wide field, and includes within its covers
nothing unworthy of inclusion.
     In the present book of 'Georgian Poetry' there are
seven newcomers: Messrs Armstrong, Blunden, Hughes, Kerr,
Prewett, and Quennell, and Miss Sackville-West.
     They all are welcome.   One of Mr Blunden's poems,
'The Child's Grave', is sheer beauty; Mr Kerr's 'The
Dead' is a gem; Mr Prewett's 'Somme Valley' and 'Voices
of Women' would justify him in any company; Mr Hughes's
'Moonstruck' is full of weird charm.   There is humour
and observation and pathos in Mr Armstrong's 'Miss
Thompson Goes Shopping'.
     Mr Quennell's 'Perception' and 'Pursuit' are full of
charm.   Miss Sackville-West has long earned a right to
inclusion in any modern anthology.
     'E.M.', indeed, has again justified himself.

43. 'A NEW ANTHOLOGY', UNSIGNED REVIEW, 'THE TIMES'

1 December 1922, 18

The opening paragraph with its further reference to the
anthology system, the third paragraph with its comments
on certain of the Squirearchy, and the fourth with its
humour at the expense of Mr Kerr, are fairly typical in
their response.   The phrase 'talented triviality' might
seem singularly apt.   Only the comment on Lawrence's
'Snake', one of the few remarkable poems in the fifth
anthology, might cause one to question the reviewer's
judgment.   As Hassall comments on the inclusion of this
poem, 'Marsh's judgment was not in all respects behind
the times' ('Edward Marsh', 1957, 501).

Mr Marsh, in a short preface to this fifth volume of
Georgian poetry, replies good-humouredly to the critics
who have begun to question the wisdom of continuing these
selections.   Into that question we cannot profitably
enter here.   The increasing prevalence of anthologies of
modern verse, very similar in detail and character, is a
phenomenon in which poetry and economics are nicely en-
tangled.   It is for the poets to agree to them, if and as

long as they will or it pays them. It is for the critic
to judge them irrespective of names and formulas.

A collection which includes Mr de la Mare, Mr Davies,
Mr Blunden, Mr Armstrong, Mr Freeman, Mr Gibson, and Mr
Graves, all at their latest and best, and Mr Abercrombie
and Mr Lawrence at their second best, is bound to be both
a choice and convenient volume for those who do not read
these poets at first hand. Three poems from Mr Monro's
'Real Property' (in our opinion his highest achievement),
Mr Nichols's 'Night Rhapsody' (from 'Amelia'), a generous
choice from Miss Sackville-West's 'Orchard and Vineyard',
and a new and admirable one from Mr Brett Young's poems,
do not lessen its appeal. In addition we have five
poets of at present slender repute, Mr Hughes, Mr Kerr,
Mr Pellow, Mr Prewett, and Mr Quennell, to stimulate our
curiosity, if not to reward it.

There remain Mr Drinkwater, Mr Squire, and Mr Shanks,
in whom, as it seems to us, the virtues and vices of
Georgian poetry are satisfactorily enthroned and popular-
ized. For although Mr Marsh may justly deny that an
'insipid sameness is the chief characteristic' of this
anthology, yet that 'lack of inspiration and comparative
finish' which he fancies hostile critics imputing to his
choice is a very constant reality. Of such a charge
certain of these poets are wholly innocent. Yet even so
fine and accomplished a one as Mr Freeman is not entirely
guiltless.

So many of these poets, we are driven to feel, are
sensitive, tolerant, and talented. They could turn out
agreeably finished verses to order on any concrete sub-
ject from a dog to a door-handle. They observe the
small details of Nature with a kindly curiosity and report
of her with a dainty daring. They lavish whimsies and
faintly provocative emotions upon situations in them-
selves often commonplace, but for the heightened speech of
passion, of imagination touching the heart of things over-
masteringly, we look almost in vain. Mr Freeman comes
near to it in such a line as 'Now, now I am but thought
kissing your thought', but so often an accomplished tech-
nique serves only a lethargy of soul, and the necessity
imposed through deficient power upon these poets of keep-
ing us awake by crafty verbal surprises soon fails of its
purpose. We weary of smiling our momentary approval of
a trick, and when the coquetry of conceits assumes the
mask of innocence, as in Mr Kerr's.

    I lingered at a gate and talked
    A little with a lonely lamb,

our smile broadens into laughter.

As with a building covered with nicely trimmed ivy or
crowded carving, we often thirst in reading this book for
something bare and stark and strong.   Mr Lawrence once
could give us it, but here he relapses into a whimsical
soliloquy over a 'golden snake', and is diffuse.   Mr
Abercrombie, who has the giant in him, gives us a poem
often fine in rhythm and in phrase ('My spirit drank my
flashing senses in', for example), but in his protracted
struggle after passion and imagination he wants art's
serenity.   Many others fail lamentably to reconcile
subtlety with sincerity - the problem above all to be
solved by the modern poet.

We have purposely stressed what we consider the grave
weakness of many poems here collected - their talented
triviality.   The beauty and insight of the others is
only more evident by comparison;   and it is good that
such poems as Miss Sackville-West's 'Evening' and Mr
Brett Young's 'Quails' should now speak to a wider public.

44.   'THE POET'S CORNER', ROBERT LYND, 'DAILY NEWS'

7 December 1922, 8

Robert Lynd (1879-1949), once highly regarded as an essay-
ist ('Y.Y.') in the Addison-'Times' leader tradition, was
appointed literary editor of the 'Daily News' (later the
'News Chronicle') in 1913, and was a middle-writer on
'The New Statesman'.   He published many books, among
them 'The Book of This and That' (1915), 'The Pleasure of
Ignorance' (1921), and 'In Defence of Pink' (1937).   He
was married to the poet, Sylvia Lynd.

'E.M.', who deserves so well both of poets and the public
as an anthologist of contemporary poetry, is evidently
becoming a little alarmed at the responsibility of his
task.

His collections of Georgian poetry, of which the
present is the fifth, have come to be regarded by many
people as a sort of Academy, and the poet whose work is
not admitted seems to them like a painter whose pictures
have been rejected by Burlington House.

'E.M.', in a prefatory note to the new volume, eagerly

denies that he is a 'kind of public functionary' - 'a pundit, or pontiff, or a Petronius Arbiter'. 'I have', he impresses on us, 'neither the sure taste, nor the exhaustive reading, nor the ample leisure which would be necessary in any such rôle.' After a disclaimer so charming and disarming, what can the critic say but 'Carry On!'? Mr Marsh, in preparing these anthologies, has performed a task that nobody else has ever attempted, and has performed it, within the limits admirably.

At the same time, I agree with those who hold that he would produce a still better anthology if he aimed at collecting the best individual poems of the year instead of specimens of the work of those whom he regards as the best poets. He frequently quotes five or six specimens from a poet whose pure gold is contained only in one or two poems. The inferior poems should be swept away, and room could thus be made for many excellent poems by writers still excluded. Every anthologist has, of course, a right to his own plan. But I think Mr Marsh's books would be improved if he made the poem rather than the poet the unit of selection.

A number of new poets have been admitted among the Georgians in the present volume. Of these, Mr Edmund Blunden and Mr Martin Armstrong have already established themselves with the reading public. I am sorry that Mr Marsh has not included Mr Blunden's beautiful 'Evening Mystery', but the selection is otherwise good. Mr Armstrong's three poems are all good - full of light and the colour and smell of the world and 'Miss Thompson Goes Shopping' shows him to have a nice humour. Another newcomer, Mr Frank Prewett's, good qualities are seen in 'Snow-buntings' and 'Voices of Women'; but why include a mere youthful gesticulation such as 'Come, Girl, and Embrace'? This is an exercise, not poetry.

Mr Peter Quennell's poems raise hopes, and Mr Richard Hughes, Mr William Kerr, and Miss Sackville West, all appear as Georgians for the first time.

Among the established Georgians, Mr de la Mare might, I think, have been represented by a still more beautiful selection of poems; but the lovely 'Corner Stone' and 'Titmouse' are here. I am glad to see Mr Squire's moving 'Elegy', with its unforgettable portrait of a dead friend, and his 'Late Snow' given, and Mr W.H. Davies's 'The Truth' is already sure of a long life. Reading Mr John Freeman, one feels at times as if one were in the midst of a beautiful landscape in which the 'going' is a little heavy, but there is no doubt of the loveliness and sincerity of his vision in 'The Evening Sky'. Mr Robert Graves is perfectly delightful in those fanciful, humorous pieces, 'Fox's Dingle' and 'The General Elliott'.

The new work of Mr Edward Shanks shows that he has def-
initely added to his skill in casting his net among the
little silver fishes.   'The Rock Pool' is an almost per-
fect sonnet, and he has not previously written a poem so
long as 'Memory' in which the emotion and the sensitive
imaginativeness have been so well sustained.

If I do not quote examples from the poets I have men-
tioned, it is because I have already written on most of
the books from which these poems have been taken.   Nor
is the list of authors I have named complete.   There is
also interesting work to be found here among the select-
ions from Mr Brett Young, Mr Harold Monro, Mr Aber-
crombie, Mr D.H. Lawrence, Mr Wilfrid Gibson, Mr Drink-
water, Mr J.D.C. Pellow, and Mr Robert Nichols.   In the
mass, with a few obvious exceptions, this contemporary
poetry is open to the criticism that it does not scale
the heights of joy or sound the depths of sorrow;   that,
even when it stirs the imagination, it does not always
move the heart.   But, perhaps, a general anthology in
any age would have been open to the same charge.   And
anyhow, a generation which possesses Mr de la Mare cannot
be called anything but fortunate in its poets.

45.   'MR MARSH'S ANTHOLOGY', 'DELTA', 'THE CHALLENGE'

8 December 1922, 214

A cantankerous and repetitious piece, this review of
'Georgian Poetry, 1920-1922' at least shows that a review-
er's suggestions (A.Y. Campbell, Frank Kendon, J.R. Acker-
ley, Edgell Rickword, and Kenneth Ashley) were to prove no
more distinguished than Marsh's choice.   Apart from
Ackerley (see No. 22), who is better known for his prose
writings, Edgell Rickword (b. 1898) alone merits further
mention.   His first book, 'Behind the Eyes', was pub-
lished in 1921, his 'Collected Poems' in 1947.   That he
has written no poetry since 1930 must be counted a consid-
erable loss.

Nine years ago the first volume of the series 'Georgian
Poetry' was published: this week the fifth appears.
The Editor, Mr Edward Marsh (who might have given his

name in full since the initials E.M. have long ceased to obscure his identity from all but the incurious) contributes a preface to the new volume. It is partly a self-diffident disclaimer of his editorial pretensions, partly a reasonable piece of self-defence against the foolish and hap-hazard criticism that greeted the last volume of 'Georgian Poetry, 1918-1919'. Mr Marsh says that the critics have asked '... who was E.M. that he should bestow and withhold crowns and sceptres, and decide that this or that poet was not to count'. He also says that the critics 'very properly disapproved of his choice of poems', and denies that he has set himself up as a pundit, or a pontiff, or a Petronius Arbiter. He conducts his self-defence with great self-depreciatory charm, an excellent method of making a lot of silly critics look sillier than their own unaided efforts could make them. It is useless to deny that 'Georgian Poetry', or rather, Mr Marsh, has done a great deal of good to certain of our poets and also to the poetry reading public. The new volume is by no means the best of the series, but it contains much really beautiful poetry (Mr de la Mare, Mr Davies and Mr Shanks all have work in it) and almost nothing that is entirely worthless. In fact it is a good anthology of the work written by certain specified poets during the last two years. Everything in Mr Marsh's garden is lovely. One cannot quarrel with him on these counts. But it can be said without carping that the book is not what it could have been, and, when one considers the title, it is certainly not what it should have been.

Mr Marsh shews himself very spiritless in saying that the critics 'very properly disapproved of his choice of poems', if I am right in supposing that, for him, this is too clumsy to be intended as a piece of irony. If he can admit their objections against his choice to be 'very proper', then he has no right to compile anthologies for anybody, especially under such a title as 'Georgian Poetry'. A man should have the courage of his convictions, and, after that admission, Mr Marsh is either a man lacking such courage or merely an easy-going, undiscriminating philanthropist, if not both. To disclaim any intention of setting himself up as a pundit may be, and probably is, true. But the fact remains that in effect, by the very fact of the circulation and popularity to say nothing of the title of Georgian Poetry, Mr Marsh does occupy that position and has done so in a sense for many years. The theory of Mr Marsh and Georgian Poets is excellent; the practice cannot be defended as Mr Marsh would defend it. At the same time I should be the last to say hard words of his generosity towards poets and public.

I found, ten years ago, that there were a number of
writers doing work which appeared to me extremely good
but which was narrowly known; and I thought that any-
one, however unprofessional and meagrely gifted, who
presented a conspectus of it in a challenging and man-
ageable form, might be doing a good turn to the poets
and reading public.

The motives could not be bettered.   Yet it is strange
that good motives and incompetence go so often hand in han
The fact is that, by including or excluding a poet's
work, Mr Marsh is actually setting a temporary Yea or Nay
against that man's name in the minds of some fifteen
thousand people, the readers of 'Georgian Poetry'.   That
number includes all the people who read serious contemp-
orary verse.   Most of them have neither the time nor the
knowledge to discriminate for themselves; they do not
habitually buy or read poetry outside the anthologies and
perhaps the books of the more popular poets, and Mr Marsh
does, therefore, occupy a pontifical position, against his
own will.   That is not to say that he is withholding or
bestowing crowns and sceptres.   If there were fifty Mr
Marshs and each one of them had ten times his critical
faculty, they would still fail to do that.   Mr Marsh's
position would not be so false if he were entering into
definite competition with the other anthologists - with
Mr Squire, Mr Davies, and Sir Arthur Methuen, who are out
after poetry and not poets.   What Mr Marsh does is to
say, in effect, 'here is the representative work of the
best twenty-one poets of our time', and most of his read-
ers take him seriously.   In his book they are re-
introduced to a challengeable selection of the poetry of
our best accepted writers - Mr de la Mare, Mr Davies, Mr
Squire, Mr Shanks, and the others.   Willy-nilly they
meet also with the newcomers.   Now there will be very few
people to quarrel with Mr Marsh's selection of Messrs
Blunden and Armstrong who are poets as good, if not better
than several of the old contributors to Georgian Poetry.
But the other newcomers - Messrs Hughes, Kerr, Prewett and
Quennell and Miss Sackville-West lag far behind.   Mr
Marsh's choice lay among more than a dozen of the less
known poets of whom only about three stand out above the
rest in so far as they stand out at all.   Poem for poem,
Mr A.Y. Campbell, for instance, does stand high above most
of the new 'Georgians': in fact I would go further and
say that he is immeasurably superior to Messrs Drinkwater,
Gibson, and Monro, who are again included in 'Georgian
Poetry'.   It is true that there is scarcely a new man
represented in any of Mr Marsh's five volumes who has not
written at least two or three fine poems, but the same can

be said of dozens of writers who have never been drawn
under the shadow of Mr Marsh's mantle.   What of Messrs
Kendon, Ackerley, Rickword, Ashley?   Even if they are no
better than Hughes, Quennell, Kerr, Prewett (and I would
undertake to shew, so far as criticism can show, that they
are better) why have they been entirely ignored?   It
appears that Mr Marsh has not succeeded in collecting
either 'Georgian Poetry' or Georgian Poets, but has fallen
into mediocrity and injustice between.   He should either
have included them all, or better still, have let most of
them wait until a future year, by which time the sheep may
be distinguishable from the goats.

It may be said that these names I have mentioned are
unknown.   That is, relatively, quite true.   But as
editor of 'Georgian Poetry' it was Mr Marsh's business to
know them, if not to have made them known, and he cannot
have lacked opportunity.   If Mr Marsh has considered and
rejected the best work of Mr Campbell, Mr Kendon or Mr
Ashley in favour of the poems that represent Messrs Hughes,
Prewett, and Quennell, then, in my opinion, he has re-
vealed a lamentable lack of taste.   If, on the other hand,
he has not considered their work at all, then he has no
justification for editing an anthology with an originally
fatuous title that at once becomes, in addition, pretent-
ious and misleading.   In either alternative he is
incompetent.

46.   'SEVEN NEW GEORGIANS', UNSIGNED REVIEW, 'THE
MORNING POST'

8 December 1922, 6

This waggish piece, reviewing 'Georgian Poetry, 1920-1922',
shows how the cricketing verse of William Kerr (see Appen-
dix, p. 406) could set the scene for a Georgian cricket
XI - 'The older Georgians are all in good form - having
played themselves in, so to speak' - and so lead inevit-
ably to the scorn of Sitwells (see Introduction, pp. 28-30).

To this volume of 'Georgian Poetry', the fifth of the
series, Mr Eddie Marsh, the editor, prefixes a witty ex-
postulation with his critics, in which he disowns any pre-
tension of setting up as a pundit, or a pontiff, or a

Petronius Arbiter.   He explains that his object in start-
ing the series was to do a good turn not only to a number
of narrowly-known poets, but also to the reading public;
and he mildly protests against the charge that he has
'merely encouraged a small clique of mutually indist-
inguishable poetasters to abound in their own and each
other's sense or nonsense'.   'To my fond eye', he adds,
'those who have graced these collections look as diverse
as sheep to their shepherd, or the members of a Chinese
family to their uncle', and he denies, with good reason,
that an insipid sameness is the chief characteristic of
an anthology which, to name almost at random seven out of
forty contributors, offers the work of Messrs Abercrombie,
Davies, de la Mare, Graves, Lawrence, Nichols, and Squire.
And, even if we cannot admit that all the verse he has
chosen is such as in Wordsworth's phrase:

> The high and tender Muses shall accept
> With gracious smile, deliberately pleased -

yet we freely confess that, to use his own metaphor, he
has never - well, hardly ever - mistaken tapioca for
pearls.
      There are seven new-comers in this new volume - Messrs
Armstrong, Blunden, Hughes, Kerr, Prewett, and Quennell,
and Miss V. Sackville-West.   It is a little surprising
that the last-named has been so long in catching the eye
of this judicious judge.   We are glad to find her 'Saxon
Song' is included, and also her freakish tribute to the
Moon, who must be very tired of being greeted with
Sidneian solemnity - as tired as an ultra-modern flapper
would be of a course of chivalrous adoration in the
Arthurian style.   The Moon is the flapper of the solar
system of planets:

> She cared not a rap for all the big planets,
> For Betelgeuse or Aldebaran,
> And all the big planets cared nothing for her,
> That small impertinent charlatan;
> But she climbed on a Kentish stile in the moonlight,
> And laughed at the sky through the sticks of her fan.

The work of Mr Blunden and Mr Hughes has had aforetime the
praise they deserve in this journal; we hope the latter
will go on writing plays, for playwrights are rarer far
than poets.   Mr Peter Quennell (did we or did we not see
his early work in an anthology of Public School verse?) is
refreshingly original, as you may see from 'A Man to a
Sunflower':

[Quotes 'A Man to a Sunflower', all 10 lines.]

Mr Prewett is no more than a peewit to us;   but Mr
William Kerr, when he makes a poem about cricketers, old
and new, is as good as a tankard of the ale they drank on
Broad Halfpenny:

[Quotes 'Past and Present', all 13 lines.]

   How's that?   Mr Armstrong is also cordially welcomed;
we like his ballad of Miss Thompson's Shopping, and his
'Honey Harvest', from the second of which we tear away a
few lines:

[Quotes 'Honey Harvest', concluding 13 lines.]

   The older Georgians are all in good form - having
played themselves in, so to speak - and we wish we had
space to quote them all, for quotation (of whole poems) is
the sincerest kind of criticism.   Mr J.C. Squire has
found a fitting line, a strong pull-drive that reaches the
boundary every time, in 'Late Snow':

[Quotes 'Late Snow', stanzas I and II.]

   Mr J.D.C. Pellow, maker of the poem about Trees in the
fourth volume, has a vision of London gone and the Thames
meadows back again:

   London Bridge is broken down;
   Green is the grass on Ludgate Hill;
   I know a farmer in Camden Town
   Killed a brock by Pentonville.

   I have heard my grandam tell
   How some thousand years ago
   Houses stretched from Camberwell
   Right to Highbury and Bow.

Finally, for we cannot do justice to all, let us end with
a stave of song from Mr W.H. Davies:

   Our kisses are but love in flower,
   Until that greater time
   When, gathering strength, those flowers take wing,
   And Love can reach his prime.
   And now, my heart's delight,
   Good night, good night;
   Give me the last sweet kiss -
   But do not breathe at home one word of this!

For the poet is yet to come who will get more than
Georgian kisses from the Muse so subtly prinking at her
mirror these days!

47. 'GEORGIAN POETRY', ARTHUR WAUGH, 'THE DAILY
TELEGRAPH'

12 December 1922, 16

Arthur Waugh (see No. 21) continues his influential sup-
port for 'Georgian Poetry'.   At the same time, although
E.M. 'has won his golden spurs with acclamation', Waugh
comments on a decline of choice.

The fifth volume of 'Georgian Poetry' sees its still
anonymous but generally recognised editor riding out into
the open, with his lance atilt.   Criticism has chall-
enged him, and pat he appears in reply to the trumpets.
His response is animated alike with spirit and with
humour.   Someone apparently has been asking 'Who is
"E.M.", that he should bestow and withhold crowns and
sceptres?'   Some one else (rather discourteously) has
whispered that the pages of 'Georgian Poetry' are given
over 'to a small clique of mutually indistinguishable
poetasters, to abound in their own and each other's sense
or nonsense'.   Whoever said that, of course, said what
was manifestly absurd;   and E.M. is well justified in his
rejoinder.   He disclaims all pretension to be 'a pundit,
a pontiff, or a Petronius Arbiter';   he has simply taken
pleasure in setting forth the work of young poets who
seemed to him promising, and he implies with reason that
the judgment which finds the poetry of Mr Abercrombie,
Mr Davies, Mr de la Mare, Mr Graves, and Mr Squire 'mut-
ually indistinguishable' must be congenitally incapable
of distinguishing between the champagne and the sherries
of the Muses.
     For ourselves, we refuse to believe that any critic
worth a paragraph's consideration can ever have descended
into such a slough of fatuity and confusion.   What has
been said, perhaps, and said not altogether without
reason, is that, while the editor of 'Georgian Poetry'
has indeed been quick to recognise the most notable verse

of the younger men, his further choice has confined it-
self somewhat exclusively to the over-elaborate, self-
conscious, and artificial developments of the hour.   It
has been content to disregard that 'one drop of human
blood', without which the poet's art soon degenerates
into mere artifice and boredom.   The editor has kept his
volumes healthily free of the worst modern extravagances
of formlessness and vulgarity; but as if from very fear
of these faults he has been apt to let his choice decline
upon a sort of moody and fastidious affectation.   Yet
even if the enterprise of 'Georgian Poetry' is not exempt
from this defect in the editorial taste, it has undoubt-
edly done splendid service to English poetry and poets.
Many young writers have caught the public eye through its
well-organised publicity, and a genuine impulse has been
given to poetic production through its quite sufficiently
authoritative encouragement.   'E.M.', in short, has won
his golden spurs with acclamation, and is fully entitled
to flourish his lance and to flaunt his favours in the
lists.
   One of the great merits of 'Georgian Poetry' has
always been its susceptibility to new reputations, and
with each fresh volume there has been much public curios-
ity about the newcomers.   In the present collection
there are seven names which have not appeared before, and
with two exceptions it cannot be said that they add much
to the treasury.   Most of the new work is very slight
and experimental; the thémes are trivial, the execution
thin.   Indeed, one of the new arrivals, who has the ad-
vantage of extreme youth to his credit, has yet to find
his feet with any degree of confidence.   Like Hotspur,
in the fever-heat of fantasy,

   He apprehends a world of figures here,
   But not the form of what he should attend.

Experience, no doubt, will bring the gifts of vision and
of fire, experience and discipline.
   The two new poets, about whom there can be no question,
are Mr Martin Armstrong and Mr Edmund Blunden, both of
them masters of a balanced style, with an absorbing loy-
alty to nature.   Both write pastoral poetry; but while
Mr Armstrong derives from Virgil through the Tennyson
tradition, Mr Blunden touches in his carefully-wrought
portraits of rustic life and character with something of
the stern simplicity of Crabbe.   The 'Honey Harvest' of
Mr Armstrong is an English Georgic, clustering with the
rich scents and colours of 'the high midsummer pomps'.

[Quotes 'Honey Harvest', stanza IV.]

This accuracy of observation and variety of tone is even
more laboriously embodied in Mr Blunden's 'April Byeway',
in which line upon line adds to the delicate intricacy of
the composition.

> All our lone journey laughs for joy, the hours
> Like honey-bees go home in new-found light
> Past the cowpond amazed with twinkling flowers
> And antique chalk-pit newly delved to white,
> Or idle snow-plough nearly hid from sight.
> The blackbird sings us home, on a sudden peers
> The round tower hung with ivy's blackened chains,
> Then past the little green the byeway veers,
> The mill-sweeps torn, the forge with cobwebbed panes
> That have so many years looked out across the plains.

Mr Armstrong and Mr Blunden are Georgians of proved
achievement, and take their place without challenge among
the leaders of the choir.

And what of the familiar faces, already established in
public favour?   One or two of them have certainly never
been seen to better advantage than in the present volume.
Mr Edward Shanks, in particular, makes a more vigorous
and vital show than he has ever done before.   The great
lack in so much of Mr Shanks's poetry has been a genuine,
sincere, and solid humanity beneath his facile and elabor-
ate decoration; he has seemed like a worker in ivory, a
carver of fantastic arabesques.   But in one dramatic
poem in the present book he reaches a note of poignant
and haunting pity and regret.   It is the reflection of a
disillusioned woman, whose love has flickered out like a
wind-blown candle-flame.

[Quotes 'Woman's Song', stanzas III and IV.]

Another notable appearance is made by Mr Harold Monro.
Two of his three pieces are allied in spirit; they echo
the inalienable claim which every lover asserts over a
scene on a field which has once usurped his heart.   This
spiritual possession is stronger than any fee simple; it
is the only 'real property'.

There are many other fine things in the volume - Mr
Brett Young's sombre, but majestic, burial at sea; Mr
Squire's grim foreboding of death faced and mastered; and
the pensive, child-like melancholy of Mr Robert Graves, in
which beats and falters the restlessness of a wondering
heart, never quite at ease in a world of miracles, nor

schooled to reconciliation with the sweet suffering of
love.   Most memorable of all, perhaps, are the wistful,
whispering melodies of Mr Walter de la Mare, songs of the
land of make-believe come true, where the dusk is a-
rustle with faëry wings, Ariel cries in the cloven pine,
and Puck's laughter mocks our dull humanity from among
the branches overhead.   Neither Georgian, nor Victorian,
nor Elizabethan, but eternal as the imagination of man, is
the poetry woven of such subtle gossamer and lighted by
such transfiguring glimpses of 'the moon of poets'.

48.   'GEORGIAN POETRY', W.J. TURNER, 'DAILY HERALD'

13 December 1922, 7

One of the reasons for Turner's refusal to contribute to
the fifth anthology had been disagreement over Marsh's
choice of his poems for the previous one (see Appendix,
p. 417).   Marsh's objections, characteristically, had
been on grounds of his poems' obscurity.   One can hear
Turner's answer in the condescending remarks on giving
beef to a baby.   It is interesting in contrast that a
poem's simplicity should be one of the reasons he gives
for his first choice of Graves.   Sassoon was at this
time literary editor of the 'Daily Herald'.

'E.M.', the editor of 'Georgian Poetry', explains that
when he brought out his first volume it was simply with
the intention of making more widely known to the public
'a number of writers doing work which appeared to me ex-
tremely good ... the first volume seemed to supply a
want.   It was eagerly bought ... and there has been no
break in the demand for the successive books.   If they
have won for themselves any position, there is no possible
reason except the pleasure they have given.'
   Naturally, 'E.M.'s' selection has satisfied nobody
fully acquainted with contemporary verse.   No selection
would.   Even that made by Mr W.H. Davies himself (one of
the few living poets whom nearly everyone accepts) is un-
satisfactory to many, as was pointed out when reviewed on
this page a few weeks ago.   But such an anthology as
'Georgian Poetry' is not meant for connoisseurs or

experts;   it is meant as an introduction to modern verse
for the general public, or for that part of the general
public which is interested in contemporary literature.
    As such it is admirable.
    It has given a great deal of pleasure to large numbers,
where a more exclusive collection, a selection of a
higher type, would have probably given no pleasure at all;
might have even alienated thousands, and prevented them
from ever troubling themselves with modern verse again.
    For just as you cannot give beef to a new-born baby so
you cannot give to the aesthetically undeveloped the
ripest and most complex art of the age.   They must grow
to it by slow degrees, and in the development of the
sense for poetry this anthology marks a definite stage.
The aesthetic sense, like all the finest human faculties,
all those powers which mark man off from the animal, is
completely unnatural.   It has to be cultivated with sweat
of the mind and agony of the spirit.   It is not to be
'picked up' idly at no expense.
    Only a constant and attentive reading of the best
poetry for many years will enable one to begin to see how
much a good writer has put into his work, and how little
a bad writer has put into his.   'Georgian Poetry' pro-
vides some sort of standard.   No one but the half-witted
could read 'Georgian Poetry' carefully without noticing
how immensely better its contents are than the verse to
be found in the magazines, or in the average literary
review;   while those who care to look up the collections
of verse popular during the nineteenth century will be
astonished to find how much higher is the standard in
'Georgian Poetry'.
    Of all the contributions in the present volume I,
personally, prefer the work of Mr Robert Graves.   I will
quote the first verse of his 'A Lover Since Childhood':

    Tangled in thought am I,
    Stumble in speech do I?
    Do I blunder and blush for the reason why?
    Wander aloof do I,
    Lean over gates and sigh,
    Making friends with the bee and the butterfly?

    That, I maintain, is exquisite.   Its simplicity hides
a perfection of expression and a direct sincerity which is
worth reams of futuristic bombast, metaphysical pretent-
iousness or vague rhetoric about generalities;   yet it is
far from being the only good work in the volume as those
who go to it with unprejudiced eyes will rejoice to
discover.

49. SHORT NOTICE, 'LIBRARIAN', 'THE SATURDAY REVIEW'

16 December 1922, 153

Unsigned short notice by 'Librarian' under 'Authors and
Publishers: a Miscellany'.

'Librarian' speaks up like 'Delta' (see No. 45) for
Edgell Rickword, but what became of Mr F.V. Branford?
Robert Graves included Branford in a short list of 'mal-
contents from the Centre and Right ..... who have no
great passion for revolution, and if the pinch came would
defend no street barricades' ('Contemporary Techniques of
Poetry', 1925), and Maurice Wollman, who included him in
'Modern Poetry, 1922-34', 19, records sadly: 'Totally
disabled while serving with the R.N.A.S. on the Somme.
Only since 1932 has he sufficiently recovered to make any
statement of his aims and methods.'

Mr Marsh's fifth selection of the work of contemporary
poets ('Georgian poetry, 1920-1922': The Poetry Bookshop,
6s. net) does not, in my opinion, cover a wide enough
field.   The object of the idea when it took form in the
publication of the first volume was, unless I am mistaken,
to help not only the public to a better appreciation of
the work of new and little-known poets, but also to help
these poets themselves in their claims to recognition.
Now many - most - of the poets represented in Mr Marsh's
fifth volume are well-established both in their own and
in the public's regard, and it would, to my mind, have
been useful as well as generous to the host of still
younger poets who have not yet reached the secure emin-
ence of their brothers, to have included more than seven
of them, even though it had to be at the expense of some
of the twenty-one elder brethren.

Not that I am not glad to see names like W.H. Davies,
Walter de la Mare, J.C. Squire, or John Drinkwater.
Their work is always a delight, and the selections here
given from their writings - and, indeed, all the select-
ions - are quite admirably chosen.   But what, for example,
of the claims of Messrs Edgell Rickword, Louis Golding,
Edward Davison?   And could no corner be found for that
poet who, though his star is bright, has strangely not yet
swum into the ken of many who scan the literary firmament?
- I mean Mr F.V. Branford.   Which raises the reflection -
not apt in this particular instance, but often - that

perhaps critics spend too much time on the work of dis-
section with their eye to the microscope, when it might be
more profitably employed scanning the heavens through a
telescope.

50.   'POETS AND POETRY', A. WILLIAMS-ELLIS,
'THE SPECTATOR'

16 December 1922, 927-8

For a note on Lady Williams-Ellis see headnote to No. 36.

Mr Marsh may disclaim as much as he likes, but 'Georgian
Poetry' has become an institution, a most typically nat-
ional institution furthermore.   We might, indeed, trace
in the history of this recurrent anthology an epitome or
microcosm of the methods of the English with institutions.
A private citizen comes along, he observes a want or an
abuse in a sphere which is entirely outside his profess-
ional interests.   He supplies the want or remedies the
abuse unobtrusively but with success.   In a moment he
finds himself a public institution with definite obligat-
ions.   He is freely abused if he does not fulfil them.
    Whatever we may think of this *ad hoc* method in other
spheres, there can be no doubt that in the case of Mr
Marsh it has been entirely successful.   'Georgian Poetry'
is a most excellent institution.   The present new volume
shows it to be adaptable without being backboneless, to be
aware of new influences and alive to new merit without
being so sensitive to fashion as to lose its definite
character.   Whether we agree with him or not, it is right
for an anthologist to have an opinion of his own and to
express it with vigour:

[Quotes penultimate paragraph of Prefatory Note.]

Now I, for example, see much to admire in what Mr Marsh
calls the 'Gravy School'.   But it seems a rule in this
world 'No prejudices no gusto', and without a genuine
appetite in the compiler an anthology becomes at once in-
sipid and obvious.   Though I for one am sorry to find here
no Sitwells and no Imagists, I would not have them in if

their inclusion meant that Mr Marsh was growing indiffer-
ent.   But if he has a right to his prejudices, we readers
have a right to ours.   At the inclusion of one poem in
the anthology I for one stand amazed.   It is a set of
verses by that admirable artist, Mr Blunden.   I have al-
ready quoted some of the stanzas to 'Spectator' readers
with surprise, but now that Mr Marsh has set the seal of
his approval upon them I am nonplussed.   The poem is
called 'The Child's Grave'.   Here is a verse of it:

This peace, then, and happiness thronged me around.
Nor could I go burdened with grief, but made merry
Till I came to the gate of that overgrown ground
Where scarce once a year sees the priest come to bury.

The idea seems to be to produce an effect of freshness and
naïveness.   The introduction of white lilies, coffins,
faithful dogs, flitting birds, and spring sunshine is
apparently a deliberate effort towards the reclamation of
these 'properties'.   To me the effort at floating these
things seems entirely to have failed and the poem to have
sunk to the level of the parish magazine serial whence it
drew its images.
Mr Blunden is one of the seven newcomers to 'Georgian
Poetry', and the rest of his poems show his work to great
advantage.   It is particularly pleasant to see the merits
of the admirable 'Cottager's Pig' acknowledged.   Of the
other poets whose work appears for the first time in the
collection the youngest is certainly Mr Peter Quennell,
who made his *début* in 'Public School Verse' about two
years ago.   His work is highly fantastic and has a pec-
uliar quality of delicacy and wildness.   A poem about a
sunflower which begins

See, I have bent thee by thy saffron hair
- O most strange masker -

is particularly successful.   Mr Quennell has just pub-
lished a volume of verse which I hope to discuss soon.
One of the most popular poems in the book will certain-
ly be Mr Martin Armstrong's delightful 'Miss Thompson goes
shopping'.   It is a long poem in rhymed couplets and
gives an account of a shopping expedition undertaken by a
maiden lady who lives alone.   All sorts of elements are
used.   There are descriptions of atmosphere, of shop-
keepers, of smells, and of states of mind - the whole most
delicate.   There is a certainty of touch and an ease in
the poem which make it extremely pleasurable to read.   Of
one of the other newly included poets, Mr Richard Hughes,

we have written lately and at length; the poems here
chosen are not perhaps his most characteristic, though in
one aspect 'The Singing Furies' represents him well.

It is exceedingly difficult to attempt any classificat-
ion of these poems in order.   With a very few exceptions
all the poems in the collection are of great interest and
most of unquestioned merit.   For sheer beauty, however,
there are two poems which the reader will probably feel
excel the rest; one of these the most exquisite in my
opinion is Mr John Freeman's 'The Evening Sky'.   Here are
the two first verses:

[Quotes 'The Evening Sky', stanzas I and II.]

This theme is repeated with a beautiful intricacy of
change in the succeeding verses.

The other is Mr Robert Nichols's well-known 'Night
Rhapsody'.   Not that sheer beauty is the only, nor,
indeed, the chief desire in many readers of poetry.
Beauty in its narrower but still apparently undefinable
sense is by no means the only quality which can be better
expressed in poetry than in any other medium.   Certain
psychological experiences and certain psychological facts
can be adequately set out in no other way.   That is to
say, that through poetry we can get into touch with
certain tracts of the mind of another person which are
sealed to other approaches.   That this has always been
felt is proved by the existence in all ages of a great
body of religious and love poetry and of certain sorts of
'heroic' verse.   The exultations, the doubts, the tri-
umphs and despairs which the spirit experienced under the
influences of religion, love and war could best be des-
cribed and uttered in verse.   It seems odd that this
should have been so often lost sight of and that poets
such as Walt Whitman, Donne, and several moderns should
have been abused because they neglected what was after all
one among several of the legitimate excellences of poetry.

A considerable proportion of the poems in this collect-
ion will be found to have for first aim the utterance of
something rather than the creation of something beautiful
(these are coarse and inexact phrases but roughly indicate
a meaning).   There is very much a place for both kinds of
poetry, and in Mr Marsh's anthology the balance has been
very well kept.

51. 'THE WORLD OF BOOKS' EDMUND GOSSE, 'THE SUNDAY TIMES'

17 December 1922, 6

This article was reprinted in 'More Books on the Table', 1923, 229-35.

Edmund Gosse (see headnote to No. 7) comments, like other critics, on a 'general identity': 'five or six passages from different poets which might ..... appear in the work of a single writer' (paragraph 7); pontifically, he finds that it was otherwise among 'the great Victorians'. He was perceptive in his judgment of Edmund Blunden, and one of the first critics to note his indebtedness to Clare. His general comments (paragraphs 11-14) give a well balanced assessment of the Georgians.

Eleven years ago appeared the first volume of a work destined, I believe, to occupy a prominent place in the history of contemporary literature. The accomplished connoisseur, who faintly conceals his name under the initials 'E.M.', was struck by the fact that English poetry was blossoming anew in a parterre which was but rarely and negligently visited. A number of young writers, actuated by similar aims, were putting forth little volumes which contained beautiful passages, but were seldom observed by reviewers or by the public. Guided solely by his own taste, he gathered an anthology out of the best of those and published it as 'Georgian Poetry'.

The success of the venture was immediate and prolonged. Poets whose isolated productions had been unnoticed woke up to find themselves famous beneath the aegis of 'E.M.'. Rupert Brooke and James Elroy Flecker were the main ornaments of the first collection, and when a second instalment came (in 1916) it was inscribed to their memory. What I hold before me to-day is the fifth volume of 'Georgian Poetry', and while the general order and character of the work remain unchanged, time has not been negligent in modification. Several writers who, in 1912, were threatening to become middle-aged, have been placed on the retired list; and death has made further inroads.

The principle on which the selection was originally conceived is identical. Seven new writers have this time been introduced, with varying advantage to the scheme. On the other hand, there are seven of the older members

who 'do not exhibit this year', as the formula runs in
the case of older Academies.   This is unfortunate, since
among the absentees are the three most energetic of the
Georgian set - Mr Masefield, Mr Ralph Hodgson, and Mr
Siegfried Sassoon.   It cannot be denied that this partic-
ular volume labours under a disadvantage from their tempo-
rary abeyance.

No previous instalment of 'Georgian Poetry' has had any
but the briefest preface from the editor's pen.   But in
this case 'E.M.' has signed a more or less facetious in-
troduction.   He takes up several objections which wond-
ering reviewers have ventured to make and he replies to
them.   His answers give me a text for a further reply,
although I am certainly not one of the reviewers to whom
he refers.   He says, with amusing exaggeration, that he
has been treated as a sort of President of an Academy,
fitted to 'bestow and withhold crowns and sceptres, and
decide that this or that poet was or was not to count'.
Well, in quieter language, that is exactly what he has
shown himself fitted to do, and, what is much more re-
markable, his competence in doing it has been almost uni-
versally admitted.

'E.M.' should bear his honours patiently, for it is
undeniable that his scheme has responded to the need for
gregarious selection which affects groups of persons, en-
gaged with unequal skill, on the same task.   Force is
obtained by eliminating the weak elements and welding the
strong together, and to do this is to found a successful
Academy.   Certainly, 'E.M.' had no such aim when he or-
iginally insisted on the recognition of certain gifted
poets who had achieved no notoriety.   But this is what
his venture has come to be.   The choice of poets included
in the list is not an arbitrary one.   It advances a
young writer to the honour of *hors concours*, (1) and the
successive biennial volumes of the publication are really
no more nor less than the transactions of the Academy of
Georgian Poets.   The diffidence of 'E.M.' is misplaced.

Another objection which, as I learn from this preface,
has been brought against the poets is that their works
display 'an insipid sameness', and that they are 'merely
a small clique of mutually indistinguishable poetasters'.
'E.M.' seems to be a master of the art of making an oppon-
ent ridiculous by exaggerating his strictures.   To say
that the admirable poets who owe much to 'E.M.'s' dis-
crimination, but still more to their own genius, are
'indistinguishable' one from another is absurd.   But the
emphasis of the benevolent editor ought not to blind us
to what is a real and a very curious peculiarity.   The
poets who have become prominent in the present century

are, with all deference to 'E.M.'s' sarcastic explosion,
remarkable for their general identity.   They form a
school in a degree which has rarely been seen in this
country, but has frequently marked the poetry of Italy and
France, and was present, with us, among the Elizabethan
lyrists.   The close resemblance of the style of Coler-
idge to that of Wordsworth at an early date is a parallel
instance.   I will name no names, because I am anxious to
avoid all offence, but in the present volume I have
marked five or six passages from different poets which
might certainly appear in the work of a single writer
without exciting the slightest suspicion of another hand.
    Among the great Victorians it was otherwise.   No one
could possibly be persuaded that a page of Browning was
written by Rossetti, or be doubtful whether a stanza was
the work of Swinburne or of Patmore.   But a strong per-
sonal note of character is lacking among many of the
Georgians, and 'E.M.' must remember that although the
shepherd knows his individual sheep by their faces, a
whole flock is apt to look very much the same to a candid
public.   When the standard of artistic merit is so high
as it is in the present case, similarity is hardly in it-
self a defect.
    Criticism of contemporaries must always be limited and
superficial, since growing organisms cannot be definitely
measured.   But in comparing the output of 1922 with that
of 1911, I have to confess that I see little evidence of
evolution, of progress.   Perhaps it is an error to ex-
pect from poetry, which is eminently a perfection of
early youth, any sign of growth.   Most of our lyric
poets have written their best pieces, and have exhibited
the fullness of their powers, before they were thirty.
But it was my hope that the new writers, now admitted to
the sacred ranks from which expulsion is impossible and
where fame becomes mechanical, would go a little further
than their forbears, and strike out in new directions.
    Of this I see but one example, Mr Edmund Blunden,
whose future will be watched with the most eager anticip-
ation.   He displays all the characteristics of a mind
inspired by the close and independent contemplation of
nature exercised in imagination.   That he is under the
spell of John Clare is evident; and is curious, since
Clare never boasted a disciple before.   Mr Blunden will
grow out of this, when he perceives that why Clare was not
a poet of the first rank was that his attention was hamp-
ered by incessant beauties, and that he lacked the gift of
selective apprehension.   Already, in the very remarkable
piece in which 'The Giant Puffball' speaks, Mr Blunden has
got beyond Clare, and I have no doubt that he will rise

much further yet.   No more interesting star has appeared
of late in our poetical heavens.

The determination to be anything rather than rhetorical
is a snare to the Georgians.   They are determined to
avoid any appeal to the movement of experience and thought.
They reject general ideas in favour of a pictorial rep-
resentation of the physical phenomena of life, and they
approach more closely than any previous school of English
poetry has done to the method of the cinematograph.   They
will have everything concrete, nothing abstract.   An ex-
ample is the clever and accurate piece of rhymed obser-
vation called 'Miss Thompson Goes Shopping', where every
artifice of style is expended on a long description, ex-
cessively minute, of a spinster's excursion down a
country town in the evening to buy articles for her
house.   It could not be more vivid in its congregation
of details, but at the end of it the reader asks what is
the use of such a catalogue of trivialities.   The poet
stands entirely outside Miss Thompson, whose footsteps he
dogs, while his photographic apparatus melodiously clicks
out its couplets.   But the result is a 'film-picture',
and nothing more.   The same almost crazy fear of being
'rhetorical' plunges the poets in occasional bathos.
They are so determined to be simple that they succeed in
being silly.   When one of the new Academicians remarks,

I know a farmer in Camden Town
Killed a brock by Pentonville,

and when another says,

I lingered at a gate and talked
A little with a lonely lamb,

they failed to ask themselves whether the confessions are
of general interest to anybody.   Coleridge, who wrote an
ode to a Young Ass, whom he hailed as 'Brother' -

I love the languid patience of thy face -

nevertheless rebuked Wordsworth 'for attaching himself to
the low in his desire to avoid the genteel'.   So diff-
icult is it to see ourselves as others see us!   But the
Georgians would do well to quit addressing poetry to
lambs and donkeys and badgers, in spite of the precedent
of W.W. and S.T.C.

If we take the contents of this volume as typical of
what is best in the poetry of the present day we may
regard the Georgians as jewellers, while the Victorians

were sculptors. The broad outline, the radiating vistas
of intellectual and moral life do not interest these
young poets in the least. Their eyes are not lifted to
the mountains, but are occupied in minute inspection of
the ground. They listen to the whisper of their own
inner feelings, and the daisy at their feet doth the same
tale repeat. The result is that they lack in some degree
the sense of proportion. They know not what to withhold,
and they sow with the whole sack. No generation of
writers, I suppose, was ever more obsessed with the charm
of nervous sensibility, cultivated for its own sake, and
not shrinking even from an apparently prosaic diction in
order to emphasise its penetration. As a French contemp-
orary has put it for them:

L'ombre émouvante est dans les choses minuscules. (2)

All this is very interesting and very sympathetic, yet
there may be a danger in this eclectic refinement of the
Georgians. They are exquisite, but poetry should not al-
ways be 'breathing through silver'. In their critical
performances we see the Georgians shrinking, as if in
physical pain, from the robustness of Mr Kipling, from the
trumpet-note of Sir Henry Newbolt, from the breadth of Mr
Noyes, from the sonority of Sir William Watson. They
hardly attempt to conceal that they think these manifest-
ations of energy vulgar.
    If, however, I have been drawn to express my conscious-
ness of some lack of variety and some narrowness of pur-
pose in certain of these sectarian singers, I am not in-
sensible to their accomplishment. They are admirable
artificers of verse, and I rejoice to find them less and
less drawn away from wholesome tradition by the lure of
metrical experiment. Apollo be praised, there is not
in this fifth volume a single piece of prose cut up into
lengths and called *vers libre*! To pass to particulars,
the passionate and wayward fancy of Mr Walter de la Mare
is still dominant, as it has been from the beginning. He
has always struck the peculiar chord to which all the
others have gone dancing, each in his own way. Land-
scape, poignantly felt and searchingly described, contin-
ues to be a leading feature of the Georgians, and Mr
Lascelles Abercrombie in 'Ryton Firs', brings the very
colour and form and smell of Gloucestershire across our
senses. Where the subjective tone prevails, the object-
ive of 'Full Moon' is welcome. I am constrained to
quote this amusing little piece, by V. Sackville-West
(Mrs Harold Nicolson), the only woman, I think, yet
admitted to the Georgian Academy:

[Quotes 'Full Moon', both stanzas.   V. Sackville-West
was, of course the second woman poet among the Georgians,
Fredegond Shove having appeared in the previous
anthology.]

   Mr Francis Brett Young is delightful in the plaintive
futility and shadowy pathos of 'The Quails'; Mr Squire
very moving in his 'Elegy'; Mr Robert Nichols - but if I
proceed I shall have to mention all the poets, or almost
all.   'E.M.' is to be warmly congratulated on his fifth
Transactions, but before 1925 I hope he will have recapt-
ured Mr Masefield and Mr Hodgson and Mr Sassoon.

Notes

1 Unrivalled, outside competition.
2 The evocative shade dwells in the minute particulars.

52.   'THE LATEST GEORGIANS', UNSIGNED REVIEW,
'THE OBSERVER'

17 December 1922, 5

_____

This is the fifth collection of contemporary poetry
which 'E.M.' has edited since 1912, when he began his
series of anthologies.   Of each of the four preceding
volumes some fifteen or sixteen thousand copies have been
sold, and the new volume will probably achieve a similar
success.   It seems clear, therefore, that 'Georgian
Poetry' has become an established biennial publication,
with a large circle of readers who, as a matter of course,
buy each volume as it appears.   It is, therefore, useful
to consider the exact aims of 'Georgian Poetry', and its
relation to the whole bulk of contemporary verse.
   Mr Edward Marsh (the identity of 'E.M.' is so generally
known that the full name may be written without indis-
cretion) tells us in his prefatory note that 'I found, ten
years ago, that there were a number of writers doing work
which appeared to me extremely good, but which was narrow-
ly known; and I thought that anyone ... who presented
a conspectus of it in a challenging and manageable form
might be doing a good turn both to the poets and to the
reading public.'   From that sentence, and from an exam-
ination of Mr Marsh's books, may be drawn the conclusion
that his eye is rather on the poet than on the poem.   In

other words, he tries, not, as most other anthologists do,
to make a collection of the best and prettiest verses
written during a specified period, but to represent those
poets whose work, taken as a whole, is most interesting
and who seem to him most likely to win for themselves
positions of distinction.   He therefore makes no attempt
to find the isolated, almost accidental, successes of in-
ferior writers, but attempts to make reputations that have
some breadth of basis on which to stand.   And in the
achievement of this object it is a matter of history (so
far as history that is only ten years old can be judged)
that Mr Marsh has been remarkably successful.

Many well-known poets of the younger generations are
included in the present book; among others, Mr Aber-
crombie, Mr de la Mare, Mr Davies, Mr Drinkwater, and Mr
Squire are represented by selections from their most
recent books.   But the chief interest in a new volume of
'Georgian Poetry' centres round the newcomers, of whom
there are this time seven: Messrs Martin Armstrong,
Edmund Blunden, Richard Hughes, William Kerr, Frank
Prewett, and Peter Quennell, and Miss Sackville-West.
Of these the first two and the last have the surest
touch, and the selections from their work are well
chosen.   That Mr Blunden and Mr Armstrong are included
for the first time comes to one with something of a sur-
prise, for their poems have already attracted a good deal
of attention; but Miss Sackville-West's name is less
generally known, and many readers will surely turn to her
solitary book of verse, 'Orchard and Vineyard', after
reading the seven examples given here of her talent, es-
pecially the vivid and neatly-written couplets of
'Sailing Ships':

> Lying on Downs above the wrinkling bay
> I with the kestrels shared the cleanly day,
> The candid day; wind-shaven, brindled turf;
> Tall cliffs; and long sea-line of marbled surf
> From Cornish Lizard to the Kentish Nore
> Lipping the bulwarks of the English shore,
> While many a lovely ship below sailed by
> On unknown errand, kempt and leisurely.

Not all Mr Marsh's Georgian poets (there are in all
twenty-one in this volume) attain that level of easy, un-
strained effect, and of technical proficiency.   Of one
or two of the new admissions, in particular, it is diff-
icult to be sure that they have not more mere cleverness
than genuine poetic impulse.   But the editor, in his
character of poetical tipster, has a right to his own

opinion, and he has shown himself, in the past, to be a
wonderfully shrewd judge.

53. 'GEORGIAN POETRY', 'C.P.', 'THE MANCHESTER GUARDIAN'

27 December 1922, 5

C.P.'s comments in this review of 'Georgian Poetry, 1920-
1922' are typical of the disappointment with which many
reviewers compared the fifth anthology with its
predecessors.

This is the fifth volume of 'Georgian Poetry', and its
right of succession can be most readily tested by compar-
ing it with the only other issue covering three years -
the one for 1913-15.   That opened with Gordon Bottomley's
'King Lear's Wife' and closed with Lascelles Aber-
crombie's 'The End of the World'.   In between it had the
best of Brooke and the best of Flecker; it had Ralph
Hodgson's 'The Bull' and 'The Song of Honour'; it had
gems from Ledwidge's 'Songs of the Fields' and James
Stephens's 'Songs from the Clay'; it had pearls from
W.H. Davies's 'Foliage' and 'The Bird of Paradise', and
the choicest pickings from 'Peacock Pie', to say nothing
of other fine things.   If this issue has but a fraction
of the wealth of the second the fault is not altogether
Mr Marsh's: relatively speaking,

No birds were flying overhead -
There were no birds to fly.

Still, with so much less wealth available the greater his
obligation, one would have thought, to avail himself of
all there was.   But in a prefatory note he disclaims any
design to 'give the best and only the best poems of the
best and only the best poets of the day'; and as only by
doing so could he have got it into proper relation to
1913-15 his new book is as we find it.
     It has some riches, of course.   In Mr de la Mare and
Mr Davies alike is an inexhaustible vein of gold: 'The
Moth', 'Sotto Voce', and 'The Titmouse' from 'The Veil',
and 'A Bird's Anger', 'The Truth', 'The Villain', and

'Love's Caution' from 'A Song of Life', place *them*, at any
rate, level with their earlier selves.   Robert Graves, too,
is as good as ever with 'Morning Phoenix', 'The Pier Glass',
'Fox's Dingle', and 'The Patchwork Bonnet', and John Freeman
only a little less good with 'I Will Ask', 'The Evening Sky',
and 'Change'.   Then Mr Edmund Blunden, who is new to the
series, made his calling and election sure with 'The Shep-
herd', and so in lesser degree did Martin Armstrong with 'The
Buzzards', and Miss Sackville-West with 'Orchard and Vine-
yard'.   But what one misses in many of the pieces is imag-
ination's dynamic, which proclaims a poem at sight as of the
blood royal and registers it at once on the tablets of the
memory and the tables of the heart.   It comes out in Mr
Abercrombie, if only in this vision of daffodils:

> Light has come down to earth and blossoms here,
> And we have golden minds . . .
> It was as if the world had just begun;
> And in a mind new-made
> Of shadowless delight
> My spirit drank my flashing senses in,
> And gloried to be made
> Of young mortality.

But the trouble with so many is that, though they can see
daffodils, can observe them with marvellous precision, in
single shape, in the mass, and in concerted movement, they
have no power first to apprehend them in terms of light
and then to transfuse them with the spirit - which is
imagination.   There was a good deal of it in the second
series, and it is a pity that the balance was not tipped
towards that with something like Gordon Bottomley's
'Britain's Daughter'.   Mr Squire's beautiful 'Elegy' was
bound to be in, and so was Mr Drinkwater's 'Persuasion',
and some, at any rate, of the Shanks and Brett Young sel-
ections.   But, good as they are, they do not compensate,
and so we are left lamenting that a book dedicated to such
a choice spirit as Alice Meynell should have fallen so far
out of its heritage.

54. 'GEORGIAN POETRY', UNSIGNED REVIEW, 'YORKSHIRE POST'

10 January 1923, 4

Although, like many contemporary notices which have been
excluded, this is little more than a summary of contents,
the notes attached are sufficiently perceptive to merit
its inclusion.

In a prefatory note to 'Georgian Poetry, 1920-22 '
(Poetry Bookshop, 6s.), the editor, 'E.M.', points out
that since the series was started, ten years ago, his aim
has been not so much to compile fully representative
collections of modern verse as to give prominence to
little known writers, who have, in his opinion, done
really good work.   Thus newcomers to the series are al-
ways of particular interest, and we wish that we could
feel more enthusiasm for those who make their first app-
earance in this new volume.   'E.M.' appears to be unduly
attracted by suave accomplishment.   Thus, although Mr
William Kerr and Mr Peter Quennell write with an agree-
able, musical smoothness, and although there is a certain
vitality of style and some original fancy in the work of
Mr Richard Hughes, we are not convinced that either of
the three has at present anything greatly worth saying.
Mr Frank Prewett has more strength and originality; he
probably has something to say, but has hardly yet found
out what it is.   The other three newcomers, Mr Martin
Armstrong, Mr Edmund Blunden, and Miss V. Sackville-West,
are in a different category.   The first two are already
quite well known, and Mr Blunden is one of the three or
four most interesting younger poets now writing.   Miss
Sackville-West, through her inclusion here, snould
greatly extend her readers.   There is nothing strikingly
original about her verse, but it is very clearly and
truly felt, and written with directness and sureness.
'Sailing Ships', for instance, from which we wish we had
room to quote, is a really valuable piece of work.
   Among thoroughly established poets, the best repres-
ented are, perhaps, Mr W.H. Davies (whose 'Love's
Caution' is a most beautiful little lyric), and Mr
Wilfrid Gibson.   A much better selection might have been
made from Mr de la Mare.   There are a number of sonnets,
good in parts, but a trifle overweighted, by Mr Drink-
water, and in a moderate selection from Mr Edward Shanks

is included one beautiful and unusual little poem, 'The
Glade'.   A good choice has been made from the very attr-
active and original work of Mr Robert Graves.   On the
whole, however, we do not think this volume of Georgian
poetry nearly so good as its predecessors, and there is
one notable omission - that of Mr W.J. Turner.   He is
sometimes obscure and extravagant, but his last book, 'In
Time like Glass', published a year ago, contained several
pieces, such as 'Love: A Dream', and 'The Forest Bird',
which should be included in any contemporary anthology.

55. 'GEORGIAN POETS', UNSIGNED REVIEW, 'THE TIMES
LITERARY SUPPLEMENT'

11 January 1923, 24

Robert H. Ross comments:

  The reviewer for 'The Times Literary Supplement' could
  only introduce a more or less irrelevant comparison
  between the poetic forms used by the Georgians of
  volume V and those in use fifty years before, and
  question rather mildly whether the Georgians were per-
  haps not too greatly absorbed in 'the new love of
  detail' for its own sake.   ['The Georgian Revolt',
  1967, 232.]

'Georgian Poetry' is now so nearly an established instit-
ution that it provokes the indignation of those who do not
belong to it.   Its editor is obliged this time to refuse
the honours so inevitably thrust upon him and to protest
that he is not a pundit or a pontiff, or even the Presid-
ent of the Royal Academy: that he is just a private
individual who ten years ago thought he saw that the
public wanted something which it had not got, tried to
supply it, succeeded to some extent, as appears from the
booksellers' returns, and has no complaint to make of
those who do not want him, provided they do not interfere
with those who do.   He adds a word or two of what his
aims have been:

[Quotes penultimate paragraph of the Prefatory Note,
omitting the opening sentence.]

These lines are open to verbal criticism, as so much of
Wordsworth is: did he mean anything by 'deliberately',
or is it just padding, and prosaic padding, too?   But
the rest makes a fair statement of a poetic ideal: poetry
should be a fit offering for gods who are high and tender;
though they are not always high when they are tender or
tender when they are high, and their 'gracious smile' must
take a larger view than our shortsightedness can always
take of what may be smiled at, of what has a grace which
defeats sadness and promises the ultimate victory that
belongs to beauty and truth.   For it must be able to wel-
come the 'Stanzas written in Dejection' - nay, and even
Lear himself.

There are twenty-one poets represented in the present
volume, seven of whom appear as 'Georgians' for the first
time.   They are Mr Armstrong, Mr Blunden, Mr Hughes, Mr
Kerr, Mr Prewett, Mr Quennell, and Miss Sackville-West.
It cannot be said that any of these introduces anything
which makes the new volume markedly different from its
predecessors.   The poems of 1922 are still, like those
that went before them, very orthodox and traditional com-
pared with those which are believed by their writers to
'be in the movement' and by other people, what is perhaps
the same thing, not to have come to stay.   And again,
compared with the poetry of fifty years ago, they are
very free in form, very detailed and descriptive in
matter, and at once very odd and very ordinary in phrase.
Of these three points the freedom in form is the least
noticeable, though it has commonly been the most dis-
cussed.   Indeed, the extravagances of freedom seem now
to be disappearing except among a small group of propa-
gandists.   The wiser men, in this as in other matters,
after being driven by restrictions to ask a great deal,
begin to see that to get it all would be a kind of
suicide.   They are learning that while the servants of
the Muse do well to throw off the chains which some of
her too-presuming officers have laid on them, they are
not to be ashamed, rather they are to be proud, to wear
her colours and be known as her men.   And perhaps they
are beginning to notice that the first and greatest of
their masters, Walt Whitman, lives most by the poems in
which he kept nearest to traditional forms, while they
may be struck by the extraordinary power of compelling
all the world to listen to him just shown by a poet who,
to-day, as forty years ago, uses the very simplest and
oldest of forms, and is not afraid to use them again and
again.   It would be a bad day for us if all our poets
were as chary of experiment and, to put it frankly, as
monotonous as Mr Housman.   But there is this question to

be asked.   How many of the poems even in this volume,
where there are very few liberties and most of the forms
are either altogether or partially traditional, were
learnt by heart this Christmas as so many of Mr Housman's
had already been?

And if there are few, why is it?   Primarily, no doubt,
because few of the poets approach the rare quality of Mr
Housman's genius.   But perhaps for other reasons too.
One of the contrasts suggested just now between these
Georgian poets and those of fifty years ago was their
trick of being at once very odd and very ordinary in
phrase.   Mr Housman does not write after the fashion of
one of these poets: 'This new mood of judgment orders me
my present duty, to face again a problem strongly solved
in life gone by, but now again proposed out of due time
for fresh deliberation.'   This is pure prose, as is seen
at once when it is no longer divided into lines.   Can
such ordinary leading-article language produce the effect
of poetry?   Is it conceivable that anybody should learn
it by heart?   It is not words of this sort that come into
our heads as we walk in a wood alone or lie in bed waiting
for sleep.

The oddness of phrase is less common, but it is also
there; and oddness is not originality.   Why, for inst-
ance, does so true a poet as Mr Blunden talk of 'hang-dog
alder-boughs'?   He knows so much more about trees than
this reviewer that it may well be that he has natural
justification for the phrase.   But it can hardly fail to
strike most readers as forced and odd.   And so, in spite
of the ordinariness of its words, such a line as that
which begins Mr Freeman's 'Caterpillars', 'Of Caterpillars
Fabre tells how day after day', is not only as dull and
clumsy as that clumsiest and dullest of all Victorian
lines, Arnold's 'Who prop, thou ask'st, in these bad days,
my mind?'   But it is even more odd; it is even
grotesque.

The other point, the new love of detail, is really more
important.   That has been growing for a hundred and fifty
years.   One sees the ascending scale: Cowper, Keats,
Tennyson, Bridges; and now the Georgians.   The first
thirty pages of this book, Mr Abercrombie, Mr Armstrong,
Mr Blunden, are all loaded with descriptive detail, often
very curious and interesting.   But does it not over-
weight the thought, the emotion, the imagination?   Will
not many readers, and not perhaps the least judicious,
feel a sense of relief when they escape from this receipt
of information and get to Mr Davies's quiet little lyric
'Wasted Hours', so almost empty of things observed, so
rich in two or three things felt and lived and loved:

> How many buds in this warm light
> Have burst out laughing into leaves!
> And shall a day like this be gone
> Before I seek the wood that holds
> The richest music known?
>
> Too many times have nightingales
> Wasted their passion on my sleep,
> And brought repentance soon :
> But this one night I'll seek the woods,
> The nightingale, and moon.

It is true that the passion for detail is not confined
to poetry: it has now spread everywhere.   Perhaps it
comes of the scientific atmosphere of the nineteenth
century; perhaps of popular education, which seems to
make people insatiable of facts, quick to sentiment, slow
to thought.   The same thing is to be seen in the novel.
Compare Scott with Dickens or George Eliot, and them with
almost any novelist of to-day.   Compare René with St
Julien l'Hospitalier, and that with the work of M. Proust.
Compare 'I Promessi Sposi' with a modern Italian novel.
Everywhere something like specialism, the minute observ-
ation of unusual things, the unintelligible language of
the craftsman or the expert, the engineer or the doctor,
have more and more taken the place of common humanity and
its ordinary ways and thoughts and words.   However, it
may be judged, it is a process to note.   Only in poetry
these discoveries of fact and specialisms of training
need to be absorbed in the larger imagination.   For
poetry, as Wordsworth said long ago, has to give pleas-
ure to men as men and not to men as specialists or ex-
perts of any kind.   Who in this volume come most ass-
ured through that test?   Who give us most poetry and
most pleasure?

Well, there is not very much to say about the contri-
butions of the more familiar Georgians.   Mr Abercrombie
has often done better work than he does in 'Ryton Firs';
it is one of several poems here which make us think of
that common fault of painters, the fault of taking a can-
vas too big for their subject and so being forced to bury
the subject in a wilderness of detail.   Mr Drinkwater
sends an interesting series of Shakespearean sonnets.
But they owe too much to their great original in thought
and manner as well as in form to add much to his reputat-
ion.

Mr Gibson and Mr Graves strike familiar notes, but Mr
Gibson has certainly made finer tunes out of them on
former occasions.   He has nothing here that has the

power of 'The Hare' or 'Geraniums' of 1911, or the beauty
of 'Reveille' of 1918.   Mr Freeman's 'The Caves' is a
beautiful thing, but it lacks the fine concentration of
'The Fugitive' of four years ago.   Mr D.H. Lawrence is as
fresh, as curious, as intensely modern, as mingled of sen-
suousness, sentimentality, and power, as usual.   His
'Snake' arrests and holds the reader.   It is seen and
felt and even thought with sincerity and strength.   And
yet its art fails!   It is almost in spite of its langu-
age ('my accursed human education') that one realizes its
power;   and how poorly and cheaply it ends:

> And so, I missed my chance with one of the lords
> Of life.
> And I have something to expiate:
> A pettiness.

The form throws immense weight on 'Of life' and 'A petti-
ness':   can either of them bear it?   They are almost as
weak as the trivial 'Led them on' and 'For a time' which
are the ignominious conclusions of the first two stanzas
of Campbell's 'Battle of the Baltic', where he only once
got the full value of his short last line with -

> By thy wild and stormy keep,
>   Elsinore!

Mr de la Mare sends six beautiful things - four from
'The Veil' and two from 'Flora'.   Here, as almost al-
ways, he is at once a child, a seer, and a spirit: for
him poetry is a secret and a mystery;   and his instrument
never fails to respond exactly to his touch;   the langu-
age has an aery lightness, the verse seems to be treading
a measure of the spirit:

[Quotes 'The Moth', all three stanzas.]

Mr Squire and Mr Nichols give us two fine winter land-
scapes.   Mr Squire's deals with snow seen from a train:
it is not saying too much to say that it can bear to re-
call the 'London Snow' of Mr Bridges, so full it is of
delicacy, tenderness, and truth.   Here are two stanzas
of it:

[Quotes 'Late Snow', stanzas III and IV.]

Mr Nichols's 'November' has not the beauty of this, but it
is one of the best descriptions of late autumn in English.
Here are a few lines of it:

A rheum, like blight, hangs on the briars,
And from the clammy ground suspires
A sweet frail sick autumnal scent
Of stale frost furring weeds long spent;
And wafted on, like one who sleeps,
A feeble vapour hangs or creeps,
Exhaling on the fungus mould
A breath of age, fatigue, and cold.

But it is time to turn to the newcomers.   There is Mr
Martin Armstrong, who brings a little masterpiece in a
difficult manner: his 'Miss Thompson Goes Shopping'.
Great poetry it is not, of course; scarcely poetry at all
in our strictest sense; but it illustrates, as do several
other things here, that recovery of the pleasure of verse
for its own sake, even when it makes no pretence of being
high poetry, which is one of the best ways in which the
twentieth century has gone behind the nineteenth to the
seventeenth and eighteenth.   And the conclusion, at least,
rises far above mere verse:

[Quotes 'Miss Thompson Goes Shopping', concluding 20
lines.]

Then there is Mr Blunden, with his charming almswomen and
very Georgian perch-fishing: full of realism and senti-
ment; partly ugly and partly tender and more than partly
true.   The same things are to be seen in Mr Hughes: his
'Singing Fires' of rain are Georgian, every note of them.
Mr William Kerr contributes eight little poems, each
pleasant enough, with the pleasure of promise rather than
of any exceptional performance.   Mr Pellow, another name
which will be new to most readers, has four poems, the
first of which is a sort of modernized echo of the Dies
Irae:

[Quotes 'When All is Said', all six stanzas.]

    Mr Prewett has some war poems, and a fine little poem
about snow-buntings.   Mr Quennell has a graceful frag-
ment called 'Procne'·   Stronger than anything by either
of these is the 'Saxon Song' of the last of the new-
comers, Miss Sackville-West:

[Quotes 'A Saxon Song', all four stanzas.]

After all the secret of verse, though some of our new
poets do not know it, is the repetition of a pattern,
something that the ear can expect, which is the same

every time and yet not quite the same.   Miss Sackville-West, at any rate, knows that, and her knowledge has helped her to make this poem what so many modern poems are not, a unity in which the first word looks on to the last and the last back to the first.

On the whole, without being able to pretend that the Georgian editor has discovered any unknown geniuses, or induced his fixed stars to shine brighter than before, we may congratulate him on proving once more that English poetry is alive and giving us some very useful hints of where to look for it.

56.   'THE GEORGIANS', UNSIGNED REVIEW, 'THE NATION AND ATHENAEUM'

13 January 1923, 585-6

This unsigned review is of 'Georgian Poetry, 1920-1922' and 'Shorter Lyrics of the Twentieth Century' (ed. W.H. Davies).

For this, the latest issue of 'Georgian Poetry', 'E.M.' offers what is, to our mind, a quite unnecessary apology. In a mood nicely balanced between indignation and concili-ation, he seeks to warn all future rivals from his path. Did he expect that the little fleet of five vessels his pains have launched over a period of a dozen years under the standard of St George, was going to ride the public seas unchallenged and unfought?   Had that been so, their timbers might just as well have rotted at their anchors. The trouble with the Georgians has been, not too many hard knocks, but too much security;   or perhaps it would be more accurate to say that their enemies have only been lightly armed corsairs, rakish craft flying the skull and crossbones of poetic nonconformity.   The actual cannon-ades of these piratical fry have made very little impres-sion;   but the force of revolt behind them has been, and is, a very real one, indicating a discontent, not only with the beautiful but narrow expression of the Georgians, but possibly even with literature itself, as the final embodiment of the sense of beauty to man.

As a period of three years has elapsed since the last

volume of 'Georgian Poetry', and there are seven new poets
among the twenty-one included in the present, judgment is
made difficult by the quality, very uneven as to contri-
bution, of the neophytes.   Mr Armstrong, of 'The Buzz-
ards', has handsomely won his election, and he has two
other pieces, one of which, 'Miss Thompson Goes Shopping',
if slight, is very elegant.   Mr Blunden can obviously
carry all the newcomers on his back, and with the except-
ion of two of them beats all the old stagers into the bar-
gain.   He has half-a-dozen landscape poems of noble, rich
content, but 'The Shepherd' ought to have made a seventh.
But 'Almswomen' is here, a poem now classic both for mem-
ory and in essential art, while 'The Poor Man's Pig' would
be a piece of remarkable evidence for the Reincarnation
Society, if such existed.   This is John Clare, not his
ghost, nor his shadow nor his emanation, but himself:

> Then out he lets her run; away she snorts
> In bundling gallop for the cottage door,
> With hungry hubbub begging crusts and orts,
> Then like the whirlwind bumping round once more;
> Nuzzling the dog, making the pullets run,
> And sulky as a child when her play's done.

What further proof can a reasonable man require?   With
this twain passed in, one has to look about rather care-
fully for the other five.   Miss Sackville-West is, per-
haps, the best, though Mr William Kerr's 'The Audit' does
deserve a hearing where there is plenty of room for a
conflicting opinion.
     Of the young veterans, Mr Davies, Mr de la Mare, and
Mr Francis Brett Young are the captains, and 'E.M.' has
done very well with all of them.   The choice of 'The
Villain' in the Davies selection was particularly happy,
for it is the image and superscription of a poet timeless
in a sense beyond what we usually associated with the
term.   'I turned my head, and saw the wind', he writes,

> Dragging the corn by her golden hair
> Into a dark and lonely wood.

That vivid impersonation is essential Davies, and we can-
not but feel his sympathy with the wind!   The poem
'Love's Caution' exhibits another characteristic.   It
contains the lines:

> A falling star:
> It was a tear of pure delight
> Ran down the face of Heaven this happy night.

Nobody can read them without calling to mind the lines of
Keats at the close of a famous sonnet.   Davies's work
carries a heap of these mementoes, and they are too fresh
and genuine for imitations.   They are the blossom, in
fact, of an intuitive memory, and show how little he is
bound to the thought or manner of any age, period, or
fashion.   Mr de la Mare's specimens are also chosen with
taste and discernment - no very difficult matter in a poet
whose New Found Land has so few suburbs to its enchanted
cities.   But all estimates as to a poet's growth or as to
the measure of his excellence in relation to the rest of
his product have to be largely guesswork in this volume,
owing to 'E.M.'s' elementary negligence in failing to give
the reader the slightest indication of the date of the
poems selected, or the volumes whence they are taken.   To
offer a bibliography at the end of the book of all the
works of the poets included in it is a futile substitute
for what we really want to know.   It was only, for in-
stance, by taking the trouble (which it was 'E.M.'s' duty
to spare us) to look into the matter ourselves that we
could see how great an advance in poetic freedom, power,
and mastery has been made by Mr Francis Brett Young.
There are four poems - a description of a burial at sea,
of a sirocco, and of the blinding and netting of migrating
quails in Southern Italy, and a fine 'Song at Santa Cruz'.
Mr Young's imagination, at once robust and pitiful, has
deepened and widened; it takes broad sweeps and is human
and direct, without dropping and wasting any of its packed,
tropical intensity.   Without doubt, he promises to take
his place beside the best of the poets now writing.   Some
of the others - Mr Abercrombie, for instance - are dis-
appointing, though Mr Freeman has made a definite improve-
ment in sharpness and closer texture - have perhaps fallen
below their wonted achievement.   A curious melancholy of
temper pervades the volume and gives an autumnal effect to
all its graces.
   Mr Davies's Davies-flavored and disarming 'Foreword' is
enough in itself to recommend his anthology to all true
readers.   Mr Davies does not think a great deal of modern
poets.   Their work, he says, 'begins and ends in descrip-
tion ', and they 'seem to lead easy and placid lives with-
out having any burning sympathies to make themselves great
as men '.   And they lack 'the sympathy and generosity of
men that drink'.   So his volume is intended as a guide to
the best short poems of the century, not the best poets,
and among them are many surprises, as he says, quite
rightly, there should be - better surprises than another
he tells us of - that 'the worst poets charged the high-
est fees for the use of their work'.   The result is just

as individual and human and original as we should
expect it to be.

57.   'NEW PHOENIX-NESTS', UNSIGNED REVIEW, 'THE WEEKLY
WESTMINSTER GAZETTE'

13 January 1923, 17-18

Unsigned review of 'Georgian Poetry, 1920-1922', to-
gether with 'A Miscellany of Poetry, 1920-1922' (ed.
William Kean Seymour), R.H. Strachan's 'The Soul of
Modern Poetry', 'The Golden Book of Modern English
Poetry' (ed. Thomas Caldwell), 'Modern American Poets'
(selected by Conrad Aiken), 'Shakespeare to Hardy'
(chosen by A. M[ethuen].), and 'A Diary for the Thankful-
Hearted' (compiled by Mary Hodgkin).
    The review is given in full to show Marsh's anthology
in the context of its contemporary rivals.

Doctor Strachan, in one of the Edinburgh Lectures on
Modern Poetry, applies to contemporary verse a verdict
passed by Professor Saintsbury on modern literature gen-
erally: it is, he says, characterised by 'a vagabond
curiosity of matter and a tormented unrest of style'.
And, having extracted this dictum for his text, he pro-
ceeds through English lyric poetry from Meredith and Mr
Hardy to Mr John Masefield and Mr Robert Nichols, and
finds no difficulty in proving its truth, or at least its
justification.   But interesting as Dr Strachan's analysis
of contemporary poetry is, it is neither exhaustive nor
complete.   No age in which the poets were entirely given
over to vagabond curiosity and torments of style could
have produced what is now the most remarkable feature of
literary activity, the revival of the Anthology.
    Not since the days between Richard Grimald's first
effort and the appearance of 'The Gorgeous Gallery' has
there been so wide an impulse to collect and dis-
seminate lyrical excellence as has reached what it· must
be hoped is its climax during the autumn of 1923.   Week
after week some new anthology by some collector of repute,
either as a taster of verse or as a former of public
opinion, has been reviewed in the literary columns of

newspapers and magazines.   Delightful, if quite erron-
eous, reports of the huge profits made by the antholo-
gists have enlivened the air and given occasion to at
least one of the collecting crowd to retort with comp-
laints of the fees charged by authors: while a certain
poet, who is also a wit, has announced his intention of
retiring to the mountains and there living in a comfort-
able frugality on the guineas earned for him by the one
poem he always insists on all the anthologists taking from
his books whatever else their idiosyncratic choice may
happen to select.   This project is not so fantastic as it
would have been ten or fifteen years ago.   The authors of
'Arabia', 'Innisfree', 'The Listeners', 'Time You Old
Gipsy Man', poems no gentleman's anthology can be without,
are still with us to give the lie to those who believe
that the war recreated English poetry, pointing to
Brooke's 'Soldier' and Grenfell's 'Into Battle', also con-
spicuous in every anthology made since 1914, to illustrate
that claim.   And in none of these poems, each of which
adds a new glory to the English lyric, is there any evid-
ence of vagabond curiosity or of tormented style.
      It is quite true that some very odd things do get into
our weekly - almost our daily - anthologies.

      What desperate hand would draw the ethereal veil
      That robes thy deathless secret?

asks Mr Frederick V. Branford on page 35 of Mr William
Kean Seymour's 'Miscellany'.   But this is no worse in its
slipshod way than the cries of 'Kinwelmersh, Hunnis, and
other respectable men of letters', which were heard among
the native wood-notes of Spenser, Drayton, and Ben Jonson
in the days of the first 'Phoenix-Nest'.
      The trouble with our Georgian Phoenix is that it has so
many nests that it is compelled to lay the same egg again
and again.   Mr Seymour, Mr Caldwell, add the incompletely
anonymous 'E.M.' have twisted straw and twig and feathers
in the several branches of the great Publisher's Tree,
and (allowance being made for the difficult business of
personal friendship and the interesting one of personal
taste) have made selection of the best work so nearly
identical as to make any two of the three books super-
fluous so far as poetry since 1870 goes, and 'From Shakes-
peare to Hardy', in some respects the best of the three,
neither an improvement on nor a really satisfactory app-
endix to 'The Oxford Book of English Verse'.   Mr Seymour
and Mr Caldwell, with a catholicity which does them inter-
mittent credit, have included not only a great many really
bad poems, but also such controversial matter as the work

of the Sitwell family, much of which made its first dust-
raising appearance in these columns;   but these vivid and
unusual poems, though they might easily be made to serve
Dr Strachan as examples of the vagabond and the tormented
quality of modern verse, cannot be said to have had any
immediate influence on either the volume or the quality
of contemporary poetry.   And it is interesting to remark
that Mr Caldwell's selection from Miss Sitwell is 'The
Mother', an early poem, the meaning of which could not
escape the dullest-witted critic, even at a first reading.
Mr Seymour is more courageous if less discriminating.   He
has, it is true, found and rescued from the iniquity of
oblivion the one and only poem Mr Hodgson is known to have
written for years.

'Silver Wedding'

In the middle of the night he started up
At a cry from his sleeping Bride,
A bat from some ruin in a heart he'd never searched,
Nay, hardly seen inside:

'Want me and take me for the woman that I am,
And not for her that died,
The lovely chit Nineteen I one time was,
And am no more,' she cried.

To Mr Seymour also belongs the credit of recognising
Mrs Lynd's verse as an adornment to any anthology.   It
must have been hard for 'E.M.' to decide between the ad-
vantage of so delightful a preface as Mr Robert Lynd has
made for his book, and the distinction of including Mrs
Robert Lynd in his list of poets.   Mr Seymour includes
among other poems her 'Fable':

[Quotes 'Fable', stanzas I-V.]

But this delicate, but unfinished piece of beauty, is
by no means the best of Mrs Lynd's published work, and in
selecting it, Mr Seymour betrays the enthusiasm which fits
him for, and the blindness or deafness which makes him un-
suited to, the business of selection.
There are indeed only two ways in which a good and use-
ful anthology can be made.   Such a collection must either
be as Mrs Hodgkin's 'Diary for the Thankful-Hearted' most
ingenuously and restfully is, a collection of poems and
prose passages chosen with a single eye (and that eye
quite unpreoccupied with literary merit), to the subject
discussed, or a collection of poems chosen by an

enlightened mind possessed by no other idea than that of
good writing.

And of all anthologists' contemporary verse, the first
both in time and in achievement is the quasi-anonymous
'E.M. who, as long ago as 1910, realised that Georgian
poetry was the stuff of which anthologies are made, even
as was the Elizabethan lyric out of which our first an-
thologies arose.   Alone among his imitators 'E.M.' con-
fines himself to the years between each successive volume
of what has now become a really great serial work.   And
to judge from internal evidence he alone has preserved
his judicial integrity.   In one of the most delightful
and disarming prefaces of modern times, he protests:

I will only say that with an occasional exception
for some piece of rebelliousness or even levity which
may have taken my fancy, I have tried to choose no
verse but such as in Wordsworth's phrase:

'The high and tender muses shall accept
With gracious smile, deliberately pleased.'

And to this stern precept 'E.M.' has manifestly ad-
hered.   Individual preference may regret the omission of
so fine a poem as 'The Old Angler' from Mr de la Mare's
work.   It is a pity that 'E.M.' instead of rifling 'The
Veil', by now well known to all lovers of poetry, should
not have included one or more of the poems which have
appeared in the Press since the publication of that coll-
ection, and it is possible that some readers may find
dullness rather than rebellious levity in one or two of
the poems by the seven new writers now for the first time
brought to the notice of readers of 'Georgian Poetry'.
But one of them, Mr Peter Quennell, has written this poem
and 'E.M.' has found it for us:

[Quotes 'Procne (a Fragment)'.]

And none of the poems is ill-made or tortured in any
sense.   Mr Lascelles Abercrombie's dream, 'Ryton Firs',
the longest poem in the book, will give point to the crit-
icism referred to in the preface that the poets of this
generation have rather too much in common, especially as
alphabetical coincidence places Mr Abercrombie with Mr
Martin Armstrong and Mr Edmund Blunden.   But relief is
not far.   The lyrics of Mr Robert Graves, the fine
'Snake' of Mr D.H. Lawrence are by themselves a justifi-
cation of Georgian poetry, and towards the end of the
book (and the alphabet) we find among the new comers a
frivolous, lovely little song beginning

> She was wearing the coral taffeta trousers
> Someone had brought her from Ispahan,
> And the little gold coat with pomegranate blossoms,
> And the coral-hafted feather fan;
> But she ran down a Kentish lane in the moonlight,
> And skipped in the pool of the moon as she ran .

['Full Moon' by V. Sackville-West, stanza I.]

Certain names are missing from 'E.M.'s' book this year, but before complaining of these gaps it must be remembered that some poets have grown restless under the increasing demands of the army of anthologists, and in refusing one claim must say 'no' to all.   And if 'E.M.' should find any of his poets less easy to shepherd now than they once were, he will easily console himself for their vagrancy in the knowledge that he is now reaping not only the distress of being imitated, but also the glory of being right, and the joy of seeing how richly in and outside of his own collections Georgian poetry is vindicating his prophetic faith in its virtue.

58.   J.C. SQUIRE, INITIALLED REVIEW,   THE LONDON MERCURY'

February 1923, 432

J.C. Squire, being himself a contributor, 'can hardly do more than record the appearance of the fifth volume of "Georgian Poetry"'.
    Squire had not felt the same constraint in writing his anonymous review of the fourth anthology (see No. 33). He repeats the opinion he expressed in the earlier review that Marsh's 'admissions are far more open to criticism than his exclusions'.
    For a note on Squire see Appendix, p. 415.

The present chronicler can hardly do more than record the appearance of the fifth volume of 'Georgian Poetry' - which, before she died, was dedicated to Mrs Meynell, and is now a tribute to her memory.   There is an apologetic preface by the editor, which should disarm a very Attila: he has compiled these volumes in order to make a wider

public acquainted with certain poets whom he thought good.
They profess to represent nobody's taste but his own, and
he does not attempt to cover the whole contemporary ground
with finality.   No apology was needed.   Like other
people, I do not always admire what E.M. admires; less
frequently, but occasionally, I admire something which he,
if his collections be evidence, does not.   Yet I do not
see how anyone who is not prejudiced or quite incompetent
can dispute that from 1912 - when Brooke, Flecker, and
even Mr de la Mare were first introduced to very many
readers by Volume I of 'Georgian Poetry' - Mr Marsh has
done far more than any other critic or anthologist to
attract attention to good modern verse.   In all he has
printed selections from forty poets.   Twenty-one are
represented in the present volume; seven of these, in-
cluding Mr Martin Armstrong and Mr Edmund Blunden, are
newcomers.

59.   HOLBROOK JACKSON, 'TO-DAY'

March 1923, 113

_____

Holbrook Jackson, but for a different reason, does little
more than 'record the appearance of' 'Georgian Poetry,
1920-1922'.   Robert H. Ross writes:

   Both in what he said and the manner in which he said
   it, Holbrook Jackson courageously did what one
   suspects most other reviewers would have preferred to
   do: he devoted precisely one short paragraph in 'To-
   Day' to a succinct dismissal of the volume.   ['The
   Georgian Revolt', 1967, 233.]

'C.P.' (see also No. 53) was to express a contrary opinion
to Jackson's in 'The Manchester Guardian', 15 March 1923:

   Whether is the gleaning of the grapes of the Georgians
   better than the vintage of Mr Edward Marsh?   That is
   the question raised by the first of these anthologies.
   In other words, do the sixty-one poets that Mr Seymour
   has assembled make, with their poems taken from the
   manuscript, a braver show than Mr Marsh's twenty-one
   Georgians, whose poems came from their published books?
   Quite the reverse is the only possible answer after

reading the miscellany with the other still fresh in
the mind.

For note on Holbrook Jackson see No. 29.

The fifth book of 'Georgian Poetry', despite the addition
of seven writers who have not hitherto appeared in this
collection, carries on a tradition of sameness.   The
quality is maintained but the freshness has departed -
which means that E.M. has more or less completed his work
as an anthologist.   He has represented a poetic mood with
fairness and accuracy, and it is not his fault that the
particular vein has exhausted itself.   The series was at
one time representative of the younger school of bards -
it is no longer so;   indeed it is a misnomer to refer to
writers like Drinkwater, Davies, Walter de la Mare, Monro,
Lawrence and Squire as 'contemporary poets of the younger
generation'.   They are nothing of the sort.   There is a
younger generation and a newer poetry more fully repres-
ented in Mr Seymour's 'Miscellany'.

60.   HAROLD MONRO, 'THE CHAPBOOK'

March 1923, 3

Article entitled 'The Publisher Speaks' in 'Editor's
Notes'.
    This piece and the next are a fitting conclusion to
the section.   Monro maintains a strangely ambivalent
attitude to his publication: it should be noted, too,
that W.H. Davies's anthology, 'Shorter Lyrics of the
Twentieth Century' (see No. 56) was also issued from the
Poetry Bookshop.
    For a note on Harold Monro see Appendix,pp. 407-8;   for
a note on 'The Chapbook' see Introduction, pp. 27-8.

'The end of "the boom" in poetry for which the righteous
have so long been praying, seems at last to have arrived'
wrote Mr J. Middleton Murry recently in an 'English
Letter' to one of the American dailies.   Yet we notice

that 'Georgian Poetry, 1920-1922' is mentioned by book-
sellers in London and many provincial towns as a Best
Seller.   The public is apparently more interested in
Georgian poets as a group than individually, for, though
all the reviewers have discussed the seven new-comers now
introduced into the series, we hear of few inquiries for
their individual books.

If there really has been a boom, we pray, with the
righteous, that its end may have arrived.   For a boom
(vile word) is the hollow product of commercial plotting,
and it is a fatal obstacle to true appreciation.   We are
told that the sales have declined lately of some even of
the greater favourites among the Georgian poets, and the
following rough figures have been given us by one who
ought to know.   They are based upon a one hundred per
cent standard.   The first figure denotes the probable
average circulation, in comparison with the others ment-
ioned, of any particular poet's works at the moment of
their highest recent popularity.   The second figure in-
dicates what is thought to be their proportionate average
circulation to-day.

Walter de la Mare 100/80; Ralph Hodgson 100/60; John
Drinkwater 100/50; Rupert Brooke 100/30; J.E. Flecker
70/60; W.H. Davies 70/50; Wilfrid Gibson 70/25; Robert
Nichols 70/20; James Stephens 60/50; J.C. Squire 60/30;
John Freeman 50/30; D.H. Lawrence 40/40; Robert Graves
40/30; Edward Shanks 40/20; W.J. Turner 30/10.

These figures, which will be seen to refer to a few so-
called 'Georgian' poets only, are of some ephemeral
interest, but they mean nothing except either that less
poetry is now being bought, or that (as our informant
believes) anthologies have been so foolishly, indiscrim-
inately, we might say unscrupulously, over-multiplied,
that their excess has now at last begun to prejudice the
circulation of individual volumes.

61.   'THE END OF THE AFFAIR',   HAROLD MONRO AND E.M.

1925

'Georgian Poetry': a Correspondence between E.M. and
Harold Monro: reprinted in 'The Chapbook', 110-11.

There is a suggestion I am so tempted to make that I really
can't resist it.   The booksellers clamour for a sixth vol-
ume of 'Georgian Poetry', and five thousand copies could
be sold - no more.   From what you have said and written
to me, I understand clearly that you have not sufficient
confidence in the material available, and I have been of
like mind, and have felt that the series might fittingly
close;   but lately I have been thinking that nevertheless
several recent books could be drawn upon without dis-
advantage.

Some of them are volumes for extracts from which I feel
certain you would not care to act as sponsor, although you
well might not be unconscious of their merits.   I will
not at present mention any names.   Naturally, several
previous contributors would be included.

Far be it from me to want to drag out a 'movement'
after it has lost its natural impetus.   But I have been
coming to the conclusion during the past few months that
just one more volume would round off the series by sugg-
esting new directions.   This view, I know, is not entire-
ly compatible with your original objects.   Nevertheless,
circumstances alter continually with the progress of the
years, and the original motives of 'Georgian Poetry' are
now slightly obscured, or have become diverted, by later
developments.

If you think there is anything in my suggestion, would
you like a preliminary investigation of all possible books
undertaken immediately in order to find out whether my
impression that a sixth volume might be possible has any
real warrant?

Even if you had to cavil, or to object, or to question;
or to doubt whether the poems that would be included were
sufficiently suitable or important, would you nevertheless
undertake to introduce such a volume into the world?

It would be a rare opportunity for you to sum up and
round off the 'movement' (I use the word advisedly in
inverted commas), and to comment upon new directions;   and
as much space as you felt inclined to use could be allot-
ted to a critical Introduction.

Yours,

Harold Monro.

My dear Harold,
I have been thinking carefully over your letter, but I
haven't succeeded in confuting the arguments which decided
us a few months ago to announce that there would be no
more 'Georgian Poetry' books.   My chief reason was that
the series seems to me to have done its work.   We set out
with the single object of stimulating public interest in

contemporary poetry, and I shall always cherish the belief
that the books had a great deal to do with the marked
growth of that interest which there has certainly been
within the twelve years since we began.   But whether
propter or merely *post* what I like to think of as our
success, there has been a pullulation of other antholog-
ies which cover much the same ground as ours, and which,
by appearing at shorter intervals, have taken the bread
out of our mouths.   If I tried to make a choice from the
poetry which has been published since our last volume, I
should find that the field has already been most effic-
iently reaped.

The other point is what you call the new directions.
In my own opinion, I have always been catholic to a
fault, but everyone must have his preferences, and mine
have been for the verse which seemed to me to be in the
direct line of tradition.   I will not say that the 'new
directions' are not in that line, *de peur*, as M. Bergeret
said, *d'offenser à la beauté inconnue*, (1) but I own that
my feeling towards their chief exponents is one of tepid
and purblind respect, which would make me quite the wrong
person to anthologize them, even if they had any wish to
be anthologized by me, which is more than doubtful.   And
I hope it isn't dog-in-the-mangerish to feel that after
being solely responsible for the previous books, I
shouldn't care to come forward as sponsor for a selection
made by somebody else from work with which I wasn't
really in sympathy; still less to make my exit with the
gesture of *moriturus te saluto* (2) which you seem to
suggest.   So I hope you won't be vexed if I stick to
what we settled.

Yours ever,

E.M.

Notes

1 For fear of injury to unknown beauty.
2 I who am about to die salute you.   Cf. *Ave, Imperator,
   morituri te salutant*: Hail, Emperor, those about to
   die salute thee (Suetonius, 'Life of Claudius', 21).

Later articles

62. 'THE NEO-GEORGIANS', ALEC WAUGH, 'FORTNIGHTLY REVIEW'

CXV (1924), 126-9

Only the first part of this article is given.
   For a note on Alec Waugh (b. 1898) see headnote to
No. 22.   See also Introduction, p. 11.

In those days so distant now as to belong seemingly to
another century, when in every month and in every seventh
periodical we read articles on 'The War and Literature',
we encountered rarely enough the note of prophecy.   No
one seemed to be more than casually concerned with the
effect of peace on literature;   no one was seriously
wondering what would happen when the immediate intoxic-
ation of war conditions was removed, when the electric
battery that had maintained at such a high pitch the ner-
vous tension of the country was disconnected.   No one
appeared to realise that peace would exert as profound and
as disturbing an influence on modern literature as had
previously the war.   The Neo-Georgians (the men who were
unknown or unnoticed before the war and had reached prom-
inence in the course of it) were expected confidently and
unreasonably to take the peace in their stride, carrying
into new conditions the manner and temper of their earlier
work.   'If they can achieve so much', the critic wrote,
'during the stress and discomfort of army life, what may
they not accomplish when peace restores to them that
leisure which is requisite for big work?'

Well, they have got that leisure now, have had it for
the last five years, and it is doubtful if there is, with
the exception of Mr Aldous Huxley, a single Neo-Georgian
who stands as high in popular and critical esteem as he
did six years ago.   The four most vital and most robust
of the later war poets have not repeated the successes
that came so quickly, if so deservedly, to them in 1917.
Siegfried Sassoon was not represented in 'Georgian Poetry,
1920-1922', and since 'Counter-attack' has published
nothing except in private and limited editions.   Robert
Graves has abandoned his fusiliers for his fairies; W.J.
Turner has become exceedingly abstruse; Robert Nichols
is apparently in a sort of halfway house between two
manners; and of the others - those whom the chance of
things withheld from service, those whose work, as in the
case of Edmund Blunden, did not receive recognition till
1919, and those again who, though serving, wrote little,
if any, war verse, of them in an equal measure.   When the
last volume of 'Georgian Poetry' appeared a number of
critics deplored in it a general absence of life and vig-
our.   Individually the poems were good enough, but coll-
ectively they presented a curious and distinctly tedious
homogeneity of style and matter.   The book contained a
considerable amount of pastoral poetry, some of which
tended to become a mere cataloguing of place names, a
type of poem that Clifford Bax parodied in 'Midsummer
Madness':

> I have seen Laister Dyke and Langley Hill,
> Old Meldrum, Ollerton and Orchardleigh,
> Manningtree (Essex), Manton, Martin Hill
> (Kent), and the spirit of England breathes in me.

The material was in the bulk uninteresting.   It was im-
personal.   It was undramatic.   It limited the capac-
ities of the universe to a number of natural objects, and
to the poet who observed them.   There is little if any
recognition of the existence of other personalities.
    Mr Edward Shanks, for example, concludes with the foll-
owing very beautiful lines a poem called 'Memory':

> This is life's certain good,
> Though in the end it be not good at all
> When the dark end arises,
> And the stripped, startled spirit must let fall
> The amulets that could
> Prevail with life's but not death's sad devices.

Then, like a child from whom an older child
Forces its gathered treasures,
Its beads and shells and strings of withered flowers,
Tokens of recent pleasures,
The soul must lose in eyes weeping and wild
Those prints of vanished hours.

But 'these amulets', 'these prints of vanished hours'
that have been described in the earlier stanzas of the
poem, are every one of them remembered pictures of natural
scenes and objects, and when the reader has realised that
he is to encounter not only in Mr Shanks's other poems,
but also in the poems of Mr John Freeman and Mr Edmund
Blunden and Mr Francis Brett Young, a further and slightly
varying series of such pictures, it is not surprising that
he should complain that there is something more in life
than rivers and sunsets and branches against moons.
    'Poetry', we can imagine him to assert, not unjustly,
'is the expression of the hopes and fears and instincts of
mankind.   And how much of the stress and turmoil of the
modern world is expressed in these admittedly graceful and
melodious but equally admittedly unemotional exercises in
pastoral poetry?   Would the last volume of 'Georgian
Poetry' be of the least value to the future historian as a
guide to the mentality of post-war England?   To what a
limited extent, surely, is this poetry the mouthpiece of
its generation.   Rarely, perhaps, has the world passed
through a period of intenser action.   Rarely has a liter-
ature been more divorced from action.   One purely nature
poet in a generation would be welcome, but to have seven
such!   And to open the Georgian book at random, such
lines as these:

I will ask primrose and violet to spend for you
Their smell and hue,
And the bold, trembling anemone awhile to spare
Her flowers starry fair;
Or the flushed wild apple and yet sweeter thorn
Their sweetness to keep
Longer than any fire-bosomed flower born
Between midnight and midnight deep,
                    [John Freeman, 'I Will Ask', stanza I.]
might have been really written by any one of them.'
    Nor (and this is considerably more important) is it
common to find these pictures of natural objects raised to
significance as they are raised in Mr Shanks's 'Memory' -
an extremely lovely thing - by their juxtaposition with
some eternal process of decay and change.   Mr Freeman is,
it would seem, content simply to describe and set on

record the various sights and sounds that have brought him
pleasure; he sets them on record very sincerely and dir-
ectly and harmoniously, but he does no more.   He not only
does not use them as a medium for the expression of a
philosophy - and there is no reason why he should - but he
does not bring them into relation with any eternal process.
There is in Mr Freeman's work no discernible attitude to
life; his poetry is a delicate instrument of appreciation,
and though

> there are fifty ways to town
> And rather more to heaven,

the cumulative effect of such poetry is not exhilarating.
It is impersonal, colourless, thin blooded.
    Some critics have, with extreme injustice, blamed for
this calm-toned atmosphere of the last two volumes of
'Georgian Poetry' the taste of their editor.   E.M., they
have contended, is only interested in the placid poetry of
contemplation.   No contention could be more absurd.   It
was E.M. who twelve years ago presented to the public, in
'a challenging and manageable form', the poetry of Rupert
Brooke, of Gordon Bottomley, of D.H. Lawrence, of James
Elroy Flecker, of Lascelles Abercrombie and Wilfrid
Wilson Gibson.   And what robust, vigorous poetry is be-
ing written now, as that of Mr Prewett, E.M. has recog-
nised and published.   There can be only one explanation
for the preponderance in these last two collections of
impersonal unemotional poetry, namely, that the poetry of
personal passion and experience is being no longer pro-
duced with the rich abundance of the war and pre-war
years.

63.   'THE "NEW" POETRY, 1911-1925', EDWARD SHANKS,
'QUARTERLY REVIEW'

January 1926, 139-53

In his earlier article (No. 27), written under the con-
straints of his editor, Shanks seemed to be groping a
little uncertainly: a more distant perspective and more
space in which to develop his ideas allow him to make here
a fair contemporary judgment.   Upon one poet he seems to
have changed his mind since the time when he and Sassoon

had tried to persuade Marsh to include Edith Sitwell in
the fourth anthology.
    For a note on Shanks see Appendix, p. 414.

It is now some fifteen years since the first faint begin-
nings of what at its height was called, without much
elegance but not without a degree of accuracy, 'the boom
in poetry'.   The wave which then raised its head has run
up the shingle and seems to have retreated again, at
least for the time.   The present, therefore, seems to be
a suitable moment for inquiring whether it has gone back
into the ocean to return in full flood, or whether it was
only one of those waves which some accident of wind or
current selects for a delusive prominence out of a
falling tide.
    That the movement, whatever it was, should have been
described as a 'boom' was not altogether the fault of the
generation which produced it.   Among the legacies which
the Victorian age left to its successors there was one,
in the sphere of literature, which has been an unqual-
ified hindrance ever since.   In that period literary
creation and literary criticism began to develop a self-
consciousness which they have not yet lost and show no
signs of losing.
    In previous ages the existence of great poets, no
matter what interest or admiration they might arouse, was
never the occasion of any twittering excitement;   they
were, so to speak, the sort of thing which it was natural
to have about.   It might, indeed, be held at any given
moment that there were none;   and that was an evil, an
accident to be regretted, but not a thing to make any one
despair of the race.   It was like childlessness in a
family;   and in the same way the appearance of a poet
caused the warm but unastonished gladness which in
healthy times is caused by the birth of a child.
    The vast and sudden material prosperity of the Victor-
ian age produced a different point of view.   It seemed
necessary that among its glories there should be a poet
great enough to be worthy of it, and, for the first time,
the interested public looked for that poet with a linger-
ing anxiety lest he should not be there to be found.   He
was in fact found and, by great good fortune, he bore a
certain resemblance, freely recognised by himself, to the
chief poet of the Augustan age of Rome.   But already the
idea was abroad that great poets were a kind of creatures
that existed in earlier times, but were not to be looked
for now.   Disraeli, writing of Tennyson to Carlyle,

clearly implied that his own time should provide the
equal of - one supposes - Byron. And when Tennyson died
there ensued a feverish search for his successor which was
as injurious to both poetry and all standards of criticism
as anything could be; and the successor was not forthcom-
ing. Morris and Swinburne were still alive and had been
virtually enthroned; but neither was young and there
seemed to be no young man acceptable even as a candidate
for greatness. Mr Kipling, who alone inherited Tenny-
son's popular favour, fine poet though at his best he is,
was not quite fitted for the position. Then, after the
brief, unsuccessful burst which we generally call 'the
Movement of the 'Nineties', poetry fell for nearly twenty
years into a greater neglect and contempt than it has ever
known in all the history of English literature.

It was not that there were not good poets to uphold the
honour of the art. It could indeed be argued that there
have been periods of greater barrenness. But with each
of the poets of that time there was something that stood
in the way of public recognition, and led the critics to
champion their favourites a shade too eagerly and too
consciously. There were Francis Thompson and Herbert
Trench. But Trench, at any rate in his more easily
assimilable poems, was getting a good gleaning from
Arnold's fields, and Thompson, though there is more to be
said of him, is not unfairly described as a splendid ana-
chronism. Mr Bridges, the spiritual heir of Thomas
Campion, went on performing his chamber-music to a very
small if delighted and intelligent audience. Among the
poets of the 'nineties there were two of importance -
John Davidson and Mr Yeats. But Davidson mixed up good
and bad so inextricably that to this day no critic has
seriously attempted the task of disentangling them, and
Mr Yeats, the one poet of the 'nineties who in English
carried that world-wide inspiration to the point of
greatness, so firmly proclaimed himself to be essentially
Irish that every one believed him.

And the reading public during these years turned away
from almost everything written in verse in a manner quite
unprecedented. The public, to be sure, was changed,
though the influences which produced the change and its
characteristics are too many and too complex for analysis
here. But it was larger and lazier, and, by way of the
novel, it was more and more deliberately being led into
pastures easier for it than the concentration of verse.
It was certainly not the same public as had made the for-
tunes of Byron and Moore, had been by no means unkind to
Wordsworth, and might have been as kind to Keats, if he
had lived a few years longer, as it later was to

Tennyson.   But these considerations do not modify the
fact that, during this time, the writer who felt verse to
be his natural mode of expression, seemed to himself and
to others to have drifted into a backwater, to have en-
gaged in an occupation that had ever less and less to do
with life.   It is a relevant fact that during these
years the poet had in almost all cases to bear the cost of
publishing his work.   It is a relevant fact that in
organs of criticism the smallest space was given to con-
sideration of contemporary verse and, even so, in a pat-
ronising and pitying tone.   There existed in short an
atmosphere of slighting inattention in which poetry could
not flourish or even maintain a healthy, if humble,
existence.

The reaction which has since taken place is generally
considered to have some connexion with the war, and indeed
the 'boom' may be considered to have begun in 1915 with
the presentation of Rupert Brooke to the popular imagin-
ation as a romantic figure.   For many persons, in some
queer way, his life and death did seem to rehabilitate
poetry, to give it once again some sort of standing as a
serious, not a trivial, human activity.   He became the
type of a war-poet, and just the sort of critic who had
spent the previous August in complaining that the Great
War had produced no Great Poetry was not ready to declare
that this was the sort of Poetry he meant.   True war-
poetry, poetry springing from the war in both substance
and spirit, was to come later, and, when it came, was
very different from Brooke's sonnets, which were the ex-
pression of an ardent civilian preparing himself to be a
soldier.   There is all the difference in the world, in
temper as in material, between his 'Blow out, you bugles,
over the rich dead', and Wilfred Owen's:

   What passing-bells for these who die as cattle?
   Only the monstrous anger of the guns.
   Only the stuttering rifles' rapid rattle
   Can patter out their hasty orisons.

The first is the abstract poetry of anticipation, the
second is poetry of concrete experience.   To this point
we shall have to return later.   In the meanwhile it is
clear that during the first twelve months of the war
there came into existence a vague but none the less power-
ful emotional craving which found more satisfaction in
both the reading and the writing of verse than in any
other form of literature.   We did not in those days know
what we were at, neither what war was nor the real nature
of our reactions to it, and in that confused, distressed

time the intensity of poetry afforded a relief and a
tonic to strained spirits.   There grew and spread widely
an atmosphere in which poetry could draw upon life.
     But, like many other things which have had a similar
fate, the poetic revival began before the war and was al-
ready in existence to be fostered by war conditions.
Perhaps there is no recent period of which our minds re-
tain a less distinct recollection, as to details at any
rate, than the three years preceding August 1914.   We
certainly have almost forgotten now that in 1913 moralists
were complaining of the modern mania for dancing, of the
unhealthy frequentation of night clubs, of the freedom of
manners prevalent among the younger generation, and of the
immodesty of women's dress.   In the same way we have al-
most forgotten that critics were speaking of a revival in
poetry some years before the war, and that by this they
meant both that better poetry was being written and that
the intelligent public was taking a more living interest
in it.   And for both these contentions they could cite
adequate proofs.   There was a movement and a stirring,
people began to argue, and even to quarrel, about poetry
as though it were really of some importance, and - what is
always a significant sign - the charlatan began to lift an
alert and interested head.
     If a date is to be fixed for this change, the year
1911, I think, will do as well or better than any other.
It saw the publication of Mr Masefield's 'Everlasting
Mercy' and of Brooke's first volume, and these - not, for
the moment, to consider their merits - caused a quite
surprising amount of serious discussion.   In the next
year came the first issue of Mr Marsh's 'Georgian
Poetry', published by Mr Harold Monro at the Poetry Book-
shop - itself another sign of the times.   Mr Marsh
claimed that English poetry had recently taken on a new
power, and in this faith he compiled his anthology which
was a greater success than its promoters had expected.
     To trace any particular movement in poetry to its ulti-
mate sources in the life of the people is hard and doubt-
ful enough when history has put all before the critic and
he is far enough removed in time to see events in some
sort of pattern.   I shall not attempt to relate this
movement to the undoubted intellectual and emotional
quickenings of the years before the war otherwise than by
saying that it was clearly one of them.   There are, how-
ever, two poets of the 'interregnum', not fully recognised
before this time, who are often credited with having in-
fluenced the Georgian poets.
     And yet I doubt whether Mr Thomas Hardy or Mr A.E.
Housman exercised more than a superficial or incidental

influence in those early days.   They were, rather, prem-
ature Georgians themselves, like guns secretly established
and waiting for the course of events to unmask them.   Cer-
tainly until this time their importance was not properly
realised.   Mr Hardy was obstinately supposed to be a vet-
eran novelist, who had turned poet, as a man might take up
a retiring post, and who deserved to be indulged in this
relaxation of his later years.   Mr Housman's 'Shropshire
Lad' existed in such isolation and was surrounded by cir-
cumstances so peculiar that it was almost impossible to
look on it as a significant part of the main stream of
English poetry.   But both Mr Hardy and Mr Housman, in
their different ways, turned from the exhausted and etio-
lated Tennysonian manner and from that Swinburnian manner
which was so fatally easy for any imitator to acquire and
so impossible for any imitator to put to the smallest
living use.   Poetry goes down the hill when poets mech-
anically look at things as their predecessors have looked
at them.   The change that occurs when they rub their eyes
and look for themselves is generally slight, or appears
slight, when criticism attempts to describe it.   But it
implies a return to reality and the novelty, whatever it
may be, is priceless.   Mr Hardy and Mr Housman achieved
this return, and each contributed a new method of using
language, Mr Hardy *compelling* words to evoke such emotions
as he chose, and Mr Housman expressing lyrical feeling in
a simple, epigrammatic, almost lapidary style.

Neither, however, has at any time been considered a
revolutionary, and yet this epithet, odd as it may now
seem to recall it, was freely applied to the Georgians of
1912, who attempted the same return with less success.
The most prominent and characteristic of them were Brooke,
Mr Masefield, Mr W.W. Gibson, and Mr Lascelles Aber-
crombie.   The first two were accused of wantonly intro-
ducing ugliness into poetry, which should be used only for
the embodiment of beautiful images.   Brooke referred with
rather rhetorical gusto to the physical details of sea-
sickness and to the more unpleasant physical signs of
senile decay.   Mr Masefield made his country brooks run
over rusty pots and pans, and dealt in the violence of
prize-fights and murder committed by a navvy on his mist-
ress.   Mr Gibson avowedly turned from his early, rather
pallid decorations to the nobility of labour, the tragedy
of poverty and views from slum-windows.   Mr Abercrombie,
besides some essays in Masefieldian violence of action,
was violent in thought and language: his muse was decid-
edly muscular, and his prosody sometimes suggested the
lumpy biceps of the Strong Man at a fair.   All four
seemed to be of Synge's opinion that, before anything else

can be achieved, our poetry must learn again to be
brutal.

All four, of course, sought the return to fact more
consciously and with fewer resources than Mr Hardy and Mr
Housman.   It was a rebellion deliberately undertaken
against the exhausted conventions of the preceding twenty
years, only in a lesser degree, not a natural and instinc-
tive new opening of the eyes, and much of the rebellious
violence was a sign of struggle and restlessness rather
than of settled inclination.   It must be observed too
that the label 'Georgian', though very happily chosen,
had, to begin with, an exceedingly vague connotation.
That first selection made by Mr Marsh included several
writers who were afterwards acknowledged to be incongruous
bedfellows.   But besides these there were poets who be-
longed to their time but can hardly be forced into the
description which roughly covers the four I have already
named.   There was James Elroy Flecker, who avowed Mr
Housman as his master in style, but who, aiming at the
creation of concrete beauty, really felt stronger affini-
ties with the French Parnassians.   Mr Harold Monro made
odd excursions into a half-world of dreams merging into
nightmare that had at moments a reality of its own.   And
there was the unassuming but very cunning naïveté of Mr
W.H. Davies's small poems upon birds, bees, flowers, and
children, which afterwards had a great deal to answer for.
Also, there was Mr de la Mare, expressing, by symbols of
magic and by magically subtle rhythms, a very human atti-
tude towards life.   In all of them, in their degrees, was
the element of novelty, the new opening of the eyes.   In
these four whom I have just mentioned it was perhaps more
natural, there was less conscious rebellion, than in the
others.   But no formula, however ingenious, can impose
the unity of a school on the first Georgians who worked
from different inspirations and in many cases were not
personally known to one another.

Then came the war, and Brooke died in the French hosp-
ital-ship off Skyros, and Flecker in the sanitarium at
Davos.   These accidental happenings touched the imagin-
ation of a public which erroneously believed it to be
characteristic of good poets to die young, and encouraged
the growth of that new atmosphere of appreciation to which
I have already referred.   The emotions of war became a
forcing-house for this very tender shoot of a poetic re-
vival.   It was inevitable that sentimentalism should
rage, and the early war-poetry was of a predominantly sen-
timental character.   Speculations have often been
attempted as to the manner in which Brooke would have
developed if he had lived.   It is possible that his poems

were only the youthful efflorescence of a genius not dest-
ined for poetry at all, that he would have excelled as a
critic, perhaps as a novelist, even more probably as a
dramatist.   What is as certain as anything can be is that
if he had survived to accompany the Naval Division in its
battles on the Somme in 1916 he would not have continued
to write in the manner of the '1914' sonnets.   These,
fine as they are, are yet typical of all the work produced
by the same crisis.   A restless, dissatisfied, intro-
spective generation, believing little in the possibility
of war, and not at all that war could ever touch it
closely, was suddenly, among infinite clamours and parox-
ysms of mixed emotions, summoned to prepare itself for
battle.   It was impossible that the poets of this gener-
ation should not be over-conscious of their own position,
of their own emotions.   The attitude of patriotism or of
self-sacrifice into which the moment threw them was, for
the moment, the sole reality.   They knew that they had
chosen to fight: the concrete meaning of that choice was
as yet only to be imagined.   It was later, when some of
them had seen real warfare in the trenches, that a more
solid and more actual war-poetry began to be written.
    The change wrought by experience may be seen if we
contrast one of Brooke's sonnets with a sonnet written
later by Mr Sassoon.   Brooke, having made, like thous-
ands of others, his heroic choice, can comprehend its
meaning only in general terms.   He cries:

[Quotes 'The Soldier'.]

    It is a beautiful poem, it is sincerely passionate.
For a contrast to it I have chosen not one of Mr
Sassoon's vivid, sharply drawn scenes of trench-life but
a sonnet no less personal than this.   He fought and
suffered: he suffered as much in the persons of the
others as in his own.   He revolted against the war and
in consequence he was withdrawn from it.   Then he wrote:

    I am banished from the patient men who fight.
    They smote my heart to pity, built my pride.
    Shoulder to aching shoulder, side by side,
    They trudged away from life's broad wealds of light.
    Their wrongs were mine;   and ever in my sight
    They went arrayed in honour.   But they died, -
    Not one by one;   and mutinous I cried
    To those who sent them out into the night.

The darkness tells how vainly I have striven
To free them from the pit where they must dwell,
In outcast gloom convulsed and jagged and riven
By grappling guns.   Love drove me to rebel.
Love drives me back to grope with them through hell;
And in their tortured eyes I stand forgiven.

The difference, not merely in degree, but equally in kind,
of self-consciousness, is at once apparent.   Brooke's
subject is the impact made on his mind by the imagined
possibility of death in certain circumstances.   Mr Sass-
oon is moved by something a great deal more definite.
His emotion is more urgent and more poignant, and the ex-
perience contained in the poem is at once richer, more
complex, and more directly expressed.   Of this nature
was the true war-poetry which began to be written when
warfare had become for many a fact of daily life.   It
makes up most of the work of Wilfred Owen and Mr Sassoon,
some part of the work of Mr Robert Graves and Mr Edmund
Blunden.   Of these, Mr Blunden, who still retains a
passionately remembering interest in his experiences of
war, seems the most likely to give us a full picture of
the life of those days.   Removal in time has not weaken-
ed his creative grasp of it, but more and more enables
him to disentangle its essential spirit from passing
accidents.
   But it was not only in writing of war that the new
poets developed.   More sprang up behind the first line,
four more times did collections of 'Georgian Poetry'
appear, and presently all sorts of anthologies of con-
temporary verse were produced.   Critics and public con-
tinued to supply at least an atmosphere of serious
attention, though, not unnaturally, there were protests
against the floods of little books of verse which this
atmosphere encouraged and against the discovery by too
enthusiastic reviewers of a great new poet twice or
thrice in every publishing season.   But before long more
serious notes of dissatisfaction began to be heard, and
certain critics, some of them entitled to be listened to,
began to find grave faults in much of the work that had
been so much applauded.   On the one hand, it was not
revolutionary, it made no innovation in technique or in
diction or in subject-matter or in thought, but continued
in the ways of the poetry that had gone before it.   On
the other hand, it was told, and by such learned and
acute-minded critics as Mr Middleton Murry and Mr T.S.
Eliot, not to congratulate itself on continuing the trad-
ition of English poetry, for a poet who merely derives
from his predecessors and presents their thoughts and
images worn and at second-hand does nothing of the sort.

Now strictly technical innovation is not at this point
of time very easy to accomplish without an altogether
disabling degree of eccentricity.   The most revolution-
ary change of recent years is that suggested by the Poet
Laureate's experiments in quantitative verse - experiments
which, however, seem likely to be more useful in sharpen-
ing the ears of poets using the customary metres than in
furnishing a new instrument for English poetry.   *Vers
libre*, of course, is no new thing, and the truth about
most *vers libre* was expressed by Mr Chesterton when he
said that it was no more a revolution in poetry than
sleeping in a ditch was a revolution in architecture.
There are exceptions.   Serious attempts have been made
in England during the last fifteen years to establish a
technique of free verse, attempts largely inspired by the
example of such French poets as M. Georges Duhamel and M.
Charles Vildrac, who themselves were chiefly concerned to
make a system out of the example of Walt Whitman.   These
attempts proved, it seems, that in free verse it is poss-
ible to achieve new effects without sacrificing the dis-
cipline, the precision, and the sensuous beauty afforded
by regular metres, but that this is done only rarely and
with great difficulty and that on the whole the few succ-
esses barely justify the many failures.   Of all the
earnest experimenters who at one time called themselves
'Imagists', only one has had anything like a consistent
success, the American writer who signs her poems 'H.D.',
and whose beautiful but minute and remote talent is to be
seen in such passages as:

> In my garden
> the winds have beaten
> the ripe lilies;
> in my garden, the salt
> has wilted the first flakes
> of young narcissus,
> and the lesser hyacinth,
> and the salt has crept
> under the leaves of the white hyacinth.

The pauses made by the short lines create a subdued,
tenderly pulsing rhythm, and the form justifies itself.
But is this anything more than a surer, because a some-
what drier and quieter, accomplishment of what Arnold
attempted in 'The Strayed Reveller'?   It is to be noted
that 'H.D.' has recently showed a tendency towards the
use of rhyme and even of fixed stanza forms.   And, with
less austere spirits, free verse, by reason of its want
of discipline, generally tempts to garrulous commonplace
or to pretentious rhetoric.   Mr D.H. Lawrence writes:

And if I never see her again?
I think, if they told me so,
I could convulse the heavens with my horror
I think I could alter the frame of things in my agony.
I think I could alter the System with my heart.
I think in my convulsion the skies would break.

- which he might not have done, if he had had even only a
metrical restraint imposed upon him.   I do not mean that
there is never any difference between free verse and
chopped, violent prose or that it is impossible for free
verse to express emotion at the temperature proper to
poetry.   I mean that this happens only with exceptional
persons or on exceptional occasions, and that nothing has
occurred to suggest that free verse contains in itself any
revivifying principle.   The way of movement seems to
be in the execution of bold variations on the customary
rhythms and perhaps in the use of such unbroken fields as
the rhymeless lyric.
The critics who demand that modern poetry should
render more fully and more richly the modern conscious-
ness and the world it lives in stand on surer ground.
The most able of the critics who have made this demand,
Mr T.S. Eliot, is also the most formidable of the poets
who have attempted to comply with it.   He began under
the inspiration of Jules Laforgue, as Hamlet or as
Pierrot, laughing bitterly at life and then more bitterly
at himself for paying life so extravagantly serious a
compliment; and, like Laforgue, he managed to free him-
self very noticeably from the conventional use of poetic
ornament and image, choosing unexpected similes as, of an
evening, 'Like a patient etherised upon a table'.   This
manner is deliberately adopted and has a coldness that is
often repellent.   But it is not just to say of Mr Eliot,
as some have said, that his is a mechanically excellent
intellect which has mistakenly strayed into poetry.   He
has at times a genuinely singing note and, if he had
chosen to write in a conventional manner, might have pro-
duced work easily recognisable as beautiful.   But his
most ambitious work, 'The Waste Land', affords an almost
exclusively intellectual pleasure, and that of two kinds.
One enjoys the effort of following his thought and en-
deavouring to ascertain his meaning.   There is also a
pleasure comparable with that to be derived from a very
superior acrostic or from one of those crossword puzzles
which cannot be solved without an exhaustive knowledge of
the Latin poets.   Mr Eliot makes in his poem - I forget
how many quotations from other more or less well-known
poems and furnishes it with notes referring the reader to

various treatises on anthropology and the like for a
proper understanding of his symbolism.   The style
suggests that the author, an acute analyst of poetic
styles, has here attempted something like an operation of
synthesis.   Having resolved Marlowe, Jonson, Dryden, and
others into their elements, he has sought to reassemble
some of these elements as constituents of a style of his
own;   but synthetic products generally lack a vital some-
thing which is to be found in the works of nature.   What
is more important to observe is that this poem expresses
a typical mood of disillusionment: the modern conscious-
ness finds the world in which it lives a waste land.
Now disillusionment may be a source of poetic emotion
like another, but it is an infertile source and, in prac-
tice, the poetry which issues from it is thin and lacking
in heat.   As a matter of fact, the modern consciousness
is ill represented by modern poetry, but perhaps most
narrowly by the poetry of disillusionment.   And, it must
be remembered, this, being a source of emotion like an-
other, may bring forth only sentimentality like another.
Mr Aldous Huxley has gone perilously near this lapse.
But then Mr Huxley seems to have deserted verse for prose,
which is perhaps a natural development.

It remains only to notice the writers who have sought
to revivify poetry by the deliberate adoption of a new
set of similes and metaphors.   Miss Edith Sitwell
believes that the senses of 'the modernist poet ... have
become broadened and cosmopolitanised;   they are no
longer little islands, speaking only their own narrow
language, living their sleepy life alone.   When the
speech of one sense is insufficient to convey his entire
meaning, he uses the language of another.'   This enables
Miss Sitwell to declare that

> Each dull, blunt, wooden stalactite
> Of rain creaks, hardened by the light,

and even to justify in prose her use of these words.   It
introduces a novelty into poetic imagery: one can only
regret that what would seem to be so important a revol-
ution in human consciousness should have resulted in poems
of so little importance.   Miss Sitwell (with whom, less
strikingly, her brothers, Mr Osbert Sitwell and Mr Sach-
everell Sitwell) has done something mildly novel in pure-
ly impressionist notation, but the intellectual and emot-
ional force of the whole family does not appear to be
equal to anything more than the occasional production of
rather lively and bizarre words, which, however arrayed,
do not mean anything in particular.   These writers are

at all points on a level with the writers of magazine
lyrics, but they disguise their status by being meaning-
less instead of maudlin, and for this they should be given
as much credit as the achievement may seem to deserve.

So much for the revolutionaries or conscious modernists.
To call all the rest traditionalists would be to beg too
many questions and to impute a unity much greater than
they themselves feel and greater than in fact exists.
But there is a distinction, hard as it may be to apply in
individual cases, between the poets who have deliberately
sought modernism along the path of one theory or another
and those who have encountered it, if at all, as led by
their own natures and experience.   It is among these that
we must look for an answer to the question whether the
poetic revival has justified itself.

It has justified itself in the sense that it has added
to the canon of our poetry an amount of new work not yet
to be estimated but certainly perceptible.   It has been,
however, disappointing.   Two of the older writers are
established.   Mr Walter de la Mare, gradually augmenting
the body of his lyrics, was suddenly seen to be a writer
who, if he had attempted no organised work on a major
scale, had nevertheless ended by completely expressing a
certain conception of life and a full cycle of experience.
His glimpses into paradise and the world of dreams, his
fairies and his goblins, attain to unity as the magical
embodiment of a philosophy.   The poem which ends:

> When music sounds, all that I was I am
> Ere to this haunt of brooding dust I came;
> And from Time's woods break into distant song
> The swift-winged hours, as I hasten along,

is a beautiful thing by itself but it means as much in its
place in his whole work as does a detachable passage from
one of Shakespeare's plays.   The same thing, that he has
produced a body of work, not an assemblage of separate
pieces, may also be said of Mr W.H. Davies.   His nature
is simpler, his experience less rich and less deep;   but
all his poetry is one in expressing an innocently sensual
appreciation of the delights of the world.

The case of the younger men is different, and though
some of them early produced work of fine quality, nearly
all of them seem to have delayed in redeeming that prom-
ise.   By delaying they have incurred the just charge of
being 'anthology poets', in the sense that their best
work is detachable and makes a deeper impression when
found isolated in anthologies than when read in their own
collections.   They have refrained from larger works, and

not one of them has yet made it plain that the growing
bulk of his lyrics can be regarded as a whole.   Mr Robert
Nichols, in his second, and first noticeable, volume,
'Ardours and Endurances', had a naïve magnificence, an ex-
uberant imagination and a power of vivid language.   But
though he has made a fine attempt at a prose play, he has
flagged in the writing of verse.   Mr W.J. Turner, by com-
bining a power of so approaching common things, as to make
them seem newly strange, with a fascinating imagery of
distant and imaginary lands, suggested that he might be
evolving a universe of his own, as consistent and exciting
as Mr de la Mare's.   But of his last two books, 'Landscape
of Cytherea' (he meant 'Cythera') is wilfully obscure and
tangled and 'The Seven Days of the Sun' is a perverse,
though witty, piece of petulant eccentricity.

These are only examples of disappointments that have
occurred during the post-war years.   Mr Blunden, working
away with quiet assurance at his two subjects, the war and
the English countryside, is producing a body of poetry that
never fails in accuracy or sincerity, though his method is
a little narrow and inelastic.   His motive is perhaps the
chronicler's desire to preserve two things which are dis-
appearing from human knowledge.   Mr Robert Graves, delving
into a subsoil to which he believes psycho-analysis has
shown him the way, may have discovered a principle of
poetic being for himself.   It may be that the revival
flags because inspiration, too violently stimulated by
events since 1914, is for a little while in need of recup-
eration.   It may be that public encouragement is suffer-
ing from fatigue similarly induced.   It is possible, as
some assert, that the wireless will rejuvenate poetry by
restoring to it the direct vocal appeal which it has been
gradually losing over a period of some two thousand years.
But it is certain that at this moment English poetry is
in a depressed and languid, though by no means hopeless,
condition.

64.   'THE "GEORGIAN POETS", OR TWENTY YEARS AFTER',
WILFRID GIBSON, 'THE BOOKMAN'

September 1932, 280-2

One of only five poets to contribute to all five anthol-
ogies, Gibson conveys here with gentle irony the

consequences of bearing that 'rather meaningless, but
surely harmless label "Georgian"'.
    For a note on Gibson see Appendix, p. 403.

To begin with let me confess that, during the last ten
years or so, I have been made sufficiently aware that the
rather meaningless, but surely harmless label 'Georgian',
which had been attached to poets of my generation, has
come to be regarded as the badge of infamy by the more
vocal of our successors.   If a young critic, or one of
the not-so-young critics, who try rather pathetically to
keep up with the boys - boys who, as likely as not, will
lead them into a blind alley and leave them, blown - if
a young critic wishes to say a really nasty thing about
another writer, he accuses him of being a Georgian poet;
and in so doing not only offers him the last insult, but
commits him irretrievably to the limbo of forgotten
things.   Yet I must own, though I myself have little
liking for literary labels and the classing of poets in
categories, that I fail to see why Georgian should have
become a term of opprobium.   'Naturally', exclaims the
reader, 'being yourself a Georgian!'   And of course it
would be of little use pretending that I can take an un-
biased view of the matter;   this retrospective review of
the work of the Georgian poets by one of themselves is
bound to sound the personal note, though not necessarily,
I trust, offensively.   At all events the bias is frankly
acknowledged, and not disguised under the cloak of
anonymity.
    Well, if I am to convince myself of the correctness of
the current attitude to the Georgian poets and of the
validity of their condemnation by these impartial young
critics, I must try to discover what precisely are the
terms of the arraignment, and attempt to state the case
for the prosecution as explicitly as I can.   It would
seem then that the Georgian poets are alleged to have
been a mutual-admiration society of third-rate poets who
all wrote dull poems to a prescribed academic formula -
a sort of co-operative company for the turning out of
standardised verse.   That does sound a pretty damning
indictment, does it not?   And yet I wonder;   though I,
as a Georgian, should be annihilated by this steam-
roller condemnation, I still have strength and impudence
enough to wonder;   and, wondering, I take up the first
volume of Marsh's anthology, 'Georgian Poetry', issued
just twenty years ago, and glance through the list of
contributors, the original Georgians.

Let me give the names of these undistinguished and un-
distinguishable and mutually imitative versifiers.   Here
they are - Abercrombie, Bottomley, Brooke, Chesterton,
Davies, de la Mare, Drinkwater, Flecker, Gibson, Lawrence,
Masefield, Monro, Sturge Moore, Ross, Sargant, Stephens
and Trevelyan; and really, you know, it would seem to me
that you could hardly find a group of poets with more
diverse gifts.   The truth is that the Georgian poets were
not in any sense a school or even a homogeneous group of
writers.   So far from being a clique, the original Georg-
ian poets were for the most part solitary individual
writers, not too young even in 1912, Edwardians indeed
rather than Georgians, who had been working out their sal-
vation, or going to perdition, each in his own fashion,
for many years before Marsh's enthusiasm and his laudable
desire to secure for them a wider public recognition
brought them into a fortuitous association; their only
real bond being Marsh's appreciation.   So far from being
a group of friends, I think I may say truly that few of
them even knew each other personally until Marsh intro-
duced them; and that to Marsh himself, though a few of
the poets may have been personal friends, most of them
were acquaintances he had made through his admiration of
their work.   (Speaking personally, I may say that I was
introduced by Marsh to most of the others; and that even
now there are four of the original group that I never met;
of the later Georgians, it would be difficult to reckon up
those I am unacquainted with.)   And as for mutual admir-
ation, such a diversity of poets was bound to possess a
diversity of taste, and I fancy that few of us felt in
entire sympathy with each other's work; indeed I know
that certain members of the group frankly disliked the
work of other members; and at least one of the seventeen
detested mine, and made no bones about it either!   So
much for the clique idea of the original Georgians!   I
realise of course that a consideration of the personal
relations of the poets is irrelevant to the real issue;
that it has nothing to do with the essential and ultimate
value of the work of the poets concerned; but it is well
to clear even irrelevant misconceptions out of the way.
It might perhaps be argued with some show of reason
that the series of volumes of Georgian poetry continued
too long, and that towards the end Marsh's taste became
more conservative, or at least less adventurous; that
there is less variety of achievement in the later volumes,
in spite of the accession of new poets to the group; and
I think it must be admitted that the editor would seem to
have fallen for a while under the influence of what has
been called the Week-End School of poets or the Bird

Fanciers. And yet, taken all in all, do not the five
volumes contain quite a remarkable amount of distin-
guished work, some of which at least, even after twenty
years of disillusion, seems destined to be a durable con-
tribution to the English anthology? Though in this
matter I am an admitted partisan, I am not an exclusive
one; I suppose it is very weak-minded of me, but I can-
not help liking many different kinds of poems, and I must
confess to an admiration of the work of many of my con-
temporaries of all ages and persuasions, and even to a
delight in expressing deferentially my appreciation of
the work of the supplanters of the despised Georgians;
and yet I doubt whether the new writers of the ten years
that have passed since the issue of the latest volume of
Georgian poetry have produced a body of work in any way
comparable.

Perhaps that is a foolish remark; indeed I am sure it
is: for it is always as silly to pit one period against
another as to pit one poet against another; unique
things are scarcely comparable; so I will confine myself
to an examination of the contents of the actual volumes
of Georgian poetry, and attempt to convince myself, if no
one else, that the work of these poets fully justified
the enthusiasm of the compiler, and that, however undesir-
able it may be for a poet to bear a label, a label which
has been affixed to such distinguished and diverse poets
as Abercrombie, Brooke and de la Mare is not one to be
lightly scorned.

It would be absurd, of course, to attempt to give an
individual appraisement of every poem in the five vol-
umes; and I have no intention of contending that all of
the forty or so poets who came to be included in the an-
thology are destined to immortality; it would take a
very young critic to conceive that anyone could be fool-
ish enough to suppose they were. It will suffice, I
fancy, if I examine the earlier volumes rather carefully
and glance rapidly through the later. It is perhaps an
invidious task; I, like Marsh, have my individual taste
and personal preferences, and his and mine do not always
coincide. If I single out the work of certain poets and
seem to neglect others, I am not passing judgment, but
only saying that the work of some poets appeals to ne
more than that of others; and, unlike many critics, I am
not proud of my limitations; I do not pat myself on the
back whenever I fail to respond to the work of another
writer. Nor do I consider myself infallible; I am too
old to play the part of a pope or of a tipster; I only
say these poets appear to me to be good poets, and you
can take them or leave them as you will, not forgetting

that no poet has seemed good to all of the people all of
the time;   that even great poets have their vicissitudes
and are only poets to some of the people some of the time;
and that, after all, it is no mean thing to have been a
poet to any of the people any of the time.

Having already enumerated the names of the original
Georgians, I will not repeat them, but merely note addit-
ions to the group as I go along.   This initial volume
opens magnificently with the first part of Abercrombie's
'The Sale of Saint Thomas', a poem which has only recently
been published in its completed form and that is, to say
the least of it, one of the most signal achievements in
poetry of this century.   Next come two of Bottomley's
loveliest things, 'The End of the World' and 'Babel';
and the group of Brooke's poems that follows includes
'The Old Vicarage, Grantchester', 'Dust', 'The Fish' and
'Dining-Room Tea' - poems that have not been entirely
forgotten.

After Brooke comes Chesterton;   and I must admit that
temperamentally I am unfitted to appreciate most of
Chesterton's work;   I do not doubt his personal sincerity,
but his rhetorical, tub-thumping manner and his trick of
using theatrically opposed antithesis, so far from con-
vincing me, induces in me the Thomas mood.   But I am not
proud of my failure to respond, nor am I ungrateful for
the pleasure some of Chesterton's work has given me.

Then comes Davies with a bunch of lyrics that surely
includes some of his best - 'The Child and the Mariner',
'The Heap of Rags' and 'The Kingfisher';   then de la Mare
with 'Arabia', 'The Sleeper' and 'The Listeners' among
others;   and even the youngest of critics scarcely denies
that Davies and de la Mare have written a poem or so
between them.   Drinkwater and Flecker are hardly repres-
ented by their best work, for the sufficient reason that
it was as yet unwritten.   And now we come to a poet
about whom I have never been able to make up my mind -
Gibson;   I can only say that for a time, quite five min-
utes after they were written, 'Geraniums' and 'The Hare'
seemed to me to be perfectly good poems;   now I am not so
sure;   so perhaps we had better leave it at that, and
pass on to a writer of undoubted genius, Lawrence, whose
'Snapdragon' is scarcely a poem written to an academic
formula.

Masefield's 'Biography' too surely sounds an individu-
al note, and is certainly less uneven than most of the
work of this, the most uneven of poets, whose Pegasus is
only too apt, in mid-flight, to drop disconcertingly into
an air-pocket!   Monro in 1912 had scarcely found himself
as a poet;   but Sturge Moore was in his full maturity

when he wrote 'A Sicilian Idyll'.   As for the rest, the
two lyrics by Ross and Trevelyan do, I think, fit into
the academic formula;   and I was never much impressed by
Sargant's contribution;   but Stephens's poems alone would
give a fine flourish to the tail of any book.   Neverthe-
less, though I consider that in this first volume we have
several poets with more than a touch of genius, and that
it contains little poor or indifferent verse, it is to the
second volume I would turn, if I were put to it to uphold
the poetic adequacy of the Georgians.   Some of the orig-
inal group are not represented; Chesterton, Sturge Moore,
Sargant, Ross and Trevelyan do not appear in this or any
of the subsequent volumes;   but there are two new-comers,
Hodgson and Ledwidge.   The book opens with Bottomley's
'King Lear's Wife', which is assuredly something other
than an exercise in academic poetic drama;   this is foll-
owed by seven of Brooke's last and loveliest poems, in-
cluding 'Tiare Tahiti', 'The Great Lover', 'Heaven',
'Clouds', and the most famous, if not the best, of the
War sonnets;   then come no fewer than nine delightfully
characteristic songs by Davies, including 'Thunderstorms',
'The Moon', 'Sweet-Stay-at-Home' and 'The Bird of Para-
dise', and seven lyrics of de la Mare's which have become
by now absorbed into the poetic consciousness of all
poetry lovers.   Drinkwater is represented by three poems,
including 'The Carver in Stone', and Flecker by six,
among which are 'The Old Ships' (surely his loveliest),
'Yasmin', 'The Gates of Damascus' and 'The Dying Patriot',
Gibson is perhaps given too many pages with his 'Hoops'
and 'The Gorse', but he is luckily succeeded by Hodgson
with two of the most remarkable of all modern poems, 'The
Bull' and 'The Song of Honour'.
     Lawrence has three characteristic poems, and Ledwidge
three that have a rather uncertain loveliness of their
own.   Then come Masefield's finest poem about a ship,
'The Wanderer', three poems in which Monro is beginning to
discover his individual note, five poems by Stephens, in-
cluding 'The Snare' and 'Deirdre';   and then the volume
closes with its most outstanding contribution - Aber-
crombie's racy and exciting dramatic poem, 'The End of the
World', a little masterpiece that has not even now re-
ceived its due recognition.
     I have mentioned the contents in detail, because it
seems to me that to merely instance these poems disposes
of the assertion that the work of the Georgians is negli-
gible, for the majority of these pieces have since found
wide acceptance, without losing the love of their first
discoverers;   and I consider that in this volume alone
Georgian poetry justifies itself.   It is impossible for

me to deal with the succeeding volumes in detail.   There
were many accessions of younger poets to the group, for
the Georgians was never a closed company;   and I can do
little here but mention their names, in the order of
their appearance, without any invidious attempt to assess
their individual merits - Turner, Squire, Sassoon, Rosen-
berg, Nichols, Graves, Freeman, Baring, Asquith, Brett
Young, Moult, Pellow, Shanks, Shove, Armstrong, Blunden,
Hughes, Kerr, Prewett, Quennell and Sackville-West.

I need scarcely repeat that I make no claim of immor-
tality for all or for even a fourth of the Georgians;
nor do I pretend that Marsh gathered all the good contem-
porary poets into his fold;   his anthology was essential-
ly one man's choice;   and I for one should have liked to
have seen several other poets included;   but as these
poets might not care now to appear under the title the
editor has chosen for my article, I will not force upon
them an unwelcome and unneeded advertisement.   Though for
purposes of convenience I have only referred to poems in-
cluded in Marsh's collection, it would be a mistake to
make a final assessment of the value of Georgian poetry
from these alone;   a good poet, especially if his charac-
teristic work is narrative or dramatic, does not necess-
arily show at his best in an anthology;   but as most of
the Georgians have now issued a collected volume, their
work can be fairly judged by all, and need not be dis-
missed, unread, with a sneer.

I suppose I should conclude by saying something of the
general characteristics of the Georgians;   every period
of literature would seem to be coloured by the contempor-
ary atmosphere - such different poets for instance as
Shelley, Byron, Keats and Moore have something, if only a
pseudo-Orientalism, in common;   but a contemporary,
breathing the same atmosphere as the poets, is more like-
ly to be struck by diversities;   and it is the diversity
of the gifts of the Georgians that seems to me their most
marked characteristic.   There would appear for example
to be little in common between the lyrics of de la Mare
and Abercrombie's 'The Sale of Saint Thomas';   but a
group of poets that includes both writers can hardly be
considered limited in its range.   Not all the Georgians
were Bird Fanciers, as some would have us think.   It is
foolish to try to confine the Georgians in a category as
it would be to attempt to do the like with their success-
ors.   Ultimately every poet must stand or fall on his
own merits;   and even a Georgian poet is entitled to a
separate trial before condemnation.

65.   'ENGLISH POETRY SINCE BROOKE', L.A.G. STRONG,
'THE NINETEENTH CENTURY'

October 1934, 460-4

Only the first part of this article is given.
    L.A.G. Strong (1896-1958) published six books of verse,
many of fiction, belles lettres, and a posthumous auto-
biography, 'Green Memory' (1961).

A movement in poetry lasts as a rule anything from fif-
teen to thirty years. Of these, the first are years of
revolution, chaos, and wild experiment.   Then the wave
sweeps to a peak, and the genius or the greatest talents
of the movement do their best work.   After that, the
movement declines.   It becomes conventional and respect-
able, till it in turn is rebelled against by a new move-
ment.   That the faltering course of English poetry from
1914 to 1930 has followed no such definite lines is due
to the war.   Besides taking toll of actual poets, such
as Owen, Sorley, Mackintosh, and of heaven knows how many
potential poets, it laid its mark heavily upon those
whom it left alive.   The natural lyric impulse of youth
was damned up, or distorted into the channels of satire
or prose.   The war may have made an Owen, but we might
as well argue that it marred a Sassoon.   Brooke was al-
most the only poet to react in the traditional way, with
results that have made it difficult to estimate his real
significance.
    In spite of the title of this short survey, a few words
about Brooke will not be out of place.   The war poems and
the circumstances of his death combined to give him an
extraordinary fame with people who as a rule read no
poetry.   His name in consequence became a battle-cry, and
the young poets were led automatically to decry him as a
kind of poetic best-seller, in the tradition of Tennyson.
Yet in actual fact Brooke was a pioneer, without whom much
of the freedom enjoyed by modern poets would have been im-
possible.   He once observed acutely that the importance
of Browning to English poetry was that he made colloquial-
ism respectable.   Brooke's importance was that he carried
on, in his different idiom, the same good work.

    And I shall find some girl perhaps,
    And a better one than you,

> With eyes as wise, but kindlier,
> And lips as soft, but true,
> And I daresay she will do.

This struck a new note.   Its debt to Housman may be
guessed, but it has a shirt-sleeved, open-at-the-neck
quality which was entirely missing from the poetry of the
time.   Brooke was a ready experimenter, and many a sub-
sequent poet who condemns him is profiting by freedom
borrowed from an unsuspected creditor.

At Brooke's death there is no doubt what poetic party
was uppermost.   Since the first of Edward Marsh's anth-
ologies, the Georgians had been the fashion.   The term
Georgian is vague, and it may seem meaningless to use one
label for a group of poets so dissimilar;   Ralph Hodgson
and W.H. Davies would upset any collective apple-cart.
Yet the phrase 'Georgian poetry' does mean something, and,
when the necessary exceptions have been made, the poets
gathered under this somewhat refined banner shared certain
qualities.   Their verse had at its worst a gentlemanly
quality.   It expressed the entirely praiseworthy react-
ions of the cultured and sensitive man of letters.   It
was soothing, reassuring.   Its outbursts of indignation
were directed against precisely the right objects, and
were timed for precisely the right moment.   The verses
were neat, and expressed with many a pretty turn of
fancy.   The ordinary things of life were observed anew,
and celebrated with a somewhat finical vocabulary.
Above all, the Georgians discovered the English country-
side.   In this they probably took the lead from a gen-
uine and highly original poet, Edward Thomas.   At any
rate, they set out, an orderly band, by footpath and
spinney, and occasionally even ventured a few yards by
themselves into the thickets.   A robust little journal,
the 'Countryman', edited and published in the heart of
Oxfordshire, includes among its list of editorial re-
quirements the warning 'Townee sentimentalising about the
country barred'.   This blunt phrase could have been in-
spired by an experience of Georgian Nature poetry.
Though the Georgians numbered among them at least one gen-
uine Nature poet, a great deal of their verse is of the

> Oh to be in Mympington
> Where maids are brown as beer

order - the fancy-bred rhapsodies of gentlemen who would
be exceedingly ill at ease in Mympington or any other
rustic spot for longer than a week-end in summer, with a
car to run them safely back to asphalt and to indoor

sanitation.   Such sap as flowed in Georgian poetry was
failing by the death of Brooke; but, since dissatisfact-
ion with the Georgians provoked the Sitwells, the scept-
ical school of Eliot, and the real revolt that has just
begun, the movement kept its importance, even in decline.

The central figure of the party was probably Walter de
la Mare.   De la Mare is a scholarly and cultured poet
with an astonishing streak of imagination.   In his early
work he retreated from the harshness of contemporary life
to a simple vocabulary and an awareness, sharp as a
child's, of a dream world.   This worked well while his
imagination was content with it; but the imagination was
powerful.   It had a macabre quality, and soon de la Mare
had recourse to prose in order to satisfy it.   Its sini-
ster discoveries would have burst the bottom out of those
delicate verses, would have convulsed and agonised the
light, supple muscles of that vocabulary.   To keep his
poetry exquisite, he had, unconsciously, to exclude from
it the full force of his imagination.   The result has
been disharmony, and, latterly, silence.

This is a cursory and probably an unfair account of a
fine poet, but it suggests a certain unsoundness in the
Georgian attitude; a suggestion which finds support from
the even longer silence of another Georgian poet, Ralph
Hodgson.   Hodgson is a poet of the utmost integrity,
with a streak of real genius, but the sympathetic reader
will suspect that often he is working at cross purposes
with his muse.   The disharmony, in his case also, seems
to lie between imagination and vocabulary.   He is a
baffling poet, and should be the subject of a long study.
His first book, 'The Last Blackbird', showed originality
and excited interest, but it was the 'Poems', published
in 1920, which won him immediate fame, and still keep
their hold upon the market.   This was one of the most
striking single volumes of the century.   The poems offer
difficulties to the critic, because the weakness of one is
the strength of another.   A too arbitrary vocabulary
which spoils one poem will be the very essence of the
next, and give it its power.   Hodgson's difficulty has
been that humanitarianism and an intense love of animals
is not easy to express in poetry, and that for the later
ferocity and directness of his mind his verse technique
has proved an inadequate vehicle.   Yeats bridged the gap
between youth and age, and made a new sinewy verse to ex-
press his mind's current.   If Hodgson has made the
attempt, we have as yet no evidence of it.

The third poet of simple vocabulary, W.H. Davies, is in
a different case.   His technique, modelled on the Carol-
ine poets, remains adequate because of the innocence and

simplicity of his vision.   Now and then, in his later
work, he gets out of his depth; but as a rule he per-
suades us easily that what he records is what he has seen,
and that there has been no leakage or overflow.   Each of
these poets has a streak of genius - Hodgson's possibly
being the strongest - and no movement to which they belong
could be negligible.   There were other genuine poets
among the Georgians.   To mention one makes the omission
of the rest unfair.   Since, however, unfairness cannot
be avoided in any brief survey, mention must be made of
the sombre and self-controlled talent of Harold Monro,
whose Poetry Bookshop did so much for poetry in England,
and of the North Country poems of Wilfrid Wilson Gibson.
  The first revolt against the Georgian ascendency was
made by the three Sitwells - Edith, Osbert, and Sacheve-
ell. *Sitwellismus*, to use a term more often in the
mouths of enemies than of friends, infused into English
poetry a welcome draught of freshness and courage.   The
attacks upon it were very much like those which are made
upon birds of bright and unfamiliar plumage when they are
unfortunate enough to get loose in the countryside.
Such attacks made *Sitwellismus* into a militant creed, and
as such it had its extravagances and its absurdities;
but its courage was as undeniable as its vigour, it was
fresh and young, and it produced some lovely work.   In
so far as it has a common character (for Osbert was a
satirist), it was concerned with the refining of sensat-
ion, and the loosening up of vocabulary by an inter-
change of sense images.   Often a lyric ingenuousness
swept aside the poets' own theories, and kept them from
becoming pedantic.   It had more immediate affinities
with music than with any other branch of contemporary
art, and to both poetry and criticism it brought a happy
impertinence which was soon seen to rest on common sense.
Edith Sitwell will always have an honourable place in the
history of English criticism, if only for tirelessly
pointing out that the inability of the man in the street
to comprehend new poetry might after all give us inform-
ation about nothing but the man in the street.   From the
first Sitwellism was abhorrent to the reigning school,
and a strong feud developed between it and the 'London
Mercury', which had become the reigning school's chief
organ.   The warfare continued in a desultory manner for
several years, all the challenges coming from the one
side, while the 'Mercury' pursued its dignified path
unperturbed.
  Once the war was over, there was something of a boom
in English poetry.   Hitherto, Cambridge had been the nest
of singing birds, but now, by way of compensation, there

gathered together at Oxford a remarkable collection of
new poets.   Almost all of them had seen service in the
war, and were therefore older than the normal undergrad-
uate.   Of these, Robert Graves had without doubt the
greatest allowance of raw genius.   A highly original
writer, owing nothing to his contemporaries and immediate
forebears (the gospel of all these poets was 'A Shropshire
Lad', but they were too conscious of it directly to show
its influence), Graves particularly admired the harsh and
ingenious Skelton, whose lessons he adapted with great
skill to the time.   A series of books, each stronger and
surer than the last, put him in a commanding position.
Then he turned philosophical, lost something of the dir-
ectness of his utterance, and with it his hold upon the
public attention.   A recent volume shows, if anything,
increased power, and suggests that he is secure from con-
temporary attention or inattention.   Robert Nichols, an-
other war poet, worked upon more traditional lines, and
at first seemed likely to add a new note to the iambic
line.   His best work has an Elizabethan quality; but
latterly he has turned away from poetry.   A third,
Edmund Blunden, takes his place at once in the great pas-
toral tradition of English poetry.   He collaborated
early in an edition of Clare, whose simple and direct
outlook upon Nature his own, though more intellectual,
follows.   Blunden and another poet, V. Sackville-West,
between them rescued English Nature poetry from the
Georgians, and restored it to its place.   It had already
been strengthened by a long poem, Masefield's 'Reynard
the Fox', which proved that it was still possible for a
man of vision to see Chaucer's England.   This poem def-
initely earned Masefield the laureateship, and will just-
ify him, whatever else he may write or leave unwritten.
   These poets all write of what they know.   I have
heard farmers discussing Miss Sackville-West's long poem
'The Land', not as poetry, but as a manual of country
matters.   This in itself would be no commendation - the
works of Erasmus Darwin might in their day have been so
discussed for the information they conveyed; but, taken
in conjunction with the fact that 'The Land' was immed-
iately acclaimed by poets, it means a great deal.   No
one would have discussed Georgian Nature poetry for the
rustic information it conveyed.   Both Blunden and Miss
Sackville-West are still, happily, writing.   They are
developing, and there is no sign that either is likely to
stop.   Nor are they by any means only 'Nature poets'.

66.   'POETRY OF THE PRESENT REIGN', EDMUND BLUNDEN,
'JOHN O'LONDON'S WEEKLY'

27 April 1935, 111 and 114

This historical view, Blunden's 'Jubilee Survey' - the
'subject ..... viewed at large' - should be set beside
the more fashionable contemporary opinions cited in the
Introduction, pp. 34-41. Five only of his 'first dozen
remarkable poets' were Georgian contributors, but it
would be clear, were it not from his own poetic practice,
where his sympathies lie.
    For a note on Blunden see Appendix, pp. 397-8.

The wise are still reading, and find no difficulty in
reading, the poems of G. Chaucer, who adorned the world
of books in England five centuries and a half ago.   I
mention this by way of suggesting that in the history of
English poetry, a quarter of a century is not a very long
period;   those apparent revolutionary changes over which
we wrangle so keenly at moments are not so tremendous
when the subject is viewed at large.   We are naturally
apt to define epochs of literature, and to mark particular
dates, books, and authors as the inceptions of new styles.
But such arrangements have always an artificial, if use-
ful, character, and lead to a great deal of retrospective
debate.   Allege that Wordsworth discovered a fresh region
of feeling and wording - and instantly a host of inquirers
will report the Wordsworthian touch as extant long before
W.W. was born.
    With this proviso, we may plunge into the current of
poetry and poetics in our days.   The nearer view, indeed,
is one of seemingly abrupt contrasts.   In 1910, I
believe, the prevailing style of verse was such as might
be understood in plain meaning at first sight.   Towards
1935, the men who have been mostly mentioned as the new
generation of poets appeared eager to set their readers
strange problems of interpretation.   In 1910, and for
some time afterwards, the kind of beauty enshrined by
poets was that of 'Flora and the country green'.   Event-
ually, the endeavour was to proclaim another goddess, who
soars in pylons and whispers in loudspeakers.   Again,
the earlier voice of this period was chiefly lyrical;
the hope was to be with Shakespeare singing:

When daffodils begin to peer ...

Later on, the pace and movement of verse became those of
painful scrutiny, broken progress - one might say elegiac,
but the word has too much of strict form in it for this
manner of meditation.

In 1910 and thereabouts, the main dispute among lovers
of poetry was that brought on by Mr Masefield's novels in
verse.   They appeared in rapid succession, were regarded
as 'sensational', sold the Reviews in which they were
first printed, and forced on everyone the question of the
poet's function.   Was he justified in introducing common
details of life into his verse: 'The room stank like a
fox's gut', and so on?   We fought hard about this -
except old hands who knew their George Crabbe, or Chaucer
again, and realized that the novelty was only on the sur-
face.   Mr Masefield's theme, after all, was not that the
ugly is beautiful, but that out of the ugly man comes to
the beautiful.   His work energized poetry and the read-
ing of it, no matter what extremes of feeling it then
aroused or now fails to arouse.

Other new voices dissipated the languor which had
crept over English poetry after too much romantic spell-
binding, too much silver eloquence.   The business of
far-off themes was not yet played out.   (In those days
it was perfectly natural for the present writer to con-
coct a long blank-verse poem on Circe and her classical
habits.)   But rising spirits perceived in the things at
hand a pleasure suited to their poetry.   They were not
quite in Mr Masefield's camp, for they had no special
design on rough-house reporting; yet, like him, they
found it 'good to be out on the road'.   Among these
poets Rupert Brooke commanded much attention.   In 'The
Great Lover', written early in 1913, he catalogued a
variety of simple things, which possibly illustrate the
poetical creed of his generation as a whole.

These I have loved:
White plates and cups, clean-gleaming,
Ringed with blue lines; and feathery, faery dust;
Wet roofs beneath the lamplight; the strong crust
Of friendly bread; and many-tasting food;
Rainbows; and the blue bitter smoke of wood....

This spirit was at the time constructive and enlivening,
and the reader went his way with an increased notion of
the possibilities in normal experience.

To the advanced guard of present-day taste, how odd,
or worse, must the absence of political motive from such

verse appear!   But that was not the hour of obvious
world upheavals.   Politics even had still a sort of
country tune, and English life was not as yet seen as
subject to vast economic and sociological tides.   I
speak of the general feeling.   To-day's communist bards
would have had no political anthems to deliver had they
been contemporaries of Brooke.   Like him, they would
have entered the World War in a vague vision of a crusade;
they, too, would have felt the kindly beauty of home as a
background for a final, an individual self-sacrifice.
Perhaps one or other of them would have seen the War in
1914 as the decisive collapse of a system?   I am doubt-
ful.

The War years called into print a legion of Soldier
Poets.   They did not much vary the technique of poetry,
most of them;   and their charm lay in their refusal to be
battered down in spirit by the barrages under which one
by one their bodies fell.   They disclosed in simple
music their excellent affections.   It took time for Dis-
enchantment - so wonderfully chronicled by C.E. Montague
- to suppress this music, and to incite another express-
ion.   In 'The Traveller' Arthur Graeme West - one of the
farthest-seeing of them all - at once recorded the devel-
opment.   The Traveller set out with Pan, Art, and Walter
Pater as companions.   They 'met with maid Bellona'.
Presently Pater dropped out, then Art, at last Pan (what
with rats, shells, and Army boots), till finally there
were the Traveller and Bellona:

> And still we fare her road alone
> In foul or sunny weather:
> Bare is that road of man or god
> Which we run on together!

In 1917 the inner revolt against War found utterance
through Siegfried Sassoon's poems, in which a powerful
technical equipment served a deep intensity of emotion,
an imaginative revelation of the state of things.   The
meeting between this poet and Wilfred Owen brought about
a new conception on Owen's part of his poetical purposes.
This young officer, who had formerly enjoyed the sensuous
richness of life and the arts in the same way and degree
as Keats had once done, now saw that he had it in him to
make his poetry a terrible witness against that War, and
all War.   He composed his book, which he did not live to
publish.   The strength of his thought, the depth of his
allusions, the universality of his mind's view, would
have made him a permanent poet even without his dis-
coveries in versification, which have instructed later
poets.

Here a word is due to the term 'The Georgians' as it
concerns poetry.   A perpetual flow of nonsense has
poured past it.   Long ago John Dryden edited a Miscell-
any of contemporary poems, and nobody complained.   During
the War period, Mr Edward Marsh kept before us a sense of
things that matter in the end by editing *his* Miscellany,
'Georgian Poetry'.   He did not treat it, as his detract-
ors would have us believe, as a coterie job.   D.H. Law-
ence was among his authors.   Mr Marsh included what he
felt to be fine poems.   There are not many persons
living who have done for literature a fraction of what is
associated with the initials E.M.

With the return of Peace, some peaceful poetry was
written.   Those who had never expected to see an English
hamlet again found their hearts touched by the sight.
But discord swelled.   The nervous debt of broken civil-
ization had to be paid.   It had to be reckoned;   and
some poets, the author of 'The Waste Land' especially,
produced the statement of account.   A style appropriate
to this neurosis was not denied.   It was manifest that
the actual War was less in the minds of the melancholy
intellectuals than the chaos which they apprehended in
the relations of man and man (and which might be crudely
illustrated by the strikes and the currency crisis of the
time).   After all, even Brooke, in August 1914,
glanced for an instant at this drab wilderness, departing
to the outposts

> Glad from a world grown old and cold and weary,
> Leaving sick hearts that honour could not move,
> And half-men, and their dirty songs and dreary,
> And all the little emptiness of love!

For almost a decade, the studied apathy and the ingenuity
of poets waiting, not very vigilantly, for daylight obt-
ained the regard of criticism.   In that dusk, any vouch-
safing of a taper's light was noted as a master-stroke.
Those who (like Mr Sassoon) broke into vigorous satire
were counted outside the rules, Blatant Beasts;   and
scored O and 1.

Such a pallid mist, with the perplexing cries and
stammerings heard through it and lost again, could not
last;   and about 1930 a younger set of poets arose whose
affair it was, and is, to say Yes or No.   They were har-
assed by the new tradition of obscurity in operation - a
strange case, when we reflect that their colour of comm-
unism would imply a language 'understanded of the people'.
But, as the unreformed republic of letters is constituted,
one only approaches 'the people' under the approval of

the literary authorities of the moment.   Apart from this,
the latest 'neo-Georgians' display a keenness in criticism
of life, and a curiosity in forms and terms, which must
mark a recapture of the real task, or pleasure, of poetry
- a making of new worlds.

It is permissible to prophesy that these writers (only
grouped here for the needs of a short statement) will out-
grow their subjection to the unfamiliar, which in proper
proportion is always a valuable influence.   They have
been beguiled (for instance) by *their* discovery of G.M.
Hopkins - a recluse with equal gift and passion for unus-
ual verbal patterns and metrical inversions - into a
quaint patchwork of style.   Their best pieces are as
confident, taut, and direct as engineering.

Who reads poetry now?   (More awkward still) who buys
it?   I am not inclined to dwell on these questions;   they
are never settled for long.   But let me name some of
those, not named above, who have written poetry during the
reign of H.M. King George V;   I will not say, the First
Hundred Thousand, but the first dozen remarkable poets
whose names must occur to us.   Thomas Hardy, Robert
Bridges, A.E. Housman, W.B. Yeats, W.H. Davies, Walter de
la Mare, Ralph Hodgson, Charlotte Mew, Edward Thomas,
Edith Sitwell, V. Sackville-West, W.J. Turner - these
alone offer a wide proof that the twenty-five years have
not been unlaurelled.   Granted that English poetry in
the past has been immensely fertile, and that every sim-
ilar period has had its harvest of momentous and fascin-
ating work, still, amid what we suppose to be modern dis-
tractions, the Muse finds her own.   The future will,
moreover, quite upset such surveys as the present brief-
est abstract, when that which was not known or guessed at
the moment of writing comes to light and is recognized -
as has happened mainly with earlier poets like Blake, and
as is happening with G.M. Hopkins, adopted Georgian!

67.   'E.M. OF THE ANTHOLOGIES', GEOFFREY GRIGSON,
'NEW VERSE'

May 1939, 52

Geoffrey Grigson attacks 'this harmless and curious fly'.
In his 'Recollections of "New Verse"', Geoffrey
Grigson (b. 1905) wrote: 'The tone of "New Verse",

strictly the tone, I regret' ('The Times Literary Supple-
ment', 25 April 1968, 410).   If one may judge from the
latest collection of his literary essays, 'The Contrary
View' (1974), the tone has changed little.   In 'A Con-
versation' with the editor of 'The Review' reprinted in
that book (pp. 230-41), he talks revealingly about 'New
Verse' and its support of Auden, and quotes William
Empson against himself: 'Oh well, the trouble about Grig-
son is that he never attacks on principle;   he attacks
because he attacks.'   He has written books on painters,
travel, and natural history.   The first of his books of
poems, 'Several Observations' (1939), was advertised on
the page facing this notice in this, the last issue of
'New Verse';   his 'Collected Poems, 1924-1962' were
published in 1963.

Only the impatient and the intolerant will be unmoved by
reading 'A Number of People' ..... which is the autobio-
graphy of Sir Edward Marsh.   Sir Edward began conven-
iently.   His father became Master of Downing.   At Cam-
bridge he knew Bertrand Russell and others.   After Cam-
bridge, friendship with Rupert Brooke started him off as
an appreciator of modern poets.   No. 1 of 'Georgian
Poetry', which he edited, sold fifteen thousand, No. 2
nineteen thousand, No. 3 sixteen thousand, No. 4 fifteen
thousand, and No. 5 eight thousand copies.   Though
equipped with a heart (he read Flecker's 'Hassan', on the
way to the Admiralty, in a flood of tears), signs that
Sir Edward was equipped with an intellect, a set of val-
ues, and power to observe truth, ideas and objects are
not provided.   The littleness of his remarks is over-
whelming, and touching.   Hurt about the declining rep-
utation of his poets, for example, he perks up again:
Why?   Because the Georgians are praised now in books by
Frank Swinnerton, Herbert Palmer, and Rupert Croft-Cooke!
It is too much, too ridiculous.
   But one must not persecute this harmless and curious
fly.   He published poems, and knew nothing of poetry, he
collected pictures and knew nothing of painting, and now
that he grows old and has retired from the service of Min-
isters of the Crown, he is more and more excited by read-
ing the mild verses of Mr Christopher Hassall.   There is
no point in this book, which is one of extreme interest
for the study of English society, where Sir Edward Marsh
makes contact with literature or the life out of which it
comes.   Every paragraph is impregnated with the gas of
English mediocrity, which, like coal-gas in the oven,

frequently paralyses, when it does not kill, the man who swallows it;   and it is moving, thoroughly moving, to find an English and a social pretence of life so typically substituted for life.   'A Number of People' is also heartening: we, who have an Auden for a Brooke, can never go back in thirty years' time to find in ourselves such an extravagant fund of twitter and trivialities.

68.   'POETRY BETWEEN THE WARS', UNSIGNED ARTICLE, 'THE TIMES LITERARY SUPPLEMENT'

16 March 1946

Only the first third of this front article is given.   It is a balanced, objective 1940's view of the Georgians.

In the *débâcle* of 1914-18 the naked and evil genius of humanity had been laid bare;   the surprise at the possibility of such an indignity made the bitterness all the more poignant;   and at the end of the period a ruined and disillusioned world was prepared to discard many of the accepted traditions and idealisms.   During the war and in the years immediately after, the sensitive, bitter but unhating voices of the war-poets were heard;   theirs was the first poetical reaction and it came as a frank exposure of pain, tragedy and waste.   These writers had a moral dignity produced by suffering and its hard experience: Suffering brings knowledge'·   At that point there could have been an easy return to a philosophy of despair and nihilism.   In a review of 'Georgian Poetry, 1911-1912', D.H. Lawrence had welcomed the new freedom from the 'Nihilists, the intellectual, hopeless people', and included in this 'dream of demolition' Ibsen, Flaubert, Hardy, and Nietzsche.   But in poets from the war, such as Edmund Blunden, Robert Graves, Osbert Sitwell, Robert Nichols, Wilfred Owen, and Siegfried Sassoon the spirit of poetry gleamed in another faith;   these men realized that the destructive quality of their own injured sensibilities had to be used for some more hopeful purpose.   Even in their more ironic moments there is the glimpse of some greater hope:

> We laughed, knowing that better men would come,
> And greater wars;   when each proud fighter brags
> He wars on Death - for Life;   not men - for flags.

After the great disillusionment which might have been
claimed as a justification of 'Nihilism', Thomas Hardy
published his 'Late Lyrics and Earlier'.   In an 'Apology'
prefacing the work he pleaded on behalf of suffering
human kind that 'Pain ..... shall be kept down to a mini-
mum', and in an able defence and explanation of his per-
sonal 'pessimism', he quoted from his earlier 'In Tene-
bris',

> If way to the Better there be, it exacts a full look
>   at the Worst.

If Shelley's words still rang true that 'A poem is the
very image of life expressed in its eternal truth', this
was the moment when a careful examination of the 'eternal
truth' and its possible relation to 'the Worst' would be
demanded of the poet.   Some had newly looked upon

> The hell where youth and laughter go,

and among their generation there was to be a strong sense
not of pessimism but of thoughtful wondering and grey
speculation.
   A dull melancholy, however, persisted, as in the 'Last
Poems' of A.E. Housman;   the concise wit of 'The Shrop-
shire Lad', was still there, but it was a shivery humour.
The reality beneath it was a clear classical despair,
since man's place was far beneath that of the gods -

> These are the tears of morning,
> That weeps but not for thee.

Yet this dread of man's impotence and insignificance did
not touch the essence of any hopeful truth, and its sad-
ness was too plain in post-war life.   Robert Bridges,
increasing the power of his quiet classicism, wrote in
more comforting tones

> Keep thou bravely for him // thought of thy morrow,
> and thy beauty for grace // of thy life's sorrow.

And the Laureate crowned his intellectual strength and
humour with the 'Testament of Beauty' which was received
in 1929 as a constructive poetical philosophy by an un-
certain and bewildered audience.

Before the first world war poets were feeling for some
solid source of inspiration; there had been a general
reaction against the Victorians, and the major figures,
such as Housman, Hardy, or Kipling, were for various rea-
sons not leaders, but themselves isolated peaks of prom-
inence.   The power of William Watson had dwindled, that
of John Masefield was not yet at its height.   It was
Robert Bridges who chiefly provided the immediate in-
fluence among the generation of poets known as 'The
Georgians'.   Their verse had been published before the
war, and anthologized by 'E.M.' with great success; after
the interruption 'E.M.'s' Georgians included many of the
most significant poets of the interim.   They continued in
various and modified forms to show the strength of mind
and the development that can mark 'the unacknowledged leg-
islator'.   The poet's power is to rule, not immediately,
by open superficial propaganda, political, social or rel-
igious, but more gradually; for it is the mind of man
which he has to reach, and which his own experience and
the emotional reactions give his words the ability to pen-
etrate.   Among 'E.M.'s' Georgians there was no self-
conscious ambition; volumes record a number of individual
poets seeking a personal and fresher sense of reality.
They were largely the inheritors of the English tradition
that has been handed down through Cowper, Thomson, Gray,
Crabbe, and Bridges.

More directly the Georgians have their roots in the
Wordsworth tradition, but the new romanticism is on a
broader basis; they are well aware of man and his
doubts, spiritual and intellectual, with an awareness
sharpened by the war.   The Nature they appeal to is
stronger and more realistic than Wordsworth dared to
suggest, partly because the years between have threatened
so much that Nature has become a more significant and
permanent valuation of man's existence.   They were
anxious from the first to relate their comprehension of
Nature with an intellectual, but sensitive, way of life
that could deal with experience in simple thought and
utterance.   There was often a quaint simplicity that
suggested not 'escapism' but a sense of values that was
intrinsically sound; W.H. Davies, for example, with his
genuine appreciation of the countryside, reached a gentle
sincerity -

    With this small house, this garden large,
    This little gold, this lovely mate,
    With health in body, peace at heart -
    Show me a man more great.

Others developed a more imaginative and ranging view of
Nature and its significance - well displayed in Miss
Sackville-West's picture of a passing countryside, 'The
Land' - or a more intellectual and classical inspiration,
which recalls the names of Lascelles Abercrombie and
Laurence Binyon.

Associated with this group was one who has been counted
the most skilful Nature poet of the era.   After the emot-
ional upheaval of the war Edmund Blunden returned to his
patrimony, the English countryside - it is part of the
abiding virtue of these poets that they were so deeply
attached to the country - and saw its significance, social
and intellectual, with a greater clarity and maturity, so
that the famous 'The Waggoner' and 'Shepherd' recall the
timelessness of the tradition.

Looking back twenty-five years, we cannot but be struck
by the urgent interest then shown in contemporary verse;
and young poets could receive patient encouragement from
many sources.   Sir Edward Marsh's 'Georgian Poetry' came
to an end amid regrets in 1922.   But the years were
friendly to the art of verse.   For a time much depended
on Harold Monro, an exquisite lyricist and the first pub-
lisher of Robert Graves;   many new names found their way
to print in his 'Chapbook'.   Mr Thomas Moult's annual
selections of the year's published poems, which continue,
were beginners.   Under the editorship of Sir John Squire,
and later Mr R.A. Scott-James, the 'London Mercury' al-
lotted a large proportion of its space to new verse.   In
later years 'Penguin New Writing' expected to include
some verse.

69.   'THE GEORGIAN POETS', ALAN PRYCE-JONES,
'PENGUIN NEW WRITING', 35

1948, 91-100

Alan Pryce-Jones (b. 1908) sees it necessary to write
more defensively of the Georgians, but his concluding sen-
tences deserve to be weighed.   His anthology of 'Georgian
Poets' (1959) gives practical illustration of the 'pleas-
ure' and 'delight'.

Alan Pryce-Jones first met Marsh in 1929.   He was
present at his eightieth birthday party, and writes about
it in 'Eddie Marsh: Sketches for a Composite Literary

Portrait, ...', 1953, 44-5. He was assistant editor of
'The Times Literary Supplement' (1948-59). His books
include 'Beethoven' (1933), '27 Poems' (1935), and
'Nelson, an Opera' (1954).

Every few years the universe sloughs off a skin. Famil-
iar objects become strange, old purposes irrelevant, ex-
traordinary beauties timeworn overnight; and all because
somebody paints a picture or somebody else writes a poem.
So, although only fifteen years divide Day Lewis's 'A
Hope for Poetry' from Harold Monro's 'Some Contemporary
Poets', a difficult effort of adjustment has to be made
before a younger generation can even understand what
Monro is trying to tell it; for in the years between
1920 and 1935 an old skin was cast, and with it went the
whole conception of life implicit in Georgian poetry.
  But what exactly *is* Georgian poetry? Its component
parts are scattered about the five-volume anthology edit-
ed by Sir Edward Marsh between 1911 and 1922: an anthol-
ogy which, to a great number of people who read it when
they were young, stood out from others by marking a stage
of advance in their own sensibility. There must be
many, like myself, now about the turn of middle age, who
chose these little books as a school prize - a welcome
change from Napier's 'Peninsular War' and Creasy's 'Dec-
isive Battles' - or accepted them as a Christmas present
from a 'clever' cousin; many whose perspective of modern
poetry still wears a faint dye from the colours, then so
brilliant, of Sir Edward Marsh's careful choice. The
names in the index behaved like dragon's teeth; they
sprang up, similar but vigorous, in a field which had
been deserted since the death of Tennyson. It was only
later that we wondered why they, and no one else, had
been elected; and then, on re-reading the prefaces, Sir
Edward was not very helpful. In the first volume, he
does not go beyond 'the belief that English poetry is now
once again putting on a new strength and beauty'; he
hopes to make his readers perceive 'that we are at the
beginning of another "Georgian period" which may take
rank in due time with the several great poetic ages of
the past'. Yet a dedication to Bridges gives the fly-
leaf a consoling air. There will be nothing explosive
in the new age, it insinuates; the revolutionaries may
be Decembrists, they will not be Reds.
  Finally, it is Monro who offers the material for a
definition. He tells how the anthology was originally
suggested by Rupert Brooke, some time before the opening

of the Poetry Bookshop in Devonshire Street and he goes on
to observe that by the fourth volume (by 1919, that is)

> a tendency towards a *Georgian* manner is noticeable.
> Some of the writers are imitating each other in choice
> of subject, or treatment, or style.   This volume, un-
> like the first, could not be taken for a haphazard
> selection from the poetry of the period.   It is too
> like the compilation of a *Group*.

The Group was formed by a process of poetic silage.
Green crops of imagery, autobiographical detail, and good
humour were made to ferment under applications of bitter-
ness imposed by the sudden collapse of a safe and friend-
ly Europe.   The basic temper of the Georgians is that of
Rupert Brooke's 'Dining-Room Tea':

> I sang at heart, and talked, and ate

- a temper which was determinedly prepared to refer its
darkest moments, even, to the Comic Muse;   but upon that
temper the war imposed an inconvenience so total that it
gained a fresh dimension.   For it was the inconvenience,
not the tragedy, of war which at first inspired the mock-
ing anger of Robert Graves, Siegfried Sassoon and, in his
own way, D.H. Lawrence.   And out of the five volumes of
poetry which appear, superficially, as anonymous strips
of matter cut from a central block, it is the angry poets
who first clamour for personal attention.
    Let us say, then, that Georgian poetry came into ex-
istence only gradually, and burst surprisingly into flame
under the burning glass of a world at war.   Or we could
call it the little quivering stump of sensibility left by
the first great amputation in our time of leisure and
prosperous calm.   That, no doubt, is one of the reasons
why the Georgians fell into such disrepute during the
Thirties.   For the war left these poets dazed, and
often, like all people struck by an unexpected calamity,
frozen into absurd attitudes;   it killed their friends,
it shocked and frightened them very much;   it cut at the
roots of their self-esteem;   it could be met with no in-
herited weapons of accepted efficacity, but only with the
postures of defence.   Faced with lightning attacks from
a world which had hitherto seemed ever kindlier and more
secure, the poets of 1919 were novices in a Ju-Jitsu
school;   knowing neither falls nor counters they fell
down and hurt themselves with a regularity which can only
too easily excite an uncharitable laugh.
    When it comes to segregating the Georgian poets from

their contemporaries, Sir Edward Marsh is more explicit.
From his second volume he excluded Chesterton and Sturge
Moore, among others, 'because they belong in fact to an
earlier poetic generation'.   At the time, no doubt, the
same objection was applied to Yeats [of whom Monro wrote
that by 1910 he 'had already published most of his best
work'].   Ezra Pound and the Imagists (apart from Law-
rence), the Sitwells, Herbert Read, the Eliot of 'Pru-
frock' and Aldous Huxley are disqualified among the young;
Binyon and Belloc among their elders.   On grounds of age,
supposedly, Hardy is also omitted, although his 'Moments
of Vision', which appeared in 1917 – the central year of
the Georgian Poetry series – tackles and defeats most of
Sir Edward Marsh's candidates on their own ground.   So
that we are left with a group which excludes equally the
direct inheritance of tradition and the experimental min-
orities most aware of a need to renew the substance of
English poetry.   What is left may not seem to amount to
much;   it contains, however, in addition to work by poets
such as Walter de la Mare and Edmund Blunden, who trans-
cend the limits of group-writing (and therefore fit only
incidentally into our scheme of Georgian poetry), some
poetry of a kind which is at present particularly in need
of rescue from oblivion: what may be called low-tension
poetry.
    This is a kind of verse which fulfils a particular
English need.   It may be compared to the English water-
colour tradition which, in the manner of Anthony Devis,
turns every landscape into a neat oblong, the colour of
wood-smoke, upon which the trees and banks spill an ord-
erly emotion of an easily-recognizable kind.   Possibly
some peasants look awestruck at a small waterfall or a
handful of gentlewomen point out to one another the
chapel on a rounded hillock.   The object of such verse
is to make a single and lucid statement, or to proceed
syllogistically to a single conclusion, and it may be
considered as the precise opposite of that poetry which
aims at a magical diffusion of power through juxta-
positions of symbolism and imagery.
    To perceive what Georgian poetry is *not*, one need only
look at the poems of Valéry being written at approximate-
ly the same time: poems which, if reduced to a syllogism,
as, for example, M Julien Benda willingly reduces them,
become comic.

        J'ai vu bondir dans l'air amer
        Les figures les plus profondes. (1)

That is Valéry's profession.   But M Benda doubts it very

much.   'Si vous voulez dire qu'il pleut et êtes vraiment
un écrivain, ne le dites pas avec clarté.   Mieux: ne
veuillez pas dire de ces choses simples qui commandent la
clarté'. (2)   This ironical gloss put upon an aphorism
of Valéry might have seemed an excellent joke to W.H.
Davies or Wilfred Gibson, to J.C. Squire or Flecker.   A
proper marriage between *la clarté* and *les choses simples*
represented to the Georgians the indisputable object of
poetry, an object to which technical skills were applied
in the hope of making it palatable; whereas to writers
of the opposite school poetry was (and is) a matter, like
ectoplasm, which must be procured at a high spiritual
tension and under conditions only obtainable after
rigorous training.

In questions of this kind exclusive opinions are seldom
either right or wrong.   And even if it be objected that
the Georgians have very few *choses simples* to display
which are not better expressed by Bridges or Hardy, they
are all the same worth an affectionate glance in search
of pleasures forgotten.

Of these the most surprising lie in the work of John
Freeman, an uneven poet rightly praised by Harold Monro
for his serenity and gravity, but then omitted (except
for a single poem) from Monro's excellent collection,
'Twentieth Century Poetry,' and subsequently quite over-
looked since his death in 1929.

Freeman is an odd figure.   He lived by day the life
of a successful business man and returned in the evening
to write poetry in a singularly un-beautiful suburb.
Memory recalls a shy, angular figure, spectacled, slow-
speaking, remote from fashion or pretension of any kind;
and the fate of the self-effacing has been his.   Yet
even a short acquaintance with the volume of Collected
Poems published in 1928, or with the posthumous volume
edited by Sir John Squire, makes the neglect into which
he has fallen seem inexplicable.   It might have been
expected that 'The Pigeons' alone - one of the most
accomplished and moving poems written in his time - would
have survived through the agency of the Apollo Society
or the Third Programme, or that memory would have been
revived by such poems, successful enough a generation ago,
as 'The New House', or the best of his sonnets:

> I am that creature and creator who
> Loosens and reins the waters of the sea,
> Forming the rocky marge anon anew.
> I stir the cold breasts of antiquity,
> And in the soft stone of the pyramid
> Move wormlike, and I flutter all those sands
> Whereunder lost and soundless time is hid.
> I shape the hills and valleys with these hands,

And darken forests on their naked sides,
And call the rivers from the vexing springs,
And lead the blind winds into deserts strange.
And in firm human bones the ill that hides
Is mine, the fear that cries, the hope that sings.
I am that creature and creator, Change.

Choses simples, if you like. Freeman has no hieratic
airs; worse, perhaps, in the eyes of later critics, he
has no pretension to wit. His muse is solemn, anxious,
tuneable, and massive - qualities not much appreciated in
conjunction. But out of his own faults, which are the
faults of all low-tension poetry - a tendency to cata-
logues, reliance on poetic formulae, a rather uneasy com-
bination of cosiness and melancholy - he knew how to pick
the necessary moments which justify a slow and friendly
reading. Nor should his prose, and in particular his
excellent life of Herman Melville, be forgotten.
    If we take the other poets of the fourth volume of
'Georgian Poetry' as representative, their first impact
is a painfully gentle one. The twin ghosts which hover
over this landscape are those of Keats and Miss Muffet.
One looks into page after page with an astonishment like
that engendered by a 'Studio Year-Book of Decorative Art'
of the same period: there is very little difference
between the inspiration which prompted Lascelles Aber-
crombie or John Drinkwater to verse and that which turned
to embroidered and appliqué panels, stained glass depict-
ing a bob-haired chorister walking towards his rickety,
but celestial, city, or 'Dryad' furniture in painted
wicker.

    The scene is a bedchamber in a one-storied house.
    The walls consist of a few courses of huge irregular
    boulders roughly squared and fitted together; a
    thatched roof rises steeply from the back wall. In
    the centre of the back wall is a doorway opening on a
    garden and covered by two leather curtains; the
    chamber is partially hung with similar hangings
    stitched with bright wools .....:

these opening rubrics from Gordon Bottomley's verse play,
'King Lear's Wife' ('Georgian Poetry', Volume Two) set the
note. It is a note of earnest communication, sometimes
arch, sometimes correctly splendid, but hardly urgent.
And yet under the Georgian crust is a constant lyric move-
ment, so relaxed that it offends most of the concepts of
poetry which have since become commonplace, but, unlike
much of the secondary verse of the Thirties, nosing firmly
towards a conclusive point, nevertheless.

From 1930 until very lately, the poet and the intellect-
ual - to the public eye - offered an overlapping, a stereo-
scopic, view.   The two ideas of poetry and intellect were
interfused, so that poet and seer became almost synonymous
terms and the function of poetry turned decisively to
present and to interpret a personal vision.   By a natural
paradox, anti-intellectual, or Surrealist, poets intellect-
ualized their art more energetically than anybody;   in
short, the making of poetry, by implication, has for some
time been almost tantamount to the construction of an ego-
centric universe, unless the publication of Day Lewis's
'Word Over All' was indeed, as seems possible, the port-
ent of a recall to order.

The Georgians held the opposite position.   Like the
poets of Dodsley's (or any other eighteenth-century)
Collection, they adopted a common attitude which aimed at
percipience, not at intellectuality.   They tried to make
universally valid statements, not to cast runes;   and
since universal validity was their aim they had no part-
icular fear of the obvious, so long as it could be salted
by fresh metaphor or given the gravity, at least, of mus-
ical speech.   Thus the mind, having no effort of focus
imposed upon it, tends to slip away from their statements;
it has been taught to expect something more strenuous of
modern poetry, to have at hand all the textbooks of the
moment, and to keep concentration alert by a regular
series of syntactical battles.

Those poets, however, whose observation is really fine,
whose language belongs to them alone, and who avoid that
peculiar chirrup which is the weakness of the conventional
Georgian (comparable to the Arthur Marshall note of ex-
hortation which shrills down the 1930s) are certainly neg-
lected.   They have been left in the trough of the great
nineteenth-century wave - since it is to the nineteenth
century that most of them belong - and left, what is more,
with the exception of Brooke and Flecker, unexamined.
Except inside the quiet world of an occasional reader in
sixth-form or provincial outpost who tries to clutch at
something up-to-date and gets it wrong, very little crit-
ical attention is given to-day to poets such as Ralph
Hodgson, Squire or W.H. Davies.   Perhaps the fact that
the surface of their verse shows no sign of strain makes
it suspect;   their regular stanzas get swallowed down
like cachets carrying their content smoothly with them
and never touching the palate.   Were the Georgians then
simply writing because they liked writing?   Or must the
absence of footnotes quoting apposite statistics from Dr
Otto Neurath, scraps of case-book and comment, twigs from
'The Golden Bough', suggest a frivolous attitude to art?

For whatever reason, they are half-forgotten.   Half-
forgotten also, perhaps, because so many of them seem to
have been driven out of business shortly after the last
of Sir Edward Marsh's volumes appeared.   Robert Nichols,
Robert Graves, Richard Hughes, Peter Quennell, Edward
Shanks, Squire, Hodgson, Francis Brett Young, Martin Arm-
strong: a haphazard list, but rivetted together by a
reluctance of the poetic faculty, or at any rate by the
decision to publish poetry chiefly as a side-line to
successes in other kinds of work.
   Why? one asks.   Why should a whole school of poets
abandon their art together?   Were they defeated by econ-
omics, silenced by powerful rivals, snubbed by the public,
discouraged by a post-war England?   Was it of choice or
necessity that they turned themselves into novelists,
journalists, editors, publishers?   Is there, in every
drawer, a volume of Last Poems tucked away waiting?   Such
questions cannot be answered.   Undoubtedly the Georgians
paid a heavy and immediate penalty for their general dis-
like of political and social stresses, their reluctance to
abandon a world in which the birth of their Group coincid-
ed with the wonderful, crystalline, unendangered summer of
1911.   But after a fresh lapse of time it is easy to set
them again in perspective: to see how much pleasure is in
them, and how much promise of the future we know;   above
all in quick exchanges between lyric impulse and deliber-
ate greyness, as in Squire's 'Meditation in Lamplight':

       O fearful, fearful Shadow,
     Kill me, let me die to escape the terror of thee!
     A tap.   Come in!   Oh, no, I am perfectly well,
     Only a little tired. ...

and, perhaps, in poems of place such as the poet's
'Winter Nightfall':

     The old yellow stucco
     Of the time of the Regent
     Is flaking and peeling:
     The rows of square windows
     In the straight yellow building
     Are empty and still;
     And the dusty dark evergreens
     Guarding the wicket
     Are draped with wet cobwebs,
     And above this poor wilderness
     Toneless and sombre
     Is the flat of the hill;

or the early poem of Blunden's which begins

    By Quincey's moat the squandering village ends.

    It is not by chance that Sir Edward Marsh is also a
collector of pictures;   for the best of Georgian poetry
is all pictorial.   When the poets come forward in person
- in love, in mourning, breathing aspiration or despair -
they generally strike a theatrical attitude out of key
with their setting.   It is then that they slip into their
notorious use of the fag-ends of a romantic vocabulary.
Frank Prewett issues a typical order:

    Come girl, and embrace
    And ask no more I wed thee;

and our reaction is sharp.   We know at once that nobody,
in life or poetry, ever spoke like that.   And even when
the great emotion of the time - the war - is on the
table, it is not the heroic or the angry poets who leave
a scar on the memory, but those whose exact statements
are driven home by the force of compassionate insight
(Wilfred Owen, incidentally, is not represented in these
volumes).
    In a wartime number of 'New Writing and Daylight',
Henry Reed summed up one aspect of the disintegration of
modern poetry in the statement that 'our critical stand-
ards have come to be based on memories, not of the "best
that has been thought and said", but merely of the lat-
est.   With our example before them, we may confidently
expect that in 1953 young writers will be reading only
each other'.   It would not lighten this dire prospect to
suggest that they should turn back to a tradition which
so evidently has done its work and died.   All the same,
the Georgians represent the last solid body of English
poetry written for pleasure, and without didactic pur-
pose.   They tried to offer not greatness but delight.
And sometimes they succeeded.

Notes

1   I have seen images from the very depths leaping in
    the bitter wind.
2   If you want to say that it is raining, and you are a
    true writer, do not say it obviously.   Better still,
    do not even think of saying simple things which need
    to be said obviously.

70.   'GEORGIAN POETRY: A RETROSPECT', B. RAJAN,
'THE CRITIC'

Autumn 1948, 7-14

This issue of 'The Critic' was dated autumn 1947 but pub-
lished in autumn 1948 (delays in printing: see editorial
note, p. 6).

Less sympathetic to the Georgian cause than the two
previous pieces, Balachandra Rajan's selective but well
reasoned article, with its obviously Leavisite leanings,
compares the 'uneven' John Freeman (see No. 69) unfavour-
ably with the non-Georgian Edward Thomas whom Leavis
championed.   His conclusion makes interesting comparison
with Alan Pryce-Jones's (No. 69).

Dr Rajan has written books on Milton (1947, 1970) and
Yeats (1965), and edited books on Eliot and American
poetry.

The poetry of the Georgians can hardly be called modern
though several echoes of it can certainly be heard in
poems which are otherwise fanatically modern.   Moreover
there is no reason for assuming that the movement thought
itself modern even in 1912 when the first of their five
anthologies was published.   The Georgians were not rad-
icals, and probably not even reformers, and unlike most
groups concerned with the future of literature, they
shared no conclusions about its immediate past.   So
their introductory preamble, fervent though it may be, is
limited to large hopes and indefinite convictions:

This volume is issued in the belief that English poetry
is now once again putting on a new strength and beauty.
Few readers have the leisure or the zeal to invest-
igate each volume as it appears;   and the process of
recognition is often slow.   This collection, drawn
entirely from the publications of the past two years,
may if it is fortunate help the lovers of poetry to
realise that we are at the beginning of another
'Georgian period' which may take rank in due time with
the several great poetic ages of the past.

This terse, but unhelpful introduction leaves open the
question of what Georgian poetry is.   The obvious answer
would be that the anthologies collect what was considered

363 Georgian Poetry 1911-1922: The Critical Heritage

to be the best poetry of their time and so represent
nothing beyond the tastes of their editor. But those
tastes were homogeneous enough, and influential enough,
to attract the attention of those literary critics who
can never feel satisfied about the status of a movement
until they have endowed it with a programme and a pedi-
gree. We now know precisely what Georgianism is, even
if Sir Edward Marsh unfortunately does not. Professor
Bullough informs us for example that there were five ten-
dencies in English poetry at the beginning of this cent-
ury and that Georgianism succeeds in combining all five
['The Trend of Modern Poetry', 2nd edition, 1941, 44-5].
Herbert Palmer sees not merely Georgianism but two
Georgian 'revolts' preceded by a 'prelude'. In keeping
with the greater subtlety of his methods he is able to
isolate not five tendencies but fourteen and to note as
the unifying tendency behind them 'a definite break with
nearly everything known as "Victorian"' and 'a revival or
preservation of the Wordsworthian tradition' ['Post-
Victorian Poetry', 1938, 75-8 *et passim*].

Mr Palmer's detailed and fastidious classifications
are enough to pacify even the fiercest of critics. It
is therefore all the more discouraging to find that his
full-dress account of what Georgian poetry is becomes
very largely an account of what it is not. Twelve of
his fourteen tendencies are negative; the positive
qualities amount to nothing more than restraint in dic-
tion and an emphasis on nature and on country life. Of
the technical innovations which are proposed, the most
drastic are the avoidance of poetic licence and the el-
imination of constructions such as 'thee', 'thou' and
'methinks'. The 'revolt' which is dramatized in chapt-
er headings is described as a protest against the
Tennysonian tradition, a generalization which is next to
useless since the same protest has been registered
(though no doubt in different forms) by the pre-Raphael-
ites and by the aesthetic movement. Mr Palmer's sign-
posts, therefore, can by themselves do little to direct
us; but the conclusions they pointed to were sufficient-
ly important to invite this rejoinder by Sir Edward
Marsh:

> I had no smallest intention of founding a school, or
> of tracing a course for Poetry to follow; for such
> enterprises I was ill-equipped, in knowledge, in
> leisure, and in self-esteem. When Mr Herbert Palmer
> draws up a list of fourteen canons by which he de-
> duces that I was guided in my choice of poets and
> poems, he pays my lucidity and my purposefulness a

compliment which they do not deserve.   I was, of
course, guided by the preferences which instinct and
training had formed in my mind;   and these can be
easily, if roughly, set forth.   I liked poetry to be
all three (or if not all three, at least two;   or if
the worst came to the worst, at least one) of the foll-
owing things: intelligible, musical and racy;   and I
was happier with it if it was written on some formal
principle which I could discern, and from which it de-
parted, if at all, only for the sake of some special
effect, and not because the lazy or too impetuous
writer had found observance difficult or irksome.   I
liked poetry that I wanted to know by heart and *could*
learn by heart if I had time ['A Number of People',
1939, 322].

These criteria would be more acceptable if 'intelligible'
meant that a poem ought not to be more difficult than it
has to be and if 'musical' meant that the sound of a poem
(which may by itself be unmusical) should help to compose
the harmony of its meaning.   Unfortunately there is no
reason for assuming that Sir Edward would find these in-
terpretations acceptable, and even if he were to do so,
the standards he accepted would still apply to several
poems which are in no sense Georgian.   Perhaps, then, it
would be more prudent to turn for our information to the
poetry, to that most Georgian of poets Rupert Brooke, and
in particular to the last lines of 'Grantchester' which
perfectly epitomize the Georgian spirit:

[Quotes 'The Old Vicarage, Grantchester', final section:
26 lines.]

The half-humorous nostalgia of the passage cannot hide
the seriousness of its demand for forgetfulness, its
search for security in the rustic peace of England.   But
the corners in which certainty is discovered are fenced
in, significantly, against 'the lies, and truths, and
pain'.   The abstractions are discussed as if they were
interchangeable, with no suggestion that they are morally
distinct and no effort to treat them as poetically un-
equal.   The Georgian universe is thus made traditional
and orderly by suppressing all elements which challenge
its stability.   Birth, death, copulation, and even sea-
sickness may enter it;   but they can only do so in ways
compatible with England's rustic serenity and with exemp-
lary sentiments about moonlight, birds and children.   If
this material is sometimes insufficiently vivid the East
and similar lands can be set against it, but though

Chimborazo and Cotopaxi may steal away our hearts for a
moment they should never be more than bright beckoning
colours which light the horizon of the Georgian country-
side.   The proof of the accuracy of this description is
that as time goes on even these colours are banished, the
realism of Masefield parodied and discouraged, and trop-
ical exoticism replaced by the wan decadence of 'Moon-
bathers' and 'The Lily of Malud'.   As the conflict of
'lies' and 'truths' in the outer world grows more stren-
uous the imagination descends with relief to the cool
brown waters of Georgia's immortal river and the scuttling
of mice in the authentic Georgian mill.   More and more
surely the constancy of nature becomes a consolation for
the waywardness of man:

    I do not think that skies and meadows are
    Moral, or that the fixture of a star
    Comes of a quiet spirit, or that trees
    Have wisdom in their windless silences.
    Yet are these things invested in my mood
    With constancy, and peace, and fortitude,
    That in my troubled season I can cry
    Upon the wide composure of the sky,
    And envy fields, and wish that I might be
    As little daunted as a star or tree.
                    [John Drinkwater, 'Reciprocity' in
                    'Georgian Poetry, 1916-1917', 132.]

Wilfrid Gibson, with even more studied innocence, dreams
of security in a house upon a hill:

[Quotes Wilfrid Gibson, 'Reveille' in 'Georgian Poetry,
1918-19', 78.]

These poems, and many others like them in the Georgian
Anthologies, should make clear enough to the average
reader, the artificial simplicity of the Georgian uni-
verse.   What may not be so clear is the extent to which
this exclusiveness is matched by a devitalized and re-
stricted treatment of language.   Drinkwater's straight-
forward generalizations about nature are neither defined
nor extended by being put into verse and Gibson's uncrit-
ical sentimentality leads him to antitheses which seem to
me irresponsible.   There is no reason why the house of
the first stanza should be 'white' and that of the second
stanza 'dark', and no explanation is provided for the
change from the 'travail of day' in the third line to the
wholly different 'rapture of day' in the seventh.   The
poem frustrates instead of rewarding analysis;   it has

nothing to offer beyond the static and simplified assertions which are available directly on its surface.   The sentimental unity it provides is so precarious that it can tolerate no reference to reality, no test of convention by the experienced fact.   It can therefore lead to no pattern of metaphorical implication, since any such pattern is certain to encourage and to unite to poetic responsiveness the active, discriminating powers of the intellect.   The result can only be that Georgian poetry degenerates into clichés and that its range of suggestion is limited and petrified by its fear of pressing beyond conventional boundaries.   W.H. Davies's poem 'The Moon' is typical of this reliance on unqualified stock responses:

Thy beauty haunts me heart and soul,
Oh thou fair Moon, so close and bright;
Thy beauty makes me like the child
That cries aloud to own thy light;
The little child that lifts each arm
To press thee to her bosom warm.
Though there are birds which sing this night
With thy white beams across their throats,
Let my deep silence speak for me
More than for them their sweetest notes
Who worships thee till music fails
Is greater than thy nightingales.

'There is', comments David Daiches, 'a peculiarly simple set of relationships here.   The relation of the poet to the moon's beauty is identified with that of a child to the moon - not the child's relationship to some quite different object .....   The poet is enclosed in a tiny little world where everyone is looking at the moon and every relationship must be a relationship to the moon'. ['Poetry and the Modern World' (Chicago), 53.]   Further analysis can only confirm this conclusion.   The child image is abandoned before any implications it may have can be developed and the birds and moonlight of the second stanza contribute nothing to the closing couplet. The elements in the design have nothing in common, beyond being bathed by moonlight in a warm and hazy unity. They cannot afford to react upon each other because such a reaction, with its growing structure of comment, would be bound to relate the poem to those realities on the exclusion of which its completeness has to depend.   The Georgian universe dare not develop.   It cannot face doubt when the meaning of doubt is destruction.   Its poetry, correspondingly, cannot release the forces of

criticism and appraisal which are inseparable from a
mature poetic language and which endow that language with
its special authority as an agent of meaning for its
generation.

The above criticisms of the Georgian outlook would be
misleading if they suggested that pastoral poetry is im-
possible in our time and that all modern pastoralists are
therefore insincere. But they may help us to understand
more clearly the stringent requirements which a pastoral
poet must satisfy. It is not enough to write of nature
exactly or to feel genuinely moved in the presence of
rivers and sunsets. It is not even enough to wed those
emotions (as no Georgian poet has wedded them) to a pass-
ionate disbelief in urban values. Pastoral poetry can
only succeed when the sensibility which nourishes it is
such that it can be wholly externalized in the objects of
nature with no sacrifice of intelligence or complexity.
If this were not so, the non-pastoral elements in the
poet's mind would involve him either in artificial ex-
clusions or in emotional judgments which would not bear
analysis. The poem would depend for its coherence on
suppression, not on the security of freely related inter-
ests, the achieved equilibrium of a fully worked-out ex-
perience. Such an equilibrium based, as it must be, on
the assimilation of facts which are superficially hostile
to the poetic thesis, is reached and preserved in modern
poetry so rarely that Edward Thomas is, I believe, the
only poet of this century who has managed to preserve it
wholly in pastoral writing. I quote for consideration,
the best known of his poems:

It seems I have no tears left. They should have
    fallen -
Their ghosts, if tears have ghosts, did fall - that day
When twenty hounds streamed by me, not yet combed out
But still all equals in their rage of gladness
Upon the scent, made one, like a great dragon
In Blooming Meadow that bends towards the sun
And once bore hops: and on that other day
When I stepped out from the double-shadowed Tower
Into an April morning, stirring and sweet
And warm. Strange solitude was there and silence.
A mightier charm than any in the Tower
Possessed the courtyard. They were changing guard,
Soldiers in line, young English countrymen,
Fair-haired and ruddy, in white tunics. Drums
And fifes were playing, 'The British Grenadiers'.
The men, the music piercing that solitude
And silence, told me truths I had not dreamed,
And have forgotten since their beauty passed.
                    ['Tears', 'Collected Poems', 1936, 26.]

Only the most honest of poets would have dared to bring
together such disparate recollections and yet convince us
of their natural unity.   The music of the poem moreover
- and this is usually a fair test - never falters in its
enactment of the meaning.   In the long stressed monosyll-
ables of the third line the physique and contours of the
very words seem to capture the colourful, lingering ex-
citement of the hunt.   The effect however is character-
istically remote.   It is not so much the incident itself,
as a subdued, slow-motion remembrance of the incident.
This suggestion of emotion recollected in tranquillity is
consolidated by 'ghosts' which serves to set the exper-
ience in memory, while 'not yet combed out' suggests with
vivid exactness the confused, strangely assorted emotions
of its texture.   The 'double-shadowed Tower' too has its
part to play among these implications, while that astonish-
ing paradox 'rage of gladness' states, as directly as is
possible in this setting, the profound ambiguity of the
poem's basic emotion.   'A kind of exultant melancholy',
Huxley calls it, 'which is the nearest approach to quiet
unpassionate happiness that the soul can know'.   ['On the
Margin', 1923, 51.   Huxley is speaking of 'October' but
his comment applies equally to 'Tears' (Rajan's note).]
That melancholy, subdued but variegated, possesses the
courtyard in an April whose sweet stirring passes with
memorable aptness into the more blatantly stirring music
of fifes and drums.   It is a music which pierces, with-
out violating, the inner theatre of the poet's solitude,
and as it does so we realize to what extent the clamour
and brilliance of the earlier recollections are broken
into and defined by silence.   So the various elements in
the experience demand each other in the name of their own
completeness and when the differences between them have
been 'combed out' they are all left ordered by the poem's
'rage of gladness'.   Such a simplification can only be
inadequate but it may perhaps serve as a map of the poem's
intentions or as a means of suggesting its unaffected
unity.   It is a unity which puts in its proper perspect-
ive the methodical artifice of Georgian writing:

> Beauty walked over the hills and made them bright,
> She in the long fresh grass scattered her rains
> Sparkling and glittering like a host of stars,
> But not like stars, cold, severe, terrible.
> Hers was the laughter of the wind that leaped
> Arm-full of shadows, flinging them far and wide.
> [John Freeman, 'Discovery', 'Georgian
>   Poetry, 1916-1917', 130:   opening lines.]

The whole poem is ostentatiously pre-arranged.   Because
Beauty and starlight are associated in poetry, Mr Freeman
begins by comparing raindrops to stars.   But he has no
sooner produced his simile than he has to destroy it with
a caveat.   The result is that, at the end of four lines,
one has discovered nothing about either stars or raindrops
and one is becoming, in addition, far too interested for
the poem's good health in the horticultural feats per-
formed by Beauty.   To cut matters short, the poem is not
held together by any unifying centre of sensation.   It is
therefore no poem but a poetic exercise and Dr Leavis is
quite justified in stressing the extent to which such
writing is 'composed' while that of Edward Thomas simply
'happens'.

> It is only when the complete effect has been
> registered in the reader's mind that the inevitability
> and the exquisite economy become apparent.   A char-
> acteristic poem of his [Thomas's] has the air of being
> a random jotting down of chance impressions and sen-
> sations, the record of a moment of relaxed and undir-
> ected consciousness.   The diction and movement are
> those of quiet, ruminative speech.   But the unobtrus-
> ive signs accumulate, and finally one is aware that
> the outward scene is accessory to an inner theatre
> ['New Bearings in English Poetry', 1930, 69].

I have tried to discuss some of these qualities as they
are presented in 'Tears', and to suggest, in addition,
the extreme complexity of feeling they make possible.
It only remains to indicate the extent to which this
pressure of meaning in Thomas's poetry defines and
tenses his most exact descriptions.

> The green elm with the one great bough of gold
> Lets leaves into the grass slip, one by one -
> The short hill grass the mushrooms small, milk-white,
> Harebell and scabious and tormentil,
> That blackberry and gorse, in dew and sun,
> Bow down to; and the wind travels too light
> To shake the fallen birch leaves from the fern;
>   [Edward Thomas, 'October', 'Collected Poems', 85.]

The third line with its stressed, labouring movement,
clotted unmercifully by the *m's* and *s's* has already some-
thing of winter's gnarled severity.   It cannot but react
upon the words which follow it and so force into the fore-
front of our attention the harsh and malignant deformity
of their surfaces.   But the effect, though inescapable,

is never allowed to gain control of the poem.   The dom-
inant rhythm is one of life, not death, a rhythm made
all the more meaningful and enduring by its recognition
of life's destructive elements.   When every allowance
has been made for the obvious differences of mood and sit-
uation its quality is not without some kinship to these
words of Cordelia in 'King Lear':

>   Alack! 'tis he: why, he was met even now
>   As mad as the vex'd sea; singing aloud;
>   Crowned with rank fumiter and furrow weeds,
>   With burdocks, hemlock, nettles, cuckoo flowers,
>   Darnel, and all the idle weeds that grow
>   In our sustaining corn.

The manner in which affirmation proceeds through the rank
chaos which normally should strangle it, is itself a con-
fession of the whole play's buoyant security, the harmony
of acceptance which it reaches through every denial and
incitement of despair.   No hint of any such vitality is
displayed, and no recognition of its poetic power con-
ceded, in the itinerary of the average Georgian cata-
logue:

>   And I will take celandine nettle and parsley, white
>   In its own green light,
>   Or milkwort and sorrel, thyme, harebell and meadow
>   sweet
>   Lifting at your feet,
>   And ivy blossom beloved of soft bees; I will take
>   The loveliest -
>   The seeding grasses that bend with the winds, and
>   shake
>   Though the winds are at rest.
>   [John Freeman, 'I Will Ask', 'Georgian Poetry',
>   1920-1922', 65]

Clearly what Freeman has to say has very little to do
with the way in which he says it.   The language is set
apart from the objects in nature which it signifies and
one's attention is drawn to the objects rather than the
language.   The properties of poetic speech are never
used, as they are in the earlier quotations, to create a
response to these denoted objects.   So the intelligent
reader's reaction to the words - their sound, their hist-
ory, and their fortuitous resemblances - is suppressed
and destroyed, instead of being utilized.   Thomas's
writing results in no such frustration; even if you be-
lieve whimsically that 'scabious' is the superlative of

'scab' you will find that fancy allowed for in 'October'.
The poem invites your active reaction to it, not your un-
critical acceptance of its counters;   its wholeness and
sincerity depend on the degree to which such reactions
lead into the poem's logic and find their fulfilment in
its structural unity.

This long digression will have served its purpose if it
has shown that the unity achieved by Thomas's poetry, and
indeed by all good lyric or reflective poetry, is essent-
ially a unity of inclusion.   The implications of the lan-
guage are made to branch out into wider and wider areas of
experience and the foundations of the poem are thus made
more secure by the range and variety of the interests it
unifies.   You cannot destroy so comprehensive a security
by attempting to belabour it with 'facts', since all such
facts, however hostile, have already been admitted into
the poem's citadel and become part of its imaginative
logic.   The Georgian unity however is essentially one of
exclusion.   Facts which misbehave in its territory are
gently but firmly exiled from its garden, and the implic-
ations of language carefully censored to exclude all ref-
erence to these unfortunate events.   One can understand
and even sympathize with the defensive anxieties which
led to these retrenchments.   Well before 1914 the acc-
epted modes of poetic feeling were beginning to disinte-
grate and the War (an embarrassing visitor in the Georg-
ian garden) only accelerated the process of their des-
truction.   Imagism tried to conceal their irrelevance by
providing them with an up-to-date exterior.   The result
was an inability to assimilate modern life, a too easy
repudiation of its obvious deficiencies, a too precipi-
tate and unconditional withdrawal into Hellas.   Georg-
ianism chose the obvious alternative: to preserve the
traditional poetic standards by confining them to those
sectors of reality which still seemed amenable to poetic
treatment.   Such measures are intelligible, even if they
are regrettable;   but they can form no basis for a living
poetic movement.   A rare and special sensibility such as
Edward Thomas's can still live naturally in a pastoral
universe;   but a whole generation of poets can only do so
by an unnatural censoring of poetic subjects.   That sup-
ervision can only result in the policing and strangling of
poetic language, the refusal to allow words their life of
implication, their power to mean more than they immediate-
ly suggest.   No tradition which is expected to live sig-
nificantly can afford to accept this destructive isolat-
ion, this confinement in Eden as the price of its surviv-
al.   It has to condemn the etiquette of the garden and
the more plausible, but still menacing, ceremonies of the

desert.   The values it regenerates must be not the prod-
uctions of an outer conformity, but the creations of the
poem's total logic, confessed and defended by its imagin-
ative unity.   We are forgetting how to create and may
soon forget how to recognize this unity;   the fashion to-
day is not for poetry but for well-dressed and respect-
able (or respectably shocking) noises.   To challenge the
authority of those noises one needs to do more than em-
bellish the landscape of Georgia with skeletons, mermaids
and sexual innuendo.   Nothing less is required than a
restoration of intelligence to its proper poetic status,
a restoration made possible by the responsible use of
language, the union of the whole mind to the object of
poetic experience.   One can only regret that no such
restoration is assumed or contemplated by the periodic
sponsors of a Georgian revival.

71.   'GEORGIAN POETRY', UNSIGNED FRONT ARTICLE, 'THE
TIMES LITERARY SUPPLEMENT'

21 November 1952, 753-5

Returning in spirit to the 'front' of March 1946
(No. 68), the writer of this article (possibly the same?)
offers one of the best short assessments of the Georgian
venture, and links its 'academic poetry' with the work of
later writers, 'even perhaps Professor Cecil Day Lewis'
(see Introduction, pp. 39-40, and Alan Pryce-Jones's
reference in No. 69 to 'Word Over All').
   Marsh was never to edit the selection from Georgian
Poetry referred to in the second paragraph.   Christopher
Hassall records:

   Edward Shanks wrote in July 1952, wanting Marsh's
   help in the making of an anthology drawn from the five
   volumes of the Georgian series;   he said he was get-
   ting more and more 'militantly disgusted' by current
   references to the movement.   'No one knows what it
   did for the poets represented in it and for the public
   appreciation of contemporary poetry in general.'   The
   Introduction, written in a 'belligerent manner', would
   tell the story of how the whole thing came into exist-
   ence.   He was however extremely doubtful whether he
   would succeed in rousing the founder's interest.   He

did not know that the recent broadcast which had
finally provoked him to action had also been heard by
'E.M.'.   Eddie himself took a more lenient view.
'I do think it was rather out of proportion', he
wrote to Frances Cornford, 'to regret that Rupert
hadn't died in 1910 because "the disaster of Georgian
Poetry would *thus* have been averted".'   [Christopher
Hassall, 'Edward Marsh: A Biography', 1959, 668-9.]

Forty years after the appearance of the first volume in
1912, and in the year of the editor's eightieth birthday,
there are signs of a revival of interest in 'Georgian
Poetry'.   Perhaps the first thing that strikes the
reader who reopens the charmingly printed volumes with
the imprint of The Poetry Bookshop is the number of names
that are still familiar, more than a generation later.
In the first volume are Lascelles Abercrombie, Gordon
Bottomley, Rupert Brooke, G.K. Chesterton, W.H. Davies,
Walter de la Mare, John Drinkwater, James Elroy Flecker,
Wilfrid Wilson Gibson, D.H. Lawrence, John Masefield,
Harold Monro, T. Sturge Moore, Ronald Ross, Edmund Beale
Sargant, James Stephens and R.C. Trevelyan.   Probably
the only poems here which are not discussed to-day by
connoisseurs of twentieth-century poetry are those of
Edmund Beale Sargant and Ronald Ross, who is known more
for his friendship with poets than for his own poetry.
Of the others the poetic reputations of Brooke, Chester-
ton, Davies, Mr de la Mare, Mr Masefield, Monro and
Stephens will almost certainly outlive the year 2000, and
a younger generation may discover beauties in Abercrombie,
Bottomley, Flecker, Gibson and Trevelyan which are at
present clouded over.
    It is difficult to think of an anthology of contempor-
ary poetry published in recent years which has more claim
to be representative of work which will endure than these
Georgian volumes.   If, as we hear, Sir Edward Marsh has
been persuaded to make a selection in one volume from all
his five, such a book will doubtless attract the reading
public.   Sir Edward's first qualification as an editor
was that he chose poems a very large proportion of which
still give pleasure.   However, in the present century an
anthologist - a gatherer of chosen flowers - is not
judged simply by this.   He is expected also to have
something called 'contemporary sensibility': that is to
say, his poets, or some of them at least, should reveal
an awareness of the problem of adapting poetry to these
unpropitious-seeming days, unless indeed - as

occasionally seemed the case with 'the Georgians' -
poetry is to become a minor art like embroidery, to be
done of a week-end in a country cottage.

Unfortunately for 'Georgian Poetry', already with its
second volume (1913-15) it had run into war. Passengers
and cargo of the craft reflected little awareness of this
war, apart from the presence of Rupert Brooke's 'The
Soldier' - a sonnet which seemed at the time to reflect
exactly the mood of the hour, and which has endured in
its power to provoke the utmost resistance in the reader.
But in the third and later volumes Sir Edward Marsh
added, among other names, those of Robert Graves, Robert
Nichols, Siegfried Sassoon, W.J. Turner, Edmund Blunden,
I. Rosenberg, Richard Hughes, Peter Quennell and V.
Sackville-West. No one could seriously reproach the
editor with being out of sympathy with the young.   On
the whole he was as lucky, or as discerning, about those
with a future as he had been with his more established
starters. The criticism he encountered was not that he
lacked sympathy with youth, but that he had no enthusiasm
for the modern movement - which was something very diff-
erent. There are, indeed, poems in these volumes which
do strike the note of the times - Mr Sassoon's war poems,
for example. But some other names are rather misleading:
Mr Graves was in his rural and 'patchwork bonnet' phase;
and there is only one poem by Rosenberg. Even Lawrence
and Mr Sassoon do not quite succeed in introducing a dis-
cordant voice into a party chosen by Sir Edward Marsh on
principles which he imagined would have appealed to
Wordsworth when he wrote of verses which

> The high and tender Muses shall accept
> With gracious smile, deliberately pleased.

It is not altogether fanciful to be reminded, by the
distinguished blue and brown 'boards' which enclose Sir
Edward's volumes, of bistre walls around a cloister or
college quadrangle; and D.H. Lawrence's presence here is
rather like his week-end visit to Bertrand Russell at
Cambridge. One feels that a poet who was not 'quite
quite' could be invited: Lawrence, in the minds of Gibson
and Abercrombie, had perhaps a bucolic or rustic North
Country air, pleasing to those whose imaginations wand-
ered affectionately among tumbled hay and pewter tank-
ards. Moreover, he had a gift which all could recog-
nize, and if it seemed untutored, well, he could be told
about rhythms, music, suitable subject-matter and the
rest. And if, when his attention was drawn to the music
of the 'Golden Journey to Samarkand', he replied, '"It

satisfies your ear", you say.   Well, I don't write for
your ear' - that was only to be expected.   Lawrence also
wrote to Sir Edward: 'If your ear has got stiff and a
bit mechanical, *don't* blame my poetry.'   Lawrence's
letters, together with those of Ezra Pound, in fact pro-
vide an excellent background to the controversies waged
around 'Georgian Poetry'.   If one can agree with some of
the views expressed by the opposition party, Sir Edward
Marsh emerges as an editor of infinite patience, kindness,
tolerance and generosity.

The first and the last volumes open with prefaces in
which the editor expresses some predilections;   in the
ones between he is a producer who remains discreetly in
the background, although his presence is always felt.
The first preface opens on a note of high hope: 'We are
at the beginning of another "Georgian period" which may
take rank in due time with the several great poetic ages
of the past.'   But even in his rôle of prophet, 'E.M.',
unlike the stimulators of other poetic movements, who
wish to draw everything into their net and condemn all
they have not caught, adds that his volume has 'no pre-
tensions to cover the field'.   This was in 1912.   In
the prefatory note to the 1920 volume the editor is no
longer a Moses showing the Children the Promised Land;
he is a shepherd, rather partial to his own little flock.
He pleads that his taste is - and always has been - per-
sonal, and not institutional.   He is no arbiter of
taste, president of a Royal Academy of Poets.   He has
only attempted to bring before a wider reading public
poets whose work had seemed to him in 1912 extremely
good, and which was too narrowly known.   He protests
against the view that 'Georgian Poetry'

> has merely encouraged a small clique of mutually
> indistinguishable poetasters .....   It is natural
> that the poets of a generation should have points in
> common;   but to my fond eye those who have graced
> these collections look as diverse as sheep to their
> shepherd.

He goes on to name 'Messrs Abercrombie, Davies, de la
Mare, Graves, Lawrence, Nichols and Squire,' whose diff-
erences of manner may be taken to vouch for the diversity
of 'Georgian Poetry'.

So far, so good.   The argument could be pushed
farther than Sir Edward takes it.   An editor should not
be a critic but a person of natural taste who has the
courage to 'like what he likes'.   Unfortunately though,
as has been pointed out, the little ship of 'Georgian

Poetry' had run into the war.   The problem confronting
poetry is referred to in the last paragraph of this pre-
face, which was written in 1922, the year of the public-
ation of 'The Waste Land':

> Much admired modern work seems to me, in its lack of
> inspiration and its disregard of form, like gravy
> imitating lava.   Its upholders may retort that much
> of the work which I prefer seems to them, in its lack
> of inspiration and its comparative finish, like
> tapioca imitating pearls.

This was the last number of 'Georgian Poetry', though the
best of Sir Edward's poets continued writing;   several of
them, like Mr de la Mare and Mr Blunden, are producing
beautiful poetry to-day.   Looking back, it may seem that
the Parthian shot of the editor was fired on the assumpt-
ion of a false diathesis between 'form' on one side and
'formlessness' on the other.   It might have been better
to draw a distinction between the academic and the kind
of revolutionary movement in contemporary poetry which was
based on a complete reinterpretation of tradition.
    A sideward glance shows what had happened.   The first
volume of 'Georgian Poetry' did really draw attention to
the remarkable continuity of a tradition still unbroken
after Tennyson.   But during and after the war that move-
ment which was an awakening of English poetry to influ-
ences spreading from Paris by way of New York, Boston and
Chicago had acquired a greater impetus than ever since in
this century.   The 'Little Review', 'Poetry' (Chicago),
the 'Egoist' and the Sitwellian 'Wheels', were all doing
noisy things unheard of within the seclusion of 'Georgian
Poetry' which, after its early rough passage reflected in
Brooke and Sassoon (but without ever taking aboard Wilfrid
Owen) was anchored in quiet waters.
    'Georgian Poetry' in fact showed that there was and is
an academic poetry in England far more worthy to be res-
pected than any other of the arts.   That this is so is
shown by the paradox that whereas 'Georgian Poetry' has
passed, as a movement, into history, many of Sir Edward's
Georgian poets are alive and writing some of the best
poetry in the language;   and of those who are dead several
survive.   The mistake - probably unavoidable - was to
regard 'Georgian Poetry' as a 'movement' when (apart from
Rupert Brooke, who might if he had lived have been the
centre of some kind of literary programme) it was really
a kind of shelter for a few poets writing poetry in a fam-
iliar style about a familiar subject-matter.
    What is, of course, true in the contrast Sir Edward

makes between the 'gravy imitating lava' and the 'tapioca
imitating pearls' is that the urgency of 'modern poetry'
is far more difficult for contemporaries to appraise than
the achievement of the best of the Georgians.   There is
something about the position of Mr de la Mare and Mr
Blunden which is likely never to be disputed, and if
English were a dead language one can imagine students
translating their poems, and attempting to write poems in
the same manner.   All the same, if English poetry in the
half-century of two world wars consisted of nothing but
poetry such as this, we should have to say that we were
living in a period of Alexandrinism, when the thundering
flow of the central tradition was lost, and we were left
with a few poets like watchmakers, putting their 14 jewels
into the miniature cases of conventional forms.   The
modern movement which began with the Imagists and Symbol-
ists, developed through 'The Waste Land' and the socio-
logical poetry of the 1930s, and has now turned towards
themes of religious orthodoxy may be seen as one sus-
tained attempt to extend the tradition of poetry so that
it can deal with the theme of man in his contemporary
situation.   It has kept the roads open for a great
dramatist or writer of epics.   Whatever its failures, it
is a movement, and if the academics attack it under the
impression that they are a movement also they are bound
to fail through a misconception of their own rôle.   For
it is the business of the academic to do perfectly the
things which have been done perfectly before, not to ex-
tend the field of their art into modern life.

When a great many misconceptions have been cleared
away, it may be seen that the Georgian poets should be
judged by their achievements, not as a movement related
to the 1920s or the 1930s.   And as achievement the work
of Mr de la Mare, W.H. Davies and James Stephens - to
choose three from the first volume - is among the most
considerable, and the least bound by factors of time, of
this century.   In this first volume there appeared Mr de
la Mare's 'Arabia', 'The Sleeper', 'Winter Dusk', 'Miss
Loo', and 'The Listeners'; by Davies, 'The Child and the
Mariner', 'Days Too Short', and 'The Kingfisher'; by
James Stephens, 'In the Poppy Field', 'In the Cool of the
Evening', and 'The Lonely God'; and by Rupert Brooke,
'The Old Vicarage, Grantchester', 'Dust', 'The Fish',
'Town and Country', and 'Dining Room Tea'.   This seems a
larger quota of poems that have remained favourites than
one can think of in any later annual.   Moreover, some of
the poems are not just anthology pieces: they are among
the most beautiful produced by their writers.   Davies's
'The Kingfisher' and Mr de la Mare's 'Arabia' are among

the purest lyrics in the language.   Again Davies's 'The
Child and the Mariner' is an enchanting narrative, un-
affected and simple, yet profound, far more successful
than the long poems by Gordon Bottomley and Sturge Moore,
which are surely dead weights on the Georgian volumes,
tremendous sops to some conscience which told these poets
that they ought to be writing big poems on big subjects.
Davies, paradoxically enough, was (apart from Mr de la
Mare) the only poet capable of writing a long poem,
because since he relied simply on recollecting and re-
creating the magic which surrounded his childhood, he was
not faced by problems of technique and subject-matter
which made the poetic idiom of Bottomley and Abercrombie
inadequate to themes that appealed to them - themes such
as Babel and the End of the World.
     Those who do not like the Georgians would doubtless
maintain that Mr de la Mare was not ever one of them.
This is true in the limited sense that an original poetic
genius can never 'belong' to anyone or anything.   Never-
theless, it is clear from reading these volumes that being
a Georgian consisted in fulfilling certain conditions, un-
stated but yet very much in evidence.   These conditions
were that a poet should use a vocabulary and forms, and
write about a subject-matter recognizably and tradition-
ally poetic.   Mr de la Mare fulfilled all these perfect-
ly, and if his poetic world lies in a mysterious territory
quite beyond any conditions, this only shows that it was
possible to be a de la Mare and a Georgian poet.   He
showed that the forms in which he first found and used
poetry were adequate to express that faith in invisible
values which he has sustained throughout a lifetime.
His philosophic strength no more demanded a revolution in
poetry than did Mr E.M. Forster's in the novel.   This
was scarcely true of Brooke, who wrote love poems which
have an affinity with love scenes in the novels of Mr
Aldous Huxley, who was fascinated by the disgusting, and
who would almost certainly have rebelled against the
Georgians had he lived.
     Mr de la Mare, Mr Blunden and Davies are all poets of
worlds with boundaries clearly separate from a great deal
of the world of actuality.   They have each perfected a
discipline of the imagination which is entirely adequate
to create their independent visions.   Their poems are
poured into the moulds of the forms they use, like wine
into bottles.   It is the quality of the wine which one
notices and not, very much, the form.   Think of a poem
by Mr de la Mare and you think of music, an atmosphere, a
charm, but you do not think of dynamic form inseparable
from content, as in works as different as an 'Epistle' of

Pope, an 'Ode' of Keats, or Mr Pound's 'Hugh Selwyn
Mauberley'.   The Georgians were in reality rather form-
less, because form had become a habit, a matter of good
manners and a sign of cultivation with them.   There was
no struggle with form at all.   This matters little with
the poets to whom it was secondary, since the content was,
as with Davies, so pure and innocent, or as with Mr de la
Mare, so obsessively dream-like that it could use any fam-
iliar form for its purposes.   The somnambulist poets who
wrote out of an instinctive poetic life were successful as
Georgians;   indeed it was an advantage never to challenge
the forms they were using.   But with more intellectual
writers, like Abercrombie or Gordon Bottomley, the habit
of form hangs on their poetry like a shabby, once-glorious
garment, and their inability to create tense rhythms is
one of the minor tragedies of such would-be tragedians.
Here, for instance, is a speech from Lascelles Aber-
crombie's interesting poetic drama, 'The Sale of Saint
Thomas':

> Fear not.   'Tis likely indeed that storms are now
> Plotting against our voyage;   ay, no doubt
> The very bottom of the sea prepares
> To stand up mountainous or reach a limb
> Out of his night of water and huge shingles,
> That he and the waves may break our keel.   Fear not;
> Like those who manage horses, I've a word
> Will fasten up within their evil natures
> The meanings of the winds and waves and reefs.

The blank-verse medium here, though handled cleverly,
forms a surface over the life of the poetry, like a dense
varnish over a painting.   This storm fails to freeze the
blood, because the movement of the verse is not terrify-
ing.   It is too literary without becoming naked liter-
ature.   With Gordon Bottomley, the verse he writes is so
much a habit, so much an academic gown, that the reader
has to pinch himself to realize that the subject of these
lines is 'The End of the World':

> The snow had fallen many nights and days;
> The sky was come upon the earth at last,
> Sifting thinly down as endlessly
> As though within the system of blind planets
> Something had been forgot or overdriven.

To-day these long poems of Abercrombie and Bottomley
seem distinguished failures, perhaps because a generation
aware of the dangers in English of the iambic pentameter

cannot view them otherwise.   In spite of several much-
advertised poetic rebellions, the work of several young
poets even to-day - notably that of Mr Christopher Fry -
shows that the over-used, facile iambic line which seems
such an accessible medium for intellectual verse can still
attract writers.   It offers the possibility of many var-
iations, but nearly all have been used already, and the
bright look of newness in this metre seems to wear off
more quickly than in any other.

The danger of anthologies conforming to a certain
taste, and appearing at regular intervals, is that camp-
followers appear whose flattering imitations of the work
of the best poets in the group tend to become parodies.
This certainly happened with the Georgians.   There were
dozens of poets - published for the most part outside the
Georgian anthologies - who produced work of the level of
these lines by John Drinkwater:

Shy in their herding dwell the fallow deer.
They are spirits of wild sense.   Nobody near
Comes upon their pastures.   There a life they live,
Of sufficient beauty, phantom, fugitive.

The lesser Georgians came to be known for lack of
vividness and acuteness in every respect.   Their images
were not sharply or clearly seen, their metre was slack,
their feelings had no pressure.   D.H. Lawrence went on
being one of their most amusing critics in letters which
Sir Edward Marsh has generously allowed to appear in the
'Collected Letters by D.H. Lawrence'.   In some comments
on a poem of Ralph Hodgson, he hits the nail on the head
with his usual apt unfairness:

And now I've got to quarrel with you about the
Ralph Hodgson poem: because I think it is banal in
utterance.   The feeling is there, right enough - but
not in itself, only represented.   It's like 'I asked
for bread, and he gave me a penny.'   Only here and
there is the least touch of personality in the poem:
it is the currency of poetry, not poetry itself.
Every single line of it is poetic currency - and a
good deal of emotion handling it about.   But it isn't
really poetry.   I hope to God you won't hate me and
think me carping, for this.   But look:

the ruby's and the rainbow's song
the nightingale's - all three.

There's the emotion in the rhythm, but it's loose

emotion, inarticulate, common - the words are mere
currency.   It is exactly like a man who feels very
strongly for a beggar, and gives him a sovereign.
The feeling is at either end, for the moment, but the
sovereign is a dead bit of metal.   And this poem is
the sovereign.   'Oh I do want to give you this
emotion', cries Hodgson, 'I do.'   And so he takes out
his poetic purse, and gives you a handful of cash, and
feels very strongly, even a bit sentimentally over it.

> the sky was lit
> The sky was stars all over it.
> I stood, I knew not why.

No one should say, 'I knew not why' any more.   It is
as meaningless as 'yours truly' at the end of a letter.

In spite of its casual tone this is perceptive criticism.
In writing of Hodgson, Lawrence is not prejudiced by per-
sonal feeling, as he is when he writes (in the same
letter) of Davies: 'He's really like a linnet that's got
just a wee little sweet song, but it only sings when it's
wild.   And he's made himself a tame bird - poor little
devil.   He makes me furious.'   Here Lawrence completely
misses the point that Davies was a perfectionist writing
very beautifully in a minor vein.   'Georgian Poetry'
made work like that of Davies possible.
   The third volume of 'Georgian Poetry' (1916-17) led
off with six poems by W.J. Turner.   Mr Blunden did not
appear until the last volume in the series, published in
1922, so Turner, whose poems appear in two volumes, is the
only 'discovery' of importance who might be described as
a mainstay of 'Georgian Poetry'.   His work illustrates
the thesis that good poetry could be written which ful-
filled the requirements of an editor who disliked work
which he considered 'formless', if the poet had that kind
of gift which rejects the modern world.   W.J. Turner, of
Australian origin, had an intense and simple vision -
though composed of more complex elements - which was only
excelled by Davies at his best.   With 'Romance', he joins
at once the small band of Georgians whose poems, whether
or not one approves of them, become part of the luggage
one carries through life;   for this poem with its wonder-
ful opening lines is as unforgettable as certain poems by
Mr de la Mare:

> When I was but thirteen years or so
> I went into a golden land,
> Chimborazo, Cotopaxi
> Took me by the hand.

> My father died, my brother too,
> They passed like fleeting dreams,
> I stood where Popocatapetl
> In the sunlight gleams.

The strange poem called 'Ecstasy', beginning 'I saw a
frieze on whitest marble drawn', has a quality of pure
enthusiasm which Turner attained perhaps twenty times in
a career of many failures, when he had not keyed his
writing up to the pitch which could produce a minor
masterpiece.

'Georgian Poetry' may have been an unfortunate name
for the series.   It had the advantage of attracting a
public to the work of a group of poets, but it all too
aptly provided a label for the work of the weakest poets
in the collection, a label which was then tagged on to
the better ones.   To the modernists, the weaker Georg-
ians represented the influences which they were trying to
resist in their own work.   For to a poet, the struggle
with language is not just a struggle with himself.   It
is also a struggle against echoes set up in his mind by
the work of contemporaries.   Hence the new writers are
always trying to drown too-familiar voices.

'The Georgians' is an unfortunate label for another
reason, because, in the best sense, the Georgians are
still with us.   If one says that Mr Norman Nicholson,
Mr Vernon Watkins and even perhaps Professor Cecil Day
Lewis are often very close to the Georgian poets, one
does not mean to denigrate them.   What is meant is that
they belong to a company which also includes Mr de la
Mare and Mr Blunden, and that they have not absorbed very
deeply into their work the aims of Mr Ezra Pound and Mr
T.S. Eliot.   In a day when editors publishing poetry and
supporting and encouraging poets have almost vanished
from the literary scene, there is every reason to pay
grateful homage to Sir Edward Marsh.

72.   'A PATRON OF ART AND LETTERS', HAROLD NICOLSON,
'THE OBSERVER'

7 June 1959

Harold Nicolson reviews Christopher Hassall, 'Edward
Marsh: A Biography'.

It seems fitting to conclude with three reviews of
Christopher Hassall's biography of the editor of 'Georgian
Poetry'.   Harold Nicolson (1886-1968) first met Marsh in
1909 at St Petersburg where Nicolson's father was ambass-
ador.   Like his father, he entered the Diplomatic Service,
but resigned from it in 1929.   He was married to Victoria
Sackville-West, one of the two lady Georgian Poets (see
Appendix, p. 413).   His many books include studies of
Tennyson, Byron, and Swinburne, and he benefited from
Marsh's 'diabolization' of his writing: the notes on the
proofs of his 'Tennyson' 'show me, in a way that heartens
rather than humiliates, how wide a gulf is fixed between
writing and good writing' (quoted in Christopher Hassall,
'Edward Marsh: A Biography', 1959, 703).   Nicolson wrote
the Introduction to Christopher Hassall and Denis Mathews
(ed.), 'Eddie Marsh: Sketches for a Composite Literary
Portrait ...', 1953, 10-11.

Mr Christopher Hassall's 'Edward Marsh' is a remarkable
biography.   It has all the qualities that are essential
to the biographical art.   It is true; it is detailed;
it is a vivid portrayal of an interesting personality;   it
shows sympathy and penetration;   it is excellently written;
it gives us the history of a period illustrated by numer-
ous anecdotes and graced by skilful portraits of contemp-
orary characters.   It is at one and the same time an an-
alysis of individual temperament and a description of life
in general.   Above all it displays an admirably balanced
sense of proportion.
Mr Hassall is aware that Edward Marsh was a prominent
Civil Servant and that he was intimately connected with
the leading statesmen and the tremendous political advent-
ures of his time.   He knows also that he was an except-
ional participant in the social life of his age and that
there were few house-parties or dinner-parties that he did
not both grace with his elegance and delight by his rich
repertory of anecdote and quotation.   Yet he has realised
that the true significance of his hero is as a patron and
benefactor of art and letters and he has wisely concent-
rated his description on these two aspects of achievement.
He mentions politics of course;   he refers to Marsh's
astonishing social energies;   yet these indulgencies are
presented merely as the background to Marsh's main pur-
pose, which was to identify, assist, advise, encourage
and warn poets and artists when at the opening stages of
their careers.   It is in this capacity, rather than as
the beloved coadjutor of Winston Churchill or the philos-

opher guide to other less eminent politicians, that
Edward Marsh will live for posterity.   It is on his
services to art and letters that Christopher Hassall
rightly throws the emphasis.

What differentiates Marsh from other famous patrons is
that he was not a rich man.   He possessed little income
beyond his salary as a Civil Servant;   such sums as he
received from royalties or from the grant made to his
family as compensation for the murder of his great-
grandfather, Spencer Perceval (which he would always
refer to as 'the murder money'), were devoted to helping
artists and poets during their years of penury.   It was
with tender delicacy that he would press these gifts upon
those whom he knew to be struggling.   'I should be
ashamed', he wrote, 'of being comparatively well-off, if
I couldn't take advantage of it to help my friends who are
younger and poorer and cleverer and better than I am.'
His charity was lavish.   But it was always distributed
with such tact as to leave behind it, not the poisons of
humiliation, but a glow of lasting gratitude.   He kept
many wolves from many battered doors.

His was a happy life.   When he was approaching eighty
a woman asked him what he would say if told that he was
doomed to die on the morrow.   His reply was immediate.
'I'd say "thanks for the party".'   It was not that his
long life was exempt from personal tragedies.   When
Rupert Brooke died he felt that the whole pattern of the
world had 'broken down'.   The cruel jealousy of Mrs
Brooke caused him deep embarrassment and mortification.
A boyhood illness had rendered him incapable of the act
of love, giving an epicene tone to his voice and appear-
ance and inducing many people to misjudge both the tend-
erness of his heart and the strong fibre of his intellect.

The five successive anthologies of Georgian poetry,
which represented the main work of his adult age, grad-
ually declined in influence.   The early _Pléiade_ that he
gathered together and which seemed to coruscate with such
fresh brilliance, tended to disintegrate as the decades
passed and to lose its lustre.   It was depressing to
recognise that those of his young poets who survived the
war were regarded by the rising generation as out of date
and that he himself was sometimes mocked at as an unfash-
ionable Maecenas.   He had endeavoured by his advice and
warnings to maintain the traditions of English poetry and
it was sad to be told by Mr T.S. Eliot, the austere
master of the twenties, that the Georgians paid too much
regard to 'pleasantness' and that 'they caress everything
they touch'.   He realised that he was perhaps too trad-
itional, too conventional, too 'catholic to a fault';

after nearly thirteen years' hard work on the Georgian
anthologies, the series was abandoned and for a while
Marsh felt himself to be 'no longer necessary'.   He was
but slightly comforted by the reflection that his venture
had had a lasting influence on English letters.   'No one
knows', wrote Edward Shanks many years later, 'what it
did for the poets represented in it and for the public
appreciation of contemporary poetry in general.'

One of the most impressive of Edward Marsh's many qual-
ities was his astonishing power of resilience.   The de-
cline in the popularity of Georgian poetry in no sense
diminished his zest for collecting and encouraging the
work of younger painters.   He had an exceptional gift for
detecting artistic talent and many famous artists of to-
day owe much to his recognition and encouragement of their
early work.   His friendship for Ivor Novello (a friend-
ship which never slackened for thirty-six years) gave him
a new passion for the theatre.   Some of his friends re-
gretted the spell cast upon him by the footlights and de-
plored the fact that his dictum that 'he would rather see
the worst play in the world than no play at all' had weak-
ened his faculties of discrimination.   There were those
even who complained that his rigid standards of literary
criticism became debased by theatrical emotionalism and
that he came in the end to attribute undue importance to
those writers who possessed a sentimental appeal or who
had a talent for dramatic narrative.

In later middle age he developed a fourth quality that
was in truth formidable.   He became the best book-doctor
and proof reader that my generation has known.   'If
Edward Marsh', wrote Somerset Maugham, 'in his relations
with people somewhat overflows with the milk of human
kindness, he makes up for it when he corrects proofs;
for then his comments are by turn scornful, pained, acid
and vituperative.'   Once again, in doctoring galley
proofs, he found himself indispensable.

And finally, at an age when most men lose their energy,
he composed his translations of Horace, La Fontaine, and
Fromentin.   The Fables of La Fontaine assuredly rank
among the models of English translation and in these he
was able to recapture his scholarship, his fastidiousness,
and his exquisite delicacy.

Mr Hassall is to be congratulated on a solid and im-
portant work excellently accomplished.

73.   'THE GOOD-NATURED MAN', RAYMOND MORTIMER,
'THE SUNDAY TIMES'

7 June 1959, 14

Raymond Mortimer reviews Christopher Hassall, 'Edward
Marsh: A Biography'.

Raymond Mortimer (b. 1895), another beneficiary of
Marsh's 'diabolization', was a fellow committee member of
the Contemporary Art Society.   When Marsh resigned from
the chairmanship after sixteen years in 1952, Mortimer's
tribute to him concluded:

> His services to the Arts, literature as well as paint-
> ing and sculpture, have been prodigious, improbable,
> fabulous.   He has offered incessant and practical
> sacrifice to the Muses; poets, and painters, and all
> of us who love the Arts, are immeasurably in his debt.
> [Quoted in Christopher Hassall, 'Edward Marsh: A
> Biography', 1959, 670.]

He also paid posthumous tribute in Christopher Hassall
and Denis Mathews (ed.), 'Eddie Marsh: Sketches for a
Composite Literary Portrait ...', 1953, 13-14.   His
books include 'Channel Packet' (1942) and 'Duncan Grant'
(1944).

Even the least angry of the young may wonder why a volume
of over 700 pages should be given to a civil servant who
anthologised living poets, translated dead ones, collect-
ed pictures, attended first nights and retailed anecdotes
in stately homes.   The answer is that Eddie Marsh served
Sir Winston Churchill as private secretary or else as
literary adviser for over forty years, and lavished his
time and money on painters and writers with unsurpassed
generosity.

Sometimes, I must admit, my curiosity flagged when Mr
Hassall was dwelling upon dim poets not yet remote enough
to have a piquant period-flavour; but his documented
picture is just the sort of book one would welcome about
the reign of Queen Anne or the Regency.   He never ob-
trudes his own partialities or dislikes.   He strikes me
as remarkably accurate, he writes clearly, and I have
noticed only one of those grammatical solecisms that used
to make Marsh raise his caracal eyebrows even higher.

So long as anyone remains interested in the England of
the last seventy years this book will be consulted: it
includes memorable stories about such a variety of per-
sons including Sir Winston, Henry James, Gosse, Bridges,
Tovey, G.E. Moore, George Moore, Bertrand Russell, Max
Beerbohm, Somerset Maugham, and Sickert.

In 1870 a granddaughter of Perceval (the Prime Minis-
ter who was assassinated by a madman) married an obscure
surgeon, the son of a penniless farmer;   and two years
later they produced their only son, the subject of this
biography.   At ten he went to Westminster, at twelve he
had by heart the first four books of 'Paradise Lost'.
In his pious home Shakespeare was allowed only in Dr
Bowdler's edition, 'The Heart of Midlothian' and 'David
Copperfield' were banned for indecency.

The boy was ill at ease with his grim father and
adored his fervent mother - a condition apt to obstruct
later love for other women.   Moreover he was permanently
unmanned by mumps just before adolescence: his voice
never broke, and he 'cultivated a capacity for friendship
which, untroubled by physical desire, could develop into
a devotion characteristically feminine in its tenderness.'

At nineteen he proceeded with a scholarship to
Trinity, Cambridge, where he was tutored by Verrall, the
great Hellenist, and made friends with the two Trevel-
yans, G.E. Moore, Bertrand Russell, Maurice Baring and
Desmond MacCarthy.   He thought these friends too cens-
orious about the sins of the flesh - especially Moore
(whose later disciples often tended to laxity).

It seems so strange that there should be people who
don't know the two ways of caring about people, the
one mainly through the senses, the other through the
mind.

This double thread in his own temperament was always
to disconcert austere friends, but helped his understand-
ing of Horace and La Fontaine, D.H. Lawrence and Mr
Forster.

Though a dazzling examinee, he seems never to have
desired an academic career, and entered the Colonial
Office, where young Mr Churchill selected him as Private
Secretary in 1905.   (Mr Hassall seems to think that
Marsh helped to fight the ensuing by-election, which
would not have been possible for a civil servant.)   He
had not much flair or feeling for politics apart from his
long devotion to Sir Winston, with whom, however, he dis-
agreed about Munich.

There was always in him something boyish, not to say

silly.   In his later years, for instance, he dismayed
some of his old friends by what they thought a blind
passion for the theatre.   This book proves that he was
not so undiscriminating a playgoer as he often seemed.
In any case he was by nature scholarly rather than int-
ellectual, enthusiastic rather than critical, a man of
wide culture in the eighteenth-century style and a friend
to highbrows rather than a highbrow himself.

His translations of Horace and La Fontaine are neat but
the diction is stale: they traduce the originals by
giving the sense without the poetry.   As a reviser of
his friends' writings he came into his own: Sir Winston
and Mr Maugham have testified magnificently to the help he
gave them, and kindness kept him always ready also to im-
prove the work of secondary writers like myself.   An app-
endix here displays his method.

Mr Hassall subtitles his book 'Patron of the Arts',
thus rightly indicating Marsh's supreme claim to attent-
ion.   Who else with so little money to spare has been so
generous to painters and authors?   The small grant he
received as a descendant of the murdered Perceval was de-
voted entirely to succour for the gifted;   and so were
the royalties he received for his memoir of Rupert Brooke.
Gertler, Middleton Murry, D.H. Lawrence, James Joyce,
Robert Graves and Dylan Thomas were among those whom he
rescued from emergencies with presents of cash.   Painters
he usually helped by purchasing their pictures, which cov-
ered the doors as well as the walls in his chambers.   His
beautiful Richard Wilson he gave in his lifetime to the
National Gallery;   all his modern pictures he bequeathed
to the Contemporary Art Society (of which he was for fif-
teen years the chairman);   and they have now been distrib-
uted among the museums of this country and the Common-
wealth.

His editorship of 'Georgian Poetry' is more controver-
sial.   The first volume appeared in 1912 with a preface
signed 'E.M.', and included work by Lascelles Abercrombie,
Gordon Bottomley, Rupert Brooke, Chesterton, W.H. Davies,
de la Mare, Flecker, D.H. Lawrence, Masefield, and James
Stephens.   Housman would not contribute: 'If you want to
get poetry out of me you must be either a relative or a
duchess, and you are neither.'   Ezra Pound refused the
two poems he had been asked for because he was about to
publish them in a volume of his own.

There was thus at first no thought of championing one
school of poetry against another.   But four further vol-
umes appeared, and in these Marsh turned a blind eye to
certain newcomers, notably Mr Eliot and the three Sit-
wells.   None of us can hope to be good judges of

imaginative work by men thirty years younger than our-
selves, but he was still in his forties and might have
been expected to show greater acumen: my sympathies were
violently and I think rightly with the innovators.   Marsh
had a narrower taste in verse, on which he considered him-
self an expert, than in painting, which he judged intuit-
ively 'by the pricking of his thumbs'.

In his fifth volume of 'Georgian Poetry' which appeared
in 1922 the new names included Edmund Blunden, Peter
Quennell and V. Sackville-West - a proof of the editor's
continuing alertness.   Yet he wisely decided not to con-
tinue the series: he had achieved his aim, which was not
to impose his individual taste but to enlarge the public
for current verse.   His first volume bowled me over
before I went to Oxford, and I retain a strong taste for
several of the contributors.   Everyone would presumably
agree about the virtue of de la Mare and D.H. Lawrence
(whose verse resists the ravages of time better in my op-
inion than most of his prose).   Let me place a word
about Rupert Brooke.

Those war-sonnets, his tragic death and Marsh's adoring
memoir lent his reputation the brief brilliance of a
meteor.   The memoir was bowdlerised to meet his mother's
requirements (could not the original version now be pub-
lished?) but she merely intensified her neurotic jealousy
and dislike of Marsh, whom she treated with monstrous in-
gratitude.

A contemporary of Brooke's who knew him far better
than Marsh said to me years ago, 'Rupert was not so nice
as people now think, but he was more clever by a long
chalk.'   Though he had a strain of paranoia, he might if
he had lived have become one of our best writers;   and
the poems written under the influence of the Metaphysicals
seem likely to survive.   Flecker also deserves in my view
to be remembered: at his best he was a master of versif-
ication whose lines, like Kipling's, lodge themselves in
the memory.

Among the sayings recorded by Marsh for their influence
upon him was one by Conrad Russell (whom we have lately
met in Lady Diana Cooper's new volume): 'I think that
one's first duty is to make life as pleasant as one can
for the people one is thrown with.'   Not content with
living up to this Marsh sought out gifted people in order
to make life as pleasant for them as he could, sacrificing
his own comfort to this purpose.   This biography forms an
extended illustration of 'Good Nature considered as a Fine
Art'.

74.   'LARGER THAN LIFE?', UNSIGNED ARTICLE, 'THE TIMES
LITERARY SUPPLEMENT'

12 June 1959, 345-6

Unsigned review of Christopher Hassall, 'Edward Marsh: A
Biography'.

In the preface to his well-written, candid and affection-
ate tribute to the late Sir Edward Marsh, Mr Christopher
Hassall tells us how, while clearing out the attic of the
tiny house in Walton Street in which Marsh spent his de-
clining years, and in which in January, 1953, he died, he
came upon 'old letters dumped in their thousands in an
area about four feet wide by six'.   It is this mass of
papers, richly supplemented by extracts from Marsh's own
letters, the verbal reminiscences of Marsh's many friends,
and Mr Hassall's own intimate knowledge of his subject
which form the sources from which he has compiled his
book.
     This material once assembled and sorted, Mr Hassall
was, then, faced with the bleak and daunting problem that
confronts all biographers - how best to synthesize it all
so as to create a true and lifelike image of his hero.
Scheme, scale and style are the hallmarks of a good bio-
graphy.   Of style it may at once be said that Mr Hassall
writes a vivid, easy English prose which, as befits a
pupil of Sir Edward Marsh, is also scrupulously correct.
Schematically he has decided that Marsh's life falls into
six distinct phases and he has organized his book accord-
ingly.   So far so good - but what of scale?   Here some
may think that he falls down.   Running to more than 700
pages, the biography contains many passages which are re-
dundant and many others which are dull.   It is in no way
disrespectful to Sir Edward Marsh's reputation as scholar,
patron of the arts, compère of the Georgian poets, Civil
servant, friend and conversationalist to suggest that his
memory would have been better served by a monograph of
the length of Carlyle's life of John Sterling than by a
biography conceived upon the massive scale of the volume
under review.   Where he might have erected a graceful urn
or an elegant small obelisk, Mr Hassall has chosen to con-
struct a literary monument analogous in size to the Vic-
toria Memorial.
     On biographical method, as upon all other aspects of

the art of writing, Edward Marsh himself held sage and
positive views.   In a note to Lord Lytton, written in
1935 while the latter was at work upon a memorial volume
on his son, Marsh referred to his own Memoir of Rupert
Brooke, published many years before in revealing terms.
'I see now', he wrote, 'that in choosing my material I
asked myself two questions: (1)   Is this essential or
helpful to the portrait I am drawing?   (2)   Should I en-
joy reading this if it were about someone I didn't know?
If the answer to *either* question (not necessarily both)
were Yes, in it went.'   How many times, we wonder as we
read this book, has Mr Hassall asked himself these quest-
ions - and the second question in particular?   There is
a lack of selectivity in his handling of much of the mat-
erial, so that one feels that large heaps of the contents
of the Walton Street attic have been bodily transferred
to another repository - this book.

Mr Hassall's preface - a model of its kind - shows
that he is keenly aware of the difficulties of re-creat-
ing upon paper a personality so essentially undramatic as
Edward Marsh, and of recording a life which was, above
all, a vicarious one, ruled by what he has very aptly
termed 'an insatiable need to be needed'.   Edward Marsh
was happy only in the reflection of those whom he admired.
Like certain stars or dead planets he could only shine in
the presence of his sun.

The book opens with a full account of the murder of
Edward Marsh's maternal great-grandfather, the Prime Min-
ister Spencer Perceval, in the Lobby of the House of Com-
mons in May, 1812.   This assassination was the occasion
of a public grant of £50,000 to Perceval's family.   It
was the residue of a portion of this money which Marsh
inherited during his lifetime, and it was this modest
capital which enabled him to give ready and generous help
to struggling young painters and writers, and to form his
collection of examples of contemporary British paintings.
While other men would certainly have made use of this in-
heritance to increase the comfort of their daily lives,
Edward Marsh regarded it as a trust to be devoted by him
to the benefit of others, and specifically to encourage
English art and literature in his day.   Beneath his bed
he kept the red leather dispatch box which Perceval was
carrying when he was shot by Bellenger in 1812, and what
he liked to call the 'murder money' was itself safely in-
vested, and the income judiciously and imaginatively
doled out to those in most need.   Had he not many other
claims to be remembered, such selflessness would be suff-
icient alone.   Almost without exception - indeed, the
only exception is the series of bitter letters from

Rupert Brooke's mother - the letters to Marsh which Mr
Hassall quotes are letters of sincere and heartfelt grat-
itude for the right aid given at the right time.

Considerable space is devoted to Sir Edward's career
as a Civil servant, but save that it brought him into
long and intimate collaboration with Sir Winston Church-
ill, in whom he found an ideal subject for his innate
need to hero-worship, this career was uneventful.   Ad-
miration for the character, attainments or physical app-
earance of others, profound diffidence about his own
gifts, formed the key to Marsh's character.   This cap-
acity for admiration led him into many charming incon-
sistencies - so that we find the severe stylist and
scholarly translator of Horace becoming an enthusiastic
follower of the successes of the late Ivor Novello's
musical comedies.   One of the great merits of Mr Hass-
all's book is that he makes no attempt to conceal these
inconsistencies, treating his old friend with a disarming
combination of affection and detachment.   Marsh's whole
personality lies embedded in the book - his kindness, his
refusal to compromise in stylistic matters, his contempt
for the slipshod in writing, his prejudices and his en-
thusiasms are all here to the life.   So, too, is his
curious quick, fluted manner of speaking and his little
verbal puns and quips.   But at times we lose sight of
him altogether.   Reading this book is like chasing a
will o' the wisp through a very dense wood.

Sir Edward Marsh was not a man of action.   Mr Hassall
makes the excellent point that the only major decision he
took in his life 'was, paradoxically, a negative one -
not to accompany Lord Gladstone to Pretoria in 1909'.
Had he accepted this offer (he preferred to stay on in
London as Mr Churchill's Private Secretary) there would,
as Mr Hassall explains, have been no 'Georgian Poetry',
little patronage of painting 'and both the work and life
(perhaps even the duration of life) of Rupert Brooke
would have been other than they were'.   To-day it is ex-
tremely difficult to assess the exact literary worth of
the movement which Marsh and Monro together dubbed 'Geor-
gian Poetry';   for it is at once too early and too late -
too early to be certain which of these poets will survive
by their own merits, too late to share the enthusiasm
which greeted the successive appearances of Marsh's five
volumes of anthology.   It is indeed baffling even to de-
termine just how far the 'movement' was a cohesive move-
ment at all, how far it was dictated by Marsh's own per-
sonal tastes.   Mr Hassall devotes many, many pages to
the making of these anthologies, and we may fancy that
literary historians of the future will find his biography

of Marsh an essential source-book into which to delve.
But, apart from Marsh himself, the central figure of the
book is Rupert Brooke, for although he died young he con-
tinued to haunt Edward Marsh for the rest of his life.
Brooke's reputation has diminished with the passage of
years, but the fact remains that Mr Hassall's account of
his relationship to Marsh, and, later, of Marsh's battles
with Brooke's widowed mother over his Memoir of her son
and the question of copyright in the poems, forms the
most interesting portion of this book.

It was in November, 1906, while staying with his
father at Cambridge that Edward Marsh first set eyes on
Rupert Brooke.   Dressed in papier-mâché armour, with a
short cloak of red, blue and gold, and wearing a scarlet
wig, Brooke, complete with property trumpet, was taking
the part of a herald in the Amateur Dramatic Club's per-
formance of the 'Eumenides'.   Just up from Rugby, Brooke
was nineteen years old and a freshman of King's.   At
this first meeting nothing of interest transpired, and it
was not until two years later that Marsh and the young
poet became friends.   The friendship once formed, Marsh
devoted himself heart and soul to encouraging Brooke, and
to helping to make him known.   During Brooke's lifetime
he aided him as Charles Armitage Brown aided Keats;
after Brooke's death he set to work to do for him what
Monckton Milnes had done for Keats.   The only differ-
ence was that Brooke was not of the stature of John
Keats.

Mr Hassall gives us in fascinating detail the hitherto
unpublished story of Marsh's conflicts with Rupert
Brooke's mother over the publication of his Memoir of her
son.   A conventional, religious woman, who disliked the
tone of some of her son's poems, and distrusted Marsh's
presentation of him to the public, Mrs Brooke seems to
have concentrated on thwarting and vexing her son's
friend in every way.   As the years went by she developed
an uncanny gift for hurting and annoying Edward Marsh -
rejecting the original and several other versions of his
Memoir, bowdlerizing it, changing passages, appearing to
agree, only to forbid publication at the last moment.
The resulting Memoir, published in 1918, was only a trav-
esty of the first draft, and it seems a pity that Mr
Hassall could not, at this distance of time, produce a
small edition of the original work.   Mr Hassall carries
us through all the complexities, the cross-purposes and
the misunderstandings of Marsh's correspondence with Mrs
Brooke.   It was an endless-seeming conflict - on the one
hand Edward Marsh, who almost felt that Rupert Brooke was
his invention, a species of sacred private property, and

Mrs Brooke, who felt that she was, after all, the poet's
mother, and who was ruthless in her determination to
defeat and humiliate Marsh.   It was Mrs Brooke who won in
the end, by leaving a will in which he was excluded from
all those rights as literary executor which Brooke himself
had wished Marsh to possess.

Apart from Rupert Brooke and the Georgian poets Marsh
had three great passions: the collection of contemporary
British paintings, a love of the theatre and a great taste
(acquired in his youth in Edwardian London) for social
life.   Mr Hassall affectionately describes the crowded
rooms at Raymond Buildings, with pictures thick upon the
walls and even covering the doors, as well as the daily
life of Marsh's household, presided over by his deaf,
devoted housekeeper, Mrs Elgy.   In his discerning en-
couragement of young painters, as well as by his purchase
of their works, Edward Marsh found the same satisfaction
as he did in anthologizing the Georgians, and this sense
of achievement, in a life from which the most immediate
of all satisfactions was denied him, brought him true
happiness.   As he aged Marsh was fortunate enough to be
able to add two other satisfying occupations to these -
his translations of Horace and La Fontaine, and his still
more remarkable translation of Fromentin's 'Dominique',
which he made for the first time available in English;
and, secondly, the task which he called 'diabolization'
and which he was uniquely equipped to carry out.   'Diab-
olization' was the art of reading the manuscripts and
proofs of his writer friends, emending their style,
pointing out inconsistencies or vulgarities, teaching
them, as he was always emphasizing, to 'listen' to what
they wrote.   Besides Mr Somerset Maugham and Sir Winston
Churchill there are many, and younger, writers living to-
day who owe a vast and permanent debt to Sir Edward
Marsh.   Amiable in every other rôle in his life, Marsh
became in this one of 'diabolizer' most salutarily
severe.   He would never give way on the position of the
slightest comma if he was convinced that he was right.
In an appendix to this volume, Mr Hassall has most appo-
sitely printed at length Sir Edward's comments on a spec-
imen book which was submitted to him for diabolization -
Mr Somerset Maugham's 'The Summing Up'.   This appendix,
together with Mr Hassall's own vivid account of Marsh's
routine and procedure during the reading and discussion
of a new book, will be of durable value and interest to
all those who are trying to write.   But it is, as indeed
it should be, Mr Christopher Hassall's own limpid and
flexible style throughout this biography which proves to
us how much Sir Edward Marsh had to offer and to teach.

Appendix
Contributors to 'Georgian Poetry'
1911-22

The contributors to 'Georgian Poetry' are listed alpha-
betically, the order chosen by Edward Marsh for four of
the five volumes (with a small modification in the second)
and reversed for volume III. Numbers in brackets after
each refer to the volumes in which the poet appeared; it
will be noticed that only five of the poets appeared in
all five, and eighteen of them in one only. The brief
critical and biographical details appended refer chiefly
to the period covered by 'Georgian Poetry', and are taken
where appropriate from contemporary sources: in partic-
ular from the Marsh Letter Collection (see 'Letters to an
Editor, Georgian Poetry 1912-22. An Exhibition from the
Berg Collection' in 'Bulletin of The New York Public
Library', January-December 1967, 277-305), and from the
notes by 'Recorder' (chiefly = Harold Monro) in 'The
Chapbook', June 1920. The whole of this issue of 'The
Chapbook' was given to 'A Bibliography of Modern Poetry
with Notes on some contemporary poets': quotations from
it are indicated by the initials 'H.M.'.

LASCELLES ABERCROMBIE 1881-1938   (I, II, IV, V)

One of the first to be invited by Marsh, Lascelles Aber-
crombie seems to have been overvalued as a poet by many
of his contemporaries. Like Robert Bridges, he achieved
the unusual distinction of publication as an 'Oxford
Standard Author' in his lifetime. Among his many books
was an early study of 'Thomas Hardy' (1912). He became
lecturer in poetry at Liverpool University (1919), Prof-
essor of English Literature at Leeds University (1922-9),
and Professor of English Literature at Bedford College,
London (1929-35). In 1935 he became Goldsmith's Reader
at Oxford and Fellow of Merton. See short memoir by

Oliver Elton, 'Lascelles Abercrombie 1881-1938', from the
'Proceedings of the British Academy', vol. xxv.

> Emotion felt through the intellect and represented by
> abstract speech characterises most of his work.   Al-
> though the sense of drama is unusually keen, the imag-
> ination fertile and the verse accomplished, the reader
> is continually baffled by the wilful way in which plain
> thought is made to appear intellectual and direct
> speech *tortured* out of its normal course.   He is, as
> it were, chipping granite with a blunt chisel and the
> result is neither satisfactory to the poet nor the
> reader.   Having overcome these difficulties the
> student will find Mr Abercrombie one of the best
> verse-writers of to-day because his intellectual force
> is such that he is bound to appeal to those who require
> more than nightingales and stars in poetry.   His in-
> fluence is to be found in a number of his contempor-
> aries. [H.M.]

MARTIN ARMSTRONG b. 1882 (V)

Martin Armstrong's first book, 'Exodus and Other Poems',
was published in 1912.   He served in France on the West-
ern Front.   Robert Nichols attacked 'Miss Thompson Goes
Shopping' in a letter to Marsh: '... too easy - the
curse of Georgian easiness.   Why, damn it - I could
write such in my sleep.'   Marsh thought it was 'exquis-
ite, and must have taken an enormous effort of thought
and skill'.   He was literary editor of 'The Spectator'
(1922-4).   His 'Collected Poems' were published in 1931.

[THE HON.] HERBERT ASQUITH 1881-1947 (III)

Herbert Asquith was son of the Prime Minister (1908-16).
He was president of the Oxford Union, and was called to
the Bar in 1907.   A captain in the Royal Artillery, he
served on the Western Front.   The reviewer in 'The Times
Literary Supplement' (25 November 1920, 772) wrote un-
flatteringly but not unfairly about Asquith's 'A Village
Sermon and Other Poems', which was reviewed with Dorothy
Wellesley's 'Poems':

> If [the two poets] had some idea to convey to us
> beyond the commonplace, or some emotion with a wide
> and noble appeal, we should not apply the microscope
> in such a manner.   Liberation is what we seek in

poetry; but if a poet only transports us from our own
prison to his, there is nothing for us but to pick
holes in the walls of our cell.

Asquith wrote four volumes of poems, four novels and a
memoir.

[THE HON.] MAURICE BARING 1874-1945 (III)

Maurice Baring, the fourth son of Lord Revelstoke, joined
the Diplomatic Service, and later became a foreign cor-
respondent to 'The Morning Post' and 'The Times'.   He
served in the Intelligence Corps, 1914, and was attached
to the Royal Flying Corps and later the R.A.F.   He was
opposed to 'representativeness', and also to the spirit
of Sassoon's and Rosenberg's war poems.   Reciprocally,
some Georgians resented the inclusion of his 'In Memor-
iam, A.H.'; its references to Hector and Achilles, Lan-
celot and Tristram, not to mention the Almighty ('You
chose the noblest way.   God did the rest') were thought
to reflect an attitude which had died with Brooke and
Grenfell.

A gentleman of social importance.   A capable govern-
ment servant both in the diplomatic service and army.
His prose is well informed and in excellent style.
His verse has a certain elegance.   It is reminiscent
but at the same time bears the stamp of his training.
[H.M.]

A prolific writer (travel, biography, literary and art
criticism, memoirs), his 'Collected Poems' were pub-
lished in 1911 and 1925.

EDMUND BLUNDEN 1896-1974 (V)

Edmund Blunden was the only new poet to be well received
by critics of V.   He served as lieutenant with the
Royal Sussex Regiment in the First World War, a time
about which he wrote memorably in 'Undertones of War'
(1928).   Early volumes of poetry appeared in 1914, 1916,
1920 ('The Waggoner and Other Poems'), and 1922 ('The
Shepherd', which won the Hawthornden Prize).   He was
Professor of English Literature, Tokyo (1924-7), Fellow
and Tutor of Merton College, Oxford (1931-44), Professor
of English in Hong Kong in 1953 (Emeritus 1964), and
Professor of Poetry at Oxford (1966-8).   'The Waggoner'

was reviewed in 'The London Mercury', probably by J.C. Squire:

> ... of all the poets who have emerged since the war
> Mr Blunden is the one whose position is most secure.
>   Mr Blunden's subject - though many of his poems
> have subsidiary subjects - is the landscape of South-
> Eastern England. He writes of it like a countryman,
> but an observant countryman. He relishes not merely
> the large and obvious effects of Nature but the small
> day-to-day occurrences. He is, that is to say, in
> the tradition of Edward Thomas, the poet, and Richard
> Jefferies, the essayist; but he has a power of music
> which surpasses them both. ['The London Mercury',
> September 1920, 624-5.]

GORDON BOTTOMLEY 1874-1948 (I, II, III, IV)

Bottomley asked Marsh to omit him from V on the plea that
he had nothing to submit: 'And don't think me ungrateful
or inappreciative about G.P.; in any success I have had
it has been by far the largest factor.' He bitterly re-
gretted this decision when he learned, in 1926, that
there were to be no more collections. See headnote to
No. 20.

> He has a fine poetic mind. He writes mainly what may
> be called psychological studies and appears to be only
> interested in the world from this standpoint. He
> gives clear and definite pictures of country life and
> scenery. In 'King Lear's Wife' he succeeds in re-
> creating the barbarous, lecherous atmosphere of early
> English life. [H.M.]

'Poems of Thirty Years' were published in 1925.

RUPERT BROOKE 1887-1915 (I, II)

Reviewing Rupert Brooke's posthumous '1914 and Other
Poems', 'Solomon Eagle' (J.C. Squire) wrote:

> Brooke's name a few weeks after his death is known to
> a public a hundred times more numerous than that which
> knew him in life. A myth has been created: but it
> has grown round an imaginary figure very different from
> the real man. ['The New Statesman', 26 June 1915,
> 281.]

Intellect and cynicism.   A child of the age: a dis-
ciple of the Jacobeans, bringing modernity to their
style.   It is difficult to tell how far his reputat-
ion was the result of a much liked and remarkable per-
sonality and of those sonnets written at the period of
his own and the nation's white hot condition of inter-
national antagonism promoted by the European War.
His influence on the poetry of the last five years is
incalculable and uncalculated.   [H.M.]

The subject of several biographies and critical works,
Brooke needs no fuller mention here.

GILBERT K[EITH]. CHESTERTON 1874-1936 (I)

Housman suggested G.K. Chesterton for inclusion in the
first volume.   Robert H. Ross comments: 'Marsh's jud-
icious mixture of a dram of the old with liberal portions
of the new, though it may have slightly vitiated the head-
iness of the new wine, did much to increase its market
value among those with untrained or traditional palates'
('The Georgian Revolt', 1967, 121).   Chesterton's first
poems, 'The Wild Knight' and 'Greybeards at Play', had
appeared in 1900, and in the remaining thirty-six years
of his life he was to publish a hundred books, his first
novel, 'The Napoleon of Notting Hill', appearing in 1904
and the first collection of Father Brown stories, 'The
Innocence of Father Brown', in 1911.   Critical and bio-
graphical studies included 'Dickens' (1906), 'Thackeray'
(1909), 'Shaw' (1910), and 'The Victorian Age in Liter-
ature' (1913).   After his conversion to Roman Catholi-
cism in 1922, many of his books dealt with religious
subjects, notably 'St Francis of Assisi' (1923) and
'Aquinas' (1933).   His 'Collected Poems' were pub-
lished in 1933.   Eleven more books have been compiled
posthumously from his uncollected writings, and over
thirty have been written about him and his work, includ-
ing Maisie Ward's biography (1944) and Dudley Barker's
(1973).   John Sullivan, author of 'G.K. Chesterton: a
Bibliography' (1968), edited 'G.K. Chesterton: a Centen-
ary Appraisal' (1974) to which W.H. Auden contributed a
chapter on the verse.   Although Chesterton was 'essent-
ially a comic poet' and wrote 'some of the best pure non-
sense verse in English', he wrote serious poems also, of
which Auden names 'The Sword of Surprise' as one which
'any poet would be proud to have written'.

The modern ballad-writer and jester.   Mr Chesterton

also writes skilful and charming lyrics in conventional
rhythms.   He is typically English.   He is never un-
interesting because of his sincerity and his humour.
[H.M.]

WILLIAM H[ENRY]. DAVIES 1871-1940 (I, II, III, IV, V)

Marsh did not know W.H. Davies when he wrote for permiss-
ion to include him in I.   Davies insisted on helping him
make the selection.   In return, he attempted to produce
work of greater finish and complexity, and to strike a
'strong note'.   Later he even allowed Marsh to cut lines
of his poems.

>These poems are as natural as a bird's song.   When the
>poet is happy he sings gaily of the sun or the moon, of
>the good drinks he has had and hopes to have.   When he
>is sad he laments, in true bird fashion, that there
>should be cruelty, greed and unhappiness .....   He is
>typically English.   He links the present with the
>past.   Though his form is conventional, his thought
>and expression are always fresh and original.   [H.M.]

Davies's first book, 'The Soul's Destroyer' (1907), was
written in, and published from, a doss-house.   His 'Who's
Who' entry used to read, 'became a poet at 34 years of
age; been one ever since'.   His 'Autobiography of a
Super-Tramp' was published in 1908.   'The Poems of W.H.
Davies' were published in 1934, and 'The Complete Poems'
(including some 113 he had suppressed) in 1963.

WALTER DE LA MARE 1873 ⁻¹⁹⁵⁶ (I, II, III, IV, V)

Walter de la Mare was one of the first poets Marsh app-
roached.   He was included in every volume - although he
several times questioned Marsh's wisdom in including him!
His first book, 'Songs of Childhood', appeared in 1902
under the pen-name of 'Walter Ramal'.   Collected editions
of his poems have appeared from 1906 to the present day.

>The poet of the unconscious.   Mr de la Mare is con-
>cerned with that supposed unreality that lies behind
>apparently real events.   He cannot see a tree without
>looking beyond it to that 'other world' in which all
>living takes place.   When he sees a child he sees all
>the phases of childhood that make up the child of the
>moment, as separate children that have lived and died.

His rhythms are entirely his own and his method of
using them follows directly on the method of his
thought. His understanding and expression of child
psychology has none of the insolent condescension that
is usually found in child-poems. He is just as succ-
essful when giving a definite and accurate picture of
a small girl finding her mother unexpectedly asleep in
her chair as he is when creating a marvellous and mus-
ical vision of Arabia from the sound of the word as it
strikes his senses. His followers are legion.
[H.M.]

W.H. Auden made an interesting critical point in his
introduction to 'A Choice of de la Mare's Verse' (1963)
21:

As the work of some of the Georgian poets bears wit-
ness, the danger of the English landscape as a poetic
ingredient is that its gentleness can tempt those who
love it into writing genteelly. De la Mare was pro-
tected from this, firstly by his conviction that what
our senses perceive of the world about us is not all
there is to know, and, secondly, by his sense of the
powers of evil.

'The Times Literary Supplement' (16 May 1912) captured
another of de la Mare's perennial qualities in a review
of 'The Listeners and Other Poems' which concludes: 'He
is not concerned with himself, but with those whispering
voices which he listens for; and often he gives us their
music, so that we know he is reporting truly what he has
heard.'

JOHN DRINKWATER 1882-1937 (I, II, III, IV, V)

John Drinkwater was the son of a schoolteacher who turned
actor, and he, though an insurance clerk for twelve
years, was likewise attracted to the stage. He spent
much of the war years working with (Sir) Barry Jackson at
the Birmingham Rep., and wrote the war play 'X = O'
(1917). As reported (Introduction, p. 6), he was
present at the inaugural luncheon for 'Georgian Poetry'.
A leading Georgian, he appears like Abercrombie to have
been overvalued by his contemporaries. Unlike Aber-
crombie, however, he has been allowed a modest place in
'The Oxford Book of Twentieth Century Verse'.

This poet has published more than almost any other

Georgian. He is *poetical* on every subject. He is
openly and plainly the descendant of the English
poets. His verse shows how well he has assimilated
and reproduced them. His thought is usually common-
place and an exhaustive examination of his work leads
to the conclusion that he expresses himself, not in
the manner that is actually natural to him, but as he
feels a poet should. He belongs to that literary
tradition that believes in the torch from hand to hand.
[H.M.]

JAMES ELROY FLECKER 1884-1915 (I, II)

Flecker was introduced to Marsh by his Cambridge friend,
Brooke. His first book of poetry, 'The Bridge of Fire',
was published in 1908, his play 'Hassan' posthumously in
1922.

The work of this poet stands almost by itself to-day
as the production of a man who believed the basis of
all verse to be *craftsmanship*. He declared himself a
disciple of the French 'Parnassian' school. He took
his art very seriously and honestly. No poem app-
eared in print until he had assured himself that it
was as finely polished and chiselled as was consistent
with its subject; and the imagery represented the
idea as exactly as was possible through the medium of
words. The definiteness of form and rhythm is con-
spicuous in his later work. ..... Flecker's in-
fluence on the 'young' poetry of to-day is too evident
to be calculated. [H.M.]

JOHN FREEMAN 1880-1929 (III, IV, V)

John Freeman rose rapidly from clerk to director of the
London Victoria Friendly Society. He became Chief Exec-
utive Officer in the Department of National Health and
Insurance. His letters to Marsh show how dependent he
was on Marsh's encouragement. He felt dissatisfied with
what he called his 'little lyrical gasps'. He was
awarded the Hawthornden Prize in 1920. His 'Collected
Poems' were published in 1928.

It is easier to say of John Freeman that his style is
good, than to read his poems for the pleasure that
style may give. There is no doubt the volume of con-
tent is disproportionate to, which is to say, in excess
of, the bulk of emotional value. [H.M.]

WILFRID WILSON GIBSON 1878-1962 (I, II, III, IV, V)

Wilfrid Gibson was a social worker in the East End of
London.   He served in the ranks in 1914, but spent only
a short time at the Front.   He was another poet present
at the inaugural luncheon, and had published several
books before that, the first in 1902; but not until
'Daily Bread' (1910) did he show his real power.   'Fires'
which followed in 1912 was a still better book.   The
finest of his works, the long dramatic poem, 'Krindleskye'
(1922), has its roots in his native Northumberland.   Al-
though his 'Collected Poems' were published in 1925, he
was to write almost as much again before his death.

> The stages of Mr Gibson's development are most inter-
> esting as a keynote to the psychology of the literary
> mind.   He began with commonplace but ornamental
> verse, tried hard to find his bent and became inter-
> esting; worked it so hard that he exhausted it, and
> has now relapsed into his first stage without that
> 'exquisiteness' that characterises the young poet.
> [H.M.]

J. Middleton Murry wrote of Gibson's 'Fires' I (1912):

> This is a very wonderful book.   Not every poem in it
> is a masterpiece, indeed; but every poem is at
> least a direct presentment of the author's sense of
> reality, so direct, so sympathetic that it is imposs-
> ible but to go on reading, and to feel that here is a
> poet who has created some new beauty because he
> sought, not prettiness, but the profounder realities
> of life ... ['Rhythm' IV, spring 1912, 35.]

ROBERT GRAVES b. 1895 (III, IV, V)

Robert Graves served in France with the Royal Welch Fus-
iliers.   After the war he became Professor of English
Literature at Cairo.   In 1961 he succeeded W.H. Auden as
Professor of Poetry at Oxford.   He was still a schoolboy
at Charterhouse when he was introduced to Marsh by George
Mallory (the Everest mountaineer and friend of Rupert
Brooke) who was then teaching there.   III did not please
Graves, but he none the less agreed to appear in each of
the later volumes.   He dedicated 'Whipperginny' (1923)
to Marsh.   Graves has published about a hundred books.
Although he is perhaps best known for his early auto-
biography, 'Goodbye to All That' (1929), one of the most

vivid books about the First World War, and for such
novels as 'I, Claudius' (1934) and 'Claudius the God'
(also 1934), he has always said that his prose was
written for bread-and-butter so that he could live to
write poetry.   'The White Goddess' (1948) is a sort of
biography of the Muse of Poetry; his craftsmanship, he
claims, is taught by service to this Muse, who is unposs-
essable and never satisfied, and he prefers those poems
inspired by her to those which are commissioned by
Apollo, God of Reason.   His first 'Collected Poems'
appeared in 1926, and in each subsequent collection (1938,
1947, 1959) he has suppressed those poems which no longer
satisfy him, often to the regret of his readers, so that
the most recent collection is not much longer than the
first.   Monro's 1920 comment serves as little more than
a literary curiosity:

> A product of the war.   Light verse of the nursery
> rhyme variety.   Occasionally there is a genuine old
> ballad feeling that makes insignificant work attract-
> ive.   The three books already published show him
> still in the chrysalis stage.   [H.M.]

Graves has since written so much so well both in verse
and prose, and has been so widely acclaimed, that
further comment here would seem unnecessary.

RALPH HODGSON 1871-1962 (II, III)

Ralph Hodgson's small early book, 'The Last Blackbird',
was published in 1907, but Marsh did not have his work
until after I was published, and was disappointed upon
first acquaintance with it.   The impact of 'The Bull'
and 'The Song of Honour' (1913), supported by James
Stephens's recommendation, won them a place in II.

> Those who say dismally that there is no poetry to-day
> to compare with the great poetry of the past are ad-
> vised to read Ralph Hodgson's poems.   They will find
> in him the real descendant of all the 'great' poets.
> He brings a freshness of mind, a wealth of language
> and imagery, and a sustained power of expression such
> as have seldom been equalled in all the centuries of
> English poetry.   He is entirely modern in spirit and
> writes in the language of the day.   He gives the lie
> to those who believe there is nothing more to be. done
> with the old forms.   As long as poetry lasts these
> poems will remain.   [H.M.]

A three-column article on his poems in 'The Times Liter-
ary Supplement', 7 October 1915, 342, concludes:

> Fundamental brainwork has long been acknowledged as
> essential to the writing of poetry; fundamental
> heart-work is as indispensable.   A man is half dead
> who exists without either; a poet without them has
> not yet been born at all .....
>   ..... as regards Mr Hodgson's [poetry] there can be
> no half-heartedness.   Nothing more 'original' has been
> written of late years.   And it depends for its origin-
> ality on its pure singleness of spirit and purpose.
> There is little of the metaphorical, very little imag-
> ery, practically no allusiveness, nothing elaborate or
> literary.   It is bare, vivid, wasteless - as near
> action as words can be.   It serves life; it serves
> beauty.   And its beauty and music is as much its own
> as its love and faith and courage are his that made it.

James Reeves ends his biographical note in 'Georgian
Poetry' (1962), 159: 'In 1924 he went to Japan and later
took up residence in the United States' - in the circum-
stances, a somewhat grandiose phrase for he lived in a
hermit's cottage.   Reeves does not mention Hodgson's
surprise reappearance in 1959 with 'The Skylark and Other
Poems': moreover the publication of his anthology coin-
cided with that of Hodgson's 'Collected Poems', shortly
followed by his death at ninety.   'The Skylark' was the
subject of a front-page article in 'The Times Literary
Supplement', 13 February 1959, 77-8.

RICHARD HUGHES b. 1900 (V)

Richard Hughes, a friend of Peter Quennell, was just down
from Oxford when he first met Marsh, who had been im-
pressed by 'Gipsy-Night and Other Poems' (1922), his
first book.   His first play, 'The Sisters' Tragedy', was
produced in London in the same year.   'Confessio
Juvenis' (collected poems) was published in 1926.   He is
better known for his novels, such as 'A High Wind in Jam-
aica' (1929).   Hassall notes: 'Hughes and Quennell had
become the pride of their first patron, but they had
leanings towards the Georgian Opposition' ('Edward
Marsh', 1959, 500).   Monro complained to Marsh that the
inclusion of little 'jingles' like Hughes's 'Poets,
Painters, Puddings' only made the absence in V of first-
rate work the more painfully obvious.

WILLIAM KERR (V)

William Kerr's poems were brought to Marsh by Ivor
Gurney, the poet and composer (not included in 'Georgian
Poetry') who ended his days tragically in an asylum.
Kerr's only book of poems, 'The Apple Tree' (1927), con-
tains (p. 19) a prose-poem on that favourite Georgian
subject, 'The Moon'.

D[AVID]. H[ERBERT]. LAWRENCE 1885-1930 (I, II, IV, V)

It is sometimes forgotten that D.H. Lawrence, who wrote
ten novels, published in his lifetime ten books of poems.
His 'Complete Poems' were published in 1957.   Marsh ar-
gued so strongly for metrical formality against Law-
rence's concept of verse 'as a bird with wings flying and
lapsing through the air' that Lawrence called him 'a pol-
iceman in poetry' and mocked him with the poem 'Grief'.
One may wonder how aware Marsh can have been of the power-
ful sexual imagery of 'Snapdragon' (I).   An anonymous re-
viewer in 'The New Witness', 9 June 1922, 366, protested:

> Only Mr D.H. Laurence [sic] could have written the
> long poem which opens [the current issue of 'The
> English Review] and no one but he would have chosen
> 'Fish' as the subject of the poem in question.
> There is a tremendous vitality about the poem which
> grips one, but we are all getting a little weary of
> Mr Laurence's sex obsessions.

> Erotic poet of the modern intellectual school of
> eroticism.   Contrary to the usual custom, he seldom
> allows his head to control his heart.   In most love
> adventures he has to tell his readers *all*, and, for
> this reason, the most innocuous and harmless objects
> become portentous and terrible agents of sexual ex-
> citement, *vide* 'The Snapdragon'.   [H.M.]

FRANCIS LEDWIDGE 1891-1917 (II)

Lord Dunsany, who had helped Francis Ledwidge to win
public recognition in Ireland, called Marsh's attention to
his work.   As an Irish Nationalist, he was at first
against the English war, but later joined the Royal Irish
Fusiliers and served at the Western Front, where he con-
tinued to write of 'fairy places' and 'the little fields
that call across the world to me'.   Dunsany urged Marsh

to use his influence to get him home 'before he is
killed .....   I think he will be a national loss if he
is killed'.   The letter is dated 31 July 1917, the very
day on which Ledwidge died at the front.   In his last
letter to Marsh, he described the magic of the German
rockets over no-man's-land: 'like the end of a beautiful
world'.

JOHN MASEFIELD 1878-1967 (I, II, III)

At first reluctant to contribute (see Introduction,
p. 18), John Masefield was eventually won over.   He succ-
eeded Bridges as Poet Laureate in 1930.   His first poems,
'Salt-Water Ballads', were published in 1902, and among
numerous works in verse and prose are two plays, 'The
Tragedy of Nan' (1909) and 'Pompey the Great' (1910);
'The Everlasting Mercy' (1911) (see Introduction, pp. 8-9),
'Reynard the Fox' (1919), 'Collected Poems' (1923);
novels, including 'Sard Harker' (1924) and 'The Bird of
Dawning' (1933);   and the autobiographical 'So Long to
Learn' (1952) - which reflects his admiration for the
craft of Chaucer.

   Three personalities are revealed in the works of Mr
   Masefield - the poet, the reformer and the seaman.
   In his first book of poems he was both poet and sea-
   man;   later the seaman became subsidiary to the reform-
   er but never disappeared altogether.   His belief in
   the beauty that inhabits man and the universe, and his
   desire to be of use in the world are the driving im-
   pulses of his poetry.   His narrative poems are better
   than contemporary prose fiction;   some of them contain
   passages of startling beauty.   There is no space here
   to discuss his art in detail.   It is only possible to
   express a strong belief in his powers, and to recommend
   him to the reading public of to-day.   [H.M.]

HAROLD MONRO 1879-1932 (I, II, III, IV, V)

Harold Monro was born and brought up in Belgium, and
settled in London in 1911.   His work as an editor and as
founder of the Poetry Bookshop is mentioned elsewhere
(Introduction, pp. 24-8).   His 'Collected Poems' were
published in 1933.   In 'How I Began', Monro wrote:

   I think I only know one thing about myself for quite
   certain, which amounts to this: that if anyone can

.   imagine an earth without poetry he need not imagine me
        one of its inhabitants.   I have never been happy,
        partly because I have never been able to read as much
        or write nearly as well as I have desired .....
        ['T.P.'s Weekly', 4 April 1913, 419.]

In 'The Chapbook' for January 1923, which consisted
wholly of an annotated bibliography of contemporary
poetry on the lines of that from which exerpts have been
quoted, occurs the note: 'As Mr Monro is the Editor of
the 'Chapbook', it is not possible for his work to be
discussed in the body of the periodical.'   Such self-
denial had not obtained in 1920, when he enjoyed - could
it have been at his own hand? - one of the longest
mentions:

        One of the most original poets of the time.   He
        stands almost alone today in his preoccupation with
        the reality of the relation of man to the earth from
        which he came.   In his early books this thought was
        firmly suppressed by the force of a merely ornamental
        and poetic diction;   afterwards rejected in favour of
        'human' interests.   In 'Before Dawn' it was recog-
        nized but was not sufficiently powerful to prevent its
        being covered by a thin veil of mysticism.   'Children
        of Love' saw it bursting its shell, and in 'Strange
        Meetings' it escaped right out into the open and took
        possession of his mind.   This discovery of his funda-
        mental belief enabled him to control his rhythms so
        that they were always subservient to, and expressive
        of, the value of their emotional content.   In 'Trees',
        for instance, it enables him to reach a height of ex-
        ultation that hardly would have seemed possible in the
        author of 'Before Dawn', who, however original may
        have been his ideas, did not entirely succeed.   From
        the technical point of view the last two books are the
        most interesting, showing as they do the poet in full
        possession of his mind.   [H.M.]

T[HOMAS]. STURGE MOORE 1870-1944 (I)

Thomas Sturge Moore was the elder brother of G.E. Moore,
the Cambridge philosopher, who was a contemporary and
friend of Marsh.   He was unenthusiastic about the plans
for 'Georgian Poetry', and made his own inclusion in it
conditional on Marsh's acceptance of R.C. Trevelyan's
'Dirge'.   Marsh capitulated, which was uncharacteristic
of him, and also accepted Moore's suggestion of Flecker

(previously proposed by Brooke); but he rejected suggestions of Yeats and Binyon. Sturge Moore's first book of poems had been published in the previous century, and he was by a year the oldest contributor. His 'Collected Poems' were published in four volumes in 1932-3.

> One of the best poets. He has a definite and well-balanced theory of the use of words and rhythm in poetry. He is always literary and intellectual. His feeling for drama is greatly evident in 'A Sicilian Idyll'. His two last books are well suited to the young, and the simplicity and directness with which he presents his images and fancies bring him nearer to the child than the work of most professional writers of poetry for children. [H.M.]

THOMAS MOULT b. 1895 (IV)

As editor of 'Voices' and rival anthologist, Moult offered - uninvited - his own work for inclusion in IV. Marsh, who usually resisted even the recommendations of close friends, must have been shaken by such a breach of etiquette. Moult's correspondence with him ends on a hurt note: he had been wounded by Marsh's failure to include him in V. After 'Georgian Poetry' was discontinued, Moult inaugurated his own series, and 'The Best Poems' of the year ran from 1922 to 1943. He has written and edited many books, but apart from two books of 'cricket poems' (1936 and 1938), the only books of his own poems were published in 1921 and 1922.

ROBERT NICHOLS 1893-1944 (III, IV, V)

An Oxford undergraduate when war broke out, Robert Nichols immediately enlisted, and was commissioned in the Royal Field Artillery in October 1914. In the following autumn, after only a few weeks' service in the front line, he suffered shell-shock, and was invalided out in 1916. Later in the war he lectured on contemporary war literature in the USA. He preceded Edmund Blunden as Professor of English Literature in Tokyo (1921-4).

Nichols sent Marsh a copy of his first book, 'Invocation: War Poems and Others' (December 1915); Marsh wrote encouragingly, and the two met in the following summer. Marsh prepared for the press his second book, 'Ardours and Endurances' (1917). Of this book John H. Johnson comments: 'In "Ardours and Endurances" there is

no spiritual centre and no core of critical and evaluat-
ive intelligence; war and poetry touch, but they are not
brought into any meaningful artistic relationship.'   (See
Professor Johnson's excellent short account of Nichols in
'English Poetry of the First World War', 1964, 42-53.)
Nichols later turned against the Georgians: they lacked,
in his words, 'a certain extreme sensibility accompanied
by a native vehemence of spirit [which] is what is needed'
Marsh felt that Nichols had 'a want of practical common-
sense'.   A shared sense of humour kept their friendship
alive despite disagreement.

A product of the War.   Almost the best example of the
professional poet, who is painfully selfconscious of
his 'mission' and determined to write as a 'poet'
should.   His war poems convey the impression that he
had his readers already in view and was striving for a
certain effect.   Some of his verse is so derivative
that it cannot be taken seriously.   The following is
one of many examples of this:

Avaunt, mild-eyed Melancholy!
Welcome, mirth and maenad Folly!

etc.   A certain promise was indicated in a poem, 'The
Tower', published in 'Oxford Poetry' (1915);   it has
not been fulfilled, perhaps owing to the war, which
has given Mr Nichols a far greater prominence than he
would have otherwise attained.   We fear this notor-
iety has made him anxious to produce in excess of his
capacity.   [H.M.]

J.D.C. PELLOW (IV, V)

Marsh first published him without permission, being unable
to trace him (see Prefatory Note to IV).   'Parentalia,
and Other Poems' was published in 1923, 'Selected Poems'
(with George Every and S.L. Bethell) in 1945.

FRANK PREWETT 1893-1962 (V)

The Canadian-born Frank Prewett was a recommendation of
Robert Graves's.   Like Graves, Owen and Sassoon, he was
treated for war-neurosis by Dr W.H.R. Rivers at Craig-
lockhart, where he met the other three poets.   Sassoon
wrote of him:

He was quite young, and the verses he was writing were
blurred and embryonic, but there was a quality in them
that interested me and raised expectations.   This was
justified by the small volume ['The Rural Scene', 1924]
which he published about five years later.   Thoughtful
and sensitive in their nature observation, these poems
have a distinctive strangeness of tone and expression.
It was a disappointment when he abandoned poetry and
became a farmer.   ['Siegfried's Journey, 1916-1920',
1945, 75.]

'The Rural Scene' had been preceded by the privately
printed 'Poems' (1921).   'The Collected Poems of Frank
Prewett' were published posthumously in 1964.   Robert
Graves, in a short biographical introduction to them,
refers to Prewett's winning an exhibition from school in
Toronto to Christ Church, Oxford, shortly before the
First World War, and then joining the Royal Artillery in
which he served first as a battery officer and later in
trench mortars.   He was invalided out in 1917 (Graves
says he had been 'seriously wounded under shell fire'),
and returned to Oxford where he graduated.   Graves knew
him when he was at Oxford in 1920 and Prewett was farming
nearby, but lost touch when they both left Oxford in 1926.

Nor did any news reach me of him until 1962.   Appar-
ently the farm had failed, his marriage had gone
wrong, and he drifted about England until the Second
World War broke out.   He then married again, and
joined a bomb-disposal squad at Birmingham during the
Blitz.   [Introduction, vii-viii.]

The 'Collected Poems' contains the text of three broad-
cast talks on 'Farm Life in Ontario Fifty Years Ago'
(1954).   His other publications include books on cattle
farming and the production and distribution of milk.

PETER QUENNELL b. 1905 (V)

Like Prewett, Peter Quennell was introduced to Marsh by
Robert Graves.   Looking through the anthology, Quennell
told Marsh that he thought most of the older contributors
had suffered from reading too much of each other's work:
'I shall write an essay tracing the decadence of English
poetry to the system of presentation copies.'   He also
disagreed with Marsh's constant objections to obscurity
in verse: 'So many of the best things of existence are
cloudy-ish.'   He published 'Poems' in 1926, and refers in

his 'Who's Who' entry to 'an early excursion into verse';
but he is best known for his writing in prose, including
a number of books on Byron, the latest published in 1974.
Like Nichols and Blunden before him, he became Professor
of English Literature in Tokyo (1930).

I[SAAC]. ROSENBERG 1890-1918 (III)

Isaac Rosenberg was educated at the Stepney Board School,
where his literary and artistic gifts were so remarkable
that he was allowed to give all his time to them.   He
left school at fourteen, and friends provided the means
to send him to the Slade.   He was encouraged in his
poetry first by Laurence Binyon and later by Marsh.
After a futile career as a soldier, he was killed during
the Somme retreat.   The passage from 'Moses' included in
III won the only wide recognition he was to achieve in
his short lifetime.   His writings were published post-
humously in 'The Collected Works of Isaac Rosenberg:
Poetry, Prose, Letters and Some Drawings', edited by
Gordon Bottomley and Denys Harding, in 1937.   It is a
sad irony that Marsh, to the value of whose friendship
many letters in the 'Collected Works' bear witness,
should have thought 'Moses' 'as a whole ... surely quite
ridiculously bad', and that Bottomley himself should, at
the time, have 'told him I thought it was worth his while
to be intelligible' (Christopher Hassall, 'Edward Marsh',
1957, 402).   Rosenberg's erratic genius has found wider
recognition since.   Reviewing the 'Collected Works',
C. Day Lewis wrote that 'Moses' 'contains some of the
finest dramatic verse of the century': 'The harsh,
broken line of this verse, its unabashed rhetoric and the
sculptural quality ..... falls gratefully upon the ears
after the Georgian jog-trot (or, for that matter, the
post-war dot-and-carry-one).'   ('The London Mercury',
August 1937, 387.)
    See also John H. Johnson, 'English Poetry of the First
World War' (1964, 210-49).

[SIR] RONALD ROSS 1857-1932 (I)

Ronald Ross's first book of verse, 'In Exile', was pub-
lished in 1906, and the verse 'Fables' in 1907.   Other
books of verse followed between 1910 and 1931, but most
of his writings concern his important work on tropical
diseases, especially malaria.   His 'Memoirs' (1923)
contain 'a full account of the great malaria problem and

its solution'.   J.O. Dobson wrote 'Ronald Ross: Dragon
Slayer' (1934); and his obituarist in 'The Times' noted:
'He slew the dragon and delivered man from immemorial
bondage'.

[THE HON.] V[ICTORIA]. SACKVILLE-WEST 1892-1962 (V)

Victoria Sackville-West had the distinction of being one
of the two lady Georgians. Her long poem, 'The Land',
won the Hawthornden Prize in 1927; her 'Collected Poems'
were published in 1933. Her marriage to the Hon. Harold
Nicolson was the subject of 'Portrait of a Marriage'
(1973) by their son, Nigel Nicolson.

EDMUND BEALE SARGANT (I)

His only book of poems, 'The Casket Songs, and Other
Poems', was published in 1911.

    Capability without inspiration.   [H.M.]

SIEGFRIED SASSOON 1886-1967 (III, IV)

Siegfried Sassoon served during the war with the Sussex
Yeomanry, and then with the Welch Fusiliers (Robert
Graves's regiment). His first volume of poems, 'Twelve
Sonnets', was published in 1911, his 'Collected Poems,
1908-56' in 1961. He is even better known for his auto-
biographical writings: the trilogy of 'The Memoirs of
George Sherston' ('Memoirs of a Fox Hunting Man', 1928,
which won both the Hawthornden and James Tait Black
prizes, 'Memoirs of an Infantry Officer', 1930, and
'Sherston's Progress', 1936), 'The Weald of Youth' (1942),
and 'Siegfried's Journey, 1916-1920' (1945).

    The best poet produced by the war. His war poems are
    exactly what is understood by the term. They are not
    'poetry' in the accepted sense, but they express in a
    vital and telling manner the disgust and revolt of a
    sensitive man against the criminal stupidity that can
    plunge a whole continent into endless misery and make
    one man the agent of another man's death ..... He
    goes directly in the path he has chosen, lamenting here
    that a harmless man should die, there that a useful
    happy life should be maimed and broken. He shouts and
    screams, he is so angry. It will be interesting to

see in the future whether the author of 'Counter
Attack' is really a poet - whether any 'peace' exper-
ience can rouse him to such height of feeling as did
the horrors of four years' war.   [H.M.]

EDWARD SHANKS 1892-1953 (IV, V)

Edward Shanks joined the 8th South Lancashire Regiment in
1914, but was invalided out in the following year.
Brooke, who had known him at Cambridge, introduced him to
Marsh, who was slow to warm to his work.   Shanks showed
an ambivalent attitude to 'Georgian Poetry' (see review
of III in 'The New Statesman', No. 27).   He at first re-
fused to be in IV, but later accepted with an admission of
coyness.   He was first recipient of the Hawthornden Prize
(1919), was assistant editor of 'The London Mercury'
(1919-22), lecturer in poetry at the University of Liver-
pool (1926), and chief leader writer of the 'Evening
Standard' (1928-35).   His 'Poems 1912-32' were published
in 1933.

   Pleasant songs and lyrics.   Most of his work is der-
   ivative - sometimes in expression, sometimes in move-
   ment.   However original Mr Shanks may seem at first
   sight, a closer inspection will reveal the fact that
   once more a poet is expressing himself by means of
   traditional poetic speech.   At times we suspect the
   author to be writing because he feels he should do so
   - not because he has a special need.   His best poem
   so far is probably the narrative entitled 'The Fireless
   Town'.   [H.M.]

In reviewing Shanks's 'Collected Poems' (1926), J.C.
Squire was, as might be expected, more appreciative,
even though 'Old friendship and old association with this
review make it difficult to discuss [his poems] with the
warmth I feel about them' ('The London Mercury',
November 1926, 93-5).

FREDEGOND SHOVE 1889-1949 (IV)

Fredegond Shove was the wife of Gerald Shove, lecturer in
economics at King's College, Cambridge, and daughter of
F.W. Maitland, biographer of Sir Leslie Stephen.   As
Robert H. Ross tactfully suggests, she is perhaps better
known for her study of Christina Rossetti (1931) than for
her poetry ('The Georgian Revolt', 224).   Marsh had long

wished to include a lady poet: Monro more than once
urged Charlotte Mew upon him; Shanks suggested Rose
Macaulay; both Shanks and Sassoon championed Edith Sit-
well.   Fredegond Shove's poems (from 'Dreams and Jour-
neys', 1918) were poorly received by critics of the antho-
logy.   'Daybreak' was published in 1922, 'Collected
Poems' posthumously in 1956.

> The one book so far published by this writer shows her
> the possessor of a strangely original mind.   She is
> able to write about rather unusual subjects in a fresh
> and natural manner.   Her poetry is like sunlight on a
> green hill.   It is always the same sun and the same
> hill, but the imagination of the beholder sees it each
> time in a new and beautiful light.   Her command of
> language and freshness of imagery in dealing with such
> a subject as 'The New Ghost' reproduces in the English
> language, with no suggestion of pre-Raphaelitism, all
> the innocence and wisdom of an early Italian picture.
> [H.M.]

[SIR] J[ACK]. C[OLLINGS]. SQUIRE 1884-1958 (III, IV, V)

J.C. Squire (see Introduction, pp. 21-2) became literary
editor of 'The New Statesman' (1913), acting editor
(1917-18), founder and editor of 'The London Mercury'
(1919-34).   His many books in verse and prose include
'Collected Parodies' (1921), 'Poems in One Volume'
(1926), and 'Reflections and Memories' (1935).   His bio-
graphy has been sympathetically written by Patrick How-
arth: 'Squire: Most Generous of Men' (1963).

> The development of J.C. Squire from journalist and
> parodist to popular poet is one of the interesting
> events of the past six years.   He has been best known
> and appreciated as 'Solomon Eagle' of 'The New States-
> man'.   Earlier in his career his desire for poetic
> expression was satisfied by witty and incisive parodies
> of poets of the past and present.   Later he became
> discontented with this method, which is but a second-
> hand business, and decided to give himself up to ser-
> ious poetry.   He succeeded admirably.   He brought to
> it all the humour and brilliance that have distin-
> guished him as a critic.   His facility in parody often
> defeats his imagination and makes a poem a mass of der-
> ivative phraseology perhaps only noticed by those who
> study the subject very carefully .....   [H.M.]

JAMES STEPHENS 1882-1950 (I, II, III)

James Stephens was slow to reply to Marsh's invitation to
I, indeed the last contributor to agree.   His letters to
Marsh reveal the dangerous facility with which he wrote:
in 1914 an average of twelve poems in two days;   in 1917
nine to fifteen poems a day!   He later suppressed 'The
Lonely God', the longest of three poems from 'The Hill of
Vision' included in I, and excluded it from his 'Collected
Poems' of 1926.   Possibly he rejected it as an epic, of
which he wrote in the Preface to the 'Collected Poems':
'A revival of epic is not to be wished;   nor, while the
general mind is steeped in what is practically a new ele-
ment, is such a revival possible ...'   He also wrote:
'The duty of a lyrical poet is not to express or to ex-
plain, it is to intensify life, and its essence is proper-
ly indefinable'.   His best known work is 'The Crock of
Gold' (1912), a prose fantasy.

> Mr Stephens records in his poems all the charm, whim-
> sicality and humour that is inherent in the Irish
> temperament.   He is never at a loss and runs through
> the whole gamut of human experience in an entirely new
> manner.   Whether he is a child or a drunken tramp, or
> an old man, woman or God sitting on His throne pitying
> someone in a public house, his self-possession never
> deserts him.   Life to him is a serious joke: every-
> thing he writes makes this clear.   [H.M.]

ROBERT CALVERLEY TREVELYAN 1872-1951 (I)

R.C. Trevelyan was the second son of Sir G.O. Trevelyan,
and elder brother of the historian, G.M. Trevelyan.   His
first book of poems, 'Mallow and Asphodel', was published
in 1898.   Five others appeared before 'Georgian Poetry,
1911-1912', and books of poems, verse, translations from
the Greeks, and plays were to follow.   The inclusion of
his 'Dirge' had been at the insistence of Sturge Moore
('There will be very few things in your book so genuinely
poetry':   see Robert H. Ross, 'The Georgian Revolt', 109).
Marsh thought the poem violated his canon of discernible
formal pattern;   among other defects, it had too many un-
rhymed lines.   Although he yielded to Sturge Moore, he
found a charitable excuse for excluding him from II: he
had 'published nothing that comes within its scope'.
Trevelyan's rival 'Annual of New Poetry' (1917) contained
the work of many of Marsh's Georgians (see Ross, ibid.,
211).

W[ALTER]. J[AMES]. TURNER 1889-1946 (III, IV)

An Australian by birth and a musician by training, W.J.
Turner was brought to Marsh's attention by Squire.   He
served in the Royal Artillery (1916-18).   His war poems
were considered realistic and bitter; his other poems
were disparaged as 'bloodless Georgian', a style which he
himself deplored and satirized.   He refused to be in-
cluded in V; admitting his obligation to Marsh, he added:
'But sometimes a devil rises up in us that will not be
denied ... a blind instinct which is too strong even for
my admiration and liking for you'.   He wrote music crit-
icism for 'The New Statesman', dramatic criticism for 'The
London Mercury', and succeeded Sassoon as literary editor
of the 'Daily Herald'.   His 'Selected Poems, 1916-36'
were published in 1939, and his other writings include
books on 'Beethoven' (1927), 'Berlioz' (1934) and 'Mozart'
(1938).

  Of the de la Mare-Hodgson school.   Very nearly all his
  work is derivative, not from the past but from his
  contemporaries.   He seems to have discovered a 'manner'
  of writing, and a close examination of his two books
  shows his imagination and vocabulary to be somewhat
  limited.   When he is not *trying* to write he can pro-
  duce 'Ecstacy', a most successful poem.   There is
  still a chance for him if he confines himself to the
  record of such subjects and impressions as have come
  to him through his own senses, not of those that he
  feels will make a good poem.   [H.M.]

FRANCIS BRETT YOUNG 1884-1954 (IV, V)

Remembered chiefly as a novelist, Francis Brett Young
published several volumes of poetry, an early study of his
fellow poet-physician, Robert Bridges (1913) and a 'Por-
trait of Clare' (1927) which won the James Tait Black
Memorial Prize.   'Collected Poems' (1919).

  Verses by a popular novelist, which show him to be a
  man of culture and intellect.   His subjects are
  mainly 'poetical'.   His treatment and expression are
  generally so derivative that to the reader they appear
  nothing more than Exercises in the Best Poetical Style.
  [H.M.]

He claimed to have invented 'the Squirearchy' (see
Frank Swinnerton, 'Background With Chorus', 1956, 156).

Select bibliography

Almost every book about the poetry of this century has
some relevance to the Georgians in general or in partic-
ular, as has almost every literary biography. To list
here even those hundreds which have been consulted in
preparing the present work, some of which are already
mentioned in references, would seem less useful than to
select a few which have especial relevance.

DEL RE, ARUNDEL, 'Georgian Reminiscences' in 'Studies in
English Literature' (Tokyo), XII (1932), 322-31, 460-71;
XIV (1934), 27-42.
Del Re came to England with Monro in 1911, and worked
closely with him as assistant and sub-editor. These
reminiscences were written while he was Professor of
English Literature at Tokyo. Although unreliable in
factual details, they are true to the times and recapture
something of the pioneering spirit shared with Monro.
GRANT, JOY, 'Harold Monro and the Poetry Bookshop', 1967.
A well researched account of that unique venture, the
Poetry Bookshop, and a sensitive appraisal of Monro as
man and poet.
HASSALL, CHRISTOPHER, 'Edward Marsh, Patron of the Arts:
A Biography', 1959.
Hassall's sympathetic study of his friend and patron is
based on Marsh's extensive papers (now in the Berg Coll-
ection, New York Public Library), and gives full coverage
to the Georgian venture.
HASSALL, CHRISTOPHER, 'Rupert Brooke: A Biography', 1964.
'If not the definitive, Hassall's will be for many years
the most authoritative life.of Brooke': so I wrote in
review ('The Times Literary Supplement', 28 May 1964,
445-7). It was not Hassall's fault that he could tell
only half the story, nor possibly his fault that he told

419   Georgian Poetry 1911-1922:   The Critical Heritage

that half at unnecessary length: his untimely death
occurred before he could make final revision.   (I have
tried to suggest, and in small part to supply, deficienc-
ies in 'Rupert Brooke: A Reappraisal and Selection',
1971.)
JOHNSON, JOHN H., 'English Poetry of the First World War',
1964.
Professor Johnson's valuable guide has a two-fold purpose:
to examine the characteristic attitudes and techniques of
the poetry of the First World War, and to test the values
embodied in these attitudes and techniques by reference
to the large artistic possibilities inherent in the
subject.   His opening chapters and those on Sassoon,
Blunden and Rosenberg are especially relevant to Georgian
Poetry.
MARSH, EDWARD, 'Rupert Brooke: A Memoir', 1918.
We know now from Marsh himself and from Hassall how much
Brooke's formidable mother impeded the writing of this
memoir.   Loyally, Hassall 'would rather the Memoir by
E.M. were not regarded as superseded but still be turned
to for its own sake, as a miniature painted on ivory'
('Rupert Brooke: A Biography').
MARSH, EDWARD, 'A Number of People', 1939.
Marsh writes wittily and gracefully about his contempor-
aries, but hardly appears himself in these memoirs.
MONRO, HAROLD, 'Some Contemporary Poets', 1920.
Joy Grant fairly calls Monro's book 'a survey rather than
an evaluation'.   This reflects both his editorial in-
stinct to bring everyone in and his unevenness as a
critic.   But his comments, like those in 'The Chapbook'
(see Appendix), are an index of contemporary opinion.
He is remarkably candid about some of the Georgians he
has published.
PALMER, HERBERT, 'Post-Victorian Poetry', 1938.
A valuable study of the Georgians by one who was never
admitted to their company (Bridges tried in vain to per-
suade Marsh to include him in the fifth anthology).
Palmer goes to foolish lengths in defining no fewer than
fourteen canons by which he supposes Marsh was guided as
an editor: the Georgians have never been taken so ser-
iously before or since.   He writes perceptively about
poets who are usually denied serious attention, and less
so about some such as Eliot who are not.
PRESS, JOHN, 'A Map of Modern English Verse', 1969.
A selective, well balanced introduction to the English
poetry of this century.
REEVES, JAMES (ed.), 'Georgian Poetry', 1962.
Much as one may quarrel with Mr Reeves's selection of
poems in this anthology, one may applaud the motives

which impelled him to make it as set out in his excellent
introduction.   The notes on the poets contain a number
of inaccuracies.
ROSS, ROBERT H., 'The Georgian Revolt: Rise and Fall of
a Poetic Ideal 1910-1922', 1967.
Tribute has been paid elsewhere to Professor Ross's book,
which is the best introduction to its subject.
STEAD, C.K., 'The New Poetic', 1964.
Independently and by different routes, C.K. Stead reaches
many of the same conclusions as Ross (the American
edition of Ross's book appeared in 1965, too shortly
after Stead's for Ross to have consulted it).   Stead
relies on intuitive response rather than scholarly
research, and writes with directness and economy.
SWINNERTON, FRANK, 'The Georgian Literary Scene', 1935.
Swinnerton uses 'Georgian' to cover the whole period, and
seems more at home with prose writers than with poets.
(See also his 'Background With Chorus', 1956.)

Index

'Harold Monro and the Poetry
  Bookshop' see Grant, Joy
Harris, Frank 23
Harrison, Austin 8-9
Harte, Bret 60
Hassall, Christopher 7, 11,
  15-16, 17, 19, 40, 52,
  133, 214, 235, 248, 268,
  349, 353-4, 372-3, 382-94,
  405, 412, 418-19
Hawthornden Prize, The 28,
  397, 402, 413, 414
Headlam, Walter 60
Heine, Heinrich 23, 215
Herbert, George 107, 140
Herrick, Robert 107
Hewlett, Maurice 25
Heywood, Thomas 107
Hodgkin, Mary 306-10
Hodgson, Ralph 2, 35, 57,
  106, 126, 128-9, 132, 133,
  155, 171-2, 182, 203, 209,
  227, 228, 251, 255, 258,
  288, 292, 294, 307, 308,
  313, 337, 340, 341, 348,
  359, 360, 380-1, 404-5,
  417
Hoffman, F.J. 45n.
Holland, Bernard 119-20
Holly, Horace 43n.
Homer 215
Hopkins, G.M. 35, 39, 348
Horace 15, 16, 196, 385,
  387, 388, 392, 394
Hoskyns, John 74
Housman, A.E. xii, 18, 38,
  60, 178, 188, 298-9,
  323-4, 325, 340, 343, 348,
  351, 352, 388, 399
Howarth, Patrick 21, 415
Hudson, Stephen 23
Hudson, W.H. 20
Hueffer, Ford Madox see Ford,
  Ford Madox
Hughes, Richard 268, 269,
  271, 274, 275, 276, 285-6,
  293, 296, 298, 338, 360,
  374, 405
Hulme, T.E. 4, 20

Hunnis, William 307
Huxley, Aldous 23, 28, 122,
  215, 317, 330, 356, 368,
  378
Hynes, Samuel 20

Ibsen, Henrik 63, 102, 350
Imagism 2, 4, 20, 22, 32-3,
  42n., 253-4, 263, 284,
  328, 356, 371, 377

Jackson, Barry 401
Jackson, Holbrook 20,
  212-13, 311-12
James, Arnold 30
James, Henry 2, 16, 387
James, William 249
Jameson, Storm 20
Jefferies, Richard 398
Jeffrey, Francis, Lord 21
Jenkins, Elinor 162
'John O' London's Weekly'
  344
Johns, Orrick 158
Johnson, John H. 183, 409,
  412, 419
Johnson, Lionel 64, 65, 142
Johnson, Samuel 16, 117,
  144
Jones, Alun R. 42n.
Jonson, Ben 74, 107, 307,
  330
Joyce, James 32, 388

Keats, John 64, 65, 85,
  100, 107, 117, 189, 208,
  214, 215, 219, 235, 241,
  247, 254, 299, 305, 321,
  338, 344, 346, 358, 379,
  393
Kendon, Frank 272, 275
Kenner, Hugh 47n.
Kerr, William 268, 269,
  271, 274, 275, 276, 277,
  293, 296, 298, 302, 304,
  338, 406

434   Index

THE CRITICAL HERITAGE SERIES

GENERAL EDITOR: B. C. SOUTHAM

Volumes published and forthcoming